History of
Long Island

BENJAMIN F. THOMPSON

History of Long Island, B. F. Thompson
Jazzybee Verlag Jürgen Beck
86450 Altenmünster, Loschberg 9
Deutschland

ISBN: 9783849678890

www.jazzybee-verlag.de
admin@jazzybee-verlag.de

Printed by Createspace, North Charleston, SC, USA

CONTENTS:

EXTRACT FROM THE PREFACE TO THE FIRST EDITION

In collecting materials for the History of Long Island, the compiler has availed himself of every source of authentic information to render the work both useful and interesting; with what success must be left to the consideration of the reader. He has avoided, no reasonable labor or expense to make his publication worthy of approbation, although he has failed to satisfy himself in accomplishing all that he anticipated on first setting out. Beauty of style and elegance of description were not among the primary objects of the compiler, his principal aim being to present a correct and full account of Long Island, constituting a valuable repository of historical and statistical information. Had he anticipated the labor and responsibility he was about to assume, with the obstacles to be encountered in his progress, he would most likely have abandoned the undertaking, even after a large mass of material had been accumulated.

Two centuries have scarcely elapsed since this fair isle, now so far advanced in population, business, and wealth, was possessed by a race of men, little more intelligent than the beasts of the forest. Consequently it must be a matter of very considerable importance to trace the progress of Its strange eventful history, mark the revolutions which time has produced, and transmit the details thereof to posterity.

A Long Islander by birth and descended from an ancestry coeval with its first settlement by Europeans, the compiler has been desirous of presenting to his fellow citizens a series of interesting facts and incidents of olden time, of much intrinsic value and highly worthy of preservation. For much valuable information derived from the kindness of several respectable individuals, he begs to express his sincere acknowledgments for the many favors thus gratuitously afforded him.

To the Sketch of the First Settlement of the Several Towns Upon Long Island, by the Hon. Silas Wood, the compiler is largely indebted, as well to Notes, Geographical and Historical, Relating to the Town of Brooklyn, by the Hon. Gabriel Furman. In relation to the geology of the island, he has availed himself of the labors and researches of William W. Mather, Esq., and others his associates, in the late geological survey of the state of New York.

In this compilation, it is presumed something will be found interesting to every class of readers; and that it may hereafter be referred to as an authentic record of facts connected with the settlement of the country, and with its colonial and revolutionary history. The author is aware that by delaying his publication many additional matters may have been obtained, but this desideratum is incident to the very nature of history, and if one should resolve not to publish till everything should be collected, his labor would never end, and what he had already procured would in the meantime be useless to others. Works of this character will always appear premature, for the reason that there is no limit to the accumulating of materials. History is progressive and new facts are constantly occurring, which can only be included in subsequent editions of a work like this. When it is considered that a single town will often afford sufficient matter for a good-sized volume, the difficulty of comprising anything like a complete history of twenty-one towns in the present publication will not only be apparent to all, but it is hoped will constitute some apology for any imperfections discoverable herein.

Hempstead, L. I., January 1, 1839.

EXTRACT FROM THE PREFACE TO THE SECOND EDITION

As History has been allowed to hold an elevated rank among the more important branches of human learning, so the knowledge which it affords must be highly useful and interesting. As a distinct species of literature, history not only teaches important lessons, but by a method also the most striking and durable, that of example. It collects the evidences and perpetuates the recollection of events long past, which would otherwise be buried in oblivion.

Local history must necessarily be more minute in its details than that which is more general, requiring equal patience and labor of inquiry, with a circumstantial delineation of facts, which would necessarily be passed over in works of larger grasp.

Many generations have come and passed away since the towns of Long Island began to be settled by our Dutch and English ancestors, and doubtless a thousand events have perished which, if known, would dissipate much of the doubt and uncertainty that now impede the progress of inquiry.

The first edition of this work having been most favorably received by the public, has imposed upon the compiler an obligation of increased exertion to render the present, in all respects, more worthy of its patronage. In addition to a thorough re-examination of town and country records, he has inspected with care and attention numerous volumes of manuscript records in the office of the Secretary of State, and the historical collections of most of the New England States. The map accompanying this work has been compiled with care, and is more accurate than any other heretofore published. By it the topography of the island will be better understood, and what has been hitherto a sort of terra incognita will be better known, and as it is hoped more favorably appreciated.

It will be perceived that the arrangement in the former volume has been altered in this edition, the better to harmonize with the chronological order of events, and to allow of the insertion of much new matter. The names of the first planters, and prominent individuals of olden time, have been inserted, from which it may be learned that most of those names are still found amongst us. A more complete series of ancient patents, and other documents affecting the titles to real estate, have been introduced, which are of importance to the towns and to their inhabitants.

Among other matters of curiosity and interest now published, may be mentioned the Mortgage of Long Island to Fenwick and Others in 1641, and the subsequent release of it. The grant of the island, with other territory, by Charles II., in 1664, to James, Duke of York; the Flushing remonstrance of 1657; the account of Captains Underbill and Scott, and the piratical career of the notorious Kidd. To these are added a full account of the terrible disasters connected with the wrecks of the " Bristol " and " Mexico," on the south shore of the island and the burning of the steamer " Lexington " In Long Island Sound.

More extended lists have been prepared of the persons who composed the different colonial and state conventions, congresses and legislative assemblies: — the signers of the charter of independence; the framers of the national and state constitutions; judges, representatives in congress; members of assembly, surrogates, clerks, sheriffs, and district attorneys, since the organization of the government.

The compiler dismisses his work, believing that he has thereby rendered a valuable service to his country, one which the inhabitants of Long Island will appreciate when he shall be numbered with the dead, and the hand that pens these lines be crumbled into dust.

Hempstead, L. I., July 4, 1843.

PREFACE TO THE THIRD EDITION

It is not a little gratifying to the compiler to be assured in a very substantial manner of the due appreciation of his historical labors, and that two editions of four thousand volumes 8vo (of more than five hundred pages each) have been disposed of in a period of ten years. A result, as regards a publication so entirely local in its character, probably without example in this country. A third being now called for, previous success demands that no reasonable endeavors should be wanting to render it in all respects more correct and valuable than it was possible for the preceding editions to be, because the means to improve them were not then known to be in existence. In pursuance of "An act to appoint an agent to procure and transcribe documents in Europe relative to the colonial History of this State," passed May 2, 1839, John Romeyn Brodhead, Esq., a talented, learned, and enterprising gentleman, was appointed to that service, who, by indefatigable labor and diligence, has enriched our stores of colonial literature with at least eighty manuscript volumes of the most valuable historical materials. These immense treasures have been carefully examined, and the compiler has thereby been enabled to enhance the value of the present edition and make it, what he is anxious it should be, a full and complete account of his native island. No inconsiderable amount of new matter of intrinsic value has been gathered by diligent research from various other sources, which, being incorporated with the former text, much contributes to its improvement. Numerous errors, which escaped timely detection in the former edition, have been carefully corrected in this, and most of its pages having been almost entirely re-written, it is hoped that greater satisfaction will be experienced by readers of the work. The history of the different churches and of the ministers who have been settled therein will be found more full; and the biographical and genealogical department more complete and satisfactory, although in very many instances where information has been respectfully solicited from individuals it has been unceremoniously denied, or very scantily afforded.

GENERAL DESCRIPTION

Long Island may be described as the south-easterly portion of the state of New York, situated between 71° 47' and 73° 57' west longitude from Greenwich, and extending from about 40° 34' to 41° 10' north latitude, and from 2° 58' to 5° 3' east longitude from Washington City; being in length, from Fort Hamilton at the Narrows to Montauk Point, nearly one hundred and forty miles, with a mean range north 69° 44' east. Its breadth from the Narrows, as far east as the Peconic Bay, varies from twelve to twenty miles in a distance of ninety, widening in a space of forty miles from Brooklyn, and then gradually lessening in width to the head of Peconic Bay. This bay is an irregular sheet of water, into which the Peconic River discharges itself, expanding in width as it proceeds eastwardly from Riverhead, and separating this part of Long Island into two distinct branches, — the northerly branch terminating at Oyster Pond Point, and the southerly branch at the extremity of Montauk; the latter branch being the longer of the two by about twenty miles.

The area of the island, including the great South Bay, may be estimated at more than two thousand square miles, or twelve hundred and eighty thousand acres. Although the island is narrow and its southern shore tolerably straight, yet Inclining considerably from an east and west line, it occupies in its whole extent about 36' of latitude. A line due south from the City Hall, New York, would pass about one and a half miles east of Fort Hamilton, and cut off the west end of Coney Island. A line drawn due east from the City Hall, enters the Island near the foot of South Fifth Street, in Williamsburgh, passes three-quarters of a mile north of Jamaica Village, leaving a greater part of Queens County on the north; it approaches the south bay, going about a mile and a half north of Babylon, and enters said bay at a distance of fifty miles from New York. Thus the whole of Suffolk County, with the exception of about thirty square miles, lies north of the City Hall.

Long Island is bounded on the west partly by the Narrows, partly by New York Bay and the East River, and partly by Long Island Sound; on the north by the Sound; on the east by the Sound and Gardiner's Bay; and on the south by the Atlantic Ocean, including the islands called the North and South Brother, and Riker's Island in the East River; Plumb Island, Great and Little Gull Island, Fisher's Island, and Gardiner's Island in the Sound; and Shelter Island, and Robin's Island in Peconic Bay.

A ridge, or chain of hills, more or less elevated, commences at New Utrecht in Kings County, and extends, with occasional interruptions and depressions, to near Oyster Pond Point in the County of Suffolk. In some parts this ridge or spine (as it is sometimes called) is covered by forest, and in others entirely naked, having stones, and frequently rocks of considerable size, upon their very summits, presenting to the geologist and philosopher a curious subject of Inquiry and speculation. The surface of the Island north of the ridge is in general rough and broken, excepting some of the necks and points that stretch into the Sound, which are, for the most part, level; while the surface south of the ridge is almost a perfect plain, destitute not only of rocks, but even of stones exceeding in weight a few ounces. On both sides of the island are numerous streams, discharging their contents into bays and harbors, affording convenient sites for various manufacturing establishments; while the bays themselves are navigable for vessels of considerable size, where they are well protected from storms and heavy winds. On the south side of the island is that remarkable feature in the geography of the country, the great South Bay, extending from Hempstead in Queens County, to the eastern boundary of Brookhaven — a distance of more than seventy miles of uninterrupted Inland navigation. Itis in width from two to five miles, and communicating with the sea by a few openings in the beach, the principal of which is opposite the town of Islip, called Fire Island Inlet, and through which most of the vessels enter the bay. In this bay are very extensive tracts of salt marsh, and Islands of meadow, furnishing an Immense quantity of grass annually to the Inhabitants; and its waters are equally prolific of almost every variety of shell and scale fish, which can never be exhausted. Wild fowl of many kinds, and in countless numbers, are found here, affording a pleasant recreation to the sportsman, and a source of profitable employment to many hundreds of individuals, who pursue it as matter of emolument. Indeed, the country generally, as well as the markets of New York and Brooklyn, are mostly supplied by the produce of this bay, and it is a mine of inexhaustible wealth. The bony fish that abound here are used extensively for fertilizing the soil, and are unsurpassed by any other manure. The beach which separates this bay from the ocean, is composed entirely of sand, which in many places is drifted by the winds into hills of the most fantastic forms, and in other parts is low and flat, scarcely rising a few feet above the level of the ocean. This beach is in some places nearly half a mile in width, and has upon many parts, a considerable growth of forest, and some tillable land, although less of the latter than formerly. Very great and extraordinary changes are constantly taking place on this beach, composed of drift sand and exposed, as it is to the continual action of the winds and the heavy waves of the wide and boisterous Atlantic. While in some parts much of the beach has been washed away, in others large accretions of alluvial matter have been made; and at the same time the sand is carried onward, so that the guts or inlets are constantly progressing to the westward. In some instances these changes have been so rapid, that persons now living can remember when some of these inlets were miles farther to the eastward than they now are. Some persons have accounted for this progressive alteration from what they suppose to be the indirect effects of the Gulf Stream, which, moving in immense volume with a velocity of five miles the hour without diminution or interruption, in an eastwardly direction, sweeping past the

American coast from the Gulf of Mexico to Newfoundland, causes a current or eddy upon the shore in an opposite direction; and its materials being composed of loose sand, are carried onward by the force of the current, and deposited in places to the westward. The existence of such a current upon the southern shore of Long Island is demonstrated by a fact of ordinary occurrence, that goods cast into the sea near the coast will soon be found floating to the west, without the agency of the wind, or other cause than the motion of the water in that direction.

The existence of this current, not being known generally to mariners, may account for some shipwrecks upon this coast. This may be presumed, as some of them would seem to be otherwise unaccountable, except from a wilful exposure of property and life, by intentional casting of vessels upon the coast. The southern shore of the island is everywhere inaccessible to vessels of a large class, in consequence of the flats and sand bars which stretch parallel with, and at a short distance from, the beach. This is usually denominated the bar, and in some places there are two, called the outer and the inner bar.

The north, or Sound shore of Long Island is very irregular, being influenced in shape and form by the numerous bays and headlands, and is fortified against the wasting effects of the waves by masses of stones and rocks, projecting in some places beyond the edge of the cliffs; and where these are not found, the coast has evidently been worn away to a considerable extent by the sea in the course of centuries. The ridge or spine of the island has some considerably high hills, and are seen at a great distance at sea, serving as landmarks to the sailor nearing the coast. One of these, called Harbor Hill in the town of North Hempstead, has been ascertained to be 319 feet above tide water; and another in the West Hills, town of Huntington, is 339 feet above the sea. There is, however, reason to believe that both are much higher than has heretofore been supposed. Long Island Sound, a Mediterranean Sea, separating the island from the main land of Connecticut, is connected with the ocean at each end of the island, and affords a sheltered line of navigation of about 120 miles in extent. The Sound proper may be said to commence near Throg's Point, where the tides by Sandy Hook and Montauk meet each other. This point upon which the general government has erected Fort Schuyler at great expense, received its name from John Throckmorton an early settler of Westchester, to whom and his associates, a patent was granted, including the land now called Throg's Neck, by Governor Kieft in 1642. Instead of Throckmorton Neck or Point, it has been corrupted to Throg's and sometimes even Frog's Point. The course of the Sound is about north-east for eighteen miles, between Stamford atid Lloyd's Neck, in which distance, the shores are rugged, the channel rocky, and interrupted by small islands and projecting points. Beyond Lloyd's Neck, the Sound opens into a noble elliptical expanse, from ten to twenty miles wide; presenting a fine view of gently rising hills and sloping valleys, forests, -and cultivated fields, beautifully intermixed. The water of the Sound is generally of sufficient depth for vessels of the largest draught, and is free from obstructions to navigation. Its length is about 150 miles, reckoning from Sandy Hook to Montauk; and its breadth in some places more than twenty; average breadth about twelve miles. The fdtce of the current between Oyster Pond Point and Plumb Island is very great, yet it is exceeded by that called the Race in the vicinity of the Gull Islands, which, when increased by a north-east storm, is tremendous.

The Bay of New York being about nine miles in length and five in breadth, has a communication with the Atlantic through a strait of about a mile broad between Long and Staten Islands. This is called the Narrows, and on each side, as well as in the channel, are forts for protecting the harbor. This magnificent bay is completely sheltered from the stormy Atlantic by Long Island, forming a noble basin, and offering a spacious and safe anchorage for shipping to almost any extent; while the quays which encompass the town, afford facilities for loading and discharging cargoes. The shipping in the harbor of New York, therefore, without the erection of breakwaters or covering-piers, is, in all states of the wind, protected from the roll of the Atlantic. Without the aid of docks, or even dredging, vessels of the largest class lie afloat during low water of springtides, moored to the quays which bound the seaward sides of the city; and, by the erection of wooden jetties, the inhabitants are enabled, at a small expenditure, to enlarge the accommodations of theirport, and adapt it to their increasing trade.

The perpendicular rise of tide is only five feet. The tidal wave, however, increases in its progress northward along the coast, till at length in the Bay of Fundy, it attains the maximum of ninety feet. Toward the south, on the contrary, its rise is very much decreased, and in the Gulf of Mexico, "is reduced to eighteen inches, while on the shores of some of the West India Islands, it is quite imperceptible; A bar extends from Sandy Hook to the shore of Long Island, across the entrance to the harbor, over whith is a depth of twenty-one feet at low water, which is sufficient to float the largest class of merchant vessels. Proceeding easterly from the city of New York, the river has a tortuous course for a distance of sixteen miles. From the battery to the mouth of Harlaem River, eight miles, the course is north-northeast, and from thence to Throg's Point, east, nearly eight more. At the bend, situated opposite Harlaem River, is the noted pass or strait called Hell Gate, which is crooked; and from the numerous rocks, islands, eddies, and currents, is somewhat difficult and dangerous, particularly for vessels of large size; and many serious accidents have occurred at this place. The danger, however, is not so great as used to be supposed, or as much so as appears from the agitation of its waters at half tide, to a stranger on his visit to the spot. At such times the water forms, by its course among the rocks, noisy whirlpools of terrific aspect, and capable of swallowing up or dashing in pieces the largest ships exposed to their influence. Besides the streams which empty into the Sound from the shore of Long Island, there are several considerable rivers of Connecticut that pour their contents into it from the north; among these may be mentioned the Saugatuc, the Housatonic, the Thames, and the Connecticut. The opinion has sometimes been advanced that the bed of the Sound was at some remote period covered by the waters of a lake; and there are many geological facts in corroboration of the opinion also entertained, that the shores of Long Island and the Island of Manhattan were once contiguous. A tradition is said to have prevailed among the Indians in that quarter, that their ancestors could once cross from one side to the other upon the rocks. These strongly resemble each other in their character and structure; and the probability of their former union, may be considered as well established as the nature of the case admits. By what extraordinary convulsion of the elements the disruption was occasioned, or how effected by natural causes, is a matter for speculation and inquiry.

SOIL AND CLIMATE

The soil of the Island is so various, that it is hardly possible to give a general description applicable to any considerable portion of it. Like the surface it has a great diversity, for while no part can be called mountainous, yet much is hilly and rough, particularly near the Sound. The largest portion is either quite level or only moderately undulating. The necks and headlands have generally a rolling surface and a deep loamy soil, slightly mixed with sand; on the south side is a flat surface, and sandy soil, occasionally modified by loam or clay, covered by a thin stratum of vegetable mould. The more elevated grounds are of a superior quality to the plains, and better adapted to most kinds of grain usually raised in this climate. Hempstead Plain is composed, in good degree of a coarse black sand or fine gravel, yet possessing, with the aid of a scanty soil, sufficient fertility to yield a rich pasture for thousands of cattle and sheep, for seven months in the year. With lime or ashes, it is rendered quite productive. Along the north side of this immense heath, in the region of Queens County Court House, and the settlement of Westbury, are some of the best farms in the county, and if the whole of this open waste was disposed of and inclosed in separate fields, the agricultural products of this portion of the island would be nearly doubled. A stupid policy, consequent upon old prejudices, has hitherto prevented any other disposition of it, than as a common pasturage. It is hoped the time is not far distant, when this extensive tract shall abound in waving fields of grain, yielding not only support, but profit, to thousands of hardy and industrious citizens. It appears that a course far more rational was contemplated by the inhabitants about a century ago and which it is greatly to be regretted, had not then been fully accomplished.

Page 198 of the town records shows, that it was voted and agreed at a town meeting in Hempstead, March 30, 1752, that the plains should be divided to every person that had any right therein, and that Jacob Smith, Richard Ellison, John Williams, John Dorian, John Birdsall, and John Foster were appointed and empowered to make such division, each person having land so laid out to him, paying the costs of laying out the same. A protest was however entered against the measure, and it is probable that it became in the end so unpopular, as to have been finally abandoned.

It was afterwards, April 1, 1755, resolved to fence said plains, for which purpose an appropriation was made, but such was the opposition, that in April 1763 the town voted to dispose of the materials which had been provided for the purpose.

Eastward of this plain and extending nearly to the head of Peconic Bay, is a vast tract of land sparsely covered with small pines and shrub oaks, portions of which only are enclosed. Although the soil of a great part of this waste is sandy and probably unsusceptible of profitable cultivation by any process heretofore known, yet many portions of it, particularly on and adjacent to the line of the Long Island Railroad, is quite loamy, and with the facilities now afforded for the transportation of manure, will become highly valuable for agricultural purposes.

Accordingly attempts are now making by enterprising individuals to redeem occasional parts of this hitherto useless territory, and it is hoped their very laudable exertions will be followed by merited success, thereby stimulating others to imitate so worthy an example.

When it is considered that this region, being allowed to remain covered with wood and other wild growth, combustible in its nature, is liable to be overrun by fires, by which great damage has heretofore been sustained, it is matter of importance that it should be used in a manner more profitable to the owners, and far more creditable to the character of the people, for intelligence and industry.

The soil of Kings County is in the aggregate possessed of a greater natural fertility than most other parts of Long Island: yet the lands about Newtown and Flushing, as well as those upon Little Neck, Great Neck, Cow Neck, and portions of Oyster Bay, are wonderfully prolific.

The numerous and extensive tracts of salt meadows and marshes, in various places, and upon the south side of the island particularly, produce an almost inexhaustible quantity of food for cattle and horses, of a nutritious quality.

The immense shell banks which heretofore existed on the sites of ancient Indian villages, have in many instances been removed, and their contents applied for fertilizing the soil with eminent advantage. Upon the southerly side of the island, as well as in the towns of Riverhead and Southold, the bony fish have been principally used for manure, and with great success. The profusion of this species of fish and the consequent cheapness of the article, will probably always insure its use in those parts of the island where they abound. It is probable that at least 100,000,000 are annually taken for this purpose.

There is reason to believe that the farmers of Long Island furnish yearly for market a surplus of beef, pork, hay, and grain, amounting to more than $150,000 in value; and in all probability the produce of the south bay is little short of the like sum. The fire-wood sent annually from the bays and harbors of this island, has amounted to at least $60,000 for the last fifty years. The value of a good part of which has been returned in ashes and other kinds of manure.

Long Island is, as has been intimated, abundantly supplied with springs, and of the purest water, many of them being made to form ponds for driving mills, which are almost indispensable to the inhabitants. The localities of these groups of copious springs, says Mr. Mather, are either at the heads of the bays, and re-enterings of the coast, or in the valleys prolonged beyond the heads of the bays, or at the heads of the small bays and marshes, branching from the main bays.

The main features, says he, of the topography of Long Island, are a range of hills from one end to the other, and occupying most of the northern half; and a nearly level plain, slightly undulating, with a very small declivity, extending from the southern base of the hills to the south shore. There are valleys through the hills, from the heads of nearly all the bays, which extend across the plain to the south shore. They have the appearance of channels, through which the water has flowed in tidal currents, before the emergence of the land from the ocean, and have either been excavated since the deposition of the strata, or else the currents setting through these channels, prevented the deposition of as much earthy matter, as in other adjacent parts. The evidence preponderates in favor of the latter supposition, and that the same general cause has acted during the deposition of the various strata, from the lowest of the depositions that have come under observation through the drift and quaternary periods, until the island emerged from the waters of the ocean, so that currents no longer flow across it. This suggests an obvious reason why such quantities of spring waters flow from particular localities.

On the south shore of the island, the same cause does not act. There the quaternary strata are all pervious sands and gravels, and the springs flow from about tidewater level, or a few feet above, and are very uniformly distributed along the coast. The sides of these valleys are almost all gravelly and pebbly, and the bottoms the same, except that in the hilly ranges, they are frequently loam and clay, covered by superficial beds of sand and gravel.

The climate of Long Island depends as much upon its Insular situation as upon the latitude in which it is situated. The influence of the sea renders it more temperate than many other places in the same latitude in the Interior. The humidity of our atmosphere and its variableness of temperature, render it perhaps less conducive to health and longevity than If it were either colder or warmer, and less liable, at the same time, to great and sudden alteration. In the summer, and generally in the afternoon, the island is almost regularly fanned by a breeze from the ocean, which renders it a desirable place of residence at that enervating season of the year. The same cause melts the snow in winter, and often before it reaches the ground. The west and south-west winds predominate in more than half the months of the year; the thermometer seldom falling below zero in winter, or rising above ninety degrees in summer; the mean temperature being about fifty-one degrees, which is the ordinary temperature of springs and deep wells.

It is well known that the temperature of places in the same latitude is modified by the elevation of the land, the state of cultivation, proximity to the sea, or large bodies of water that do not freeze, and by the course of the prevailing winds. The temperature of the air is supposed to decrease in the same latitude one degree for every 590 feet of elevation above the level of the sea. The elevation of Mexico being 7,217 feet above the sea, in latitude 19° 18', reduces the temperature to that of places on a level of the sea in latitude 33° 30'.

The United States are less elevated above the sea than Europe, and the differenceis in favor of a milder climate with us. The climate of this country has been estimated to be from ten to fifteen degrees colder than the corresponding latitudes in Europe. From the description of the climate of France and Italy by the Roman writers a few years before the Christian era, the temperature of those countries could not have been materially different from that of the United States at present. Their rivers were frozen solid, and the earth covered with snow more or less of the winter. Experience shows that rivers do not congeal with any degree of solidity until the thermometer is as low as twenty, and in the United States in the latitude of Italy. The thermometer at present is seldom below twenty more than a few days during the winter. To produce the effects described, must have required quite as severe frost as now prevails in the same latitude in the United States, if not more so; and the same causes which have produced the change in the climate there, will have the same effect here, so far as they are common to both countries. The clearing up and cultivating the country is the most powerful cause that has contributed to this effect, and will have a great influence in meliorating the climate of the country. The trees which cover an uncultivated country, shield it from the rays of the sun, and deprive the earth of the heat derived usually from that source. It is proved by experiment that the temperature of improved land is ten degrees greater than wood land.

Evaporation and rain are sources of cold, and are more abundant in a country covered with timber; more moisture is supposed to evaporate from the leaves of a given quantity of green timber than from the same extent of water. The influence of these causes is lessened by cultivation; the earth becomes warmer and drier, and the temperature of the air is increased. The air from the sea has also a powerful effect on the climate; the sea being eight or ten degrees warmer in winter and colder in summer than the earth, and in proportion as the country is cleared, the air from the sea penetrates further into the country, moderates the heat in summer and the cold in winter; and operates to render the temperature of the seasons more mild and uniform. The climate is also affected by the course of the winds. Formerly upon Long Island the north-west was the predominant wind in the winter months, and the north-east wind generally prevailed in the spring and sometimes in the fall; but at present, as before observed, the west and south-west are predominant in more than half the months in the year. These winds either come from the sea, or blow over a country less cold than that traversed by the north-west and north-east winds, and of course more mild and temperate.

The climate here is evidently undergoing a change, and becoming more uniform than heretofore; the winters are less severely cold, and the summers not so scorching hot. The extreme cold, and its long continuance in some seasons at intervals of eight or ten years, is probably attributable to the effect of large bodies of floating ice which is formed at the Pole, and being detached from the great mass, is brought by the prevailing currents towards our coast, thereby disturbing the ordinary course of the seasons, and making the air, while passing our latitude, much colder and of longer continuance than it would otherwise be.

Thus in the year 1816 there was frost upon Long Island in every month of the year, and the corn was killed almost universally by the fifth of September. The same cause occasioned the cold summers of 1836 and 1837, but not to the same extent, the floating ice being less extensive, or was carried by the winds further from the shores.

Long Island does not present as much variety to the observation of the philosopher and geologist as some other parts of the state; yet there is probably enough to warrant the belief of its gradual formation by natural causes, and that a greater part of the island, if not the whole, has been reclaimed from the ocean. The discoveries made by deep excavations of the earth in various places, seem to have left this point no longer a matter of uncertainty or doubt with those who carefully consider the subject. The reasonings and conclusions which these surprising developments have given rise to, are, to the scientific inquirer, most curious and interesting. Dr. Ebenezer Emmons says that Long Island, the Atlantic district of the state, is a gift from ocean's waves, or from Neptune's hand, sands washed from the deep by waves from the broad sea breaking upon the skirts of land, and casting up the debris of a wasted continent. It stretches far away in a south-east direction, in the form of an immense ridge of sand and drift, or in more common language, is an alluvial formation of a very porous character. It rises 300 feet above the sea. It is the grand rendezvous for birds of passage. Here they resort from the arctic regions, and find a retreat from the pinching frost of a northern winter; and from the tropics, to escape a burning sun, and find protection from the heats of summer. Fruit trees bloom at Easthampton a week later than in the interior of the state and a fortnight later than at the west end of the island. The harvest is also later, but the frosts are later by a month than the average of the state, and three weeks later in the western parts of the island.

If we except the drift upon its northern slope, or that which faces the Sound, Long Island has been reclaimed from the ocean; it is based undoubtedly upon a reef of rocks, which first formed a bed whereon the waves washed up the sand, and this has continued to accumulate to the present time. The Hempstead plains, whose soil when washed is merely a white beach sand, is destitute of the elements essential to fertility. It bears light crops, and produces moderately well for a season, yet soon fails even with special nursing.

It is abundantly demonstrated that very extensive alterations have taken place, and are still in progress upon the shores, and within bays and harbors, by the inroads which the sea is incessantly making in some places, and the large accretions to the land in other locations.

Land slides, or the slipping or the tumbling down of banks and high cliffs, are common on the island, of which there are many examples on the north coast. In consequence of the sea washing away the base of the cliffs, large masses slip off and sometimes slide into the sea.

The washing away the base of the cliffs, conjointly with land springs, which in some localities convert the beach of sand into quicksand, cause the mass of superimposed materials to flow off from the slippery clay beds, oftentimes carrying with them the trees and shrubs, and sometimes without changing their relative position. Many years since, a pond, skirted with marsh containing trees, was situated near the edge of the cliff, near Sweezey's landing. Mr. Skidmore stated, that one of his brothers, when young was playing with another lad in this pond, when the water in it was higher than usual. The water burst its barrier, and flowed with the sand of the cliff so suddenly into the Sound, as to uproot and bear away the trees, even in the marsh around it. The two boys were hurled also down the cliff with the descending torrent, trees, mud, and sand, into the sea, and the brother of Mr. Skidmore was so much bruised thereby that he died in consequence thereof.

The more extensive and extraordinary marine encroachments of the kind have been and are now in continual operation upon the south shore of the island, the materials of which it is generally constructed, being incapable of opposing any considerable barrier to the violence of winds and waves, especially during the existence of heavy storms, driving with inconceivable force and augmented energy, against the soft and yielding substance of the headlands and beaches.

Its effects and ravages are perceptible to the most common observation from one end of the island to the other; yet probably in no one place so palpable as about Gravesend, and particularly in the neighborhood of Coney Island. John Van Dyck, Esq., recollects when the beach at Coney Island was composed of high and extensive sand-hills, where it is now a flat and level beach, sometimes covered by the tides; and he has cut grass upon a part of the beach which is now at a considerable distance in the sea. At other places where the water was of sufficient depth to float vessels of fifty tons, it is now solid ground. Mr. Court Lake, of the same place, aged seventy-nine, states that his grandfather, about no years ago, cut a quantity of cedar posts upon a part of Coney Island which is now two miles in the ocean; and that he has himself cut fire-wood at a place now a mile and a half from the shore. There was also a house upon Pine Island, owned by one Brown, the site of which is now a great way at sea; and that Plumb Island was once covered by fine timber, where there is none now, the greatest part of the land having washed away.

The coast of Long Island on the south side, from Montauk Point to Napeague Beach, a distance of about ten miles, is constantly washing away by the action of the heavy surf against the base of the cliffs, protected only by narrow shingle beaches of a few yards or rods in width. The pebbles and boulders of these beaches serve as a partial protection to the cliffs during ordinary tides in calm weather, but even then, by the bouldering action of the surf as it tumbles upon the shore, they are continually grinding into sand and finer materials, and swept far away by the tidal currents. During storms and high tides the surf breaks directly against the base of the cliffs, and as they are formed only of loose materials, as sand and clay with a substratum of boulders, pebbles, gravel, and loam, we can easily appreciate the destructive agency of the heavy waves, rolling in, unbroken from the broad Atlantic. The destruction of land from this cause is less than one would be led to suppose, but still it is considerable. The road from Napeague Beach to Montauk Point, which was originally at some distance from the shore, has disappeared in several places by the falling of the cliffs. There are no data by which to estimate the inroads of the sea on this coast, as this part of the island is held in common by many associated individuals, who use it for pasturage, and it is inhabited by three herdsmen only, who are frequently changed, and who live several miles distant from each other.

From Napeague Beach to two miles west of Southampton, the south coast of Long Island is protected by a broad and slightly inclined sand beach, which breaks the force of the surf as it rolls in from the ocean. From

Southampton, westward, the coast of the island is protected by long narrow islands, from one mile to five or six distant from the main island.

Some parts of the north shore of the south branch of the island, from Montauk Point towards Sag Harbor, are washing away, but not so rapidly as on the south side of this branch of the island.

The eastern parts of Gardiner's and Plum Islands, which are composed of loose materials, are washing away in consequence of the very strong tidal currents, and the heavy sea rolling in upon their shores from the open ocean. The action upon these coasts is so rapid as to attract the attention of the inhabitants, and calculations even have been made, as to the time that will probably elapse before they will have disappeared. Rocks (boulders) that have formed a part of Plum Island, may now be observed at low water a mile or more from the present shore.

Little Gull Island, on which a light-house is located, was disappearing so rapidly a few years since, that it became necessary to protect it from the farther inroads of the ocean by encircling it with a strong sea wall.

Napeague Beach is mostly drifting sand, piled up into little hills or ridges, with marshy places and wet sand between them. Much of the surface between Sag Harbor and Easthampton, and toward Southampton, is in its natural state, a loose and drifting sand. One place was observed near Wainscott, where there were deep and broad wheel tracks on the loam, where the sand had recently drifted off. An old man present remembered that, when he was a boy, a whale had been dragged across that place, partly supported by wheels.

Between Canoe-place and Riverhead, the country is a deep drifting sand, except where the wind cannot act upon it. The same is true of the region from Canoe-place, west, through the central parts of Southampton, Brookhaven, the northern part of Islip, and across Huntington, where it communicates with the great southern plain of Long Island. The country is almost entirely in its wild native state and no house or hut is to be seen for many miles.

On the north branch of the island, the same character of drifting sands may be seen in patches, more or less extensive, between the villages of Riverhead and Mattituck, and westward toward Middle Island.

Oyster Pond Point is wearing rapidly away, by the combined action of the waves during heavy north-east storms, and the strong tidal current, which flows with great velocity through Plum Gut. A small redoubt, about one quarter of a mile west of the Point, is nearly washed away; and Mr. Latham, the owner of the farm, says, that several rods in width have disappeared since his remembrance. During the heavy storm of the 12th October 1836, the sea made a clear breach over about one quarter of a mile of the eastern part of the point, washed away all the light materials, and cut a shallow channel, through which the tide now flows. The effects of this storm were very marked at many localities on the north shore. The cliffs were undermined, and crumbled or slid down, exposing the geological structure, and presenting beautiful coast sections of the strata. The time subsequent to the storm until the winter set In, was devoted exclusively to meandering the coast on the north part of Suffolk County, in order to Inspect in detail the geological structure and phenomena of the alluvial and tertiary deposits.

The destroying action of the sea upon the headlands and cliffs, where currents and a heavy surf beat against the coast, has been considered. Another effect of the sea Is, the formation of marine alluvion. It results from the deposition of the materials transported coastwise by tidal and marine currents, and by the action of the waves in the direction of the prevailing winds and storms. The winds which produce the greatest transport of alluvial matter on the coast of Long Island (with the exception of particular parts where there are local exceptions in consequence of the form of the shore, or direction of current), are from the north-east, during the heavy north-east storms. These storms bring in a heavy sea from the ocean, which, rolling obliquely along the shore, aided by the powerful tidal currents, sweeps the alluvia in a westerly direction. The north-west winds, are nearly as powerful as the north-east, and blow for a much longer period in the year; but do not bring an ocean swell, and the waves which they raise fall upon the shore in a line nearly perpendicular to the trend of the coast; so that their effect is to grind the pebbles and gravel to sand by the action of the surf, rather than to transport them coastwise. In this way, outlets of small bays are frequently more or less obstructed by bars, shoals, and spits, formed by the tidal currents sweeping past their mouths, and depositing the materials in the eddy formed by the meeting of the currents. If the strongest currents and prevailing winds be coincident in direction, the outlet of the harbor will of course be found upon the leeward side.

Almost every bay, inlet, and marsh upon the north coast of Long Island, as well as the south, where they are not protected from the sea by the long sandy islands mentioned in the preceding article, have their outlets blocked up entirely by the materials deposited, or so nearly as to leave only narrow entrances. Strong currents set along the shore, and these, aided by the oblique action of the surf, roll the pebbles and sand up on the beach, which, on the retiring of the waves, are swept again into the surf, having described a semi-circular line, and perhaps progressed several feet by the action of a single wave. This mode of transport is seen almost everywhere on these coasts. The cliffs are undermined, and the coarser parts of their wrecks are thus tumbled along from time to time, by each succeeding storm. The particular local effect of such causes can only be fully understood by visiting the localities, or having accurate detailed topographical maps, like those now in progress under the supervision of the superintendent of the National Coast Survey. It is hoped that those maps of Long Island will be published before the geological survey of the state of New York shall have been completed, in order that an accurate, detailed map of this part of the state may be formed, so as to illustrate the numerous important geological details. The transporting action above alluded to, has been the most effective agent in the formation of the marine alluvions of Long Island. This island has been composed of one principal, and several small detached islands, which are now connected with each other and with the main island. The east end of the island from Montauk Point to Napeague Beach, seems to have been at some former time, two separate Islands, which have since been connected with each other and with the main island by the westward currents sweeping along detrital matter, derived from the continual destruction of cliffs of loose materials. Napeague Beach is five miles long, a great part of which is loose, drifting sand, enclosing marshes and salt ponds. This beach is so low in some places that the tides frequently overflow it. The skeleton of a whale is said to be now imbedded in these sands.

The land on both sides of Montauk is gradually wearing away by the action of the water. The road, which was formerly at a distance from the edge of the cliffs, has already disappeared in many places from the undermining action of the sea, and stumps of trees are found on the north side below low water mark. Indications of iron are occasionally seen along the banks and gullies, and an ochre brown oxide of iron occurs in a considerable bed, a mile and a half from Napeague. A small but lively spring, slightly chalybeate, on the north shore near Oyster Pond, discharges into the bay. It was freely used by the Indians as a medicine. The water is very cold, and its temperature appears to be uniform.

At Fort Pond Bay, a few miles east of Napeague Beach, a narrow strip of shingle, frequently overflowed by the tides, separates the Atlantic from this bay, which is separated from Long Island Sound by a beach sometimes open, but often blocked up with sand. Great Hog Neck and Little Hog Neck, near Sag Harbor, were once Islands, which have been united by a sand and shingle beach, and the latter with the main island. Farrington Neck, a few miles west of these, was an island which is now united by the main island by a low beach. That part of the township of Southold, which is situated on the main island, was originally three islands, now connected with each other and with the main island by beaches and marshes of alluvial formation. The effects of alluvial action can be distinctly seen on the map of Oyster Pond Point. It shows where two of the islands, which were once separated from the east end of the north branch of Long Island, have been connected by a beach and sand-spit, enclosing a large pond, with an outlet only wide enough for a mill sluice. A tide mill is constructed at this outlet.

Those long points of alluvion, called sand-spits, projecting from the land in the line of the eddy currents, and formed by them, are very common, and are, in fact, the unfinished beaches which will eventually obstruct the outlet of harbors and bays, and connect islands with each other. An interesting alluvial formation is now in progress on the north and north-west sides of Lloyd's Neck, in Huntington, and formed entirely by the deposit of the coarse detrital matter swept along by the current from the destruction of the high cliffs in the vicinity. This deposit is about one quarter of a mile broad, partly marsh and salt pond, protected by a high bank of shingle piled up and continued westward, so that the present outlet of the pond is half a mile further west than it was within a recent period; the shingle having been continually swept westward, while the flux and reflux of the tide through the narrow channel keeps its outlet open.

The hilly region of Long Island shows the character of the drift deposits better perhaps than any other portion of our country, except the south-eastern part of Massachusetts. Some of these hills present elevations and depressions of a hundred feet or more, and the highest point of them is 404 feet above the ocean. The ridges which extend through the island, are interrupted in many places, where channels seem subsequently to have been made across them. The country around Montauk Point, or what is called Shawango Neck, once an island, shows this hilly character of the drift to as great advantage as perhaps any other on Long Island.

The hills have a nearly uniform character, round-backed, with deep valleys, without any approximation to regularity, unless their tendency to a bowl-shape be so construed. The valleys have no outlets, and the water that falls or drains into them, either sinks into the soil, or collects so as to form pond holes.

The hills are in form like potato hills, but disposed helter-skelter, and are from twenty to eighty or one hundred feet high. At the Shinnecock hills, west of Southampton village, near Canoe Place and at Dix Hills, the same characters of the drift hills are observed, but on a smaller scale.

The ponds and small bays on the south side of Long Island, in the townships of Southampton and Easthampton, frequently have their outlets closed by beaches formed by the detrital matter swept coastwise by the tidal currents and the waves. The long sandy islands on the south coast of Long Island, which protect it from the heavy waves of the Atlantic, are doubtless formed by the same cause. Long Beach is a sand-spit, extending from Ben's Point, near Oyster Pond Point, westward four and one-fourth miles; and has been formed by the detritus swept coastwise, and deposited in the eddy currents.

This beach gives safety to Oyster Pond Harbor, by serving as a natural breakwater. Two sand-spits were observed in Cold Spring Harbor, resulting from causes similar to those above detailed.

The headlands and cliffs on this part of the island are continually wearing away by the action of the sea; and the materials of which they are composed, consisting principally of clay, sand, gravel, and pebbles, are transported by tidal currents, and deposited in other places. The tidal currents, in sweeping along the headlands and cliffs, undermine them, and, transporting the materials from which they are composed, form shoals, block up the mouths of small inlets and creeks, so as to form freshwater ponds, by preventing the ingress of salt water, throw up sand beaches in front of marshes, form sand-pits across the mouths of harbors, and connect islands with each other and the main land.

Huntington Bay, certainly one of the best on the island, is of alluvial origin. By reference to the map of Long Island it will be seen that this bay is formed by two necks of land, Lloyd's Neck on the west and north-west, and Eaton's Neck on the east and north-east. Lloyd's Neck, which was originally an island, has been connected with the main island by a low sand beach, now overflowed at high water. Eaton's Neck was formerly a cluster of four islands, which have in some way been connected with each other and with the main island. A sand-spit, one and one-fourth mile in length, and from ten to twenty rods in width, makes out into the harbor from the southwest part of Eaton's Neck, and adds much to its safety; as also a similar one from the south-east part of Lloyd's Neck.

There is abundant evidence that this harbor, and the safety of the smaller ones in the vicinity, are the result of alluvial action. The materials composing the sand beaches and spits which I have mentioned, are precisely like those now thrown up by the action of the surf; they consist of pebbles, gravel, and fine siliceous sand, interspersed with water-worn shells belonging to genera and species now living on the coast; and they are destitute of boulders, which characterize all those low places formed by the degradation of the superincumbent materials.

The beach connecting Eaton's Neck with the main island, is three and a half miles in length, and ten to thirty rods in width. Mr. Gardner, who keeps the light on Eaton's Neck, informed me, that some years since, a vessel, during a violent storm, having been driven upon this beach, and an excavation made to get her off, marsh mud was found beneath the sand near tide water level, precisely like that in a small marsh on the opposite side of the beach, clearly indicating the manner of formation at that place.

On the north-west part of Eaton's Neck, a sand-beach, one-half or three-fourths of a mile in length, has been thrown up in front of a marsh containing several acres. It has formed rapidly since the remembrance of Mr. Gardner, who says he has seen sloops, loaded with wood, float in places now some feet above tide-water level.

The long stretch of beach connecting Eaton's Neck with the main island,is continued three-fourths of a mile eastward, and is, a part of the way, formed in front of cliffs which it protects from the farther encroachment of the sea, and for the remaining distance, lies in front of a small pond skirted with marsh, which formerly communicated with the sea by means of a creek now filled with alluvial sand.

An extensive salt marsh is in process of formation in Glen Cove. The salt marshes near the head of Little Neck Bay, occupy several hundred acres, and that at the head of Flushing Bay some thousands.

A sand-beach, one-fourth of a mile in length, has been formed between Long Island Sound and Crab Meadows, through which a creek, entering obliquely from the northwest, passes in a serpentine direction through the marsh. By the action of violent winds, the finer particles of sand are formed into hillocks, which are very slowly moving inland.

At Fresh Pond Creek is a similar sand-beach. The small pond at that place communicates with the sea by means of a small creek, which is often filled by alluvial sands, so as to prevent the ingress of the salt water. The obstruction has sometimes been removed by digging, and at others, the water, rising in the pond, bursts its barrier, and finds its way to the ocean, removing every obstacle, and making the channel deeper even than before.

At Sunken Meadows is a sand-beach one-half mile in length, through which a creek enters obliquely from the north-east. Mr. Abraham Smith says this beach has extended thirty rods in an easterly direction since his remembrance.

On the north part of Crane's Neck is a shingle beach, about a mile in length, between Flax Pond and the Sound. The pond is skirted with marsh, and communicates with the sea by an opening called Flax Pond Gut. The tidal current is so strong on this part of the coast, that the finer materials have been carried onwards; while the coarser, consisting of pebbles, varying in size from a marble to two or three inches in diameter, have been left to form this beach. A large proportion of the finer materials appear to have been swept to the south-west part of the neck, where, having been deposited, they form shoals, and a long sand-beach between the sea and a marsh of several acres in extent. This sand is used in sawing marble.

By the action of water on the headlands, sand-spits have been formed across the mouths of Old Man's, Drown Meadow, Setauket, Stony Brook, and Smithtown harbors. They are rendered safer by these alluvial deposits, but they afford shelter only to vessels of small burthen, on account of sand-bars, which extend from the extreme points of the sand-spits across their entrances, which, I am informed, in some instances, are moving westward.

Land-slides, on a small scale, are a very common occurrence on the north coast of Long Island. They are in some places caused by the sea undermining the cliffs, so that the superincumbent masses crack off at a short distance from their edges, and slide down to a lower level, carrying with them trees and shrubs, and sometimes without even changing their relative position. These phenomena are common along the north shore, but they are more striking and numerous where there are clay beds, and particularly so where the clay slightly inclines towards the sea. Where the cliffs are high, they present an appearance of steps, in consequence of the successive slides.

Another cause of slides is the undermining action of land-springs, which often convert sand into quicksand, so that it flows from the cliffs, and bears along with it the superincumbent masses: but in most instances, they are caused by springs, rendering the upper surface of clay-beds slippery, so that large masses from the cliffs slide down upon the shore, and even into the sea. Several acres have thus slidden off at once, and sunk in level from twenty to one hundred and fifty feet. By this means, ravines of considerable extent are frequently formed by successive slides along the line of these springs, and in some instances these valleys form the only places for roads to the beach. A great number of examples of these slides may be seen at Petty's Bight, between Hudson's and Roanoke Points, and between Eastbrook and Sweesey's Landing. One of the most remarkable slides is at Fresh Pond Creek. The land, having there slidden down within the reach of the surf, is carried away at high tides, and during storms, thus allowing new slides to take place in succession. The degradation of the land on this part of the coast, on individual farms, is comparatively trifling, but in the aggregate, during a series of years, it is matter of some moment. Itis a loss that cannot be remedied except at too great an expense; but the loss is local, not general, for the materials washed away from one place, are deposited in another, and as much land is probably recovered from the sea, as is destroyed by it.

Sand-dunes are low hills of loose sand, which have been piled up by the wind like drifting snow heaps, and, like them, are frequently changing their magnitude and position; so that, in some places, productive lands are buried by the moving materials, while in others they are uncovered by their removal. An instance was mentioned to me of land in Southampton having been Inundated by sand, and after a lapse of about fifty years. It was uncovered by Its drifting off. On sea-coasts, and in some other places in the Interior of a country, the atmosphere is often clouded during high winds with the lighter particles of drifting sand, while the heavier are rolled along on the surface. Every obstacle which creates an eddy current in the wind, as a rock, fence, bush, or tree, causes a deposit of sand, which often serves as a nucleus of a hillock. The sand-banks, when first formed, present almost as much variety of outline and form as snowdrifts after a snow-storm. Examples were observed on the north shore of Long Island during the heavy winds of October, where heaps of drift sand, two or three feet deep, were formed in a few hours behind boulders and blocks of rock, which created eddy currents in the wind. Sand-banks, several feet deep, were observed in some of the ravines next the beach, that had been formed between the time of the storm of the 12th, and the time observed on the 17th of October. A small pond near Horton's Point has been converted into a meadow by the drifting sand filling it up, within the remembrance of Mr. Horton of Southold.

The sand-dunes along the shore are so prominent as to mark the line of coast in many places, when seen at the distance of several miles, presenting a very broken, undulating or serrated outline of white hillocks, from ten to forty feet high. On almost all the beaches are hillocks of drift sand, and in many places the high bluffs on the north coast are capped with them. Jacob's Hill, north-west of Mattituck, was once much higher than Cooper's Hill east of it; but the sand has blown off, so that it is now much lower at the former place. Some arable land has been covered over, and red cedar trees have been buried by the drift sand. The grounds occupied by the dunes are exceedingly irregular in form; in some places covered with small round-backed hills, with deep, irregular or bowl-shaped valleys, formed by the wind scooping the sand out where it is not confined by the roots of the scanty vegetation that gains a foothold in some places.

The south shore of Long Island, from Napeague Beach to Southampton, is skirted with a line of sand-hills, presenting a very irregular, broken appearance in the distance. Napeague Beach is covered for a considerable breadth, with loose, drifting sands, forming small hillocks, of almost every variety of shape. The South Beach of Long Island is almost entirely a line of hillocks, and is composed of a chain of long narrow islands of sand, from one to six miles from the main land.

Three kinds of sand are found on Long Island, viz: siliceous sand, garnet sand, and iron sand. These sands are mixed with each other in variable proportions. They result, as has before been remarked, from the degradation of land, the disintegration of boulders, and the grinding up of pebbles by the action of the surf.

The siliceous sand is found everywhere along the coast, and constitutes most of the soil of the island. In some localities it contains grains of red and yellow feldspar; in others, grains of black hornblende. Much of it is of good quality for the manufacture of common glass, for sawing marble, and for making mortar.

Red garnet sand is not uncommon on the shore. In some operations this sand may perhaps be used as a substitute for emery. The most interesting localities are at Oyster Pond Point, and the shore between Old Man's and Miller's Place.

Magnetic iron sand is found in small quantities along the whole coast of Long Island where the surf beats on the shore. It is so abundant in some localities after storms, that perhaps it may be collected for blotting sand and for iron ore. Layers of it, two or three inches thick, are seen in many places.

Garnet and iron sands both occur more abundantly after storms; and the reason is, that the surf, as it rolls upon the beach, carries the various kinds of sand along with it, and during the reflex of the wave the water washes back the lighter grains, leaving the heavy sands behind. Each wave repeats this process, and the garnet and iron sands thus accumulate in layers. The same principle is applied in the artificial separation of metals and ores from sand and pulverized rocks in metallurgic operations.

Salt marshes are very extensive on the coast of Long Island, and they are of much value for meadow lands. These alluvions result from a combination of several causes. The first step in their formation is, the deposit of a sand or a shingle beach, by marine currents sweeping along detrital matter, and depositing it in the eddy currents in front of shallow bays and re-enterings of the coast, so as to shelter these spaces from the action of the surf, if they were before exposed to it; they are also made shallower by the sand and silt carried in by the tide, the deposits from the surface waters of the adjacent country, and by sand drifted from the beach. Not only marine animals and plants, by their growth and decay, add new matter to the gradually shoaling pond or bay; but the accumulation of drifted sea-weed, trees, &c., serve to increase the alluvion at every successive storm. These various causes combined, gradually shoal the water with alluvial depositions, until marsh grass finally takes root upon the surface. In the formation of these marine alluvions, vegetable remains far exceed the other materials in volume, so that an imperfect marine peat results. The marine peat observed in most localities is of inferior quality; it is light and spongy, containing undecomposed vegetable matter.

Sand-stones, conglomerates, and brown iron ore, are continually forming, in small quantities, in several localities, by the action of mineral springs, and by the decomposition of pyrites. At Broad Meadow Point, called also Iron Point, two or three miles east of Riverhead in Suffolk County, this recent sand-stone may be seen, at low water, in thick, solid masses. It may also be seen in the sand cliffs between Roanoke Point and Mattituck Inlet.

Alluvial sand-stone was observed in many places along the north coast of the island, formed by the chalybeate springs depositing iron as a cement between and around the grains of sand and gravel. Many large blocks that had tumbled from the cliffs, are lying on the shore. At Hudson's Point a chalybeate spring flows from the ravine, and has caused the yellow and reddish color of the sands, and the aggregation of sand into rock. A chalybeate spring is supposed to exist on Farrington's Neck, upon the farm owned by Judge Osborn. The water sinks into the sand a short distance from the spring. A number of similar springs exist in other parts of the island.

The sands and clays on some parts of West Neck are of beautifully bright and delicate colors. The principal number of the sands are red, light and salmon color, buff, light and deep yellow, white, gray, and black; and of the clays, blue, brown, white, gray, bright and mottled red, and bright and mottled yellow. At the brick yards, of which there are several, making five or six millions of common and stock bricks annually, the clay is at least sixty feet thick. The beds dip about 20° east. Some of the sand beds are as red as if formed of the sand from the disintegrated red sand-stone of New Jersey. Some of the white sands of West and Lloyd's Necks, are pure enough for the manufacture of flint glass.

Lignite occurs abundantly in the sand and some in the clay beds. Some of it is pyritized and some changed to hematite; some is wood partially decayed. Fort Hill cliffs are from ninety to one hundred and twenty feet high at this place. In one of the pebble beds, great numbers of geodes of limonite were observed, and in many places, the limonite had cemented the pebbles, gravel, and geodes into a conglomerate. Iron abounds here, and many tons could easily be collected on the shore.

Nodular masses of iron pyrites are not uncommon in the pebble beds of Suffolk County, and by their decomposition, form brown oxide of iron or hematite, enveloping the adjacent substances which serve as nuclei, and cementing them together into solid rocky masses of sandstone and conglomerate. When nodules of clay, or decomposable stones are thus enveloped, geodes of brown hematite are the result. These are abundant at the high cliff on the north-east side of Lloyd's Neck, in Huntington. Where these geodes are numerous, a kind of ferruginous conglomerate is formed of gravel, pebbles, and geodes. At the above locality, the geodes and conglomerate were confined to a stratum only a few inches in thickness. Two geodes were found filled with water.

The filtering of clay in suspension in water, is another cause now forming sand-stones and conglomerates; but they are too easily crumbled to be useful. Salt was formerly manufactured to a considerable extent on the eastern part of Long Island, by exposing sea-water to the action of the sun and wind, in shallow wooden vats constructed for that purpose; but the business was found not worth pursuing, and is now nearly if not wholly discontinued.

The erratic blocks of Suffolk County are of some importance, as they furnish the only rocks for buildings and walls. Some of these blocks are of great size, weighing from one to five hundred tons. At Horton's Point in Southold, the boulders and blocks of granite and gneiss cover the beach under the cliff. They fall from the upper stratum, like the boulder stratum of Brown's Point and other places. A few blocks only of conglomerate, of the red sand-stone formation, were seen.

On the north shore opposite Greenport, the cliff had been washed away at its base, so as to expose its stratification, the base consisting of sand, gravel, and pebbles, horizontally stratified. In the town of Riverhead, from Roanoke Point for two or three miles east, the shore is skirted by a high cliff, principally of clay and sand. Boulders are seen in the greatest profusion along the shore. They, as well as the pebbles, lie at the depth of twenty or thirty feet below the surface of the earth at this place.

At Roanoke Point and for three or four miles east a large proportion of the blocks, boulders, and pebbles are of red sand-stone and trap rock. In some places these rocks form one-third of the mass. The sand-stone is of the coarse, fine and fissile varieties, and often quite micaceous. The trap is greenish, compact, vesicular, and amygdaloidal.

In Brookhaven a block of gneiss was seen a few rods from the road, on the north side, about a mile from Coram, but it is scarcely probable that it is in place, as rock has not been found distinctly in place, on the island, except near Hell Gate. Boulders are abundant on the hills, south of the road between Coram and West Middle Island.

At or about Wading River, they are in great profusion. One block that had been blasted, gave one hundred cart loads, and many others were seen still larger. On the beach a mile or more from Wading River, a block of fine-grained limestone was found, containing serpentine. It was precisely similar to the New Haven verd-antique marble. Green-stone boulders and blocks were not rare in the same vicinity.

Between Miller's Place, and Old Man's the surface is pebbly, with blocks and boulders of gneiss and granite. Near the latter place the hills are steep, and elevated about 100 to 120 feet above tide-water, with a loamy soil. Many blocks of one hundred tons or more were seen, and at a place half a mile east of Old Man's is a nest of five or six of these enormous blocks; but only a few boulders of green-stone, and a single one of red sandstone, were observed from Miller's Place to Smithtown.

Fragments of a block of porphyritic granite were seen near Setauket, similar to that in the vicinity of Reading, and of Sterling and Killingly, Conn. It had been blasted and made into a wall. About halfway from the village in Smithtown to Stony Brook a boulder of about two tons was observed, composed of a coarse conglomerate, with a siliceous cement; the pebbles in it were from the size of a hazelnut to a six pound shot.

In Huntington, at Dix Hills, the same character of hills was observed as at Shinnecock and Montauk. A boulder of serpentine, containing diallage, was seen on the roadside a little west of Comac.

Ferruginous conglomerate, in pebbles and small boulders, and a ferruginous sand-stone, with limonite as a cement, are common in the hills that begin on the west side of Smithtown valley, and extend to Huntington. Fossil wood was found in some of the masses of brown iron ore and ferruginous sand-stone. A single large pebble, or small boulder of brown iron stone, was found with the iron stone containing the petrified wood, three miles north-west of Comac.

Red granite, white granite, gneiss, slaty hornblende rock, and a kind of sienite composed mostly of hornblende, are common, as boulders and pebbles between Comac and Huntington.

On Lloyd's Neck, granular white limestone and dolomite, hornblende slate, hornblende rock, granite, porphyritic gneiss, and common gneiss were seen among the boulders both in the drift deposits and on the shore where they had been washed out of their former positions.

Granite, gneiss, and trappean rocks are the most abundant among the boulders. On West Neck, the boulders are rather common; and among them, granite, gneiss, porphyritic gneiss, trap, and hornblende slate are the most common.

Near Jericho, the road leads into the swells of the hills, and these are like those of the chain of hills stretching through the Island, composed of loamy gravel, with an abundance of pebbles and boulders. The red Iron stone, brown Iron ore, and ferruginous conglomerate, were seen more abundantly between Jericho and Oyster Bay, than in any other part of the island. The boulders and pebbles consist in most part of granite, gneiss, quartz rock, mica slate, talcose slate, chlorite slate, with some hornblende rock, and the latter is massive, laminated, and fibrous in texture. A few boulders of serpentine containing anthophyllite were seen a mile south of Norwich, among loose stones collected from the fields.

Granite, gneiss, and hornblende gneiss were the principal rocks seen among the boulders and blocks of the north coast of Oyster Bay; but on the north shore of Oak Neck, blocks of granite with yellow feldspar were seen. Blocks and boulders extend out also at Kidd's Point, Barker's Point, Hewlett's Point, the Stepping Stones, and generally along the projecting parts of the north-west coast of North Hempstead, on all of which the shore is washing away, more or less rapidly.

About half a mile south of Manhasset, near the dwelling of the late Judge Schenck, is an enormous block of granite, undoubtedly an erratic block, estimated to contain 800 cubic yards above the surface of the ground, and to weigh nearly 2,000 tons. It may be the rock described by the late Dr. Mitchill, in Bruce's Mineralogical Journal as containing 20,400 cubic feet.

Granite and gneiss form the largest portion of the boulders and erratic blocks of Great Neck. In some of these masses, granular epidote is very abundant, forming nearly one-half the mass. A large nest of these blocks may be seen at high-water mark on the north-east shore of Great Neck. Boulders of tremolite, like that on Cow Neck, were seen in several places on Great Neck.

In the town of Flushing, boulders of green-stone trap predominate from the village to Little Neck Bay. Three miles from Flushing many boulders of gray sand-stone were noticed. They are composed of grains of quartz and feldspar, most of which are rounded, and the latter are in a state of decomposition, forming white pulverulent, or crumbling grains, which give a whitish color to the masses of rock. Boulders of trap were numerous, mixed with granite, gneiss, &c., on the hills around, and in the ravines that enter the valley at the head of Little Neck Bay. One kind of boulder about Whitestone, to which this place probably owes Its name.is what appears like a decomposing granite rock. Itis light-colored, almost white, from the feldspar decomposing to form kaolin.

In Newtown, trap boulders predominate in the loam and gravelly loam of the hills on the Jamaica road from Halletts Cove and also on the Flushing turnpike.

The Jamaica hills, which skirt the great southern plain, have the same general characters as Montauk, Shinnecock, and Dix Hills. Their soil is richer, however, in consequence of the partial decomposition of a different class of rocks that predominate in the detritus. These materials also constitute the mass of the hills from Jamaica to Williamsburgh and Brooklyn. The excavations and stone fences for six miles toward Jamaica, show the boulders to great advantage. The hills are of sand and gravel, on which are seen boulders and blocks of granite, gneiss, and green-stone from 100 pounds to 100tons weight each, but the very large ones are rare. They are dug and blasted to make cellar walls and underpinning for buildings at Southampton. Most of the pebbles of the gravel beds are of white quartz, intermixed more or less with those of granite, gneiss, mica slate, red sandstone, and red oxide of iron.

This latter mineral is found in all the gravel beds of the quaternary formation, from Montauk Point to Brooklyn. It is composed of iron in brilliant grains, like sand firmly aggregated, but of a red color.

In Southold, the surface is generally a loamy gravel, or light loam. Boulders abound about Horton's Point, and thence to Rocky Point; also north-east of Oyster Pond Harbor, on the hills. They are numerous on the points at the extremities of the beach, and along the shores. Those on the hills and shore consist mostly of red granite and gneiss.

Many curious blocks of granite, gneiss, and hornblende rock occur on the north shore of Southold, showing quartz, granite, and trap veins cutting through them. Plum Island, Gardiner's, Gull, Fisher's, City, Harts, Ram Island, the Brothers, and Riker's Island all contain an abundance of boulders and blocks similar to those of Long Island.

There is one circumstance connected with these boulders which we will mention, on account of the bearing it has upon some questions in the scientific part of geology. We will state only general facts, without entering at this time into the minute details, or the conclusions to be drawn from them. The boulders and blocks vary in size from a pebble to masses weighing several hundred tons, and are mostly found on the range of hills running through the island, and between them and the north shore. The boulders and blocks are contained in a stratum which is inter-stratified with deposits of sand, clay, and gravel, and is often exposed along the coast. Some of the blocks, when first disinterred, exhibit scratches upon one or more of their sides. Rocks, like those occurring on Long Island, are found in Rhode Island, Connecticut, and along the Hudson River; and they are so similar in their mineralogical characters and associations, as to lead to the conclusion that they were originally derived from those places. Again, as we progress westward from Montauk Point to Brooklyn, along the north shore, there is a regular succession of the groups of boulders, pebbles, and gravel, corresponding to the successive changes in the rocks on the north side of the Sound. For example, the boulders on the east end of Long Island are like the granite, gneiss, mica slate, green-stone, and sienite of Rhode Island and the east part of Connecticut; further westward, opposite New London and the mouth of the Connecticut River, are boulders like the New London and Connecticut River granites, gneiss, and hornblende rock; opposite New Haven are found the red sand-stone and conglomerate, fissile and micaceous red sand-stone, trap conglomerate, compact trap, amygdaloid, and verd antique; opposite Black Rock are the granites, gneiss, hornblende, quartz, and white limestone, like those in Fairfield County; and from Huntington to Brooklyn, the trap (compact, crystalline, &c.), red sand-stone, gneiss, granite, hornblende rock, serpentine and crystalline limestone, are found identical in appearance with those of the country between New Jersey and Connecticut.*

The fact of the perfect correspondence of the mineral characters, and the associated minerals of these pebbles, boulders, and blocks, with those narrow beds on the main land, has already been alluded to; but another fact of as great Importance is, that these blocks, &c., are in a southerly direction from those beds, and this direction is generally different from the line of bearing of the strata. These facts Indicate that the boulders and blocks have been transported by some natural means from their original location to the one they now occupy. The size of some of these masses, many of which weigh 600 tons or more, and the fact of their being imbedded in sand, gravel, and loam, and that they repose upon the same materials, forbids the idea of their transport having been the result of powerful currents of water. Mountain streams often transport blocks of many tons' weight to considerable distances, but never across beds of loose materials like clay, sand, and gravel without removing them also. The theory of the transport by ice, corresponds more closely with facts, than any other which has been proposed. The occurrence of these boulders and blocks, as it were, in nests, on the north side of the hills, and generally on elevated grounds, strongly favors this view of the subject. The facts collected in relation to the erratic blocks and boulders are more numerous, and are an extremely interesting subject of Investigation, in consequence of the Important conclusions which may be drawn from them. A single one of these blocks at Oyster Pond Point was blasted a few years ago by Mr. Latham, and with it was built a stone wall eighty rods long, three feet high, and of proportionate thickness; and enough of the same, he thinks, remains in the earth, to construct twenty additional rods of wall. The upper soil at Brooklyn is generally a yellowish sand and sandy loam; below is a loam and gravel, containing a great number of boulders, blocks, and pebbles. Below the boulders' bed, is a series of strata of sand, gravel, and clay, in which shells are said to be frequently found.

Green-stone, serpentine, red sand-stone, granite, gneiss, &c., form the mass of the gravel and boulders' beds.

Between Flatbush and Brooklyn, the country is sandy gravel and sandy loam, like all the great southern plain of the island, to the base of the hills. A little west of East New York, the railroad enters the range of hills, and is excavated for a considerable distance from ten to thirty feet. The materials thrown out consist of loam and hard pan, containing multitudes of boulders, blocks, and pebbles of green-stone, granite, hornblende rock, gneiss, red sand-stone, and serpentine.

The same characters of soil and boulders continue to Brooklyn. The hilly region from thence to Bedford, Flatbush, and Bath is similar to that described, as also are the plains of Flatbush, and the rest of the great plains of the island. About a mile west of Bath, in New Utrecht, boulders of green-stone are very abundant, with some black serpentine and red sand-stone; and these, with a heavy loam and some gravel, form the soil of the country around.

The clays of Suffolk County are so abundant and varied in their character, as to be adapted to various useful purposes. The beds are extensively wrought in some places, and the clays are mostly used for the manufacture of bricks, from four to five millions of which are annually made at West Neck in the town of Huntington alone. Lumps of white clay were frequently seen imbedded in the sands of the south part of Long Island, along the route of the railroad, where the excavations had exposed them, in Jamaica, Hempstead, and Oyster Bay towns.

On the east side of East Neck, a bed of white clay occurs of a superior quality for stone ware. It is overlaid with variegated sands of brown, yellow, white, and red. These sands are used for castings at New York, Boston, and other places. The white clay of Eaton's Neck is of the finest quality for making stone ware, and superior to that of South Amboy. It is sold for one shilling a bushel.

At Fresh Pond Creek, flesh or salmon-colored clay occurs, also on the land of Wm. W. Mills, a mile south of Stony Brook. He dug a well 180 feet deep, passing through a stratum of clay five feet thick near the surface, then sand and gravel till the solid rock was reached at the bottom. Near Setauket is a yellow ocherous sand, ten bushels of which yielded two and a half of ochre.

White clays, which have the external characters of potter's clay, occur on West Neck, Lloyd's Neck, Eaton's Neck, East Neck, and Little Neck, between Centre Port and North Port.

Brown clays, suitable for stone ware, and others for coarse pottery, abound in many places in the west part of the country. Both the white and brown clays are carried to distant parts of these manufactures. Some of the clays have the external appearance of good fire clays, but actual experiment only can determine their fitness for this use. These clays contain no lime, and therefore are far less likely to melt in the fire than ordinary clays.

Some of the clay beds on West Neck and Lloyd's Neck are ocherous, and perhaps they may be profitably used in the manufacture of yellow ochre.

Clay beds must not be expected everywhere in the county — still they exist in most parts at greater or lesser depth. In some places the strata are very much waved, bent, and contorted; indeed they were not observed in any place to be continually horizontal for any great distance, so that where a clay bed emerges upon the surface, it may within a few rods plunge so deep below, that a well 100 feet in depth will not reach it. The clay beds are associated with strata of gravel, sand, and pebbles, with which they alternate. The clays toward the east part of the country lie at a greater depth than they do near Huntington.

Fossil wood, or lignite, has been found in several places in the clays, and in their associated beds of sand and gravel, but in no instance in sufficient quantity for fuel. Sometimes it appears like charcoal, in others it is changed to iron ore, either hematite or pyrites. It was seen on Lloyd's Neck, Eaton's Neck, East Neck, Little Neck, and Mount Misery; and has been found in many places from twenty to one hundred feet below the soil. Fossil wood was found in digging a well at Sweesey's Landing. Mr. Skidmore dug a well here 180 feet deep and found a stick of wood of considerable size at sixty feet. On the east side of Lloyd's Neck, fossil wood was found, showing the ligneous texture as distinctly as the wood itself. It has also been found near Cold Spring, on East Neck, and at Eaton's Neck; at Newtown the body of a tree was found at forty-five feet, and others at East Woods, at forty feet, with the bark adhering.

Fossil shells are said to have been found in several places by persons worthy of credit; and it is only remarkable that in deposits of this kind more have not been observed. Recent shells are so common on the soil where they have been used as manure, by the inhabitants, or left in heaps, or scattered round the sites of ancient Indian villages, that even where they have been thrown up in digging wells, they may not have been observed. Although the most particular attention was directed to all the phenomena connected with the banks of shells so common near the shores of Suffolk County, yet not an individual shell was observed which was not perhaps identical with the species now existing in the adjacent waters; and none of these banks were buried under other materials, than light drift sand or recent alluvial wash from the adjacent hills.

Shells are said to have been dug up in almost every well in the hilly range of the island. Shell banks are very numerous, from some of which thousands of cart loads have been removed and spread over the lands to increase their productiveness. They decay very slowly, and act to afford lime for a long time to the soil and vegetation. Several shell banks were observed between Canoe

Place and Saboneck Neck, Cow Neck, and Farrington's Neck, near the shore and generally near the heads of the small bays and on their sides; sometimes bare and sometimes covered by one or two feet of drift sand. There is another near Old Man's Harbor, from which large quantities have been taken for manure.

The subject of fossil shells should excite the attention of our farmers; for where such shells are found, it is very often the case that extensive beds of marl occur, which would be of Inestimable value in a district where manures are so necessary and expensive as on Long Island. The heaps of shells on. the old village sites of the aborigines are used as a manure, and as they decay slowly, their fertilizing effects continue for a long time. At the brick, yards, on West Neck, bones and shells are said to have been found in the clay. At Brown's Point, Southold, a bone is said to have been dug from the sand-bank twenty feet below the surface, between two layers of clay. It is white in color, eighteen inches long, two inches in diameter, with large roundish heads.

Shells were dug from a well, at ninety feet, at the head of Cow Neck, as well as marsh mud. Also at Prospect Hill and Brooklyn. Oyster shells were found at great depths on the ridge of hills north-west of Jamaica, and in many other places, but very rarely on the plains, south of the hills. Shells of both oysters and clams were dug up at eighty feet below the surface, by Isaac Overton, on the Bald Hills, south of Coram; and at Sweesey's Mills, Brookhaven, at twenty-four feet. Shells and a log eight or ten inches in diameter, and ten feet long were dug up at West Rocky Point at seventy feet. Oyster shells were found at Coram at forty feet. At Middletown, on the farm of John Howell, a shell was found thirty feet below the soil. On the farm of Zophar Mills, near Wading River, round clams and oyster shells were found at sixty-five feet.

The celebrated Dr. Samuel L. Mitchill in 1826 presented among other things, to the New York Lyceum of Natural History, the left side of the lower jaw, with the symphysis of the chin, and two grinders, belonging to a fossil animal, like a mammoth, found at Southold, between high- and low-water mark; and fragments of clam and oyster shells, found at Brooklyn Heights, fifty feet below the surface, and others found on digging for the site of the present Navy Yard, at the Wallabout.

Pyrites (sulphuret of Iron), a yellow and brilliant ore, which has so often, when found, excited expectations of rich gold mines, occurs in many places in the clay beds of Suffolk County. It is usually found in the dark blue clays containing lignite, and in many instances the substance of the original vegetable is replaced by this beautiful but deceptive mineral. This mineral is so easily distinguished from gold, that it need not be mistaken for that precious metal. Gold is so soft that it can be cut by a knife like lead; but pyrites is brittle, and so hard as to strike fire with steel, and when put on the fire burns and gives a sulphurous odor. Should this mineral be found in large quantities, it might be used with advantage in the manufacture of copperas and alum. It was seen more abundantly at the clay pits on West Neck and Little Neck, near Huntington, than in any other locality. We have in our possession a beautiful specimen of sulphuret of iron, found in the clay beds of North Port, and the material is said to be very common in that locality, to the great annoyance of the workmen employed in digging clay for the purpose of transportation.

Peat, although not very abundant in Queens, Kings, and Richmond counties, is very common. Many localities were observed. Those of the most importance are near Newtown. From a bog one mile westerly from Newtown, peat of a very superior quality has been dug for more than fifty years, and it is much used by some of the inhabitants. An extensive marsh of peat, which is probably deep and of fine quality, lies near the road from Williamsburgh to Jamaica, and is called the Cedar Swamp.

There may be about 30,000 cords of peat in this swamp. Small bodies of this combustible were seen in the ranges of hills in Kings and Richmond counties. A meadow of two or three acres of ligneous peat was observed about a mile north of Jamaica. The owners of quagmires or quaking meadows will do well to examine them. Before many years have elapsed, these bogs will become valuable, where they are now regarded as nearly worthless. The inferior qualities of peat will, under judicious treatment, in compost heaps, make a valuable manure.

Peat occurs in the heads of the ponds on Shinnecock plains; at Cold Spring Bay, several places in quantity; Canoe Place, and in the Mill Pond above the head of Mecoxe Bay.

Many of the swamps and marshes, where this combustible abounds, are overgrown with bushes and trees; but those which are free from timber are generally covered with moss and cranberry vines. The latter variety trembles when walked upon. The peat is so soft below the surface, that a pole may be thrust down many feet. Coal and wood are now so expensive, that peat must come into general use among a large class of people; and it ought to be worth at least $1 per cord in the swamp, where wood is worth $3. Marine peat, which is abundant in the salt marshes of Long Island, and the adjacent islands, is of an inferior quality, and is not worth notice as a combustible, though it may be of great value as a manure, when rotted with lime. The relative proportion of salt marsh on the coasts of Kings, Queens, and Richmond counties is much greater than that of Suffolk. These marshes are now forming, and have been for an unknown period of time. In some places they are washing away; in others they steadily increase in extent. I have been credibly informed that grass now grows on a marsh near Rockaway, where vessels have floated within the memory of my informant. On Coney Island, also, Mr. John Wyckoff says, that many places which were ponds and pools, within his recollection, now produce good crops of grass. A very aged man recollects having seen the surf roll in at the foot of the upland, north of the marsh, toward the east end of Coney Island. A broad marsh now intervenes between the upland and the beach. Numerous local facts of this kind, of less remarkable character, might be brought before the public; but in an economical point of view, the mere expression of the general fact, that the marshes, as an aggregate, are steadily increasing, is sufficient. These are valuable on account of the salt grass, of which they yield an abundant crop. The soil is very rich; in fact, it is composed mostly of organic matter mixed with some lime and saline substances, and can be made to produce valuable crops. It is scarcely possible that another generation will pass away, before the suggested improvement will be made on some of these rich alluvions. The value of land on Long Island will not always allow these marshes to be as unproductive as they are at present. Many of them might also be employed to advantage in the manufacture of salt from sea-water, both by allowing it to freeze in winter, and by solar evaporation in summer. It is well known that it is the fresh water only that freezes — thus rendering the brine much stronger; and that it can be so concentrated, until the salt separates, in a crystalized state. The disadvantage in winter would be, that only one crop of crystals could be obtained; but an area of sixty acres, divided into compartments of ten acres each, communicating with each other, so that six feet of water could be let into the first, would give for a single crop from 25,000 to 30,000 bushels of salt.

The principal marshes of Long Island are Napeague Marsh; one between Sagg Pond and Mecoxe Bay, east part of Shinnecock Bay; between Moriches and Great West Bay; between Ocombamack Neck and Fire Place; between Ocombamack Neck and Patchogue; between Patchogue and Nicolls' Neck; the very extensive one from Nicolls' Neck to Rockaway; and those about Jamaica Bay and Coney Island.

There are also many on the north shore of Long Island, the principal of which are at Acabonick, Oyster Pond, Riverhead, Wading River, Smithtown Harbor, Crab Meadow, Lloyd's Neck, Oyster Bay Harbor; between Peacock and Oak Neck, Musquito Cove, north part of Cow Neck, Little Neck Bay, Flushing, Williamsburgh, Brooklyn, and Gowanus.

The salt marshes of Suffolk County are estimated to cover an area of 55 square miles; of Queens County, 40 square miles; Kings, 12 square miles; and Richmond, 9 square miles; making an aggregate of 116 square miles, or 74,246 acres, of marsh alluvion of the south coast of New York, exclusive of the extensive marshes on the south coast of Westchester County, which would probably swell the aggregate to 125 square miles, or 80,000 acres.

The headlands, generally, on the north shore of Queens County are washing away. The blocks of rock, which were once imbedded in the loose soil of the island, are seen on the beach extending out far beyond low-water mark.

At Oak Neck, Fox Island, and Matinecock, as well as at Middle Island, (commonly called Hog Island), the boulders extend far out at low water, and demonstrate the encroachment of the sea on the land. Middle Island and Oak Neck are parts of a peninsula which lies between Oyster Bay and Long Island Sound. They were once islands, but have been connected with each other, and with Long Island, by beaches formed of detrital matter swept from the headlands of Middle Island and Oak Neck. Extensive salt marshes are forming under the protection of these beaches, and are materially increased by the sand drifted from them. These beaches are observed to vary in form and magnitude, being sometimes increased or diminished in particular by the effects of a single storm. Fox Island (so called) was once an island, but is now connected with Oak Neck and Long Island on the east by a long beach. A long sand-spit, of a mile and a half in length, extends to near Peacock's, where it is cut off by an inlet, which communicates with the extensive marsh between Fox Island and Long Island. This beach and spit are derived from the materials washed from Fox Island and Oak Neck. Peacock's Point is also washing away. Stumps and logs of wood are seen below low-water mark. Matinecock Point, a mile or more west of Peacock's, must have washed away rapidly. A long point of boulders and blocks stretches far out into the Sound at ebb tide. This was once an island, which is also connected with Peacock's by a long sand beach. Another ancient island, now connected with Long Island on the south-west by a beach, is very near Matinecock on the west. These two islands and beaches enclose a large pond, the inlet of which is through a mill sluice between them. Mr. Jacob Latting, who is an old and respectable inhabitant and has been a resident in the vicinity more than half a century, informed us, that these have been worn away many rods within his recollection. Mr. Latting pointed out to us the position of the beach between Peacock's and Fox Island during the revolution. The beach then dammed up the outlet of a marsh, through which a small stream ran, and a trunk was put in the beach in 1778, to allow the water to drain through, in order to prevent flooding the meadows. We saw the trunk in its original position. The beach has since made out about 200 yards in front of where it was at that time. He observed that these beaches are subject to considerable variations by storms, the materials being tumbled along either eastward or westward, according to the direction of the wind.

Sands' Point, on which a light-house has been long built, was washing away so rapidly some years since, that it became necessary to protect it by building a strong seawall along the shore. A reef of rocks, the remains of ancient lands, extends out some distance, from the shore. The wall has afforded a protection against the encroachment of the sea, and about an acre of land has been added to that belonging to the United States, in consequence of the alluvial action of the surf depositing the sand and shingle in the eddy on the south side of the Point. Mr. Mason, the keeper of the light-house, communicated these facts, and many others of much interest. The broad and extensive sand-beach south of Sands' Point, a mile or more in length, was, since his remembrance, a salt marsh covered with grass. The materials swept from Sands' Point, and deposited on the edge of the marsh, have been drifted and washed over its surface.

At and near Kidd's Rock, three-quarters of a mile eastward of Sands' Point, the wasting of the cliffs from the effects of the waves is very evident. The cliffs present mural escarpments towards the Sound, but the hills slope down gradually on the other side towards the salt marsh. This elevated land was formerly an island, but alluvial causes have formed a salt marsh where the water was sheltered from the sea. The wasting of the cliffs has caused the formation of long beaches — one connecting Kidd's Point with Sands' Point, and the other connecting with the high grounds south-east of the marsh on the west side of Hempstead Harbor. A small inlet through the north end of this beach allows the tide to communicate with the marsh. Boulders and blocks are seen imbedded in the strata forming the mural escarpments, and the shore below is also strewed with them. They also extend some distance from the coast, indicating that a considerable breadth of land has been washed away. The boulders protect the shore for a time, but the smaller ones and the shingle are gradually ground up by the action of the surf, and washed away; and during storms and high tides fresh inroads are made. The beach between Kidd's Point and Sands' Point covers a part of the marsh, the ooze and marine peat of which may be seen at the foot of the beach at ebb tide. This indicates that high land, or else a beach, was once farther seaward, to afford protection for the formation of that part of the marsh. Only a few acres of high land remain at Kidd's Point, and if it should continue to be washed away as heretofore (and much expense would be necessary to prevent it) , a century or two would be sufficient to effect its entire removal. Kidd's Rock, as it is called, is a remarkable erratic block, which was imbedded in the loam of the tertiary formation. It has been undermined by the action of the sea, and has slid down to the shore, and cracked into many large fragments. These fragments probably weigh at least 2,000 tons; and several sloop loads of them have been shipped to New York for building stone. It is hornblendic gneiss, and some of its masses abound in epidote. It is a durable stone, and will stand any exposure unchanged.

Several companies of diggers for Kidd's money have expended much time and labor at this place. Mr. Noah Mason, former keeper of the light-house on Sands' Point, related many amusing anecdotes of their mode of operating, and the ceremonies practiced, some of which seem almost sacrilegious. The superstitions connected with these gold hunters, are a rarity of this enlightened age. The rock called Kidd's Rock, at Kidd's Point, threequarters of a mile east of Sands' Point, is not the same known by that name a century ago. Mr. Mason stated that Kidd's Rock was formerly the extremity of the point, but was long ago undermined by the waves. He remembered having seen it, as an insulated rock, some distance from the shore, but it has since disappeared. The rock which lately went by that name, now a mass of fragments, is a group of huge blocks of hornblendic gneiss, some of which will weigh several hundred tons. Had the money diggers known which was the genuine Kidd's Rock, it might have saved the trouble of searching here.

In some parts of Long Island, almost every boulder and block has had an excavation made by its side.

Barker's and Hewlett's Points have also been worn away by the actions of the sea; but the Sound is here so narrow, that the destructive agency of the waves is not so great, as at the localities before mentioned. Many others, where the same effects are in progress, on the west and south-west parts of Long Island might be mentioned, but they are less marked in their results, because they are not so much exposed to the fury of the surf, from broad sheets of water. Coney Island, which is mostly alluvial, is rapidly washing away on its south side, where it is exposed to the full force of the ocean swell. A new direction given to the tidal currents by some recently formed bar, is probably the cause, Mr. Wyckoff, who lives near the ocean, remarked that the sandy part of the island was a mile broad not many years ago, though now it is not more than half that breadth. Every storm made a sensible difference. Some years before, the sand-hills south of Coney Island House were covered with small pines and bushes, and in a single night, during a violent storm, the trees and bushes and much of the earth were washed away. It would seem that the remainder of this island is fast yielding to the destructive influence of the ocean, and a century more may leave few traces of what is now Coney Island. At low water, remains of an ancient salt marsh can be seen about a mile east of Mr. Wyckoff's on the edge of the beach. This is conclusive evidence that this part of the island is fast washing away.

The beaches at Middle Island, Oak Neck, Fox Island, Peacock's, Matinecock's, and Sands' Point, which are formed by the accumulation of the sand and shingle, swept from the adjoining headlands by marine currents, and the oblique action of the surf, have already been mentioned. Other beaches, but not so extensive, occur on the north coast of Queens County. Sand-spits are unfinished beaches, and long points or tongues of land, formed of sand and shingle, by the transporting action of currents and the waves.

In Cold Spring Harbor a sand-spit extends from the west shore obliquely nearly across. It is formed by the north-east storms driving in a heavy swell, which washes away the high banks at the south point of land, between Cold Spring Harbor and the entrance to Oyster Bay. The materials are transported, by the currents and waves, and deposited to form this spit.

A sand-spit has formed nearly across Hempstead Harbor, about three miles south of the mouth of the bay, and two miles north of the village of

Montrose, near the head of the bay. It extends from the west shore, in an easterly direction, nearly across the harbor, leaving a deep inlet of one hundred, to one hundred and fifty yards wide, next to the eastern shore. It is owing to the same cause as the spit at Cold Spring. This spit is probably a thousand yards in length, but is not materially affected by storms. The detrital matter, now swept coastwise, is carried through the inlet and deposited in the inner harbor. Two large shoals have thus been formed, and it is said they are evidently becoming shallower every year, and at no distant time will form a considerable addition to the land. A small spit extends from the eastern shore a short distance north of the east end of the large one. Another spit, which extends on the west side of the bay, from the high bank on the west side of the harbor towards Kidd's Point, is separated from this point only by an inlet of thirty or forty yards, through which the tide flows into the marsh behind Kidd's Island. It is formed from the detrital matter both of this bank and of Kidd's Point.

A spit of some hundred yards in length extends from the north, partly across the mouth of Cow Bay. It is derived from the detritus of some high banks in the bay, and Barker's Point on the north.

The beaches and spits we have been considering are trifling in extent and importance when compared with the Great South Beach of Long Island. This is a line of alluvial sand and shingle, extending from Napeague, in Easthampton, to the mouth of New York Bay, a distance of 104 miles; and having a direction of about west-south-west. It is not continuous, but is divided by inlets, communicating with the bays which are situated between this and Long Island, and through these inlets the tide ebbs and flows. At Quogue, and several places east of this, Long Island communicates with the beach, either by marshes or by the upland; but westward, for about seventy miles, a continuous line of bays, from half a mile to six miles broad, extends uninterruptedly, and separates the beach entirely from Long Island. This Great Beach is a line of spits and islands. One of the islands is about twenty-five miles long, with a breadth of a few hundred yards. They are all narrow and long; and when above the reach of the surf, they are covered by a labyrinth of hillocks of drifted sand, imitating almost all the variety of form which snow-drifts present after a storm.

Rockaway Neck is the only locality west of Southampton where the upland of Long Island approaches near the alluvial beach. The land through this distance is increasing in area by constant depositions. The beach at Far Rockaway, and for many miles east and west, is undergoing frequent local changes. The surf frequently washes away several rods in width during a single storm, and perhaps the next storm adds more than had been removed by the preceding. The sea frequently makes inlets through the beach to the bays and marshes, and as frequently fills up others.

The inlet to Rockaway Bay, called Hog Island Inlet, is continually progressing westward by the oblique action of the surf driving the sand, gravel, and shingle in that direction. The deposit of these materials on the west end of the island beach tends to obstruct the inlet to the bay; but the strong tidal current during the flow and ebb of the tide washes away the east end of Rockaway beach as rapidly as the other forms. The inlet is thus kept open. Mr. Edmund Hicks, of Far Rockaway, has been long a resident here, and to him we are indebted for the fact just mentioned. He knows Hog Island Inlet to have progressed more than a mile to the west within fifty years.

New Inlet is the main inlet from the ocean to the Great South Bay. It was formed during a storm not many years ago.

Crow Inlet and Jones' Inlet are undergoing changes analogous to that of Hog Island Inlet.

Barren and Coney Islands are a part of the Great South Beach of Long Island.

Coney Island has already been referred to as washing away by the waves and marine currents. It is alluvial, with the exception of a very small tract of tertiary, and is separated from Long Island by a small creek which winds through the salt marsh. Mr. Wyckoff, who has lived for many years on the island, remembers when this was a broad inlet; but it has been gradually filled up with silt, organic alluvions and drift sand, until it is reduced to its present size.

The south part of Coney Island is a labyrinth of sand dunes, formed by the wind, which present almost every imaginable shape that such material can assume. These hillocks are from five to thirty feet high, with a few straggling tufts of beach grass, and clumps of bushes half buried in the drifted sands. They owe their origin to a tuft of grass, a bush, or a drift log, serving as a nucleus. As the grass grows, the drifted sand settles among its leaves and partly buries it, and the process is renewed for years until a sand-hill is formed. On the contrary, where there is nothing to bind the sand together or shelter it from the wind, it drifts away, leaving deep hollows. Drifted snowbanks afford an apt illustration of the sand-dunes of the south beach of Long Island, and in a high wind we can realize, in a small degree, the sand storms of the African and Arabian deserts.

It has been remarked that some of the islands and sand-pits of the Great South Beach, are continually receiving accessions on the west. Long bars form in the prolongation of the beaches, so that each successively overlaps the other, the entrance being from south-west to north-east. They project in echelon from east-north-east to west-south-west. Many of these shoals, formed at some distance from the land, are gradually driven landwards by the surf, and make new additions to it. During the investigation of the various alluvial causes now in action on this coast, we easily trace the origin of this great sand beach of more than one hundred miles in length. In Europe there is no deposit of similar character to compare with it in extent.

The encroachments of the sea upon the east end of Long Island have before been mentioned. Vast masses of the cliffs of loam, sand, gravel, and loose rocks, of which Long Island is composed, are undermined and washed away by every storm. The water of the ocean coast is almost always found to have more or less earthy matter in suspension, much of which, except during storms, is derived from the grinding up of the pebbles, gravel, and sand by the action of the surf.

This earthy matter is carried off during the flood tide, and in part deposited in the marshes and bays; and the remainder is transported seaward during the ebb, and deposited in still water. It is estimated by Mr. Mather, that at least 1,000 tons of matter is thus transported daily from the coasts of Long Island, and probably that quantity on an average is daily removed from the south coast, between Napeague Beach and Montauk Point. This shore of fifteen miles probably averages sixty feet in height, and is rapidly wearing away. One thousand tons of this earth would be equal to one square rod of ground, of the depth of sixty feet. Allowing this estimate to be within the proper limits, more than two acres would be removed annually from this portion of the coast.

Nearly one-half the matter coming from the degradation of the land, is supposed to be swept coastwise. There are many evidences that the east end of Long Island was once much larger than at present, and it is considered probable that it was connected with Block Island, which lies in the direction of the prolongation of Long Island.

From Culloden Point, a reef of loose blocks of rock projects, similar to those points on Hog Island, Oak Neck, &c., where they are known to result from the degradation of the land. Jones' Reef, north-west of Montauk Point, is similar, and Shagwam Reef, a little further west, projects three miles from the shore. It is ascertained that black fish are rarely found except about a rocky bottom. It is also known, that such a bottom of loose blocks of rock, is found wherever the natural soil of Long Island and the adjacent islands has been washed away by the sea. These facts, with the well-known extensive fishing grounds for black fish around Montauk Point, and particularly on the south shore, and between Montauk Point and Block Island, give much probability to the idea, that a great extent of land has been washed away by the sea.

But if these evidences were insufficient, the present rapid degradation of the coast in that vicinity, the constant tranportation of matter westward upon the Great Beach, and the extent of this beach (more than one hundred miles long, with a breadth of one hundred to one thousand yards), which is the result of this action, would, by most minds, be deemed conclusive.

The masses forming the erratic block group, and terrain de transport, are composed of blocks, boulders, pebbles, gravel, sand, loam, and clay, which are formed of the broken-up rocks reduced to various degrees of fineness, and transported a distance from their original situation.

The surface of Kings County is a fine example of the boulder formation, or the erratic block group, which is formed of the sand pebbles, rolled stones, and boulders brought often from an immense distance, and by the force of aqueous or diluvial action brought together within certain boundaries. It is also called drift, an expressive term, which conveys a distinct meaning of the geological theories relative to this interesting subject of scientific inquiry.

In looking over the surface of the county we have a great variety of rocks and minerals presented to our view, some of which must have come from a considerable distance, but how this was accomplished is not easy to explain.

The erratic blocks of Suffolk County, and the facts relative to their general distribution, were before alluded to. These blocks are the only wall stones and building stones on Long Island and the contiguous islands, with the exception of a small tract of gneiss in places near Hell Gate. The boulders and erratic blocks are found on the surface, and imbedded in a series of strata forming the range of hills which extend through Staten, Long, Plum, and Fisher's Islands. The boulders on Long Island are rarely found south of the hills, but on the north they are observed, both imbedded and on the surface, extending to the north shore. The varieties of rock forming the boulders in Suffolk County were mentioned before as being exactly similar, in all their characters, to rocks of granite, gneiss, mica, slate, homblendic rocks, sienite, green-stone, serpentine rocks, verd-antique, red and gray sand-stones, &c., which occur in place in a northward direction from the localities where they are now found. It has also been observed that the general direction of these boulders forming beds of similar rock in place, does not coincide with the line of bearing of the strata, or the direction of the hills. In Queens and Kings counties the same general facts are observed. Granite and gneissoid rocks predominate on the hills and shore from Oyster Bay to Little Neck Bay; and thence to Brooklyn green-stone rocks are most abundant. The various rocks occurring on Long Island as erratic blocks, are much used for fences, wall stones in wells, cellars, and basements of buildings. They are nearly indestructible by atmospheric agents, and will therefore be very durable. The sea-wall at Sands' Point is built of fragments of the boulders found in the immediate vicinity.

Some of the erratic blocks are of great magnitude. Hundreds of them have been seen that would weigh fifty tons each. Kidd's Rock has already been mentioned as a large erratic block, the fragments of which cover an area of ten to fifteen square rods, and weigh at least 2,000 tons. A large block was seen about half a mile south-south-east from the churches at Manhasset

Village, called Millstone Rock, and from an observation of its cubic contents, it was estimated to weigh 1,800 tons.

Some blocks of limestone, weighing from one to five tons each, were seen on the beach at Kidd's Island, half a mile from Sands' Point, which are precisely similar in mineralogical characters to the range of limestone extending from Barnegat to Pine Plains in Dutchess County.

The rocks or boulders most frequently met with in Kings County, are large detached fragments of trap rock brought probably from the Palisades on the North River. It is very hard to work, but of great excellence for buildings. Its name is derived from the Swedish trappe, a stair, on account of its general resemblance to a stairway. This is finely illustrated at Bergen Hill, N. J., where the regular succession of lifts may be plainly seen. It also forms a large hill on Staten Island, where it is now quarried for building stone.

Blocks of granitic rock are seen on a small hill by the road from Sag Harbor to Easthampton; and near the latter place, on the shore, the surf frequently uncovers the drift that underlies the superior sands and clays. It is of unknown thickness, and contains quartz pebbles of a yellow color, intermixed with those of granite, sienite, green-stone, and hornblende rock. Crossing Napeague beach and marsh, the hills of drift commence, and extend with some interruptions to Montauk Point. It is in many places overlaid by sandy and gravelly materials, and in some places by clay. The drift formation is well exposed to observation along the south shore of the island, for nearly ten miles west from Montauk. Boulders are frequently seen in the hills west of Three Mile Harbor, of from forty to sixty tons' weight. In digging wells in Easthampton, thin layers of clay are sometimes found in the sand and gravel beds. In Southampton, boulders occur in abundance on the hills south and south-west of Sag Harbor and on Hog Neck. In the range of hills between Sag Harbor and Canoe Place, the boulders are numerous, composed of granite, gneiss, mica slate, talcose slate, green-stone trap, and hornblende rocks.

Adjacent to these, were blocks of tremolite, of a yellowish gray color, and a species of gray amphibole, nearly like the edenite of Orange County. On the north shore of Oak Neck, masses of granite, containing yellow feldspar, were observed. We have never seen granite in place similar to this. Red sand-stone, and a few boulders of green-stone, also occur here.

A boulder weighing three or four tons, of dark green serpentine, containing radiated anthophyllite was found half a mile south-west of the head of Little Neck Bay. A large boulder of gray tremolite was found on the east shore of Cow Bay, in Plandome. Boulders of steatite and of talcose rock, containing anthophyllite, were seen near the head of Little Neck Bay. Boulders of green, black, and sandy green serpentine, like those of Hoboken and York Island, are found at Brooklyn, Williamsburgh, and Jamaica. Boulders of a peculiar rock, composed of the materials of granite, with the feldspar in a state of decomposition, are found at Flushing, Williamsburgh, Brooklyn, and on Staten Island. Boulders of granular white limestone, sometimes containing tremolite, occur at Hog Island, Lloyd's Neck, Oak Neck, Sands' Point, Hewlett's Point, Flushing, and Williamsburgh. They are similar to the limestones of Westchester County. Near Fort Hamilton, serpentine, green-stone, and red sandstone, with some granite and gneiss, like those of York Island, form the mass of boulders.

Sands and loams interstratified with beds of gravel, pebbles, boulders, and clay, form the strata of Long Island, and a large part of Staten Island.

In a scientific view these beds are extremely interesting. Siliceous, garnet, and iron sands are the principal varieties. The first skirts the whole coast of Long Island and the contiguous islands, and beaches, as well as Staten Island, except along the edge of the salt marshes on its western shore. It is generally very white, containing particles of red and white feldspar, mixed with a few grains of black hornblende and magnetic oxide of iron. Some of it is sufficiently pure to make white glass. Large quantities of the sand from the Great South Beach, are shipped to New York and from thence into the interior, where it is employed for sawing marble, making glass, and for various other purposes which, though of little importance, cause a large consumption of the article. Garnet and iron sands cover the beaches in many places, but they are seen more abundant after storms, when the surf separates these heavy sands from those which have a less specific gravity. In many places they may be collected in quantities after storms. Garnet sand may be used as an imperfect substitute for emery, and for blotting sand. The iron sand is extensively used for the latter purpose, and in some places it is employed as an iron ore. A forge in Connecticut is entirely supplied with this ore, which is made directly into bar iron.

Clays are not very abundant in Queens, Kings, and Richmond counties. White and blue clays, like those of West Neck, Lloyd's Neck, Eaton's Neck, &c., are found on Middle Island and the eastern shore of Hempstead Harbor; but they are so near the water level, where they were seen, that there is little probability of their being extensively useful. The white clay on the western side of Middle Island is very pure, lying in view at highwater mark, and perhaps extending higher in the bank, but covered with sand which has slidden from above. Reddish loamy clay was seen in the deep excavation of the streets through the hill between Brooklyn and Gowanus. An imperfect sandy brick earth occurs on the hills about one mile north of Jamaica. At this place from 300,000 to 350,000 bricks are made per annum.

On Hempstead Plains the wells are dug from 60 to 120 feet deep, through beds of gravel and sand, before water is reached; this is a little above the level of the ocean. The wells gradually decrease in depth thence to the shore.

The springs of Long Island are numerous, and present some phenomena worthy of consideration. Around the heads of the bays and re-enterings of the coast along the north shore of Long Island, copious springs break out very little above tide-water level. In some instances they boil up through the sand and gravel so as to form a brook at once; in others, several springs break out at the foot of the bank, and, uniting their waters, form a stream. The numerous mills and manufactories on the shores of many of the re-enterings of the northern coast of Long Island, which have no apparent streams communicating with their ponds to renew the supply of water, attract the attention of most observers. The water of these springs is very pure, in consequence of its having been filtered through beds of nearly pure siliceous sand and gravel. It is thrown out at the level of tide-water, or at a higher level, where there are strata impermeable to it. Some of the most remarkable of these springs, which are applied to manufacturing purposes, are about Hempstead Harbor, at the head of Little Neck Bay, at the head of Cold Spring Harbor, and the south-west part of Oyster Bay Harbor.

In most parts of Long Island, water is not found in quantity, and is not permanent, except at about the level of the ocean, in consequence of the porous nature of the strata.

In some places there are local deposits of clay and loam inter-stratified, which are basin-shaped and contain the water. Springs are as abundant and copious on the south side of the island, as on the north; but they break out at greater distance from the shore. In consequence of the surface declining almost insensibly from the hills. The great plain of Long Island extends from the base of the hills south to the ocean, descending but a few feet to the mile. On most of the farms in the interior, artificial means are resorted to, to procure a supply of water for cattle and other farm stock. A basin-shaped excavation is made in the soil, and puddled with clay, and into this the surface waters are conducted during rains. They are called watering holes, and are a striking feature of the farming economy of the island. Fossil shells and lignite are not unfrequently found in digging wells in the chain of hills which extends through the island. Such facts should be preserved, as they may lead not only to important scientific truths, but to practical results applicable to agriculture. It is well known that most of the valuable marls contain fossil shells and charred wood or lignite. The observation of such facts may lead to the development of rich marl beds, and these might be of inestimable value to the agricultural interests. Clay beds similar in character to that which overlies the green marls of New Jersey have been observed on West Neck in Suffolk County. Marls may yet be found of a similar kind, connected with the same series of strata, as in New Jersey. No gneiss rock was seen in situ on Long Island, except at Hell Gate, Hallet's Cove, and a few localities along the shore, within a mile or two of these places. The rocks are gneiss, hornblendic gneiss and hornblende slate. The strata are nearly vertical, and range north 20° east and south 20° west. The hornblendic gneiss and gneiss are quarried at Hallet's Cove, and are used for basement walls. They are easily dressed with the hammer, durable, and unchanged by atmospheric causes. Gneiss is a very common rock and is found sometimes in large masses of several tons' weight. It is the rock which forms the foundation of Manhattan Island and is to be seen cropping out, or denuded, not only along the East River, but nearly all over the island above Twenty-fourth street. It is composed of the sedimentary deposits formed by materials. It is formed of mica, feldspar, and quartz, and may be known by its shining, scaly structure.

In addition to what we have said upon the soil of Long Island in the preceding pages, Mr. Mather makes the following observations, which are deemed of too much value to be omitted.

The soils of these counties are very variable, but at least four-fifths of the surface may be characterized by the terms sandy loam and loamy sand. There are many tracts of land where the soil is a heavy loam, and even a stiff clay; and others of a pure sand, which drifts, and is piled by the action of the wind. The variation of the soil is due to the different strata which form the country. Beds of sand and gravel are interstratified with those of loam and clay; and where irregularities occur in the contour of the ground, arising from denudation, a field of a few acres may exhibit almost every variety of soil, from a pure sand to a stiff clay. The art of the farmer is here put in requisition to modify the natural texture of the soils, and fit them to receive nutritive and stimulant manures with the greatest advantage. The heavy soils are dressed with sand, and the light soils with loam and clay, with a view to transform the whole into a loam of such texture as to make a pulverulent soil, and yet have it sufficiently argilaceous to retain a suitable quantity of water. The cultivated soils within twenty miles of New York are so much modified by art, that their natural qualities could scarcely be determined without geological investigation. Many of the farmers expend from $50 to

$70 per acre for street manure once in two or three years, and they are well repaid for their enlightened views and liberal expenditures. The soil is naturally very poor on the plains, but those parts which are well cultivated have become very productive. Street manure, yard manure, composts mixed with lime, rotted sea-weed, on which hogs and cattle are yarded, ashes, barilla, bone manure, and fish are those in common use. Street manure probably exceeds all the others in quantity, and the bays and inlets on the coast, together with the Long Island railroad, offer great facilities for its transport into the interior of the island. The marsh mud, and " muck " of the meadow, and the estuary mud, would make a valuable manure on the light soils. Lime answers very well on the light soils of Long Island, and the farmers will find it to their advantage to use it on their lands, first putting it in heaps to slake thoroughly, and then spreading it with other manure on the soil. On a considerable portion of Long Island the bony fish, called hard-heads or mossbunkers, have become the principal article for fertilizing the soil; and the crops thereby produced are so abundant as to be almost matter of astonishment.

These fish weigh from one to two pounds each, and are either spread directly upon the land, or mixed with other substances to decompose. In some instances, as at Southold, two or three hundred thousand, and it is even said a million, have been caught at a time; and there are probably more than one hundred million used annually upon this island. The sandy land in Suffolk County could hardly be cultivated to advantage without the aid derived from these fish.

Mr. Mather is of opinion that they are not used by the farmers of Long Island in the most economical manner.

From five thousand to fifteen thousand, he says, are spread over the ground, Instead of being ploughed in. The soil is generally light, and the animal matter passes through it by the filtering action of water, so that its fertilizing effects are nearly exhausted by a single crop.

The object in using ashes is to keep the arid soils moist by the attraction of the potassa for water, and thus afford moisture, and a stimulating alkali to the growing plants. A great error in their use is to let them remain in heaps long exposed to the weather, an idea prevailing that ashes are improved by this means, and that if used in their raw state, they would injure the crops. The fact is, that when used fresh, too many are used; as they contain a large proportion of potassa, and prove a too powerful stimulant to vegetation; but when exposed to the weather, the potassa deliquates by Its attraction for moisture, and is removed by rains, leaving little except the inert earthy matter.

Silt, or creek mud, has been used with considerable advantage in some parts of Brookhaven; it is generally obtained from the bottom of bays, where there is very little action of the tide, and where the decomposed vegetable and animal matter has been long accumulating. The long eel grass is pulled up with iron rakes, which bring up the decomposed matter with it.

On the subject of the geology of Long Island, Dr. Mitchill has some remarks which are too valuable and interesting to be passed over. His examinations were principally confined to the north shore of the island, and to the islands in the East River.

" The Brothers," he observes, " are two small islands, lying upon the side of the ship channel in the East River, and called the North and South Brother. Their foundation is rocky, and has hitherto resisted the impetuosity of the waves and currents by reason of its hard structure. Both these, and the detached rocks and reefs around them, differ in no respect from the general character of the others."

Riker's Island lies in the middle of the Sound, nearly opposite the mouth of Flushing Bay; the banks are of considerable height, but by no means so rocky as the last mentioned. There is, however, a conspicuous mass of granite upon it, and several smaller rocks scattered about. From the loose and gravelly material of which it consists, its sides are gradually crumbling down and washing away, notwithstanding it is thickly spread with rocks and stones, the remains of former washings and encroachments of the water. Of Long Island, the Doctor observes, that the faces of the country upon the north and south sides are very different from each other. On the north it is elevated, uneven, and much variegated with hill and dale; while on the south the traveler discovers little else than a flat surface, sloping gradually toward the ocean. Indeed, that part north of the ridge not only resembles the opposite shores of the main land in its general appearance, but also in its fossils, and mineral productions. It appears to have been separated from the continent, during the lapse of ages, by the encroachments of the salt water. The occurrence of no horizontal strata, and the frequency of vertical layers, lead to the conclusion that they are certainly in a state of primeval arrangement. The probability is, says Dr. Mitchill, that Long Island and the adjacent continent were once contiguous, or only separated by a small river; and that the strait which now divides them, was formed by successive inroads of the sea. This appears likely, from the fossil bodies on both shores having a near resemblance; from the rocks and Islands lying between them being found of similar materials; from the fact that the distance is small; and that where the shore is not composed of solid rocks, there the water continues to make great encroachments, and to cause the high banks to tumble down, as may be seen in many places upon the north shore of the island, and as is most particularly the case at Newtown, at Montauk, and elsewhere, at this day.

To the eastward of Hell Gate all the considerable rocks are solitary masses of granite. These are scattered over the upland and along the shore between high and low water. These rocks may be found represented in a great variety of forms and aspects, from the finest and most compact textures to the coarsest and most easily broken. In the town of North Hempstead, not far from Manhasset, is one of the largest rocks of the kind. It is known in the records of the town by the name of Millstone Rock, and contains more than twenty thousand cubic feet. The appearance of the island on the south side of the hills induces the belief that the whole extent of level land between them and the sea is a dereliction of the waters. Its horizontal strata, its sandy and gravelly quality, and the rounded and waterworn surfaces of Its quartzy pebbles, all lead to such a persuasion.

The land, besides, is very bare of vegetable mold, as well as rocks, and the timber generally of a smaller growth. The shells of marine animals are more frequently met with in digging wells; though it is said that, towards the west end of the island, the remains of testaceous creatures have been found at considerable depths on the north side of the ridge. Between Long Island and the continent there are several shoals, with rocks scattered over them, which are apparently sunken or wasted islands, showing the extraordinary leveling power of the waves. One of these shallow places, whose rocks are bare at low water, lies off the extremity of Cow Neck, and occupies several acres almost in the middle of the Sound. From the injuries these shoals inflict upon vessels, they are called The Executioners. Another sandy spot, of many acres, with several large rocks appearing here and there above the little water that covers it, stretches far toward the main channel from the bottom of Great Neck. These rocks are called The Stepping Stones, from a tradition of the Indians, that at some former distant period their ancestors could cross over here to the main. At Oldfield Point, Crane Neck, and Mount Misery the land has been frittered away for a considerable extent, leaving a considerable area covered with rocks, visible at low water. Some facts remain to be mentioned to explain the rapid currents and dangerous navigation of Hell Gate. This is a strait, one of whose sides is formed by Long Island and the other by Parsell's and Manhattan Islands. Between the two latter, Harlem Creek empties itself. There is a small quantity of solid granite here, and the shores and intervening rocks and reefs almost entirely consist of it. Such a compact body impedes, on the Long Island side of it, the direct flow of the water of the Sound in a north-east and southwest direction so completely, that the current is forced to take a short and sudden turn around the point of Parsell's Island. This change of direction is nearly at a right angle with the ridges and strata of rocks which formerly connected the two islands; and such has been its impetuous and irresistible force, that the dams of solid rock which nature had constructed across, have been broken down and carried away, and nothing but their ruins are now perceptible. The foaming and agitation of the water over and among these rocks has given rise to the whimsical appellations of Pot, Frying-Pan, Gridiron, &c. Hog's-Back, Hallet's Point Reef, Mill Rock, Middle Reef, and South Rocks, are plain and instructive monuments of the ancient arrangement. They are portions of strata remaining after all the rest had been swept away by the force of the current. On the shallows and flats of the South Bay, where there is little current, except the swell and recession of the tides, certain vegetables delight to grow. The sand and mud, which had before been moveable, now become fixed. This process continues until the new island rises above common tide, and receives no more nutriment from the water. These are the islands and marshes of great extent, scattered almost the whole length of Long Island, and are of great value for the sedge which grows upon them. Hog Island in Hempstead Bay, and Coney Island, have been thus formed.

It is a universally conceded fact, that so much of Long Island as lies southerly of the ridge of hills, is of secondary formation; while it has been concluded that the remainder is of primeval construction. Yet there are many facts and circumstances which, if they do not prove the contrary, are in such hostility with It, as to be entirely irreconcilable to the idea that the north side of the island has always existed as it now is. Some of these facts have been with considerable pains collected, and are derived from such sources, as to be entitled to our entire belief. On the subject of mineralogy, Dr. Beck says, " the mineralogy of Suffolk County is similar to that of Kings and Queens. Thus it contains hematite iron ore, but not in large and important beds. Iron pyrites and lignite are also associated with a white astringent clay, as on other parts of Long Island, while magnetic iron sand and garnet are found along the whole sea-shore. It is indeed so abundant in some places, especially after storms, that it may perhaps be profitably collected for the purpose of reduction."

Sand and gravel, mixed with marine shells, are found at considerable distances below the surface in digging wells and excavating the earth for other purposes. These are found almost universally fifty feet and more below the soil in Brooklyn, New Utrecht, Flatbush, and Newtown. The shell of a periwinkle was found forty-three feet down at New Utrecht. In Newtown, carbonated wood, sometimes alone and sometimes incrusted by pyrites, was raised from the bottom of a shaft fifty feet deep. In Bushwick, at forty-five feet, the body of a tree was found by the workmen lying across the well, and had to be cut away to allow them to proceed. Wood has also been found at great depths a little east of Westbury meeting-house. A well was dug by Messrs. William and John Mott in 1813, at Great Neck, three miles north of the ridge; and at the distance of thirty feet, on the upper surface of a stratum of loose dark red earth, lay shells of clams, oysters, and scallops; at fifty feet a piece of wood was found, soft, rotten, and decayed. Its ligneous character was, however, perfectly distinguishable. On the land of Mr. Andrew Napier three miles west of Jamaica village, during the same year, several pieces of wood were found twenty-five feet below the surface. A well was dug some years since near the Narrows at New Utrecht, and shells of clams and oysters found at sixty-seven feet; the shell of the large murex (periwinkle) was discovered, very little damaged, at two hundred and fifty feet. President Dwight, who travelled through Long Island in May, 1804, mentions that on the eastern border of Hempstead Plain, some workmen, who were digging a well, found a log of wood, three feet long, apd one in diameter, at the depth of one hundred and eight feet; the exterior was decayed for nearly an inch, the rest perfectly sound. In digging a well in the same neighborhood, a short time after, the greater part of a tree was discovered at the depth of one hundred feet. A part of the wood, says the Doctor, was put upon the fire, and burned very well. A well was dug in the summer of 1843 upon the farm of Robert T. Hicks, near Glen Cove, and at the depth of ninety feet, the workmen encountered the body of a tree, supposed to be chestnut, more than two feet in diameter.

In the town of Huntington, about the middle of the island, the people, says he, were induced to believe there was a silver mine in a particular spot; with the inquisitive spirit usual in such cases, they dug to a considerable depth, and in their progress, found a tree, with its branches, buried in solid earth thirty feet below the surface; the branches being chiefly decayed. At Newtown, a deep pit was sunk in the side of a hill in 1804, for the purpose of forming an ice-house. The hill is about twenty rods from the shore of the East River at Hallet's Cove, and fifty feet above high-water mark. At the depth of twenty feet, the workmen threw out a great many frogs, lodged in the coarse gravel. Their color was not so vivid as common; in other respects they resembled the common frog of this country. General Ebenezer Stevens, on whose land it was, observed them, and, although torpid at first, in a short time they recovered all the activity of their species. Mr. Henry Demilt, about thirty years ago, dug a well upon the west side of Cow Neck, half a mile from the shore, and at the depth of thirty-four feet came to a stratum of creek mud and shells, the stench from which was such, as induced him to abandon his design.

The late Mr. William Allen, in digging for water at Manhasset in 1824, found a quantity of oyster shells seventy-eight feet below the surface, and obtained water at one hundred and two feet. The earth at the bottom of the well was a clean white sand, like that found upon the beach, intermixed with rounded pebbles.

Anthony Sherman, while digging a well in the year 1808, for Mr. Lodowick Havens, upon Shelter Island, at the depth of fifty-seven feet found an Indian stone pestle, beautifully polished; also abundance of clam shells, mixed with beach sand and gravel.

Mr. Abraham Van Alst, at Bushwick, some years since, found a log of wood, well preserved, at forty feet below the soil; and several others in the same town, who dug wells, were compelled to abandon them on account of the filthy creek mud found at the bottom, which rendered the water unfit for drinking.

Jeremiah Johnson, Esq., states that a well was dug about forty years ago by a Mr. Kolyer, at a place called Clam Battery, in Newtown; and at the depth of seventy feet, was discovered a quantity of shells, mixed with what resembled shore sand; that Doctor Pater, in digging a well about thirty years since at New Utrecht, came (at one hundred and twenty feet below the soil) to a stratum of salt meadow resembling that in the neighborhood. And the same gentleman says, that, while he was commanding officer at Fort Green, during the year 1814, a well was constructed there, under his direction, for the use of the garrison, and at the depth of seventy feet clam shells and sand were found, which had every appearance of having been at a former period washed by the sea.

Selah B. Strong, Esq., of Setauket, L. I., says that his grandfather, the late Judge Selah, in digging a well near his mansion on the Neck, where he then resided, shortly before the Revolution, found a large tree in a horizontal position, about forty feet below the soil, and in a good state of preservation.

Dr. Dwight, in the account of his tour upon Long Island, observes as follows:

" When we commenced our journey on this island, I proposed to my companions to examine, with a continual and minute attention, the stones of every size which should be visible to us, throughout all the parts of our progress. This examination was made by us all with great care, and was extended to the stones on the general surface; to those washed out in hollow roads; to those uncovered on the summits and sides, and at the bottom of hills; to those found in the deepest valleys, and to those which were dug out of a considerable number of very deep wells.

" The result of this examination was, that all the stones which we saw, were, without any exception, destitute of angles, limited by an arched exterior, appearing as If worn by the long-continued attrition of water, and in all respects exactly like those which in a multitude of places were found on the beach of the ocean.

" In ten or twelve instances, possibly a few more, we observed small rocks of granite on our road. Every one of these exhibited what I thought plain proofs of having been washed for a considerable length of time, and strongly resembled rocks of the same kind which have been long beaten by waves. I will not say that no other traveler would have considered these rocks as exceptions; but to my eye they exhibited manifest appearances of having been long worn by water. If this opinion be admitted, we did not find, in a progress of more than two hundred miles, a single stone which did not exhibit proofs of having been washed for a considerable time.

" On Montauk Point the stones have a different aspect, being angular, and having the common appearance of the granite rocks so generally found in New England.

" After we had passed Jamaica in our way to New York, we found a similar change in the stones; most of them being angular, and presenting no evidence that they had ever been washed. Between these limits the stones are universally aquatic, if I may be allowed, for the sake of succinctness, to give them that name.

" From this extraordinary fact, it would seem a natural conclusion that the great body of this island, or perhaps more properly the materials of which it is composed, were at some former period covered by the ocean; and that by some cause, which cannot now be discovered, were thrown up into their present form.

" That Long Island was once united with the main, towards its western end, has been believed by a great multitude of persons from a bare inspection of the scenery. The narrowness and winding of the straits in many places, the multitude of intervening rocks and islands, the projection and course of the points between this island and the counties of New York and Westchester, and the general aspect of both shores, have produced this opinion in minds which have been formed to very different modes of thinking."

From this train of accumulated facts, and the conclusions to which they necessarily lead the mind of the inquirer, it can hardly be denied that the alluvial character of the greater part of Long Island is placed beyond the pale of controversy, or even a rational doubt, in the opinion of those who have given to the subject any considerable attention. We have been the more particular upon this interesting portion of its geology, because it constitutes an important part of the natural history of Long Island, and is a subject of curiosity as well as of very considerable utility.

DISCOVERY OF LONG ISLAND

There are traditions among the Spaniards and Dutch, showing that this part of the world had been visited by Europeans, long before the renowned Hudson sailed up the noble and majestic river that now bears his name. Others have supposed that they had discovered sufficient proof. In the western part of our state, of its having been occupied at some very remote era, by a race of men further advanced in the arts, and particularly in that of defensive warfare, than could be reasonably conceived of those who inhabited the country at the period of the discovery by Hudson.

Of the early history of this highly celebrated navigator little is now known, further than that he was born in England about the year 1580, had received a thorough education and was a distinguished seaman. Under the auspices of a private association, formed in England in 1607 to discover a northwest passage to India, at whose expense an expedition was fitted out, it was determined to give Hudson the command of It. Having however failed after two voyages to the north in 1607 and 1608, Hudson abandoned the project and retired to Holland, probably induced by exertions making there to form a company for establishing a commercial intercourse with the West Indies.

In 1611 he suffered by the ferocious conduct of his crew, who rose against him on the high seas, placed him in an open boat with his son and seven of his men, and left him to his fate. He was of course never heard of more.

No traces of a civilized people have ever been discerned upon this island, nor any evidence whatever to warrant the belief that other than savages ever possessed it previous to the arrival of our European ancestors in the early part of the seventeenth century.

We may therefore reasonably infer, in the absence of any proof to the contrary, that Hudson and his adventurous crew were the first white people that set foot upon the pleasant shores of Long Island.

It must be acknowledged that none, among other claimants for the honor of the first discovery of this part of the new world, has succeeded in establishing a title equally plausible with that of the celebrated Florentine navigator, John De Verrazano who in the details of a voyage made by him in 1524, in the good ship " Dolphin " (with a description of the places visited), might lead a careless or inattentive reader to conclude that he actually entered the harbor of New York, eighty-five years in advance of the ardent, enlightened, and adventurous Hudson. Particulars of this voyage were communicated by himself to his majesty Francis I., and are contained in the collections of the New York Historical Society, published in 1841. If from the local descriptions of this renowned captain, it can be reasonably inferred, that he entered the bay of New York, it remains to be explained, why attempts to colonize the country, or even to establish commercial intercourse with the Inhabitants, were not sooner made. The first historian of New Netherlands, Dr. Adrien Van der Donk — who resided here about 200 years ago — mentions no discoverer of the country prior to Hudson, but affirms, as De Laet and other old historians have done, that to Hudson, as agent of the Dutch East India Company, is solely due the glory of this most memorable discovery.

Amid the conflicting claims of ancient navigators on this point it is more discreet to credit those authorities, especially, which best harmonize, and where there is less ground for doubt. The amiable and learned Chancellor Kent, in his admirable discourse, pronounced before the Historical Society of New York in 1828, very properly observes, that " the discovery of the Hudson [River] and the settlement of our ancestors upon its borders, is a plain and familiar story. Our origin is within the limits of well attested history. This at once dissipates the enchantments of fiction; and we are not permitted, like the nations of ancient Europe, to deduce our lineage from super-human beings, or to clothe the sage and heroic spirits who laid the foundations of our empire, with the exaggerations and luster of poetical invention. Nor do we stand in need of such machinery. It is sufficient honor to be able to appeal to the simple and severe records of truth."

It may consequently, we conceive, be reasonably assumed as a fact, admitting of no plausible doubt, that Hendrick Hudson and his brave crew of eighteen men, in the " Crescent " or " Half Moon " (of eighty tons), were the first white people who landed on the sandy shores of Long Island. He was by birth an Englishman, and had made other voyages previously, in the service of some enterprising merchants of his own nation. As they were discouraged by his failure to discover the long-sought passage to India, Hudson offered himself to the Directors of the Dutch India Company, whose objects were principally traffic with Africa and America. On the 4th of April, 1609, accompanied by his son, this heroic adventurer left Amsterdam, sailing first to the north toward Nova Zembla, and returning thence south, reached the latitude of Carolina, from whence turning north again, until the 3rd of September, 1609, "they came to three great rivers," the largest of which they entered. Two of the rivers mentioned were probably what are now called the Narrows and Staten Island Sound; and the third being the " northermost," with a shoal bar before it, and ten feet of water, was doubtless Rockaway Inlet, which is laid down on De Laet's map, as a river intersecting Long Island. In a work, entitled History of New York, by Joseph W. Moulton (one of our most intelligent antiquarians) which exhibits as much industrious research of studious accuracy as any historical volume can claim, it is stated, that when Hudson first arrived in the waters of Sandy Hook, he found them swarming with fish, and sent his men to obtain a supply. It may therefore be presumed (as they went on shore) that they landed upon a part of Coney Island, in the present town of Gravesend, being the nearest land; and if so, the Canarsie Indians were the first to hail the approach of the long-to-be-remembered discoverer of Long Island.

More than 233 years ago, then, the chivalric Hudson anchored upon the shores of this island, then thickly populated with the natives of the soil. It is related of him that on the 4th of September, 1609, he sent a number of his men on shore in a boat, who, according to the words of his Journal, " caught ten great Mullet, a foot and a half long, and a Ray as great as four men could haul into the ship." Here, he says, they found the soil of white sand, and a vast number of plum trees loaded with fruit, many of them covered with grape vines of different kinds. They saw, also, a great quantity of snipe and other birds; and on the morning of the 12th they rode up into the mouth of the great river. Judge Benson says the name of the river was Shat-te-muck. The natives crowded to the shores on beholding so strange a sight as a large ship, and men so different in appearance and dress from themselves, and speaking a language also, which it was impossible they could understand. The emotions which they felt, and the opinions and conjectures they must have formed on that most novel and interesting occasion, may be imagined, but can never be known. Such a curious combination of circumstances was well calculated to excite fearful apprehensions in the minds of an ignorant and unsophisticated people.

The following remarks of the Hon. Daniel Webster, in reply to an invitation to attend the celebration of the Pilgrim Society, at Plymouth, Mass., December 20, 1845, are too beautiful and appropriate to require any apology for their insertion:

" it was," says he, " on the third day of September, 1609, that a small vessel, which for five or six months had been tossed on the ocean, sometimes on the coast of Nova Zembla, and along the fixed ices on the northern sea, and sometimes as far south as the Chesapeake, at last made her way within the protection of the land.

" She showed a small and tattered flag, bearing a modest Crescent. She herself was called the " Half Moon." The man who trod her little deck, with the authority of master, was Henry Hudson. She was now riding inside of Sandy Hook, and her little Crescent, dimmed by time and weather, was displayed over what is now the outer harbor of New York. Here was the origin of New York.

" Henry Hudson was a man, whose enterprising character, active life, and lamentable end, render him one of the most interesting personages in our early American annals; but he little thought what he had done, either for himself, or for posterity, when he brought civilization to the mouth of the river which now bears his name. According to the fancies of those times, he was seeking a passage to India; and, like others, was, no doubt, disappointed to find, that he had run against a continent.

" When he looked over the bay, and into the river, and upon the high mountains, and unbroken wilderness, which presented themselves, what a country was before him! But it was a country, the extent or importance of which, he did not at all comprehend. Disappointed in his hopes of getting to India by this route, he was thinking of fishing, furs, and the profits of trade with the Indians — not of large and permanent settlements — not of the transfer, from Europe, of political power. In time to come, and of ultimate empire. And what a future, what a history to come, was before that country, the first step in the settlement of which he had then taken !

"That future, however, was not discovered; that history to come had not displayed itself, even faintly and dimly, to the most sagacious minds of the age. The early voyagers to this continent, adventurous and enterprising as they were, yet looked principally to the finding of mines of gold, and to making sudden acquisitions of wealth. The real and true Importance of the discovery and settlement of North America, hardly appears to have been perceived by any. It lay in the future, and was concealed from sight."

The natives are described by De Laet as manifesting all friendship when Hudson first landed among them. They were c10thed, he says, in the skins of elk, foxes, and other animals. Their canoes were made out of the bodies of trees; their arms were bows and arrows, and the arrows had sharp points of stone fastened to them with hard pitch. They had no houses, he says, but slept under the blue heavens; some on mats made of brush or bulrushes, and some upon leaves of trees. They had good tobacco, and copper tobacco pipes; also pots of earth to cook their meat in. After their first acquaintance, they frequently visited Hudson's ship. They were the deadly enemies of the Manhattans, and a better people than they; who, says our author, have always conducted toward the Dutch in a cruel and inimical manner.

Heckewelder relates, that from the best accounts he could obtain, the Indians who inhabited Long Island were Delawares, and early known by the name of Matauwakes, according to De Laet and Professor Ebeling.

Long Island at this time had various appellations, as Metoac, Mectowacks, Meitowax, Matanwake, and Seawanhacky, or "Island of Shells;" and this appears to have been the most current appellation. Itis sometimes called Matanwax and Paumanake. Some of this variety are evidently but different ways of spelling the same word, and others may have been conferred by the neighboring nations, the Manhattans, the Nehantic or Mohegan tribes. It is the better opinion that the land was in most places destitute of timber; and that the population of the tribes had been much diminished in consequence of Incessant contests and bloody wars among them, which threatened the extermination of the whole race. The timely arrival of the white people, and the protection they afforded, may have been the means of saving them from destruction by their enemies.

It appears to us, of this day, somewhat extraordinary or rather surprising that the Dutch Government did not at once avail itself of the prominent advantages which this wonderful discovery presented to the ambition, not to say cupidity, of a powerful and highly commercial people. Yet it seems they manifested no disposition whatever to improve the opportunity thus afforded, to render the event of lasting consequence to themselves by colonizing the island of Manhattan, together with the adjacent shores of Long Island and New Jersey. Indeed, so slow were they to perceive or appreciate its vast importance to themselves, that it was not until 1615 they obtained a footing on the former, nor upon the latter before 1620. The periods of the commencement, and the progressive settlements of the several towns, will exhibit the comparative enterprise of the Dutch and English.

THE LONG ISLAND INDIANS

The origin of the American Indians is one of those curious problems in the history of man, that has given occasion to much ingenious conjecture, and has been a standing subject of speculation and inquiry among antiquarians and philosophers in every age, and among every civilized people, since the discovery of the country. Thus far the investigation has not been attended by any very satisfactory results; and from the peculiar intricacy of the subject itself, there is little hope for entire success. It seems to have been taken for granted that the race were originally from another country, and both Asia and Europe have been assigned as the quarter from which they must have passed to America; that they either came by the way of Behring's Straits, or may have been driven by accident or misfortune from some distant island, to which their ancestors may have arrived in the same way. If it be as necessary to account for the existence of other animals found here, as for the native Indians, a difficulty arises from the supposition that many of the tropical animals could never have existed for any length of time in a region so intensely cold as Behring's Straits; and if these are admitted always to have been here, the argument is equally strong in favor of man. If the argument for emigration be of any force, it is just as strong in favor of the idea that Asia and Europe may have been peopled from America, as the contrary. The Indians may have been equally indigenous as any other class of animals; and if they were originally planted here by the common parent of nature, they must necessarily have been endued by the same kind author with capacities and instincts graduated to the condition in which they were destined to live, and to subserve the great purposes of their creation.

The Rev. John Heckewelder, before mentioned, a learned and ingenious Moravian missionary among the American Indians, who acquired much knowledge of their language, character, and habits, observes, that from the best information he could obtain, the Indians inhabiting Long Island were Delawares, and those of York Island, Monseys, or Minsi. Their name, say they, is derived from Monissi, signifying a peninsula. The Delawares owned, and were spread over, the whole country from York Island to the Potomac. They claimed to have been very numerous and possessed of a great many towns, some on the above-named river, some at or near the mouth of the Susquehanna and about the bay, a number on the Delaware (or Lennape wihittuck, as they called it), and a great many in the Jerseys, called by them Scheyichbi. The Alinsi always composed the frontiers, dwelling in a circle-like form, from Long Island to and beyond Minnissink. That when the Europeans first arrived at York Island, the great Unami, chief of the Turtle tribe, resided southward, across a large stream or bay, where Amboy now is. That from this town a very long sand bar extended far out into the sea (Sandy Hook). That at Amboy, and all the way up and down these large rivers and bays, and on the great islands, they had their towns. The Mahiccanni were those who inhabited the country bordering on the North River, and the Delawares (or Lenni-Lennape) to the south of them.

Yet the former (says Heckewelder) acknowledge their origin from the latter, and are proud in calling them their grandfathers. They say that their great-grandfathers (the Delawares) are at the head of a great family, which extends to the north, east, south, and west. The fact is, the Delawares call all nations exclusive of the Mengua and Wyandotts (or Hurons), Noochwissak, that is to say. Grandchildren. The Delaware word for island is Manatey, and that of the Monseys is Manachtey. The Delawares were never conquered by force of arms, by the Mingoes or Five Nations, which included the Maquas (or Mohawks); yet it has been supposed that some, if not all, of the Long Island tribes were, previous to the arrival of the white people, tributary to the Mohawks. The settlement of the Dutch on York Island and the western part of Long Island, necessarily interrupted the former freedom of communication between the latter and those who were tributary to them. Great confusion occurs in Indian history, in consequence of numerous appellations given by various tribes to the same nation, leading many to suppose them to be different and distinct people. As an example, it is asserted by Mr. Heckewelder, that the Mengua, Maqua, Mingoes, Iroquois, and Trokesen are one and the same people, and comprehend the whole of the six confederate nations, including Cocknewagoes. The name Iroquois is French, and Trokesen is Dutch. Again, the Wyandotts, Delemattenos, and Hurons are one people. This diversity of names for the same nation or tribe was not peculiar to them, but the same sort of variety was applied in like manner to places, and particularly to Long Island generally as has been mentioned. These different names may all have implied one and the same thing, and were applied according to the language or dialect of as many distinct nations or tribes.

With the exception of the Eskimos, it has been conjectured that all the American tribes possess the same cardinal distinctions and the same physical characteristics. The differences which existed among various tribes in temperament, stature, or mental powers, may in great measure be accounted for upon grounds less improbable than the supposition of their having been a different race of men. The Indians of Long Island, whatever may have previously been their conduct toward one another or to distant tribes, were less troublesome to their white neighbors than the Indians north of the Sound. Nor does it appear that any formidable conspiracy ever existed with them to destroy the settlers, as was attempted, but too successfully, upon the main. The white people, by forming distinct settlements in different parts of the island, and separating the tribes, probably prevented any such combination being formed, if it were ever intended. The white population were distinguished for their prudence and vigilance; and the first dawning of hostility would create alarm, and the means of defense be instantly resorted to. That difficulties sometimes occurred with a single tribe, and might have been provoked by the improper conduct of the whites themselves, it is reasonable to believe. The story of their griefs, or the wrongs they may have endured, can never be known; and they and their sufferings are equally buried in oblivion. Their written language, so far as they possessed any, was entirely of a symbolic character; and both deeds, contracts, and treaties were signed by a mark or symbol — as the figure of a hatchet, pipe, bow, arrow, &c., each chief having his own appropriate mark. It was not uncommon, upon the death of a sachem leaving no son, or none but an infant, for the widow to assume and exercise most of the functions which her deceased husband had done. She was then called the sunk squa, or squa sachem; and the records of the different towns present examples of deeds being executed in such cases by female sachems. In some instances the sachem nominated a person to act as guardian for his son during his minority. Wyandanch, the Long Island sachem, appointed Lion Gardiner, and his son David Gardiner, as guardians to his son Wyancombone; and these persons actually affixed their names to conveyances on behalf of their ward. This singular appointment appears by the records of Easthampton to have been made in 1660, and continued till the young sachem came to the age which would authorize him to act for himself. Pending the Indian war in New England in 1675 (designated as Philip's War), which threatened the extermination of the white people on the main, it was apprehended by the eastern towns on Long Island, that the Indians here might be induced to unite with those hostile Indians to destroy them also; and thereupon such prudent and precautionary measures were adopted as effectually prevented the consequences of such an union, if any such was in contemplation. The accounts of Philip's wars would be highly entertaining, but for the unfeeling barbarities, and cold, calculating horrors of savage warfare which mark every stage of their progress. For, not contented with the destruction of cattle and grain, the plunder of goods, and conflagration of dwellings, they murdered all they met without discrimination of age, sex, or condition; beheading, scalping, dismembering, and mangling their wretched and unfortunate victims in a manner too revolting for recital.

The Algonquin or Chippeway race of Indians is one of the most numerous in existence, and there is little doubt but that all the tribes anciently in New York and New England, were of this race, if we may be allowed to consider identity of language as proof of the fact. The vocabulary of the Narragansett tongue, recorded by Roger Williams, shows them to have been of the same stock. The Mohegans were progenitors of the other tribes in New England who spoke the same tongue. So were the tribes in Maine. The Delawares, or Lenni-Lennape, were of the same family; and their language has been pronounced by competent judges the most perfect Indian dialect in existence. The Iroquois, or Six Nations, once dreaded by all the other tribes from the Atlantic to the Mississippi, are Algonquins. This tribe extends from the mouth of the St. Lawrence to the Mississippi, and northward to the Great Slave Lake. On the western side of the Mississippi is another great Indian family, the Sioux. In the south of the United States we have four tribes — the Chickasaws, Chocktaws, Cherokees, and Creeks; of the latter the Seminoles are a part, whose towns were destroyed by General Jackson, their chiefs slain, and those who escaped death, effectually dispersed. The different and somewhat singular opinions which have existed upon this subject are amusing, although few of them are very satisfactory to the antiquary. The Rev. Thomas Thorowgood, in 1652, published a quarto volume to prove the American Indians to be the Jews, who had been lost to the world for more than two thousand years. Roger Williams seems to have entertained a similar opinion, as appears by his replies to questions propounded to him by an European correspondent. Cotton Mather, a curious and wonderfully prolific writer of the seventeenth century, affirms the same; and supposes that the devil seduced these Jews from their own country, to get them (as he expresses it) out of the way of the " Silver Trumpets of the Gospel." Boudinot, in his book entitled The Star in the West, conjectures the Indians of America to be the " long-lost tribes of Israel; " and last, though not least, may be mentioned our distinguished fellow-citizen, Mordecai M. Noah, Esq., who has composed a learned and ingenious dissertation to prove them to have been originally Jews, and a part of the lost tribes of his nation.

It is one of the peculiar traits of Indian character, and one which is apparently universal, that while the business of procuring food is the duty of the men, all other labor, however arduous or degrading, is devolved upon the women. The use of the axe and other domestic implements is considered by these self-created lords as beneath their savage dignity; while to the weaker sex it belongs to plant corn, make and mend garments, build wigwams, and attend to all the drudgery of rearing children and other family affairs. Revenge is with them a cardinal virtue, and to endure pain with heroic fortitude a quality worthy of high admiration. In short, to be proof against suffering, however exquisite, and to be destitute of all sympathy for that of others, is a characteristic of the savage in every part of the world.

In Denton's History of New York, published in 1670, we find the following interesting matter on the subject of the Long Island Indians:

" Long Island," says he, " the west end of which lies southward of New York, runs eastward about one hundred miles, and is in some places eight, in some twelve, in some fourteen miles broad; it is inhabited from one end to the other. On the west end is four or five Dutch towns, the rest being all English to the number of twelve, besides villages and farm houses.

" To say something of the Indians, there is now but few upon the island, and those few no ways hurtful, but rather serviceable to the English, and it is to be admired, how strangely they have decreased by the Hand of God, since the English first settling of those parts; for since my time, where there were six towns, they are reduced to two small villages, and it hath been generally observed, that where the English come to settle, a Divine Hand makes way for them by removing or cutting off the Indians; either by wars, one with the other, or by some mortal disease. They live principally by hunting, fowling, and fishing; their wives being the husbandmen to till the land, and plant their corn. The meat they live most upon is fish, fowl, and venison; they eat likewise polecats, skunks, raccoon, 'possum, turtles, and the like. They build small moveable tents, which they remove two or three times a year, having their principal quarters where they plant their corn; their hunting quarters, and their fishing quarters. Their recreations are chiefly foot-ball and cards, at which they will play away all they have, excepting a flap to cover their nakedness. They are great lovers of strong drink, yet do not care for drinking, unless they have enough to make themselves drunk; and If there be so many in their company, that there is not sufficient to make them all drunk, they usually select so many out of their company, proportionable to the quantity of drink, and the rest must be spectators. And if any one chance to be drunk before he hath finisht his proportion (which is ordinarily a quart of brandy, rum, or strong-water) the rest will pour the rest of his part down his throat.

" They often kill one another at these drunken matches, which the friends of the murdered person do revenge upon the murderer, unless he purchase his life with money, which they sometimes do. Their money is made of a periwinkle shell, of which there is black and white, made much like unto beads, and put upon strings. For their worship, which is diabolical, it is performed usually but once or twice a year, unless upon some extraordinary occasion, as upon making of war or the like; their usual time is about Michaelmas, when their corn is first ripe, the day being appointed by their chief priest or pawaw; most of them go a hunting for venison. When they are all congregated their priest tells them if he want money, their God will accept of no other offering, which the people believing every one gives money according to their ability. The priest takes the money, and putting it into some dishes, sets them upon the top of their low flat-roofed houses, and falls to invoking their God to come and receive it, which with a many loud hallows and outcries, knocking the ground with sticks, and beating themselves, is performed by the priest, and seconded by the people.

" After they have thus awhile wearied themselves, the priest by his conjuration brings in a devil amongst them, in the shape sometimes of a fowl, sometimes of a beast, and sometimes of a man, at which the people, being amazed, not daring to stir, he improves the opportunity, steps out and makes sure of the money, and then returns to lay the spirit, who in the meantime is sometimes gone, and takes some of the company along with him; but if any English at such times do come amongst them, it puts a period to their proceedings, and they will desire their absence, telling them their God will not come whilst they are there.

" In their wars they fight no pichtfields, but when they have notice of an enemie's approach, they endeavor to secure their wives and children upon some island, or in some thick swamp, and then with their guns and hatchets they way-lay their enemies, some lying behind one, some another, and it is a great fight where seven or more is slain.

" When any Indian dies amongst them, they bury him upright, sitting upon a seat, with his gun, money, and such goods as he hath with him, that he may be furnished in the other world, which they conceive is westward, where they shall have great store of game for hunting and live easie lives.

"At his burial, his nearest relations attend the hearse with their faces painted black, and do visit the grave once or twice a day, where they send forth sad lamentations so long, till time hath worn the blackness off their faces, and afterwards every year once they view the grave, make a new mourning for him, trimming up the grave, not suffering of a grass to grow by it; they fence their graves with a hedge, and cover the tops with mats, to shelter them from the rain.

" Any Indian, being dead, his name dies with him, no person daring ever after to mention his name, it being not only a breach of their law, but an abuse to his friends and relations present, as if it were done on purpose to renew their grief. And if any other person whatsoever that is named after that name doth incontinently change his name, and take a new one, their names are not proper set names as amongst Christians, but every one invents a name to himself, which he likes best, some calling themselves Rattlesnake, Skunk, Buck-horn, or the like. And if a person die, that his name is some word which is used in speech, they likewise change that word, and invent some new one, which makes a great change in their language. When any person is sick, after some means used by his friends, every one pretending skill in physick, that proving ineffectual, they send for a pawaw or priest, who sitting down by the sick person, without the least enquiry after the distemper, waits for a gift, which he proportions his work accordingly to. That being received, he first begins with a low voice to call upon his God, calling sometimes upon one, sometimes on another, raising his voice higher and higher, beating of his naked breasts and sides, till the sweat runneth down, and his breath is almost gone, then that little which is remaining, he evaporates upon the face of the sick person three or four times together, and so takes his leave.

" Their marriages are performed without any ceremony, the match being first made by money. The sum being agreed upon and given to the women, it makes a consummation of their marriage, if I may call it. After that he keeps her during his pleasure, and upon the least dislike turns her away and takes another. It is no offense for their married women to lie with another man, provided she acquaint her husband, or some of her nearest relations with it, but if not, it is accounted such a fault that they sometimes punish it with death. An Indian may have two wives or more if he please; but it is not so

64

much in use as it was, since the English came amongst them, they being ready. In some measure, to imitate the English in things both good and bad; any maid before she is married doth lie with whom she please for money; without any scandal or the least aspersion to be cast upon her, it being so customary, and their laws tolerating of it. They are extraordinary charitable one to another, one having nothing to spare, but he freely imparts it to his friends, and whatsoever they get by gaming or any other way, they share one to another, leaving themselves commonly the least share.

" At their canticas or dancing matches, where all persons that come are freely entertained, it being a festival time, their custom is, when they dance, everyone but the dancers to have a short stick in their hand, and to knock the ground and sing altogether, whilst they that dance sometimes act warlike postures, and then they come in, painted for war with their faces black and red, or some all black, some all red, with some streaks of white under their eyes, and so jump and leap up and down without any order, uttering many expressions of their intended valor. For other dances they only show what antick tricks their ignorance will lead them to, wringing their bodies and faces after a strange manner, sometimes jumping into the fire, sometimes catching up a fire-brand and biting off a live coal, with many such tricks, that will affright, if not please an Englishman to look upon them, resembling rather a company of infernal furies than men. When their king or sachem sits in council, he hath a company of armed men to guard his person, great respect being shown to him by the people, which is principally manifested by their silence. After he hath declared the cause of their convention, he demands their opinion, ordering who shall begin. The person ordered to speak, after he hath declared his mind, tells them he hath done; no man ever interrupting any person in his speech, nor offering to speak, though he make never so many a long stop till he says he hath no more to say. The council having all declared their opinions, the king after some pause gives the definite sentence, which is commonly recorded with a shout from the people, every one seeming to applaud, and manifest their assent to what is determined. If any person be condemned to die, which is seldom, unless for murder or incest, the king himself goes out in person (for you must understand they have no prisons and the guilty person flies into the woods) where they go in quest of him, and having found him, the king shoots first, though at never such a distance, and then happy is the man can shoot him down, and cut off his long (tuft of hair on the top of the head) which they commonly wear, who for his pains is made some captain or other military officer.

" Their c10thing is a yard and an half of broad c10th. Which is made for the Indian trade, which they hang upon their shoulders, and half a yard of the same c10th, which being put betwixt their legs, and brought up before and behinde, and tied with a girdle about their middle, hangs with a flap on each side. They wear no hats, but commonly wear about their heads a snake's skin, or a belt of their money, or a kind of a ruff made with deers' hair, and dyed of a scarlet color, which they esteem very rich.

" They grease their bodies and hair very often, and paint their faces with several colors, as black, white, red, yellow, blue, &c., which they take great pride in, every one being painted in a several manner. This much for the customs of the Indians."

This rare and curious production is beyond all doubt the first essay toward a history of the Colony of New York. It was composed by Daniel Denton, youngest son of the Rev. Richard Denton, first minister of Hempstead, who came with his father from Stamford in 1644. He was an active and intelligent man, assisted in the settlement of Jamaica, and was a magistrate there several years. In 1664, he purchased, in conjunction with John Bailey and Luke Watson of Jamaica, of certain Staten Island chiefs, a tract of land in New Jersey, on a part of which Elizabethtown now stands. He soon after released his interest in the purchase to John Baker and John Ogden. In 1665 he and Thomas Benedict represented Jamaica in the General Assembly of Deputies at Hempstead, which formed the code called the "Duke's Laws." Several editions of this Interesting history have within a few years been given to the public, the most valuable of which is that published in New York in 1845, with an introduction and notes by the Hon. Gabriel Furman of Brooklyn, who deserves the thanks of every lover of American history.

The character of this work for accuracy of description, both as regards the manners and customs of the aborigines, as well as the colonists, is admitted by all who have had an opportunity of verifying it by collateral and contemporaneous evidence.

In respect to the arts of life. Itis believed that the Long Island Indians were in many respects in advance of most other tribes, and especially those in the Interior of the country, and were at the same time less inclined to war and depredation, although some of the historians of New England, and Hubbard in particular, have conferred upon them a different character. But it must be admitted that one Instance mentioned by the latter will bear a very different construction, and is strong evidence of the prejudice generally entertained against the aboriginal Inhabitants of islands. That they were objects of persecution and oppression from some of the more powerful tribes upon the main, and upon the North River, is a matter of historical certainty, and were only effectually relieved by the protection afforded them from the white people, after colonization had made considerable progress in nearly every part of the Island.

The smallpox made at different times awful havoc among several tribes, particularly in 1662, and the introduction of ardent spirits and other Intoxicating drinks, with other co-operative causes, served to lessen their numbers rapidly, and in half a century from the beginning of the settlements by Europeans, more than one-third was deducted from the former native population, which probably one century before comprised nearly a quarter of a million, including Staten Island.

In religion, like most pagan nations, they were to a great extent polytheists and idolaters. Their good and evil spirits were very numerous, to which they ascribed whatever of happiness or misery was experienced. On this account they early became an object of importance to those engaged in missionary enterprises, and in 1653 the Rev. Mr. Leveridge was employed to labor among the Long Island Indians. The Rev. Mr. James also devoted much attention to those on the eastern part of the island after his settlement at Easthampton, and in 1741 the Rev. Mr. Horton was engaged to devote himself exclusively to instructing them, which he did for several years, but to how much advantage is a matter of uncertainty, as the account left by himself only extends to three years out of eleven which he gave to this work.

The Rev. Sampson Occum succeeded Mr. Horton in endeavoring to instruct and convert his Indian brethren of this island, and was followed many years after by the Rev. Paul Cuffee, a native of considerable worth and talent, who continued among them till his death.

Sampson Occum, the Indian clergyman, was a native of Connecticut, born at Mohegan on the Thames, near Norwich, in 1723, and was the first Indian pupil of the Rev. Eleazar Wheelock of Lebanon in 1743, at the age of nineteen years, where he remained four years. About 1755 he went to Montauk as a teacher, but being afterwards licensed to preach he was ordained by the Suffolk Presbytery August 30, 1759. He continued at Montauk, preaching occasionally to other tribes, ten years. He next engaged in a mission to the Oneidas, where he continued till 1765 when he accompanied the Rev. Mr. Whitaker to Europe. Being the first Indian preacher that ever-visited England he of course attracted much attention, the houses in which he officiated being continually thronged. Between February i6, 1766, and July 22, 1767, he delivered in England and Scotland between three and four hundred sermons. He collected, it is said, above $40,000 for the establishment of schools among the American Indians, the King, before whom he preached, subscribing $1,000. In 1786 he removed with many of the Connecticut Indians and some from Long Island to the Stockbridge tribe, at Brothertown, Oneida County, where he spent the remainder of his days, and died July 14, 1792, in the sixty-ninth year of his age.

OF INDIAN MONEY, TRIBUTE, &C.

The frequent mention of wampum, or seawan, in all the early histories of this country, occurring as it does in nearly every contract or negotiation with the Indian tribes, and the well-known circumstance of its being used during the first half century of our American settlements as the circulating medium of trade and commerce (carried on both among the Indians and the white people), require that some account should be given of an article in many respects so important and valuable.

Wampum, as it was called by the English (from wampi or wompi, signifying white), or seawan, as it was termed by the Dutch, had obtained almost universally among the savage races upon this continent.

On the banks of the Hudson, as well as upon Long Island, on the shores of the Mississippi, and even on the borders of the Niger, in Western Africa, the custom of using shells as money is found to have been equally common. The tribes of our country were unacquainted with gold or silver, but as something was necessary in their place, resort was naturally had to the manufacture of wampum, as an article more convenient and portable than skins or other things, sometimes used as the medium of exchange. The only wonder, in these days of paper money, is that the facility of procuring the material out of which it was made did not so far depreciate its value as to defeat the purpose of its manufacture. But this wonder ceases when it is known that wampum besides its use as money, was extensively used as an ornament of dress, as a consideration in treaties with other tribes where shells were not found, and as the price of peace and protection from hostile aggression, in the form of tribute. Besides which there was much difficulty in the making of it, the operation being a delicate one, requiring considerable skill, and the manufacturer was generally destitute of the necessary instruments for the purpose.

Wampum, then, was composed of shells, or strings of shells, of a particular form and size, and constituted not only the money of the Indians, but served likewise as an ornament to their persons — the women and chief men in particular. It distinguished equally the rich from the poor, and the proud to the humble. It was a tribute from the weaker to the powerful, the conquered to the conqueror. It ratified treaties, confirmed alliances, sealed friendships, cemented peace, and expiated all sorts of crime, even murder, for the wampum belt washed away the memories of all blood that had been shed, and of every injury that had been inflicted. It was probably considered by these simple people the highest evidence, in most cases, of personal wealth, and the exhibition of power and influence. The mode of preparing it is thus described by one who witnessed the operation. " it is made (says he) by clipping of clam shells to a proper size, drilling a hole through the middle, and then rubbing them smooth upon a large stone; after which they are placed upon strings, the white and black being sometimes intermixed." Mr.

John Josselyn, who visited this country in 1633, says of the Indians, " their beads are their money, of which there are two sorts, blue and white; the first is their gold and the latter their silver. These they work out of certain shells, so cunningly, that neither Jew nor devil can counterfeit it. They drill and string them to adorn the persons of their sagamores and principal men and young women, as belts, girdles, tablets, borders for their women's hair, bracelets, necklaces, and links to hang in their ears. . . . King Philip, coming to Boston, had a coat and buskin set thick with these beads, in pleasant wild works, and a broad belt of the same; his accoutrements were valued (says the writer) at £20. The English merchant giveth them 10s. a fathom for their white, and as much again for their blue beads." In Roger Williams' Key, it is observed, that one fathom of wampum or Indian money is worth 5 shillings sterling. In a short time after the settlement of the country by the white people, wampum had become so indispensable an article of domestic commerce that its value was made a frequent subject of legislation, and was often regulated by proclamation of the governor. In 1673 it had become so scarce that it was publicly ordered, that six white or three black should pass for a stiver or penny.

This article was known under various names, as wam-pum, wampum-peague, wampeague or wompampege, and sometimes as peague only.

There were two kinds of this article: white and black. The latter was sometimes known as Suckanhock, and was more valuable than white. The name comes from the Indian word sucki, meaning black. The white was made most frequently from the stem or stock of the meteauhock or periwinkle, while the black was manufactured from the shell of the quahaug (Venus mercenaria) or large round clam. The Indians broke off about half an inch from the inside (which was of a purple color) and converted it into beads. Before the introduction of awls and thread, the shells were bored through with sharp stones, and strung upon the sinews of small beasts, and when interwoven of a hand's breadth, more or less, were called a belt of seawan or wampum.

A black bead, the size of a straw, about one-third of an inch long, bored longitudinally and well polished, was the gold of the Indians, and was always esteemed of twice the value of the white. Either species, however, was considered by them of much more value than any European coin. An Indian chief, to whom the value of a rixdollar was explained by the first clergyman of Renselaerwyck, laughed exceedingly to think the Dutch should set so high a price upon a piece of iron, as he termed it. Three beads of black and six of white were equivalent, among the English, to a penny, and among the Dutch, to a stuyver. But with the latter, the equivalent number sometimes varied from three and six, to four and eight. One of Governor Minuit's successors fixed, by placard, the price of the " good splendid seawan of Manhattan " at four for a stuyver. A string of this money, a fathom long, varied in price from five shillings among the New Englanders (after the Dutch gave them a knowledge of it) to four guilders ($1.66 ½) among the Dutch. The process of trade was this: the Dutch and English sold for seawan their knives, combs, scissors, needles, awls, looking-glasses, hatchets, hoes, guns, black cl0th, and other articles of Indian traffic; and with the seawan bought the furs, corn, and venison of the Indians upon the seaboard; who also, with their shell money, bought the like articles from Indians residing in the interior of the country. Thus, by this species of circulating medium, a brisk commerce was carried on, not only between the white people and the Indians, but between different tribes of the latter. It was also the tribute paid by the vanquished to those (the Five Nations for instance) who exacted contribution. In the form of a belt, it was sent with all public messages, and was preserved as a record of important transactions between nations. If a message was sent without the belt, it was considered an empty word, unworthy of remembrance. If the belt was returned, it was a rejection of the offer, or terms accompanying it. If accepted, it was a confirmation, and not only strengthened friendships but effaced injuries. The belt, with appropriate figures worked into it, was the record of domestic transactions. The confederation of the Five Nations was recorded in this manner. Cockle shells had, indeed, more virtue amongst Indians than either pearls, gold, or silver had among Europeans. Seawan was, indeed, the seal of a contract — the oath of fidelity. It satisfied murders and all other injuries, purchased peace, and entered into the religious as well as civil ceremonies of the natives. A string of seawan was sometimes delivered by the orator in public council at the close of every distinct proposition made to others, as a ratification of the truth and sincerity of what he said; and the white and black strings of seawan were tied by the pagan priest around the neck of a white dog suspended to a pole, and offered as a sacrifice to T'halonghyawaagon, the upholder of the skies, and the god of the Five Nations.

The seawan was manufactured most abundantly and in considerable variety upon Long Island, the shores of which abounded in shells, and was called, for this reason, Seawanhacky, or "Island of Shells." The poquanhock or quahaug, and the periwinkle were very plenty; and for this reason, in all probability, it was that the Mohawks, the Pequots, and other powerful tribes, made frequent wars upon the Long Island Indians, and compelled them to pay tribute in this almost universal article of trade and commerce. The immense quantity that was manufactured accounts for the fact, that in the most extensive shell-banks left by the Indians, it is rare to find a whole shell; all having been broken in the process of making wampum. And it is not unlikely that many of the largest heaps of shells still existing are the remains of a wampum manufactory.

The French, at one period, undertook the imitation of wampum by substituting porcelain for shells. If it had succeeded, this might have proved a profitable adventure; but the Indians at once discovered the artifice, and the manufacture of earthen money was of course given up. The Dutch and English made great quantities of the article from the genuine material; and the greater mechanical facilities which they possessed, gave them a wonderful advantage in the manufacture. But the consequence, as might be expected, was to diminish its value in proportion to its abundance. At the commencement of the European settlements, and in all purchases from the natives, wampum always constituted a part of the price; and this, with a few articles of c10thing, of comparatively trifling value, was exchanged sometimes for large tracts of valuable land.

Hazard, in his collection of state papers, says that the Narragansets procured many shells from Long Island, out of which they manufactured Indian money; and that they likewise oftentimes compelled the natives of the island to pay them large tribute in wampum. Dr. Edwards supposes that all the tribes upon Long Island, Staten Island, and Manhattan Island were in like manner tributary to the Six Nations, of whom the Mohawks were the most numerous and formidable tribe. Itis well known they were more extensively dreaded than any other of the northern tribes; so much so, that even the name of Mohawk excited sensations of fear and alarm in the minds of children and young people of other tribes. The Pequots or Pequods, in the day of their power. Inhabited the country about Stonington, Groton, and New London. To the north of them were Mohegans, of whom Uncas was chief, as Saccacus was of the Pequots, at the beginning of the white settlements. The Pokanokets, or Wompanoags possessed the southern part of Massachusetts and the eastern part of Rhode Island, of whom Massasolt was chief, who was succeeded by his son Philip, having his royal seat at or near Bristol. Further to the west were the Narragansets, a powerful tribe, who gave name to the beautiful bay situated between Point Judith and Seaconet. Their sachem was Canonicus, whose death occurred June 4, 1647, when he was succeeded by his nephew, Miantonlmoh, who was afterwards slain by Uncas at the instigation of the white people. All these tribes were guilty occasionally of hostilities upon the Long Island Indians, particularly those nearest, at Montauk; and they were reluctantly compelled to purchase indemnity and protection by an annual tribute of wampum, corn, &c.; while the Indians on the western part of the island were as continually harassed by tribes on the north and west, generally called the River Indians.

In 1655 a large body of Indians, consisting of five hundred from New Jersey and the North River, landed at New Amsterdam, where, being provoked into hostilities, they did considerable injury. Thence they went to Staten Island, where they committed great havoc. A part of them crossed to Long Island and threatened the settlement of Gravesend; but the Indians there refusing to join them, they retired without doing material damage. In 1649 murder was perpetrated at Southampton, and the town was at the same time greatly alarmed at the hostile appearance of the Indians in that neighborhood. Many outrages, and even murders, were likewise committed in the Dutch towns during the year 1652. In 1645 the town of Southampton ordered one-half of the militia company to bring their arms to the church upon the Lord's day. And in 1651 the town of Easthampton ordered the inhabitants to bring their arms with them to church under the penalty of twelve pence for every neglect. In 1681 the Indians plundered a store in Huntington, and threatened the family of the owner in a violent manner.

The Montauks were doubtless superior in numbers and war-like skill, at a former period, to any other of the Long Island tribes, and this superiority was acknowledged by the payment of tribute. It is abundantly evident from several early writers of New England, that the Pequots, the most powerful tribe in Connecticut, had at one time subdued the Montauks, whereby the whole of the Long Island Indians came into subjection to the Pequots; which was acknowledged by the payment of an annual tribute, for some years at least. But after 1637 they considered themselves in subjection to the English, and paid them, for their favor and protection, the same amount of tribute which they had previously paid to the Pequots. In 1650, in consequence of their failure to discharge this annuity, the New England commissioners sent Captain Mason to Long Island to require payment of the tribute due from the Indians, and to make arrangements for more punctuality in future. In 1656 the Montauk chief visited the commissioners at Boston, acquainting them that he had paid the tribute due from him, at Hartford for ten years past, but that it was in arrear for the four last years, in consequence of the war in which they had been engaged with the Narragansets. On this account the commissioners consented to release the payment of the arrears. It is not very easy at this day to perceive the propriety or justice of the imposition of this tribute by the white people. The Pequots, who had also been tributary to the English in 1650, remonstrated against the injustice of exacting any further tribute from them. In answer to which, the commissioners said it was imposed in 1635, on account of the many murders they had previously committed. It was exacted from the Long Island Indians, it seems, under the pretense that the whites had afforded them protection from their red brethren, to whom they would otherwise have been forced to pay tribute.

Governor Winthrop, in his Journal, 1637, says that " The Indians sent in many Pequots' heads and hands from Long Island and other places, and sachems from Long Island came voluntarily, and brought tribute to us of twenty fathoms of wampum each of them." From which it appears incontestably that the Long Island Indians were often involved in wars, and that they dealt freely in the blood of their enemies, also, when the opportunity offered. In 1633, says the same author, the barque " Blessing," which had been sent to the southward, returned. She had, he says, been at an island, over against Connecticut, which is fifty leagues long, the east end being about ten leagues from the main, but the west end not one mile. The Indians there, he continues, are very treacherous and have many canoes so great as will carry eighty men. And again, that in 1636 Mr. Withers, in a vessel of fifty tons, going to Virginia, was cast away upon Long Island, seven of his men being drowned in landing, some got in a boat to the Dutch plantation, and two were killed by the Indians, who took all such goods as were left on the shore. In 1638 Janemoh (called also Ninigret, Ninecraft, and Ayanemoh) sachem of Niantic, passed over to Long Island and rifled some of the Indians who were tributary to them. The sachem (says Winthrop) complained to our friends of Connecticut, who wrote us about it, and we sent Captain Mason, with seven men, to require satisfaction. In 1643, the Indians on the western part of Long Island having, as they conceived, been misused by the Dutch, took part against them with their neighbors on the main. In consequence of this event, a convention of the leading Indians was held at Rockaway, L. I., when Penowits, their great chief, addressed the Dutch agents from Manhattan, and in his speech upbraided them for their ingratitude toward the natives, touching their kindness to them in former years. At this meeting it appears that the venerable Roger Williams of Providence was present, having come to New Amsterdam to take passage for Europe, and by his timely and benevolent mediation and assistance peace was happily re-established, not only with the Long Island Indians, but with those more distant tribes who had participated in the contest.

In Gookin's History, it is remarked that the Pequots were a very warlike people about forty years since (1624), at which time they were in their meridian; that their chief sachem held dominion over divers petty sagamores, over part of Long Island, over the Mohegans, and over the sagamores of Quinipiac; yea, over all the people that dwelt on Connecticut River, and over some of the most southerly inhabitants of the Nipmuck country about Quinebaug. Another writer observes, that when the Dutch began the settlement of New York, all the Indians on Long Island and the northern shore of the Sound, on the banks of the Connecticut, Hudson, Delaware, and Susquehanna rivers, were in subjection to the Iroquois or Five Nations, and within the memory of persons then living, acknowledged it by the payment of tribute. As a proof, it is mentioned that a small tribe near the Sugarloaf Mountian, in 1756, made a payment of £20 a year to the Mohawks.

Tammany was a celebrated Indian chief of the Delaware or Lenni-Lennape tribe, and was living after the arrival of Penn; his residence being it is said on the spot where Germantown now stands. Societies named from this chief have been formed in New York and otherwhere, the place of whose meeting is called a wigwam; Indian costume and phrases were also originally adopted by these associations; but they are now much out of use. Some historians have doubted the fact of the Long Island Indians having been tributary, as stated by various writers. The Dutch (says the venerable Samuel

Jones), finding all the Indians within and adjoining their settlements on Long Island tributary to the Mohawks or Five Nations, probably concluded from thence that all the Indians upon the island were so also. On the contrary, says Mr. Jones, a tradition once prevailed among the Montauk Indians that their ancestors had wars with the Indians on the main, who conquered them, and compelled them to pay tribute. This confirms the assertion, so often repeated, that the Narragansets once held dominion over a part of Long Island at least, and probably sometimes compelled the natives to assist them in war against their enemies. When the English commissioners met at Hartford in 1650, Uncas came to them with a complaint that a sachem of Long Island had killed some of his men, had bewitched divers others, and himself also; and anxiously desired of the commissioners that he might be righted therein. About a year after the death of Miantonimoh, Ninigret it appears undertook to organize a plan for extirpating the English, and sent a messenger to Wyandanch, the Long Island sachem, to procure his cooperation in it. Instead of listening to his proposition, Wyandanch seized Ninigret's messenger, bound him, and sent him to Captain Gardiner, the commander at Saybrook Fort. From thence he was sent under a guard of ten men to Hartford. But being windbound in their passage, they were obliged to put into Shelter Island, where an old sachem, the eldest brother of Wyandanch, lived. Here Ninigret's ambassador escaped, and thus he was informed that his plan had been discovered and defeated. After the peace of 1654 between the Montauk Indians and those upon the main, the Long Islanders, pretending to visit Ninekunet at Block Island, slaughtered of his men near thirty persons at midnight, two of whom were of great note. After which Ninigret surprised some of the Long Island Indians upon Gull Island, and killed many of them; for which massacre the general court of Connecticut demanded several hundred fathoms of wampum as a satisfaction. On November 3, 1669, the Montauk chiefs acknowledged the governor of New York as their chiefest sachem.

In 1761 the Indians had so diminished on Long Island, as in some places to have entirely disappeared, while in others they were greatly reduced; and even the once powerful Montauks could at that time number only thirtyeight families, and one hundred and ninety-two souls. This number was further reduced, in 1783, by the emigration of a considerable number of their tribe to Oneida County with the Rev. Sampson Occum.

OF THE DIFFERENT INDIAN TRIBES OF LONG ISLAND

The Indians on Long Island, on the arrival of the white people, were found divided into distinct tribes, or perhaps more properly, collections of families, having different names, and exercising an independent authority or control over separate portions of territory; and these tribes had, moreover, each their chiefs and head men, called sachems or sagamores, exercising authority in the conduct of public affairs, questions of war, treaties, and the payment of tribute. From the sachems of the different tribes, and sometimes from a few other head men associated with them, the lands were purchased by the white people, and from them have descended the titles to most if not all the real estate upon Long Island. Motives of honor, justice, and humanity, as well as true policy, dictated the propriety of this course by strangers, coming to settle a country already occupied by those who were the ancient and rightful tenants of the soil. The price to be paid was always agreed upon by the parties, and good faith, it is believed, was in most cases observed on the part of the white people.

The principal tribes or clans inhabiting the island at that distant period and occupying particular portions of territory, were thirteen in number, being the undisputed claimants of the tracts of land, over which they exercised political jurisdiction.

The Canarsie Tribe claimed the whole of the lands now included within the limits of Kings County and a part of the town of Jamaica. The principal settlement was probably about Flatlands, where there is a place which yet retains the name of Canarsie, and was, perhaps, the residence of the sachem. The last of the tribe is known to have died about 1800. The inhabitants, in the infancy of the settlement, had much difficulty with this tribe, and were compelled to erect places of defense, to prevent the consequences of surprise. The immense piles of shells at this place and upon Bergen Island, show their number must at one time have been very considerable.

The Rockaway Tribe were scattered over the southern part of the town of Hempstead, which, with a part of Jamaica, and the whole of Newtown, was the bounds of their claim. The greater part of the population was at Near Rockaway, and as far west as the present site of the Marine Pavilion. Those Indians who resided at the head of Maspeth Creek in Newtown, were a portion of this tribe, as deeds for land there were uniformly executed by the Rockaway sachem, which could not have been the case had the Maspeth Indians been a distinct tribe. This tribe had likewise a settlement upon Hog Island, consisting of several hundred acres, situate in the waters of Rockaway Bay. The banks of shells in different places are very large. Mangwobe was their sachem in 1650.

The Merrick, Meroke, or Merikoke Tribe, as they have been differently denominated, claimed all the territory south of the middle of the island, from Near Rockaway to the west line of Oyster Bay; and were, in all probability, at some former period, a part of the Massapequa, or Marsapeague tribe. A part of the lands in the town of Hempstead was purchased of this tribe. They had a large settlement upon Hicks Neck, and other necks between that and the village of Merrick.

The Massapequa, or Marsapeague Tribe had their principal settlement at the place since called Fort Neck; and from thence eastward to the bounds of Islip, and north to the middle of the island; that being the usual boundary of all the tribes by a kind of common consent. The only remarkable battle between the whites and Indians was fought with this tribe, when their fort was taken and demolished by a force under the command of Captain John Underhill, about the year 1653. Their sachem in 1640 was Tachapausba.

The Matinecock Tribe claimed jurisdiction of the lands east of Newtown as far as the west line of Smithtown, and probably to the west side of Nesaquake River. This was a numerous tribe, and bad several large settlements at Flushing, Glen Cove, Cold Spring, Huntington, and Cow Harbor; and they possessed, from their local advantages, the means of subsistence very abundantly.

The Nesaquake, or Nissaquogue Tribe possessed the country east of the river of that name to Stony Brook, and from the Sound to the middle of the island. The extensive shell-banks near the village of Nesaquake show that it was the site of a considerable settlement, and probably the residence of the sachem.

The Seatalcot, or Setauket Tribe claimed from Stony Brook to the Wading River, and was one of the most powerful tribes in the county. They inhabited the sides of the different creeks, coves, and harbors, and also Little Neck (now called Strong's Neck), which is supposed to have been a royal residence.

The Corchaug Tribe owned the remainder of the territory from the Wading River to Oyster Ponds, and were spread along the north shore of Peconic Bay, and upon the Necks adjoining the Sound. They probably claimed Robin's Island also. In 1640 their sachem was Momowata.

The Manhasset Tribe possessed Shelter Island, Ram Island, and probably Hog Island. This tribe, although confined to about 10,000 acres, could, as tradition affirms, bring into the field at one time more than five hundred fighting men. Poggatacut, chief of this tribe in 1640, was a brother of Wyandanch, the sachem of Montauk, as was also Nowedina, chief of the Shinnecocks. The death of Poggatacut in 1651 was an important event with the Indians, who transported his body to Montauk for interment. In removing it, the bearers rested the bier by the roadside leading from Sag Harbor to Easthampton, where it remained through the night. A fire was built by the Indians who excavated the earth in remembrance of the event, which excavation after a lapse of nearly 200 years is still visible. An Indian rarely passes the spot who does not clear out whatever may have fallen into the hole, the place being considered by them holy ground. A pious duty thus devolves upon them to preserve the memorial of an important event in the history of their nation. This chief was not at all friendly to the white people, and would doubtless have exerted himself for their extirpation, in the early part of their settlement had he not been restrained by his brother, Wyandanch.

The Secatogue Tribe adjoined the Massapequa Tribe on the east, and claimed the country as far east as Patchogue. The farm owned by the Willet's family at Islip is called Secatogue Neck, and was, it is supposed, the principal settlement, and probably the residence of the sachem. It was sometimes called Sickete-Wachy.

The Patchogue Tribe extended their jurisdiction east from that place to Westhampton, and, as some think, to Canoe Place. The main settlements must have been Patchogue, Fireplace, Mastic, Moriches, and Westhampton.

The Shinnecock Tribe claimed the territory from Canoe Place to Easthampton, including Sag Harbor and the whole south shore of Peconic Bay. Their sachem was Nowedina in 1640. The Rev. Paul Cuffee, son of Peter, was of this tribe. He was a man of some eloquence, and of considerable powers of mind, although his education was limited. He was on the whole a useful and respectable man, and labored to much advantage among his Indian brethren of Montauk and Shinnecock for several years. He was said to be the second of seven sons, and grandson on his mother's side of the Rev. Peter John, who labored also among the natives of the island after the departure of the Rev. Sampson Occum, and lived to the age of eighty-eight years, having been born in 1714. His son Paul was born at Brookhaven March 4, 1757, and lies buried about a mile west of Canoe Place, where the Indian church then stood. Over his grave a neat marble slab has been placed, with the following inscription:

" Erected by the New York Missionary Society in memory of the Rev. Paul Cuffee, an Indian of the Shinnecock Tribe, who was employed by that society, for the last thirteen years of his life on the eastern part of Long Island, where he labored with fidelity and success.

" Humble, pious, and Indefatigable in testifying the Gospel of the Grace of God, he finished his course with joy, on the 7th of March, 1812, aged 55 years and 3 days."

Stephen Cuffee, a brother of Paul, died aged eighty-four years at Riverhead, August 23, 1845. Obediah and Vincent, sons of the Rev. Paul Cuffee, are now living, both respectable men.

The Montauk Tribe had jurisdiction over all the remaining lands to Montauk Point, and probably included Gardiner's Island. The sachem of this tribe was of so much consequence as to have been acknowledged the Grand Sachem of Paumanake, as Long Island was sometimes called. Wyandanch was their sachem in 1640.

These thirteen tribes or families were probably members of a general union or confederacy, for mutual safety and protection; and to prevent the difficulties of divided councils, some one of the chiefs or sachems was authorized to act as head or leader of the rest, without whose advice and concurrence no great political measure was adopted.

At the time of the first arrival of the white people Wyandanch, the Montauk chief, was invested with this supremacy and was dignified with the title of Grand Sachem of Paumanake, or Long Island. The newcomers treated him with a like deference, and thus did much to conciliate his friendship and gain the esteem and confidence of all the other tribes.

Montauk thus became the seat of royal authority and the center of power among the Long Island Indians. Evidences of this supreme power are still manifest, the principal of which is the remains of the Great Fort, situated on the east side of Fort Pond, which was about 100 feet square, having a ditch at the foot of the glacis, and was probably palisaded with the trunks of fallen trees. The location was well selected for protection and defense, and must have been quite sufficient against any attack which Indian ingenuity could have devised.

The lands in Kings County were, it is supposed, purchased by the governor of New Netherlands from the natives, by whom they were disposed of to the settlers; but in all the English towns, purchases were in all cases made by the planters directly from the Indians, for which patents of confirmation were subsequently procured from the governor. It is well known that the Indian inhabitants paid little attention to the cultivation of the land, except the raising a small quantity of corn; but depended mainly for subsistence upon the flesh of deer and other wild game, in addition to the great abundance of fish, clams, and oysters, found on every shore, and in every creek and harbor on the island. Besides their canoes, some of which were very large, and their bows and arrows, the only other materials of art among them were some rude vessels of earth hardened in the fire, fragments of which are yet sometimes found. The manufacture of wampum, and Its use as money, are evidence that, however simple or limited the business of any people may be, some sort of circulating medium seems indispensable. Governor Winthrop speaks of the superior elegance of the wampum made by the Long Islanders in the year 1634. The Dutch and English, as well from necessity as convenience, resorted to this species of domestic exchange, the value of which was adjusted by common consent and general usage.

The religious notions of the Long Island Indians are described in a communication from the Rev. Sampson Occum, an educated Indian minister, published among the valuable collections of the Massachusetts Historical Society.

His words are, " They believe in a plurality of Gods, and in one great and good Being, who controls all the rest. They likewise believe in an Evil Spirit, and have their conjurors or pawaws." This ceremony was so odious in the opinion of the white people, that the Duke's Laws of 1665 enacted that "no Indian should be suffered to pawaw, or perform worship to the devil, in any town within this government."

The language of the Montauk Indiansis supposed to have been the same with that of all the Long Island Indians, differing little from that of the Narragansets and other New England tribes.

It has been contended that no more than two original languages ever existed among the American Indians north of the Roanoke, the Delaware and the Iroquois, — the languages of the different tribes from Mississippi to Nova Scotia being, at most, particular dialects of the Delaware language. The structure of the Indian tongue is admitted to be different in many respects from all other known languages, ancient or modern.

The Rev. Doctor Buell in a letter to the Rev. David Bostwick, May 9, 1761, speaks as follows of the Rev. Sampson Occum: — "As a preacher of the gospel he seems always to have in view the end of the ministry, the glory of God and the salvation of men; his manner of expression when he preaches to the Indians is vastly more natural, free, clear, and eloquent, quick, and powerful, than when he preaches to others. He is the glory of the Indian nation." And it is added by another, that " while he was in England he was an object of much attention." He however failed at all times to maintain his character for sobriety and occasionally fell into Intemperance. In a letter which he wrote to the Presbytery of Long Island, June 9, 1764, he confesses " to have been shamefully overtaken with strong drink, by which, (he says) I have greatly wounded the cause of God, blemished the pure religion of Jesus Christ, blackened my own character, and hurt my own soul." Much of the epistolary correspondence of Mr. Occum is possessed by the Historical Society at Hartford, and is in many respects quite interesting. His wife was an Indian woman by whom he had seven or eight children, none of whom were of any note.

OF THE DUTCH GOVERNMENT

The hope of discovering (as has been observed) a north-west passage to India, which had long been a favorite project of the maritime powers of Europe, and even at this time scarcely abandoned, was the propelling motive of several voyages undertaken by Hudson in the early part of the seventeenth century. Two of these were made in 1607 and 1608, in the service of an English association formed for the purpose, which, being at length discouraged by the want of success, gave up the enterprise. On his third voyage, while employed by the Dutch East India Company, with a picked crew of about twenty men, English and Dutch, after crossing the ocean, he ran down the coast from Newfoundland to 35° 4' north latitude, to ascertain whether a passage might not be discovered through the continent of North America. Retracing his route, he entered Delaware Bay on the 28th of August, 1609, but declined to explore it on account of the intricacy of the channel. Following the eastern shore of New Jersey, he anchored his ship, the " Half Moon," on the 3rd of September, 1609, within the beach at Sandy Hook; and after sailing up the river as far as Albany, again put to sea and arrived safe in Europe on the 7th of November, following.

Although disappointed in the main object of the voyage, the Dutch Company believed they might establish a profitable trade in furs with the natives upon the North River; and repeated voyages were afterwards made, that excited the ambition of private adventurers, which the Company endeavored to prevent, by obtaining a decree of the States General in their own favor, thereby securing a monopoly to themselves. This took place March 27, 1614, and produced very considerable attention among those who were animated by the spirit of adventure. Accordingly, the merchants of Amsterdam and Hoorn fitted out five ships, of which the " Tiger " and " Fortune " were commanded by Adriaen Block and Hendrick Corstiaensen (or Christiance) in the service of the company. They accordingly set sail from Holland the same year, and arriving at Manhattan, erected a fort and a few dwellings thereon or in its immediate neighborhood, with the consent of the natives. The former of these navigators is supposed to have been the first white person that passed the difficult and fearful strait, which he called " The Hellegat," after a branch of the river Scheld, in East Flanders; and going through the Sound on his way to Cape Cod, he gave name to Block Island (called by the Indians Manisses) , having ascertained that Long Island was of larger dimensions than any other he had seen, and that it was an island.

The honor of this discovery has, however, not remained uncontested, whatever the fact may be, but is claimed by some writers for a certain other individual, Thomas Dermer, who, it has been alleged, on his way to Virginia, in a small barque in the month of May, 1619, sailed between Long Island and the main land. In the account which has been published of his voyage, and speaking of this passage, he says, " wee found a most dangerous cataract amongst small rocky islands, occasioned by two unequal tides, the one ebbing and flowing two hours before the other." But as this was six years after Block's arrival in America, the latter will, we presume, continue to share the entire credit of ascertaining the insular position of Long Island. He must have been at all events a bold man, who could summon resolution enough, for the first time, to adventure the frightful whirlpool of Hell Gate. The purpose of Block's visit to Manhattan, was trading with the Indians for skins, and making further discoveries in behalf of those composing the Dutch East India Company. By some accident, it has been asserted, his vessel was burned, and he constructed another near Manhattan in the summer of 1614, this being, it is supposed, the first water craft built by white people within the limits of the United States, and with this he navigated the Sound as above mentioned. She was a yacht forty-four feet long, eleven wide, and called the " Restless."

The great West India Company of Holland was chartered by the High and Mighty Lords, the States General of the United Belgic Provinces, on the 3rd of June, 1621, and was to continue twenty-four years with a pledge of renewal at the end of the term. It was modelled after the charter to the East India Company, with which body it was designed to co-operate in extending national commerce, in promoting colonization, in crushing piracy, but above all, in humbling the pride and might of Spain.

By their charter the West India Company was invested with the exclusive privilege of trading and colonizing on the coast of Africa, from the Tropic of Cancer to the Cape of Good Hope, and in America, from the Straits of Magellan to the remotest north, while the right of subscription to the stock of this great monopoly was open to all the world. The States General themselves subscribed half a million pounds and for its encouragement gave the Company as much more. Thus incorporated, this Company became the sovereign of the central portion of the American colonies, and exerted its power to a very considerable extent for more than forty years.

It is reasonable to presume that an informal alliance or mutual understanding was immediately had between the Dutch settlers and their Indian neighbors, that being an indispensable pre-requisite to the safety of the new colony and likewise to the full enjoyment of internal trade and commerce. The main object of the Company it seems was not so much to improve the agriculture of the country, as to secure the advantages of a commercial depot upon the western continent, and the fur trade of the north and west, by the Hudson and Mohawk rivers. The establishment of a fort and trading house upon Manhattan Island, and another at or near Albany, was a primary consideration with the adventurers, to which the improvement and settlement of the country were entirely secondary.

Although the annals of this interesting period are in a considerable measure defective and unsatisfactory, yet enough has been preserved to show how the settlement of the country commenced and gradually progressed, from the first rude beginnings to the full establishment of regular government and a commerce of considerable extent and importance. In 1623 and 1624, the Company fitted out two ships laden with goods, which arrived safe at New Amsterdam (now New York), in one of which it is supposed came Peter Minuit (or Minnewit), a native of Westphalia, not as governor, but more properly as chief commercial agent and superintendent, in behalf of his constituents, the West India Company. This person afterwards assumed or was invested with the powers of director-general, or governor of New Netherlands, and Isaac de Razier was appointed secretary. The council consisted of Pieter Bylvelt, Jacob Elbertsen Wissink. Jan Janssen Brouwer, Symen Dercksen Pos, and Reynert Harmenssen. The first Indian conveyance (yet discovered) made to the Dutch was executed in 1623 for land upon Manhattan Island, the settlement of which took the name of Nova Belgica or New Belgium, which was afterwards changed to New Amsterdam, and the entire territory claimed by the Dutch took the name of New Netherlands, both of which last appellations were continued during the existence of the Dutch government on this continent.

King James, about the same time, granted a patent to a London company, under which they also laid claim to New York. The Dutch and English both contended for the proprietorship of Long Island, upon the ground of prior discovery of the country; the principle having generally been adopted by the European powers, as a part of the conventional law of nations, that all new discoveries should enure to the nation under whose authority, or by whose citizens they were made. And it was now alleged by the English that Sebastian Cabot had, while in their service, discovered the whole of North America from thirty to fifty-eight degrees of north latitude; that many voyages had been made to different parts of the coast by different English navigators previous to the year 1606; and that King James had, by letters patent, in that year granted all that part of the continent between thirty-four and forty-five degrees of north latitude, to Sir Thomas Gates and others, with permission to divide themselves into two companies; the first to be called the London Company, and the other the Plymouth Company.

In consequence of these conflicting claims of territory, both powers endeavored to strengthen their authority by encouraging and extending their settlements upon this continent. The English, however, mostly confined their operations to New England, while the Dutch claimed New York and New Jersey, with the country as far east as the Connecticut River.

In February, 1623, the privileges of the West India Company were extended, by an enlargement of their charter, and powers which were before immense were considerably increased. The Company had thus become nearly sovereign and independent, and could conquer whole provinces at pleasure.

For it will be seen that they had power to erect fortifications, administer justice, maintain a police; declare war and make peace, with the consent of the States General; and with their approbation appoint a governor, or director-general, and all other officers, civil, military, judicial, and executive, who were bound to swear allegiance to their High Mightinesses, as well as to the Company.

The director-general and his council were invested with all powers, judicial, legislative, and executive, with hardly an appeal to any superior authority.

Thus were commenced and carried on the settlement, affairs, and trade of this part of the new world; and there, says the historian Bancroft, were the rude beginnings of New York. Its first age was the age of hunters and Indian traders; of traffic in the skins of otters and beavers; the age when the native tribes were employed in the pursuit of game, and the yachts of the Dutch in quest of furs penetrated every bay, basin, and inlet from Narragansett to the Delaware. It was the day of straw roofs, and wooden chimneys, and windmills.

Director Minuit embarked for Holland in the spring of 1632, in the ship " Union," accompanied by Jan Lampo, sheriff of New Amsterdam, and carrying 5,000 beaver skins, on account of the Company. They were driven by stress of weather into Plymouth, where the vessel was seized, but after considerable expense and difficulty was finally released.

The return of Minuit rendered it necessary that another director-general should be appointed over New Netherlands, and Wouter Van Twiller, of Nieukerke, one of the clerks in the employ of the West India Company, and a near relative of the patroon Van Rensselaer, received that high and responsible office. He arrived at Fort Amsterdam in April, 1633, in a ship of twenty guns, with fifty-two men, and having on board, for the service of the province, 104 soldiers, the first purely military force in New Netherlands. He had been in this country before on commercial business, and was therefore not altogether unknown to many of the inhabitants. He appears early to have devoted considerable attention to the encouragement of agriculture, of which he set a commendable example. He had a plantation of some extent at Red Hook, in the south part of Brooklyn, and another upon Nutten (now Governor's) Island. He was probably not sent with the sole intention of superseding Minuit, but with the additional purpose of examining the condition and resources of the country, purchasing lands from the natives, promoting the trade in peltry, and advancing, as far as possible, and in every way, the interests of his employers. Such (says Moulton) appears to have been the motives and object of the delegation of Wouter Van Twiller to New Netherlands. Though it has generally been conceded, or asserted without contradiction, that he was commissioned director-general, and arrived at Fort Amsterdam in June, 1629, yet there is not sufficient authority for the assertion, and none for the common opinion, that he was the first director or governor. He may have been invested by the College of XIX., through the intervention of the Commissioners of IX., and department of Amsterdam, with powers tantamount to those of a director-general, or governor-in-chief for the time being. Indeed, this appears to have been the fact. But he took with him no supersedes for Minuit, because he is named on record as director, a year after the arrival of Van Twiller. Moreover, there cannot be assigned, from the state of Minuit's affairs at this time, any reasonable cause for the suspension of his authority. Commerce was then prosperous and increasing. In return for the imports from the department of Amsterdam, amounting within the three years, from 1628 to 1630, inclusive, to 113,277 guilders, the exports were 191,272 guilders. If, as has been suggested. Van Twiller came " a wolf in sheep's c10thing," he stayed no longer than was necessary to examine the fold and mark his intended victims. Intrigue may have scattered the seeds of faction, and Van Twiller may have remained long enough to see them germinate. It is certain that factions about this time convulsed the infant colony; and perhaps this cause, combined with favoritism, and succeeded by mismanagement, may have accomplished the recall of Minuit, and the confirmation of Van Twiller in undivided and established authority. Meantime let us retrograde in our history, and follow methodically the progress of events.

In 1634, the Dutch West India Company failed, in consequence probably (among other reasons) of the extravagance of its agents, each one preferring his own, to the interest of his employers. It was found that Fort Amsterdam alone had cost them 4,172 guilders, and the whole province of New Netherlands, 412,800. Yet Van Twiller remained in authority till he was succeeded by William Kieft, who arrived at Manhattan on the 28th of March, 1638, in the " Herring," a ship of 280 tons. Authentic history presents a very imperfect account of Van Twiller's administration, or of the events of the period in which he had the superintendence of affairs; but a work of exquisite humor, in which fiction builds upon the ground-work of truth, has fully amplified his renown; and the name of Diedrick Knickerbocker, his panegyrist, will forever remind posterity of the imperturbable gravity and unutterable ponderings of " Walter, the Doubter." He died in Holland in 1657.

The commerce of the colony during these few years was much increased, for it appears that from 1624 to 1635 the number of beaver skins exported from New Amsterdam was 80,182, and of other skins 9,347, valued together at 725,117 guilders. During Kieft's administration, settlements began to be made in Kings County, and near its close, or very soon after, in the eastern part of Suffolk, particularly at Southampton and Southold, The respective settlements under the Dutch and English in the several towns were nearly contemporaneous, and were all considerably advanced within the period of forty years; although there does not appear to have been any union or combination among them until the formation of the Ridings after the conquest in 1664. In the Dutch towns the lands were chiefly, if not universally, purchased from the natives by the governor, and by him granted out, as they were wanted, to individuals or companies; but in the English towns within the Dutch territory, the lands, as we have seen, were procured by the settlers immediately from the sachems and head men of the several tribes; while in the territory independent of the Dutch, the lands were bought from the Indians at first, with the consent of the agent of the Earl of Stirling, and afterwards by their own immediate contract with the natives. In the case of grants to companies by the Dutch governor, the lands were subsequently divided among individual inhabitants by lot; and in all other cases, of purchase inhabitants were deemed entitled to a quantity of land proportionate to the amount paid by each toward the purchase, and the expenses of the patent by which it was confirmed. Indeed, long after the settlement of the several English towns (in the distribution of the common lands), the number of acres apportioned to each individual was in exact ratio with the sum contributed to the original purchase, or to the expenses incident to obtaining patents, and other charges of a public nature. Thus, in the town of Hempstead the portions allotted to individuals differed from ten to two hundred acres. In a few instances large and valuable tracts were purchased by associations of individuals for their particular use, and have remained private property ever since, as is the case with the lands of Montauk and Shinnecock. A few towns only have at this time any lands improved as a common for pasture or for grass. Jamaica possesses a considerable tract of meadow land, which is rented out for the benefit of the town, or cut by the inhabitants themselves; so has Oyster Bay; and the town of Hempstead has more than twenty thousand acres of plain and meadow, used only as public commons. The English and Dutch harmonized in their religious creeds and opinions, which were those taught in the confession of faith adopted by the Assembly of Divines at Westminster in 1642. The Congregational form of church government generally prevailed till 1747, when the Presbyterian was adopted as better suited to preserve purity of doctrine and more efficient discipline. In many towns a minister was found among the first settlers, and the organization of churches was deemed a matter of primary importance. In the Dutch towns the governor claimed the sole right of licensing preachers, by which he virtually made himself head of the church, and the source of all ecclesiastical authority. Symptoms of superstition and a spirit of intolerance were early manifested, but not to the same extent as in some parts of New England. Heretics were objected to by all, among whom were included the unoffending Quakers, who seem to have been equally discountenanced by Dutch and English and, in some instances, treated with great severity. During the administration of Governor Stuyvesant, John Bowne, a very respectable member of the Society of Friends, was actually transported to Holland to answer for his heresies, and in 1702 Samuel Bownas, a Quaker preacher, was confined in the jail of Queens County for more than twelve months on the same charge. It may be said that perhaps this sort of persecution has existed, to a greater or less extent, in all ages; but the inconsistency seems more apparent, and the incongruity greater, with those who for conscience sake had fled from the same kind of oppression in a foreign country, and sought an asylum in this, that they might here enjoy unmolested perfect freedom, civil and religious. Even such, however, with all their zeal for equality and justice, could persecute in turn, and endeavor to exclude from the pale of society and fellowship, the simple-hearted Quaker, who asked only the privilege of thinking for himself, and imparting his opinions freely to others.

The States General of the United Belgic Provinces, in their grant to the Dutch West India Company in 1621, reserved to themselves the power of commissioning the governor whom they should appoint. The object was a politic one, and intended to connect the interest of the Company with the mother country, and, by its influence and authority, secure a partial control at least over the colony; and in 1623, when the Company fitted out two ships for the purpose of establishing trade here, Peter Minuit was sent out by them under the title of Director-General of New Netherlands, which was, in fact, but another name for governor; and with him came a number of Walloons (natives of French Picardy and southern Belgium), some of whom settled on the west end of Long Island, and from whom the Waal-bocht (or Walloon Bay) received its name. The practice of slavery was introduced in 1626, if not sooner; and the Dutch carried on a considerable traffic in slaves between Africa and Virginia. Some were even carried there in Dutch vessels, it is said, as early as 1620.

There is reason for the belief that tobacco was cultivated, to considerable extent in some portions of the province, at an early period of its settlement, as well for use among the Dutch, to whom the article was considered almost a necessary of life, as for trade and exportation. To prevent some prevailing frauds in its manufacture, and to preserve its high reputation for excellence, at home and abroad, an act was passed, called the " Tobacco Statute," In 1638, a copy of which is as follows:

" Whereas the Hon. Director and council of New Netherlands have deemed it advisable to make some regulations about the cultivation of the Tobacco, as many Planters' chief aim and employ is, to obtain a large crop, and thereby the high name which our Tobacco has obtained in foreign countries is injured — to obviate which, every Planter is seriously warned to pay due attention that the Tobacco appear in good condition; that the superfluous leaves are carefully cut away; and further, that the Tobacco which is sponged is not more wetted than is required. That what is intended to be exported from New Netherlands be first carried to the public store-house, to be there examined, weighed and marked, and to be paid there the duties which are due to the company; to wit, five of every hundred pounds, in conformity to the grant of the company. And for all which we appointed two inspectors under oath. Those who transgress this ordinance shall lose all his Tobacco by confiscation, and besides arbitrarily corrected and punished. And further, that no contracts, engagements, bargains or sales, shall be deemed valid, except those written by the secretary, while all are warned to conform themselves to this statute at their peril. Done at Fort Amsterdam, August 19, 1638."

William Kieft, who succeeded Wouter Van Twiller as governor of New Netherlands in 1638, remained in office for nine years. During his administration, he was beset with difficulties of every kind. The Swedes, he conceived, encroached upon him at the south, and the English on the east; while in 1645 and 1646 he was involved in extensive wars with the Indians, both upon Long Island and the main. Toward the close of his administration, was fought the great battle between the Dutch and Indians, in that part of Horse Neck called Strickland's Plain, now included in the town of Greenwich, Conn., in which many were killed on both sides — the Dutch being, however, in the end victorious.

Intelligence being received that Pennowit, an Indian chief of Long Island, was secretly abetting these hostile attempts upon the white people, a body of 120 men under Captain Pietersen, Major Underhill, and Peter Cock, were ordered to Schouts Bay, where they landed, marched to Hempstead, and dividing their force, attacked the Indians in their settlements, of whom they destroyed more than 100 with a loss on their own side of only one killed and three wounded. Some brutal outrages were alleged to have been committed, said to have been countenanced by Director Kieft and Counsellor La Montagne, who superintended the expedition to Long Island which took place in the spring of 1644.

It has been noticed that about the time of Kieft's arrival here, Minuit, his predecessor, came to the Delaware, with the purpose of planting a Swedish colony at Christina. He came, it seems, with a ship of war and a transport, on board of which were a large number of foreigners. The Director-General, considering this an intrusion upon his territories, sent a remonstrance, which, it seems, was not much regarded by him to whom it was addressed. The records which have been best preserved, commence with the administration of Kieft; from which time to the conquest, they are tolerably full, although great additions may doubtless be obtained in Holland. He remained here till August 16, 1647, being one of the council of his successor. He then sailed with the riches he had accumulated, for Europe, in the ship " Princess," with many other passengers, among whom was the Rev. Evarardus Bogardus, the first minister at New Amsterdam. The ship was wrecked on the coast of Wales, about six weeks after, and every soul on board perished. The conduct of this governor has been generally condemned by posterity, and the manner of his death was deemed by many a just punishment for his offences. But great allowance ought doubtless to be made for the causes of irritation and perplexity that beset him. His possessions were environed on all sides by emigrants from Europe, and portions of territory supposed to be within his jurisdiction were claimed by persons from New England, who commenced settlements within a few hours' ride of Fort Amsterdam, and particularly upon Long Island. The unjust, and sometimes cruel massacre of the natives, countenanced, as was conjectured, by the governor, created much discontent, and led his superiors to disapprove his policy, and require his return to Holland.

Of the administration of Kieft, serious complaints were made, charging him with nothing less than tyranny, extortion, theft, murder, and other crimes of a most heinous nature, and were transmitted to the Directors of the West India Company, in 1644. They were displeased on account of the wars in which he had embroiled the Company, and the consequent diminution of their revenues. They consequently desired the appointment of Peter Stuyvesant, which was signed by the States General July 28, 1646, on which day he was sworn into office.

It should be here mentioned that articles of confederation had been entered into between the plantations of Massachusetts, Connecticut, Plymouth, and New Haven, with others in combination with them August 29, 1643, and confirmed by commissions appointed for that purpose September 7 following. From which time they were called the United Colonies of New England.

This was intended as a perpetual league of friendship and amity, for offence and defense, mutual advice and succor upon all just occasions, and the management of their joint affairs was to be confided to commissioners, two from each jurisdiction, to meet once a year, and oftener if necessary, any six of whom when met, to settle and determine the business in question. Said annual meetings were to be held successively at Boston, Hartford, New Haven, and Plymouth.

Stuyvesant arrived in the colony May 27, 1647, and assumed the responsibilities of his office. Peace was soon restored with the hostile Indians, and such arrangements entered into with the United Colonies of New England, as to enable him to maintain a tolerable good understanding with them during the residue of his administration. He was well aware that the state of relations between this province and the other colonies to the east were not of the most friendly character, and therefore that sound policy required their early settlement. Consequently he addressed himself to the respective governors, expressing his desire to live at peace and good fellowship with them. These letters with the answers thereto will be found in the Appendix. He remained in the office of governor till the conquest in 1664. All the powers of government — executive, legislative, and judicial — were vested in him and his council. He directly or indirectly appointed or commissioned all the public officers, framed the laws, and decided all important controversies. He moreover heard all appeals from subordinate magistrates, and required them to send such cases as were pending before them to the council, to be decided as they saw fit. In April, 1660, the governor ordered the magistrates of Rusdorpe (Jamaica) to refer a certain cause, then pending before them, to the council, to be heard and determined; and the magistrates of Middleburgh (Newtown) on another occasion were required to do the same. There were few or no lawyers at this time in the province, there being, it may be presumed, little or no need for that class of men. The first of this profession known here in that capacity was Dr. Adriaen Van der Donck, who was educated at the University of Leyden, and came to America in a barque, belonging to the patroon of Renselaerwyck in 1642, and resided at the said manor, holding the office of schout, combining the duties of judge and sheriff to some extent. On removing to New Amsterdam, he acted as chamber counsel, there being no competitor; he was not allowed to practice in the courts. He became in 1646 owner of the tract now known as Yonkers, and in 1650 signalized himself by a remonstrance to the States General upon the abuses of power in the colony, and in 1653, by his learned and interesting description of the country. Stuyvesant also directed churches to be built, installed ministers, and even directed them when and where to preach. He excluded those whose tenets he did not approve, and finally assumed and exercised the sole prerogative over the public lands. The Indian title was extinguished by him, and no purchase could be made of the natives without his leave and approbation. He granted at his pleasure, to individuals or companies, parcels of land for settlement and cultivation, subject to such conditions and payments as he thought proper to impose. And from the frequent complaints made by the delegates of the different towns, it appears that he exercised this prerogative in a capricious and arbitrary manner; refusing lands to some, and making large and extravagant grants to others, his favorites and political partisans. The Dutch towns seem to have been settled by degrees, without any previous concert of individuals, and remained for a time without any immediate organization of courts for administering justice. Nor does it seem that they entered into any arrangement for self-government, but left everything to the will and pleasure of the governor, who appointed officers in the several villages, with more or less power, and without any uniformity as to their number, title, or duration of office. As population increased, the people were permitted to nominate magistrates, to be approved of by the governor; but their powers were not defined by any general law, and therefore their acts frequently became matter of difficulty and complaint. In 1661 the governor established a new court, with greater and more definite authority than before. The magistrates subsequently chosen and approved were authorized to decide controversies between master and servant, seller and buyer, landlord and tenant; and to take cognizance of all breaches of the peace and various other misdemeanors; the Dutch courts generally proceeding according to the maxims and principles of the " civil law," which may perhaps properly be considered as the " common law " of the Dutch empire.

The English, who settled the towns of Gravesend, Newtown, Flushing, Jamaica, and Hempstead, became, from unavoidable necessity, though reluctantly, Dutch subjects; but were allowed to hold lands, enjoy liberty of conscience, and employ their own ministers; although in their choice of magistrates it was required that the approbation of the governor should be obtained, to authorize them to proceed in the discharge of the duties of their office. Hempstead and Gravesend were incorporated towns, yet the assent of the governor was equally required to sanction their election of magistrates; but it was alleged in these instances to be mere matter of form. They were also authorized by their charters to elect a schout (or constable), and a clerk (or recorder), to take and preserve the minutes of town meetings. The magistrates were vested with power to try causes, both civil and criminal, with a limited jurisdiction as to the amount in controversy, and the nature of the crime; and also to make ordinances or by-laws, for the welfare and good government of the towns, respectively. Flushing was also partially incorporated, but restricted by the terms of its charter from electing any other officer than a schout or constable, with power to preserve good order, heal differences between neighbors, and report all important cases to the governor for his consideration and decision. This town was afterwards endowed with the power of nominating magistrates, like the other towns; and such was likewise the case with Newtown and Jamaica.

The general practice in towns subject to the Dutch was for the people to choose double the number of persons required, out of whom the governor selected and commissioned those who should serve as magistrates. In towns independent of the Dutch, the people elected annually a certain number of officers, denominated townsmen; whose duty it was to superintend the concerns of the town, and to take cognizance of all trespasses upon town lands. They were associated also with the magistrates in making such prudential rules and regulations, as they mutually considered the public good required (except such as related to the admission of settlers and the disposition of lands), but which were to be submitted to the consideration of the town meetings to be approved or disallowed by them. The authority of the townsmen, as well as of the justices, extended to such matters as concerned the police of the town and such minor duties, as related to the making and repairing of fences, prescribing the time and manner of feeding the common lands, planting the common fields, &c. The towns in Suffolk County were not subject to the control of any colony, nor had they any political connection with each other before the conquest, except certain conventional agreements entered into, for specific purposes. Being too remote from Europe to derive any protection from that quarter, and having no political alliances here, the whole power of government was retained by, and vested in the primary assemblies of the people; an instance of a pure democracy which, apparently, answered all the ends of government in those days of honest simplicity. The people elected their magistrates and all other civil officers, and established courts, which decided causes with or without the Intervention of a jury, according to the discretion of the court itself, subject to the ultimate decision of the town meeting (then called the general court) if either party was dissatisfied with the determination of the particular court. The patents, or ground briefs, issued by the Dutch governors, were made by authority of the mother country, and usually commenced as follows: " We, director and council, residing in New Netherlands, on the Island of Manhattan, under the government of their High Mightinesses the Lords, the States General of the United Netherlands, and the privileged West India Company," &c. The first patents enrolled bear date one year after the arrival of Governor Van Twiller; but there are no records remaining in the Secretary's office of the proceedings of the Dutch Government during his administration. In 1640 a few English emigrants from Lynn, having contracted with the agent of Lord Stirling for a parcel of land upon Long Island, undertook a plantation on the west side of Cow Neck and near the head of Cow Bay, afterwards called Howe's Bay from Lieutenant Daniel Howe, who was the conductor of the expedition, and sometimes Schouts Bay, from the circumstance of such an officer being sent to arrest the settlers. The jealousy of the Governor led him to direct the Secretary Van Tienhoven with the under-sheriff and twenty-eight men to repair to the place, and ascertain by what pretence these Englishmen had thus intruded upon his territory. They brought six men to New Amsterdam on the 15th of May, 1640, who, being examined, confessed that they came from Lynn, under the direction of Mr. Farret, agent of Lord Stirling, the truth of which there was some reason to doubt. The temper of the Governor is represented as rash, and disposed to tyrannize over those whom he was appointed to govern. He is said sometimes to have sported with the rights of the people, rejecting, without reason, the names of magistrates presented for his approbation. In consequence of the illegal and offensive conduct of the government, a remonstrance was presented by Captain Underbill on behalf of himself and others upon Long Island, in which they declare it to be right and just to defend themselves. It bears date May 20, 1653, and enumerates the grounds of complaint to be the knavish conduct of the Secretary Van Ruyven, the retention of lands from those who had bought them from the Indians, unlawful taxes, and the taking of the tenth part of their crops, butter, cheese, &c., for the support of a set of tyrants who prey upon the industrious peasant. They compare the oppressive measures of the government to the inquisition, and state very many causes of grievance, which exhibit the odium in which the governor and his officers were held.

This paper seems to have been addressed to the council rather than the Director, and was probably intended to produce discord between them. The government, it was evident, was neither suited to the people, nor calculated to afford them the desired protection. The laws were very Imperfect, and many of them not at all adapted to the exigencies of the people; and to aggravate the matter, the governor and council were either Indisposed or incompetent to remedy many Important defects in the administration of civil and criminal justice. The sense of public insecurity in time produced a spirit of general discontent, and the people finally, with great unanimity, resolved to state their grievances to the governor, and demand redress. Accordingly, the burgomasters of New Amsterdam called upon the several Dutch towns to send delegates to a convention in that city, on the 26th of November, 1653. They met, and adjourned to the nth of December following; at which time delegates from the city, from Brooklyn, Flatbush, Gravesend, Newtown, Flushing, and Hempstead convened, and after mutual consultation, and discussion of various matters, adopted a remonstrance, which was ably drawn and expressed in spirited but decent language:

" To the Honorable Director-General and Council of New Netherlands together, to the Council of the high and mighty Lords, the States General of the United Provinces: —

" The humble remonstrance and petition of the colonies and villages in the province of New Netherlands, humbly show:

" We acknowledge a paternal government, which God and Nature has established in the world for the maintenance and preservation of peace, and the welfare of men, not only principally in conformity to the laws of nature, but according to the law and precepts of God, to which we consider ourselves obliged by his word, and therefore submit to it. The Lord, our God, having invested their high Mightinesses, the States General, as his ministers, with the power to promote the welfare of their subjects, as well of those residing within the United Provinces as of those at this side of the sea, which we gratefully acknowledge; and having commissioned in the same view some subaltern magistrates, and c10thed them with authority to promote the same end, as are the Lords Directors of the privileged West India Company, whom we acknowledge as lords and patroons of this place, next to your Lordships, as being their representatives.

" We settled here on a mutual agreement and contract with the lord patroons, with the consent of the natives, who were the first proprietors of these lands; of whom we purchased the soil at our own expense, and transformed a wilderness, with immense labor, into a few small villages, and many cultivated farms, encouraged by the privileges which we obtained, and whose preservation is dear to us.

" The deep homage and profound respect which we feel for the Government of the United Netherlands consisting and coagulated from various nations of the world: That we, leaving at our own expense, our country and countrymen, voluntarily choose to submit to their protection, and being now immatriculated in their body under our sovereign, the high and mighty Lords, the States General whom we acknowledge:

" This being considered, we humbly solicit that this our remonstrance and petition may be received and well construed without being misinterpreted."

The remonstrance then sets forth their apprehensions of an arbitrary government being established, rendering life and property unsafe. That injustice towards the natives might lead them to commit outrages upon them. That officers are appointed contrary to law, and without the choice of the people. That many obsolete laws are liable to be put in force, by which many may be exposed to danger without knowing it. That much delay hath occurred in the execution of grants to those who had right to expect them. That large tracts of lands are conveyed to favored individuals to the injury of others. They then conclude as follows:

" As we exert ourselves to reduce all our griefs to six points, in the hope they will soon be redressed agreeable to the privileges of our country, when all discontents shall cease, a mutual harmony be restored and our anxiety relieved.

" We apply, therefore, to your wisdom to heal our sicknesses and pains. We shall remain thankful, and consider any further application needless, as we should otherwise be compelled to do.

" Upon which, humbly soliciting your Honors' answer on every point or article, in such a manner that we may remain satisfied, or proceed further, &c., as God shall direct our steps.

" Your Honors' suppliant Servants,

" Arent Van Hatten, Martin Creiger, P. L. Vander Grist – New York
Frederick Lubberson, Paulus Vander Beek, William Beekman – Brooklyn
John Hicks, Tobias Peeks – Flushing
Robert Coe, Thomas Hazard – Newtown
William Washborn, John Somers – Hempstead.
Peter Wolverton, Jan. Stryker, Thomas Penewit – Flatlands
Elbert Elbertson, Thomas Spicer – Flatbush
George Baxter, James Hubbard – Gravesend."
"Done, Dec. 11, 1653."

To this remonstrance the governor and council delivered no formal answer, but entered a reply upon their minutes; denied the right of some of the towns to send deputies, particularly Brooklyn, Flatbush, and Flatlands; and protested against the meeting altogether in their observations, the governor and council reflect much on the English as the authors of the public discontents, and especially upon George Baxter from Gravesend, to whom they evidently impute the draft of the remonstrance. Baxter had been an ensign, and Hubbard a sergeant in the British service, and are so named in the charter of Gravesend. They seem to have been men of talents and capacity, and were very often entrusted with the management of the affairs of that town. In 1642, Governor Kieft appointed the former his " English secretary, to write his letters, with a salary of two hundred and fifty guilders a year, in consideration of his knowledge of the English language, and of the law." He was continued in this office by Stuyvesant, and afterwards appointed one of the commissioners to negotiate a treaty at Hartford in September, 1650. Having been educated in the principles of English liberty, he could not consistently countenance the tyranny of the governor; his opposition to which made him the victim of executive persecution, and he was obliged to leave the country to escape his resentment. On December 13, 1653, the deputies presented another remonstrance, in which they declare that if they cannot obtain redress or protection from the governor and council, they must appeal to their superiors m the Netherlands. This so irritated Stuyvesant, that with true Dutch resolution, he ordered them " to disperse, and not to assemble again upon such a business."

At this period the country was overrun with robbers, and there appeared to the inhabitants who suffered by their depredations no mode of obtaining either relief or protection. As the only alternative, the magistrates of Brooklyn, Flatbush, and Flatlands, united in forming a military company against " robbers and pirates," and established a patrol in each village, April 7, 1654. On the day following, the governor issued his proclamation against certain robbers, who he states " had been banished from New England, and were wandering about on Long Island."

In the same year the governor refused to confirm the election of Baxter and Hubbard, who had been chosen magistrates for Gravesend; although they were among the original patentees of the town, had often previously been elected to the office of magistrate, and enjoyed the confidence of their fellow citizens in every situation.

Their rejection excited so great a ferment in Gravesend, that the governor found it necessary to go there personally to appease it. It is stated in the records of November 23, 1654, that the governor went to Gravesend, and to effect! his purpose was obliged to avail himself of the influence of Lady Moody.

Of Governor Stuyvesant, it is observed by Judge Benson, " That he was of the profession of arms, and had lost a leg in the service, which was supplied by one of wood. His skill and experience must have been very useful to him, as he was incessantly vexed with the marauding clans of the Mohegan family upon his New England possessions. He was in great difficulty with the Swedes on the Delaware; and his neighbors on the Connecticut were also a source of annoyance and perplexity. In 1655 he succeeded so far on the

94

south, as to oblige the inhabitants at the place now called New Castle, to swear allegiance to the Dutch authorities. The protracted and unhappy disputes between the English and Dutch, in relation to boundaries, were finally terminated amicably, by commissioners, who met at Hartford, September 19, 1650, and by whom it was agreed, that upon Long Island a line run from the westernmost part of Oyster Bay, and so in a straight and direct line to the sea, should be the bounds between them — the easterly part of the island to belong to the English, and the westernmost to the Dutch.

In pursuance of this determination, it was voted at the session of the General Assembly, convened at Hartford sometime after, that Mr. Wyllys and Mr. Allyn should go over to Long Island, and settle the government there according to agreement heretofore made. It is matter of record that Connecticut, on the receipt of the charter of April 20, 1662, asserted a claim to the whole of Long Island, and at a general assembly held May 12, 1664, they declared as follows:

" Whereas his majestic hath bin Graciously pleased to confirm unto this Colony By charter all that part of his dominions in New England, Bounded as in the sayd charter is exprest wth the islands adjoining. This court doth declare that they clayme Long Island for one of those adjoining islands exprest in the charter, except a precedent right doth appeare approved by his Majestic. This court doth desire and request the Worshipful Govt Mr. Math. Allyn, Mr. Wyllys and Captain Young to goe over to Long Island, and to settle the English plantations on the Island under this government, according to instructions given them. The aforesaid committee are here Authorised to errect and constitute Quarter courtes or appoynt other fitt persons for the Keeping of court for the Administration of Justice, that all cases may be tryed according to lawe (life, limbe, and banishment excepted) and to doe there endeavors so to settle matters that the people may be both Civilly, peaceably and religiously Governed in the English plantations, so as they may win the heathen to the knowledge of o" Lord and Saviour Jesus Christ, By their sober and religious conversation, as his Majestic o' Lord the King requires, in his gracious letters patents, granted to his subjects here in this colony, and in cases of crimes of a capitall nature, they are to have liberty to take the opportunity of the courts of Fairfield or Hartford; the like liberty they have in case of reviewe; they may also give oath to those that are accepted by this court as freemen on the Island, and to doe what else they judge may conduce for the good of the colony."

The commissioners accordingly came upon the island in. June, 1664, organized courts in some of the towns, established rules for the collection of rates, &c.; but these arrangements were frustrated almost immediately thereafter, by the arrival of the English and their conquest of New York, whereby Long Island became annexed to, and a part of the possessions of the Duke of York. This event was, it seems, not altogether unexpected; for on the 1st of November, 1663, the governor of New Netherlands, apprehending that the English had a design to invade the Dutch territories, convened a meeting of the magistrates of many of the towns at New Amsterdam. This meeting was composed of the magistrates of New Amsterdam, Renselaerwyck, Beverwyck, Harlaem, Bergen, Staten Island, Flatlands, Flatbush, Brooklyn, Utrecht, and Bushwick; but they adjourned without effecting anything. The Dutch government, by its continued oppressions, had become generally unpopular; so much so, that even the Dutch inhabitants were greatly disgusted with the administration, and the English were, of course, extremely anxious for the change.

The English towns under the Dutch jurisdiction had long determined on the first convenient opportunity to withdraw themselves from its authority. They had held a meeting at Hempstead during the winter, and agreed to put themselves under Connecticut, as some of the eastern towns had already done; and in consequence of these proceedings being made known to the government of Connecticut, the General Assembly of that colony, on the 10th of March, 1663, appointed two commissioners " to go to Long Island to settle the government on the west end of the island, as above stated." " The English," says Smith, " were every day encroaching upon the Dutch." The following copy of a letter from Governor Stuyvesant to the West India Company, July 21, 1661, shows the state of things at that time:

" We have not, (says he) yet begun the fort on Long Island, near Oyster Bay, because our neighbors lay the boundaries a mile and a half more westerly than we do; and the more as your honors, by your advice of Dec 24th, are not inclined to stand by the treaty of Hartford, and propose to sue for redress on Long Island and the fresh water river, by means of the State's ambassador.

" Lord Stirling is said to solicit a confirmation of his right to all Long Island, and importunes the present king to confirm the grant made by his royal father, which is affirmed to be already obtained. We have advice from England that there is an invasion intended against these parts, and the country solicited of the king, the duke, and the parliament, is to be annexed to their dominion. And for that purpose they desire three or four frigates, persuading the king that the company possessed and held this country, under an unlawful title, having only obtained of King James leave for a watering-place on Staten Island in 1623."

In November, 1663, the English inhabitants convened at Jamaica to concert measures of relief against the oppression of the governor and council. The number assembled on that interesting occasion was so great, that the government did not think it advisable to attempt either to interrupt their proceedings or to disperse the meeting by force.

CLAIMS OF THE ENGLISH TO LONG ISLAND, AND THE CONQUEST OF NEW YORK

King Charles I., on the 22nd day of April, 1636, made a request of the corporation for New England, called the Plymouth Company, to whom a charter had been granted by King James I. In 1620, to issue their patent to William Alexander, Earl of Stirling, for Long Island and the islands adjacent. This request of his majesty was assented to by the company, and a grant or patent issued accordingly. The earl thereupon gave a power of attorney to James Farret on the 20th day of April, 1637, thereby constituting and appointing him his agent to manage and dispose of the lands thus conveyed to him from the Plymouth Company.

This power of attorney, after reciting the issuing of the patent as aforesaid for a certain Island called Long Island, with all and every of the islands thereunto adjoining, and stating his desire for Improving the same, concludes as follows:

" And I the said William, Earle of Stirling, doe hereby empower and authorize him, (the said Farret,) for mee, my heyres, executors, administrators, and assignees, and for every one of us, to let, set, mortgage, sell or by any other means, for present summe or sums of money, or for yearly rent, to dispose of the said lands of the said islands, or any part or parcell of them, for such time or times, terme or termes of years, for life or for lives, as my said attorney, upon the advice of the Right Worshipful Jno. Winthrop, Esquire, Governor of Boston colony, in the said New England, most tending to the preservation of the public peace, the improvement of trade and commerce, and the due execution of justice, in obedience to the lawes of God, and as much as may be, agreeable to the lawes of England."

In pursuance of this authority the said agent released to Edward Howell and others June 12, 1639, the territory now embraced in the town of Southampton, which was confirmed by the Earl August 20, 1639.

Farret was further authorized and permitted, by the said power, to take up and dispose of, for his own use, twelve thousand acres upon Long Island or the islands adjacent. In consequence of which he afterwards made choice of Shelter Island and Robin's Island, in Peconic Bay, which, as will be seen hereafter, he sold to Stephen Goodyeare of New Haven, on the 18th of May, 1641. It will be seen hereafter that Farret on the 20th of July this year mortgaged that portion of Long Island not possessed or claimed by the Dutch, for the sum of £110, which he was obliged to borrow for the " relief of his necessities," not having received from Lord Stirling, since he had been in his service, anything for his support or maintenance. The colony of Connecticut, after the reception of their charter in 1662, asserted a claim to Long Island under the clause of their charter which annexed to that colony the " islands adjacent." And the assembly at Hartford, on the 12th of May,

1664, formally resolved that it belonged to their jurisdiction, and appointed the governor and two other persons to " come upon the island in that behalf, to establish quarter courts and other courts for the administration of justice, provided their judgments should not extend to life, limb, or banishment; " and all capital cases were ordered to be tried at Fairfield or Hartford. The commissioners thus appointed came upon the island, and convening a meeting at Setauket in the summer of 1664, made a few decisions upon disputed claims among the inhabitants, and took some further measures in the execution of their delegated powers. The final arrangements were however for some cause delayed, and eventually frustrated by the arrival of Colonel Richard Nicoll in August, 1664, with a considerable naval force to take possession of New Amsterdam, in pursuance of an extensive grant of territory, made the 12th of March preceding, by King Charles II. to his brother James, Duke of York and Albany, and the consequent surrender of the city by the Dutch. The country included in this grant is thus described:

" All that part of the main land of New England, beginning at a certain place called or known by the name of St. Croix, adjoining to Nova Scotia in America, and thence extending along the sea-coast unto a certain place called Pemaquire or Pemaquid, and so up the river thereof to the furthest head of the same as it tendeth to the northward; and extending from thence to the river Kenebeque, and so upwards by the shortest course to the river of Canada northward; and also all that island or islands commonly called by the several name or names of Meitowacks, or Long Island, situate, lying, and being towards the west of Cape Cod and the Narrow-Higansetts, abutting upon the main land between the two rivers, there called or known by the several names of Connecticut and Hudson's river. Together also with the said river called Hudson's, and all the land from the west side of Connecticut to the east side of Delaware Bay; and also all those several islands called or known by the names of Martin's Vineyard and Nantuck's, otherwise Nantucket, together with all," &c.

On the execution of this extensive grant to the Duke of York, who is also styled Earl of Ulster, and Lord High Admiral of England, Ireland, &c.. Constable of Dover, Lord Warden of the Cinque Ports, and Governor of Portsmouth, he forthwith commissioned Richard Nicoll (who had been Groom of the bed-chamber to his Highness,) to be his Deputy Governor within the lands and places mentioned in the charter, with all the powers conferred upon the duke by said letters patent. This instrument is dated at Whitehall, April 2, 1664; but it should be premised that the king had previously obtained from the grandson of the Earl of Stirling, a release of the grant formerly executed to him by the Plymouth Company, and for the consideration of £300 sterling.

April 26, 1664, a commission in the following words was issued by the king to Richard Nicoll, Sir Robert Carr, George Cartwright, and Samuel

Maverick, Esquires, as joint commissioners to demand and take possession of the country, &c.

"CHARLES R.

" Charles the Second, by the grace of God, King of England, &c., to all, &c. Whereas we have rec'd severall addresses from our subjects of severall coloneys of New England, all full of duty and affection, and expressions of loyalty and allegiance to us, with their humble desire that we would renew their several charters, and receive them into our favourable opinion and protection; and several of our coloneys there, and other our loveing subjects have likewise complayned, differences and disputes arisen upon the limits and bounds, whereby unneighborly and unbrotherly contentions have and may arise, to the damage and discredit of the English interests; and thatt all our good subjects residing there, and being planters, within the severall coloneys, do not enjoy the liberty and privileges granted to them by our severall charters, upon confidence and assurance of which they transported themselves and their estates into those partes, and we having received some addresses from the great men and natives of those countreys, in which they complayne of breach of fayth, and acts of violence and injustice which they have been forced to undergoe from our subjects, whereby not only our government is traduced, but the reputation and credit of the christian religion brought into prejudice and reproach with the Gentiles and inhabitants of those countreys, who know not God, the reduction of whom to the true knowledge and fear of God; is the most worthy and glorious end of all those Plantations; upon all which motives, and as an evidence and manifestation of our fatherly affection toward all our subjects in those severall coloneys of New England, that is to say, of the Massachusetts, Connecticutt. New Plimouth, Road Island and the Providence Plantations, and all other Plantations within that tract of land known under the appellation of New England; and to the end we may be truly informed of the state and condition of our good subjects there, that soe we may the better know how to contribute to the farther improvement of their happyness and prosperity; Know yee, therefore, that wee, reposing speciall trust and confidence in the fidelity, wisdome and circumspection of our trusty and well beloved Colonell Richard Nicoll, Sir Robert Carr, Knight, George Cartwright and Samuel Maverick, our commissioners, and doe give hereby and grant unto them, or of the survivors of them, (of whom we will the sayd Colonell Richard Nicoll, during his life, shall be always one,) and upon equal division of opinions to have the casting and decisive voyce, in our name to visitt all and every the severall coloneys aforesaid, and also all power and authority to heare and receive, and to examine and determine all complaynts, appeals in all causes and matters, as well miletary as criminall and civill, and proceed in all things for the providing for and settling the appeals and equity of the said countreys, according to their good and sound discresions, and to such instructions as they or the survivors of them have, or shall from time to time receive from us, in that behalfe, and from time to time, as they shall finde expedient, to certify us or our privy councill of theire actings or proceedings touching the premises, and for the doeing thereof, any other matter or thing relating thereunto, these presents or the enrolment thereof, shall be unto them, and every of them, a sufficient warrant and discharge in that behalfe. In witnesse whereof we have caused these our letters to be made patent. Given at our court at Whitehall, the 26th of April, 1664. BARKER."

The Dutch inhabitants, by the vigilance of their governor, were, as has been seen, not ignorant of the intentions of the English court; for the record states that on the 8th of July, 1664, intelligence was received from Captain Thomas Willet, an Englishman, that an expedition was preparing in England against the New Netherlands, consisting of two frigates of forty and fifty guns, and a fly-boat of forty guns, having on board three hundred soldiers, and each frigate one hundred and fifty men; and that the forces then lay at Portsmouth waiting for wind. News arrived also, from Boston, that the forces had already sailed from Europe.

The burgomasters were thereupon called together, to concert measures for defense; the fort was ordered to be put in better condition, and spies were sent to Milford and other places for intelligence. Boston was doubtless in the secret; for the court of Massachusetts had, in the May preceding, ordered a supply of necessaries for the use of the ships on their arrival. These were four in number, one of which was called the " Guerney." it was intended to rendezvous at Gardiner's Island, at the entrance of Long Island Sound, but the vessels parted in a fog about the 20th of July. The new governor and Sir George Cartwright were, it seems, on board the " Guerney," and fell in first with Cape Cod. The other ships, with Sir Robert Carr and Samuel Maverick (commissioners), were rightly concluded to be driven to the eastward. After dispatching a letter to Governor Winthrop of Connecticut, requesting his assistance, Colonel Nicoll proceeded to Boston, the other ships got safely into Piscataway. Endicott was then governor of Boston, but was grown old, and incapable of business. On the 27th of July the commissioners made a formal request in writing, " that the government of Boston would pass an act to furnish them with armed men, who should begin their march to the Manhattans on the 20th of August ensuing; and promised that if they could get other assistance, they would give them an account of it." This application was without success, attributable perhaps (as Smith says) to their disaffection to the Stuart family, by whose persecutions the former inhabitants of that colony had been driven from Europe.

One of the ships, the " Guerney," entered the bay of New York several days before the others arrived, and as soon as they had come up, Governor Stuyvesant sent a letter, dated August 19, 1664, directed to the commanders of the English frigates, by the hands of John Declyer, one of the chief council, the Rev. John Megapolensis, minister, Paul Lunder Vander Grist, and Mr. Samuel Megapolensis, doctor in physic, with the utmost civility, to desire the reason of their approach, and continuing in the harbor without giving notice of their coming, as they ought to have done. Colonel Nicoll answered the next day, with a summons, as follows:

" To the Honorable the Governor and chief council at the Manhattans.

" Right worthy Sirs,

" I received a letter by some worthy persons intrusted by you, bearing date the 19th of August, desiring to know the intent of the approach of the English frigates; in return of which, I think it fit to let you know that his Majesty of Great Britain, whose right and title to these parts of America is unquestionable, well knowing how much it derogates from his crown and dignity to suffer any foreigners, how near soever they be allied, to usurp a dominion, and without his Majesty's royal consent to inherit in these, or any other of his Majesty's territories, hath commanded me, in his name, to require a surrender of all such forts, towns, or places of strength, which are now possessed by the Dutch under your command; and in his Majesty's name I do demand the town, situate on the island, commonly known by the name of Manhattoes, with all the forts thereunto belonging, to be rendered unto his majesty's obedience and protection, into my hands. I am further commanded to assure you, and every respective inhabitant of the Dutch nation, that his Majesty being tender of the effusion of Christian blood, doth by these presents confirm and secure to every man his estate, life, and liberty, who shall readily submit to his government. And all those who shall oppose his Majesty's gracious intention, must expect all the miseries of a war, which they bring upon themselves. I shall expect your answer by these gentlemen, George Cartwright, one of his Majesty's commissioners in America, Captain Robert Needham, Captain Edward Groves, and Mr. Thomas Delavall, whom you will entertain with such civility as is due to them, and yourselves and yours shall receive the same from,

" Worthy Sirs,

" Your very humble Servant,

" Richard Nicoll." " Dated on board his Majesty's ship the Guerney, riding before Nayack, the 20th of

Aug. 1664."

Governor Stuyvesant promised an answer to this summons the next morning, and in the meantime he convened the council and burgomasters. The Dutch governor was a good soldier (says Smith) and had lost a leg in the service of the States. He would willingly have made a defense; and refused a sight of the summons both to the inhabitants and burgomasters, lest the easy terms offered might induce them to comply with the proposals of the invaders. The burgomasters, however, insisted upon a copy, that they might communicate it to the late magistrates and principal burghers. They called together the inhabitants at the Stadthouse, and acquainted them with his excellency's refusal. Governor Winthrop, at the same time, wrote to the governor and council, strongly recommending a surrender of the city. On the 22nd of August the burgomasters came into the council-chamber and desired to know the contents of the message received from Governor Winthrop, which Stuyvesant still refused. They nevertheless continued their importunity; and he, in a fit of anger, tore it to pieces; upon which they protested as well against the act as its consequences. Having determined upon a defense of the country, Stuyvesant wrote a letter in answer to the summons; in which he fully denied the right of his Majesty, the King of England, to the territory; and setting forth the reasons why the title was in the Lords, the States General:

" That by virtue of a grant and commission given by the said Lords and mighty States General to the West India Company, in the year 1621, with as much power, and as authentic, as his said Majesty of England hath given or can give to any colony in America, as more fully appears by the patent of the said Lords, the States General, by them signed, registered, and sealed with their great seal, and shown to the deputies; by which commission and patent together, and by divers letters, signed and sealed by the said Lords, the States General, directed to several persons, both English and Dutch, inhabiting the towns and villages on Long Island, by which they are declared and acknowledged to be their subjects, which makes it appear more clear than the sun at noon day, that the claim of England is absolutely to be denied.

" Moreover (says the governor) it is without dispute, and acknowledged by the world, that our predecessors, by virtue of the commission and patent of the said Lords, the States General, have, and without control and peaceably (the contrary never coming to our knowledge), enjoyed Fort Orange about forty-eight or fifty years; the Manhattans forty-one or forty-two years; the South River forty years; and the Fresh Water River about thirty-six years. And that though the governors and commissioners of his Majesty had often quarreled about the bounds of the Dutch possessions, yet they never questioned their jurisdiction itself. On the contrary, in the year 1650, at Hartford, and the year before at Boston, they treated upon the subject; which is a sufficient proof, that had his Majesty been well informed, he never would have given a commission to molest and endamage the subjects of the Lords, the States General; and less that his subjects would attempt any acts of hostility against them. Consequently, if his said Majesty were well informed of all that could be spoken upon this subject, he would not approve of what expressions were mentioned in your letter. And in case that you will act by force of arms, we protest and declare, in the name of our said Lords, the States General, before God and Men, that you will act an unjust violence, and a breach of the articles of peace, so solemnly sworn, agreed upon, and ratified by his Majesty of England and my Lords, the States General; and the rather, for that to prevent the shedding of blood in the month of February last we treated with Captain John Scott, (who reported he had a commission from his Majesty,) touching the limits of Long Island, and concluded for the space of a year. As touching the threats in your conclusion, we have nothing to answer, only that we fear nothing but what God (who is as just as merciful) shall lay upon us, all things being in his gracious disposal; and we may as well be preserved by him with small forces as by a great army."

While the Dutch governor and his council were contending with the burgomasters and people in the city, the English commissioners had published a proclamation to the inhabitants of Long Island, encouraging them to submit, and promising them the king's protection and all the privileges of loyal subjects. How far this flattering promise was afterwards fulfilled, will appear from the proceedings that took place at Hempstead in 1665, when a code of laws for the colony was promulgated; by which it turned out that, so far from enjoying all the privileges of British subjects, they were entirely excluded from the benefits of a general assembly, or the right of choosing persons to represent them in the government. This proclamation was as follows:

" By his Majesty's command. Forasmuch as his Majesty hath sent us by commission, under his great seal of England, amongst other things to expel or to receive to his Majesty's obedience all such foreigners as have, without his Majesty's leave and consent, seated themselves amongst any of his dominions in America, to the prejudice of his Majesty's subjects and the diminution of his royal dignity; we, his Majesty's commissioners, declare and promise, that whoever, of what nation soever, will, upon knowledge of this proclamation, acknowledge and testify themselves to submit to this his Majesty's government, as his good subjects, shall be protected in his Majesty's laws and justice, and peaceably enjoy whatsoever God's blessing and their honest industry have furnished them with, and all other privileges with his Majesty's English subjects. We have caused this to be published, that we might prevent all inconvenience to others, if it were possible; however, to clear ourselves from the charge of all those miseries that may any way befall such as live here, and will not acknowledge his Majesty for their sovereign, whom God preserve.

Richard Nicoll, Robert Carr, George Cartwright, Samuel Maverick.

" In his Majesty's frigate the Guerney, August 20, 1664."

As soon as it was ascertained by Stuyvesant's letter that he was averse to a surrender, officers were sent to obtain volunteers in the western towns on Long Island as far as Jamaica and Hempstead. And preparations were also made by those on board the ships for an immediate attack upon Fort Amsterdam. These movements, and probably the persuasions of those around him, induced Stuyvesant to write again to Colonel Nicoll on the 25th of August, in which letter he declares that though he would stand the storm, yet, to prevent the spilling of blood, he had sent John De Decker, councilor of state; Cornelius Van Ruyven, secretary; Cornelius Steenwyck, major; and James Cousseau, sheriff; to consult, if possible, of an accommodation. Nicoll, who by this time knew the dispositions and wishes of the people, answered immediately, from Gravesend, that he would treat about nothing else than a surrender. The Dutch governor next day, the 26th, agreed to a treaty and surrender, on condition the English and Dutch limits were settled mutually by the Crown and the States General.

The English deputies, agreed upon in this negotiation, were Sir Robert Carr, George Cartwright, John Winthrop, the governor of Connecticut, Samuel Wyllys, one of the assistants or council of that colony, and Thomas Clarke and John Pynchon, commissioners from the General Court of Massachusetts Bay. Whatever these persons should agree upon, Nicoll promised to ratify. At eight o'clock in the morning of the 27th of August, 1664, the commissioners on both sides met at the governor's farm (or Bowery), where articles of capitulation were agreed to and signed. These articles were twenty-three in number, and were so framed as to protect the inhabitants in their rights, civil and religious, as citizens of the new government; to remove or remain at their pleasure, and to carry on trade and commerce as British subjects; the ports to be open to the Dutch vessels for six months; public writings and documents to be carefully preserved. All persons in office to remain therein till the time of a new election; previous differences and contracts to be determined according to the manner of the Dutch; the officers, military, and soldiers to march out with their arms, drums beating, colors flying, and with lighted matches; and those disposed to continue in the country to have fifty acres of land set out for each of them.

Favorable, however, as these articles were to the inhabitants the Dutch governor refused to ratify them until two days after they were signed by the commissioners.

Governor Winthrop, on seeing the letters patent to the Duke of York, informed the English on Long Island that Connecticut had no longer any claim to the island; that what they had done for them was for the welfare of peace, and quiet settlement of his Majesty's subjects, they being the nearest organized government, to them under his Majesty. But now that his Majesty's pleasure was fully signified by his letters patent, their jurisdiction had ceased and became null.

The report and determination of the commissioners concerning the boundaries of his Royal Highness, the Duke of York's patent, is as follows:

" By vertue of his Majesties commission, we have heard the dilierences about the bounds of the patents to his Royall Highnesse the Duke of Yorke and his Majesties Colony of Connecticutt; and having deliberately considered all the reasons alleaged by Mr. AUyn, Sen'r, Mr. Gould, Mr. Richards and Captaine Winthrope, appoynted by the Assembly, held at Hartford, the 13th of October, 1664, to accompany John Winthrop, Esqr. (the Governor of his Majesties Colony of Connecticutt) to New Yorke, and by Mr. Howell and Captaine Young of Long Island, why the sayd Long Island lie under the Government of Connecticutt, which are to long here to be recited, wee doe declare and order that the southern bounds of his Majesties Colony of Connecticutt is the sea, and that Long Island is to be under the Government of his Royal Highnesse the Duke of Yorke, as is expresst by playn words, in the said patents respectively. And also by vertue of his Majesties commission and by the consent of both the Governors, and the gentlemen above named, wee alsoe order and declare, that the Creeke or River, called Momoronock, which is reputed to be about twelve miles to the east of Chester, and a lyne drawne from the east poynt or side, where the fresh water falls into the salt, at high water marke, north, northeast, to the line of the Massachusetts, be the Western bounds of the sayd Colony of Connecticutt, and all plantations lyeing westward of that Creeke and lyne so drawne, to be under his Royall Highnesse Government, and all plantations lyeing eastward of that Creeke and lyne, to be under the Government of Connecticutt.

" Given under our hands at Fort James in New York, on Manhattans Island, this 30th day of November, 1664.

Richard Nicoll, George Cartwright, Samuel Maverick."

" Wee the under written, on behalfe of the colony of Connecticutt, have assented unto this determination of his Majesties commissioners, in relation to the bounds and limits of his Royall Highnesse the Duke of Yorke's patent of Connecticutt, Nov. 30th, 1664.

John Winthrop, Mathew Allyn, Nathan Gould, James Richards, J. Winthrop."

The following is a copy of a letter addressed by Governor Nicoll to Captain John Youngs, commandant of the militia of Suffolk:

"Sir: — You are, by these presents, required to take an exact list of ye names of those on Long Island, who have taken up arms, under your command, for thier king and country, with ye place of thier usual dwelling, and deliver them in a roll, to ye end and purpose that I may hereafter, upon all occasions, and in this place, be ready to gratify those who have so eminently expressed thier affections: 2dly, That those arms may still remain in the same hands, for ye service of king and country; and that the officers, upon any sudden occasion, may know whether to send, to assemble the same men againe, who are to repaire to thier colonies in such cases, unless the deputyes of ye severall townes shall otherwise agree, upon the better ordering ye militia of this island, for ye future; wth deputyes shall, in convenient time and place, be summoned to propose and give thier advice in all matters, tending to ye peace and benefit of Long Island. I desire you will impart this letter to all your ffriends and neighbors, with is all at present from your assured ffriend.

" Richard Nicoll."

"N. Yorke, Oct. 29, 1664."

The invasion of New Netherlands, at a time of profound peace between England and the States General, was, in the opinion of Governor Stuyvesant, too preposterous to be attempted by an armed force, and therefore he determined to postpone an immediate surrender, in the hope that assistance might arrive from the fatherland, in season to repel any hostile movement against the province of New Netherlands. While negotiations were pending between the commissioners and the council, Stuyvesant dispatched the following letter to his superiors in Holland — a letter which, if actually forwarded, was not received in time to be of any avail:

" Honorable, wise, prudent, and very discreet Gentlemen: " Whereas, the bearer of this, Simon Cornellis Gilde, informs us he intends to pass, in silence, this night through Hellgate, to escape the approaching force and attack of the English frigates, which arrived five or six days past, so are these lines only intended to inform your Honors of our perilous and very alarming situation to which we are actually brought. Your Honors may see, by the annexed documents, that Long Island is gone and lost. This capital last Saturday, and again this day, summoned to surrender, and want of soldiers, ammunition and victuals; join to all this the pusillanimity of the citizens, entirely without any expectance, or even hope of any aid or relief; and in fear, if they make any resistance, and were conquered by the threatening English (who are daily reinforced from New England) , to loose with thier property, thier lives, wives and children.

" it is evident from all these circumstances, that the place cannot hold out long. Time does not permit to insert how the company is scolded and cursed by the inhabitants, in regard that notwithstanding the so often renewed and successive warnings and remonstrances from time to time, no attention has been paid, and none of the solicited succor obtained. Yea, it is loudly and openly proclaimed, to the contempt and shame of your faithful servants, that your Honors by premeditation, abandoned the inhabitants, if ye did not intend to expose them for sale, and endeavored to devote them to slaughter, because, as they say, ' ye did come them hither, and compelled them to settle in a country in which your Honors never possessed any right or property.'

" Having, last Friday provided the citizens, at the request of the burgomasters, with some powder and balls, the guns of the city and fort, and our breast-works cleaned and laden, there remained yet about 1300 lbs., partly new and partly old damaged powder. It cannot be for your Honors a difficult task to calculate how far this may reach, and what at last and ere long the event must be — namely, the total ruin and loss of this so fruitful country. If thier High Mightinesses and your Honors take the least interest in relieving such a large number of innocent individuals, then. Right Honorable Gentlemen, it ought to be undertaken without delay. It cannot be effected, but by a sufficient force of men and vessels, or before long the hope of recovery shall be entirely lost. The shortness of time and the various alarming occupations, not permitting to lengthen this letter, we with cordial, though painful salutations, recommend your Honors to God's protection, and remain, Honorable, wise, prudent, and very discreet Gentlemen,

Your faithful servant,

P. Stuyvesant."

" Fort Amsterdam, Sept. 1, 1664."

Governor Stuyvesant was permitted, after the surrender, to retain his real estate upon the Island of Manhattan, a portion of which is still possessed by his descendants. He made a visit to Holland the next year, but returned and spent the remainder of his days at his farm in the Bowery. Judge Benson says, he came here from Brazil, having lost a leg in the attack upon Tobago. He was a brave and honest man, and no doubt felt keenly the loss of the colony to the Dutch. Had he lived to witness the re-capture of the province by his countrymen a few years after, he would most likely have been reinstated in office. But his death took place in February, 1672, at the age of eighty years. His body was deposited in a vault in the chapel which he had erected, now the site of St. Mark's Church, on the wall of which is a tablet, with this inscription: " In this vault lies buried Petrus Stuyvesant, late Captaine Generall and Commander-in-Chief e of Amsterdam, in New Netherlands (now called New York) and the Dutch West India Islands."

OF THE ENGLISH COLONIAL GOVERNMENT

The English having got peaceable possession of the country, the new governor and council proceeded with due expedition to organize the different portions of it under one system of civil government. Connecticut gave up her claims to Long Island, and part of what she had seized upon the main. The boundaries having been fixed, as we have seen, by the commissioners on one side of the Sound, upon the other that colony was bounded by a line running north from the Sound at Marmaroneck Creek, thus confining her within ten miles of the Hudson. About to lay the foundation of a province, destined to become an important auxiliary to the commercial power of England, his excellency was desirous of changing not only the names of places, but, also, as far as possible, the habits and manners of the Dutch inhabitants. In compliment to his patron, the Duke of York and Albany, the city of New Amsterdam became New York, and the great northern trading depot, sometimes called Beverwyck and Fort Orange, was changed to Albany. The latter place underwent few alterations in its municipal regulations, while New York lost most of her ancient distinction. A mayor, aldermen, and sherif were substituted for Burgomaster, Schepen, and Schotit. The governor selected the individuals of his council, and exercised jointly with them the entire executive, legislative, and judicial powers.

Captain Thomas Willet of Plymouth, who had been selected by Governor Stuyvesant in 1650 to aid in compromising the question of boundary with New Haven, and who gave the earliest intelligence of the intended invasion of New Netherlands by the English, was in 1665 appointed mayor of the city; and Captain John Underbill, another very distinguished individual, was made high sheriff of the North Riding, upon Long Island.

It very early became a matter of indispensable and pressing necessity, that laws and ordinances should be passed, adapted to the (then) condition of the colony, and as effecting a uniform mode of administering justice in the several plantations upon Long Island, now for the first time united under one and the same administration. The English common law very generally prevailed in those towns previously associated with the New England colonies, but in the Dutch towns a different order of things prevailed. The Governor saw and appreciated the importance of the crisis now arrived, and, with the advice and concurrence of the council, issued a circular letter, of which the following is a copy, to the inhabitants of the several towns upon Long Island, and the town of Westchester:

" Whereas, the Inhabitants of Long Island have for a long time groan'd under many grievous inconveniences and discouragement occasioned partly from their Subjection, partly from their opposition, to a forreigne Power, in which distracted condition, few or no Lawes could be put in due Execution; Bounds and Titles to Lands disputed, civil Libertyes interrupted, and, from this Generall confusion, private dissentions and animosities have too much prevail'd against neighbourly Love and Christian Charity. To the preventing of the future growth of the like Evils, his Majesty (as a signall grace and honour to his subjects upon Long Island) hath at his owne charge, reduc't the forraigne power to his obedience, and by Patent, hath invested His Royall Highnesse the Duke of Yorke, with full and absolute Power, in and over all and every the particular Tracts of Land mentioned, with said Powers by commission from His Royall Highnesse the Duke of Yorke, I am deputed to put in Execution. In discharge therefore, of my Trust and Duty, to settle good and Known Laws within this Government, for the future, and receive your best advice and informacon in a general meeting; I have thought fitt to Publish unto yo", that upon the last day of this present ffebruary, at Hempstead upon Long Island, shall be a general meeting, which is to consist of Deputyes chosen by the Major part of the ffreemen only; which is to be understood of all Persons Rated according to their Estates, whether English or Dutch, within your severall Townes and Precincts, whereof you are to make Publication to the Inhabitants foure dayes before you proceed to an Election, appointing a certain day for that purpose. You are further to impart to the Inhabitants from mee. That I doe heartily recommend to them the Choice of the most Sober, able and discrete Persons, without partiality or faction, the fruite and benefitt whereof, will return to themselves, in a full and perfect composure of all controversies, and ye propagation of true Religion amongst us. They are alsoe required to bring with them a Draught of each Towne Limitts, or such writings as are necessary to evidence the Bounds and Limitts, as well as the right by which they challenge such Bounds and Limitts, by Grant and Purchase, or both. As alsoe to give notice of meeting to the Sachems of the Indians, whose presence may in some cases be necessary. Lastly I doe require you to assemble your Inhabitants and read this Letter to them, and then and there to nominate a day for the Election of two Deputyes from your Towne, who are to bring a certificate of their Election (with full power to conclude any cause or matter relating to their Several Townes) to mee at Hempstead upon the last day of ffebruary, where (God willing) I shall expect them.

" Your assured ffriend,
Richard Nicoll."
" Fort James, New York, Feb. 8, 1665."

The Convention met at the time appointed, consisting of the following deputies:

New Utrecht. Jaques Cortelleau, Younger Hope.
Gravesend. James Hubbard, John Bowne.
Flatlands. Elbert Elbertson, Roeloffe Martense.
Flatbush. John Striker, Hendrick Gucksen.
Bushwick. John Stealman, Guisbert Tunis.

Brooklyn. Hendrick Lubbertsen, John Evertsen.
Newtown. Richard Betts, John Coe.
Flushing. Elias Doughty, Richard Cornhill.
Jamaica. Daniel Denton, Thomas Benedict.
Hempstead. John Hicks, Robert Jackson,
Oyster Bay. John Underbill, Mathias Harvey.
Huntington. Jonas Wood, John Ketcham.
Brookhaven. Daniel Lane, Roger Barton.
Southold. William Wells, John Youngs.
Southampton. Thomas Topping, John Howell.
Easthampton. Thomas Baker, John Stretton.
Westchester. Edward Jessup, John Quimby.

At this meeting was promulgated a body of laws and ordinances for the future government of the province, which were called, by way of distinction, the " Duke's Laws," copies of which were furnished to the deputies, and filed in the clerk's offices of the different counties, where, or in some of them, they remain to this day. Of this code, an analysis has been prepared, which, it is presumed, embraces its principal provisions in a condensed form.

" All actions of debt, account, slander, and actions on the case concerning debts and accounts are to be tried in the jurisdiction where the cause of action arose. Debts and trespasses under five pounds to be arbitrated, and if either party refuse, the justice to choose arbitrators, whose award to be final. All actions or cases from five to twenty pounds to be tried at the sessions, from whence there should be no appeal. Any person, falsely pretending greater damages or debts than are due, to vex his adversary, to pay treble damages. If the action be entered, and the parties compromise It, yet the agreement is to be entered by the clerk of the court. Upon the' death of any person, the constable and two overseers to repair to the house of deceased, to inquire after the manner of the death, and whether he left any last will or testament. But no administration to be granted, except to the widow or child, until the third session after the party's death. The surplus of the personal estate to be divided as follows: one third to the widow, and the other two-thirds among the children, except that the eldest son shall have a double portion. All amercements and fines, not expressly regulated by law, to be imposed at the discretion of the court. No justice of the peace, who hath set upon or voted in any cause, to have any voice in the court to which appeal is made. Parties appealing, to give security; and in criminal cases they shall also give security for good behavior until the matter is decided. No arrest to be made on the Sabbath, or day of humiliation for the death of Charles the First, of blessed memory, or the anniversary of the restoration of Charles the Second, except of rioters, felons, and persons escaped out of prison. Persons necessarily attending courts, to be exempt from arrest. All arrests, writs, warrants and proclamations to be in the name of his Majesty. All assessments to be made by the constable and eight overseers of the parish, proportionable to the estates of the inhabitants, and justices of the peace to be exempt from assessments during their continuance in office, payments to the church only excepted. Persons of known ability when imprisoned, to pay for their support, till the second day of the next session after their arrest, and longer if there be a concealment of property. To rebuke an officer with foul words, so that he depart through fear without doing his office, shall be taken for an assault. A servant or workman convicted of assaulting his master or dame, to be imprisoned. No foreigner or stranger to have attachment against an inhabitant without giving security for costs. No justice of the peace, sheriff, constable or clerk of the court while in office, to be attorney in any case, unless assigned by the court on request. No Christian to be kept in bond slavery or captivity, except persons adjudged thereto by authority, or such as have willingly sold or shall sell themselves. Every town to set out its bounds within twelve months after they are granted, and once in three years the ancientest town shall give notice to the neighboring towns to go the bounds betwixt their towns, and to renew their marks; the time for perambulation to be betwixt the 20th and last of February, under the penalty of five pounds for neglect thereof; and owners of adjoining lands to go the bounds betwixt their lands once a year, if requested, under penalty of ten shillings. No person to follow the business of brewing beer for sale, but those skilled in the art. The name and surname of every inhabitant in the several parishes to be registered; and the minister or town clerk shall truly and plainly record all marriages, births, and burials in a book to be provided by the church-wardens. Nobody to be buried except in public places, and in the presence of three or four of the neighbors, one of whom shall be an overseer of the parish. Persons punishable with death are those who shall in any wise deny the true God and his attributes; those who commit any willful and premeditated murder; he who slays another with a sword or dagger, that hath not any weapon to defend himself; those who lie in wait; poisoning, or any other such wicked conspiracy; lying with any brute beast, (and the beast to be burned); man-stealing; taking away life by false and malicious testimony; denying his Majesty's right and title to his crown or dominions; treacherously conspiring or publicly attempting to invade or surprise any town or fort within this government, or resisting the King's authority by arms; children above the age of 16, and of sufficient understanding, smiting their natural father or mother, unless thereto provoked or forced in self defense. Married persons committing adultery with a married man or woman, or any single person having carnal connection with a married man or woman, both to be grievously fined and punished, as the governor and council, or court of assize shall think meet, not extending to life or member. Any man lying with mankind, as he lieth with a woman, both to be put to death, except he or she be under 14, or be forced. Cattle and hogs to be marked with the public mark of the town and the private mark of the owner; and horned beasts to be marked upon the horn. Every cause of £5 or under to pay a tax of 2s. 6d.; if £10, 5s.; from £10 to £20, 10s.; and for every £10 more, 2s. 6d.

" Whereas the public worship of God is much discredited for the want of painful and able ministers to instruct the people in the true religion, and for want of convenient places capable to receive any assembly of people in a decent manner, for celebrating God's holy ordinances, ordered that a church shall be built in the most convenient part of each parish, capable to receive and accommodate 200 persons. To prevent scandalous and ignorant pretenders to the ministry from intruding themselves as teachers, no minister shall be admitted to officiate within the government, but such as shall produce testimonials to the governor, that he received ordination either from some protestant bishop or ministers within some part of his Majesty's dominions, or the dominions of any foreign prince of the reformed religion; upon which testimonials the governor shall induct the said minister into the parish that shall make presentation of him. Ministers of every church to preach every Sunday, and pray for the King, Queen, Duke of York and the royal family; and to marry persons after legal publication or license. No person to be molested, fined or imprisoned for differing in judgment in matters of religion, who profess Christianity. Church-wardens to report twice a year of all profaneness, sabbath breaking, fornication, adultery, and all such abominable sins. No person employed about the bed of any man, woman or child, as surgeon, midwife, physician or other person, shall exercise or put in practice any art contrary to the known rules of the art in each mystery or occupation. Courts of sessions to be held three times a year, and continue three days. The constable to whip or punish any one, when no other officer is appointed to do it. All sales and alienations of property, to be by deed or last will and testament. No condemned person to be executed within four days after condemnation, and the person executed to be buried near the place of execution. A woman causelessly absenting herself from her husband, and refusing to return, shall forfeit her dower. Every parish minister is enjoined to pray and preach on the anniversary of the deliverance from the gunpowder treason, Nov. 5, 1605; on the 30th of Jan., to manifest detestation of the barbarous murder of Charles I. In 1649; and on the 29th of May, the birthday of Charles II. of blessed memory.

" If any person commit fornication with any single woman, they shall both be punished, either by enjoining marriage or corporal punishment, at the discretion of the court. Persons guilty of perjury to stand in the pillory three several court days, and render double damages to any party injured thereby. Apprentices and servants absenting themselves from their masters without leave, to serve double the time of such absence. Every town to have a marking or flesh-brand, for horses. No ox, cow, or such like cattle, to be killed for sale or for private use without notice given thereof to the town register. No person to be a common victualler, or keeper of a cook-shop or house of entertainment, without a certificate of his good behavior from the constable and two overseers of the parish; nor suffer any one to drink excessively in their houses after nine o'clock at night under the penalty of two shillings and six-pence. No purchase of land from the Indians shall be valid without a license from the governor, and the purchaser shall bring the sachem or the right owner before him, to confess satisfaction. No one to sell, give, or barter, directly or indirectly, any gun, powder, bullet, shot, or any vessel of burden, or row-boat (canoes excepted,) with any Indian, without permission of the governor, under his hand and seal; nor sell, truck, barter, give or deliver any strong liquor to an Indian, under penalty of forty shillings for one pint, and in proportion for any greater or lesser quantity; except in case of sudden extremity, and then, not exceeding two drams.

" To be father, brother, uncle, nephew, or cousin-german to any party in a trial, shall exempt a juror from serving, if objection be made before he is sworn, but not afterwards. No person to reveal the dissenting vote of a juror on arbitration, under the penalty of ten shillings. Every town, at its own expense, shall provide a pair of stocks for offenders, and a pound for cattle, besides prisons and pillories in places where courts of sessions are held. The value of an Indian coat, to be given to any one who shall bring the head of a wolf to any constable upon Long Island, provided it be killed upon the island.

" The court of sessions in each county shall take the proof of wills, which, with the wills, are to be transmitted to the " office of records " at New York, when the executors shall receive a copy thereof, with a certificate of its being allowed, attested under the seal of office.

" The town marks for horses upon Long Island shall be as follows: for Easthampton, A; Southampton, B; Southold, C; Seatalcot, D; Huntington, E; Oyster Bay, F Hempstead, G; Jamaica, H; Flushing, I; Newtown, L Bushwick, M; Brooklyn, N; Flatbush, O; Flatlands, P New Utrecht, Q; and Gravesend, R. At this early period the present town of Riverhead was included in Southold, and the town of North Hempstead, in Hempstead."

The delegates who attended this first provincial assembly under British authority were so entirely satisfied with the result of its deliberations, with their interview with the Governor, and the information imparted by him, as to the liberal views and intentions, of his Royal Highness the Duke of York and his Majesty the King, toward his new subjects, that they drew up and subscribed an address, filled with expressions of gratitude and loyalty, and of which the following is a copy:

"March 1, 1665. "To his Royal Highness the Duke of York. " We the deputies elected from the several towns upon Long Island, assembled at Hempstead in general meeting, by authority derived from your royal Highness under the Honorable Colonell Nicolls as deputy governor, do most humbly and thankfully acknowledge to your royal Highness the great honor and satisfaction Ave receive in our dependence upon your royal Highness, according to the tenor of his sacred Majesty's patent, granted the 12th day of March, 1664; wherein we acknowledge ourselves, our heirs and successors forever, to be comprised to all intents and purposes, as therein is more at large expressed. And we do publicly and unanimously declare our cheerful submission to all such laws, statutes, and ordinances, which are or shall be made by virtue of authority from your royal Highness, your heirs and successors for ever: As also, that we will maintain, uphold, and defend, to the utmost of our power, and peril of us, our heirs and successors forever, all the rights, title, and interest, granted by his sacred Majesty to your royal Highness, against all pretensions or invasions, foreign and domestic; we being already well assured that in so doing we perform our duty of allegiance to his Majesty, as freeborn subjects of the kingdom of England, inhabiting in these his Majesty's dominions. We do further beseech your royal Highness to accept of this address, as the first fruits in this general meeting, for a memorial and record against us, our heirs and successors, when we, or any of them, shall fail in our duties. Lastly, we beseech your royal Highness to take our poverties and necessities, in this wilderness country, into speedy consideration; that, by constant supplies of trade, and your royal Highness's more particular countenance of grace to us, and protection of us, we may daily more and more be encouraged to bestow our labors to the improvement of these his Majesty's western dominions, under your royal Highness; for whose health, long life, and eternal happiness, we shall ever pray, as in duty bound."

The inhabitants of Long Island were far from agreeing with the opinion of their deputies; were greatly displeased with the servile language of the address, and probably not less dissatisfied with many of the provisions now for the first time introduced by the new code. It was quite apparent that the people were to be allowed no share in legislation, and there was no intimation or encouragement that another assembly would be convened in the colony. Open and direct censures were freely indulged toward their representatives, and in some instances with such severity of language, that the Government thought proper to interfere.

Accordingly at a court of assize, held at Fort James, October, 1666, it was resolved, " that whoever thereafter should in any way detract or speak against the deputies signing the Address to his Royal Highness, at the general meeting at Hempstead, should he presented to the next Court of Sessions, and if the justices see cause, they should then be bound over to the Assizes, to answer for the slander, upon plaint or information."

The laws and ordinances thus made and promulgated, with occasional additions and alterations, from time to time, continued to govern the colony, until the first provincial assembly, convened by Governor Dongan, in 1683.

In addition to other matters which occupied the convention at Hempstead in 1665, Long Island and Staten Island (and probably

Westchester) were erected into a shire, called after that in England, Yorkshire, which was in like manner divided into separate districts, denominated Ridings The towns now included in Suffolk County, constituted the East Riding; Kings County, Staten Island, and the town of Newtown, the West Riding; and the remainder of Long Island, the North Riding of Yorkshire. Staten Island was detached from the West Riding by an order of the governor and court of assize in 1675, and permitted to have a jurisdiction of itself. In 1683 it was erected into a separate county by the name of Richmond.

The names of several of the towns were, it is supposed, changed at the aforesaid convention. In consequence of which, Midwout was called Flatbush; Amersfort was altered to Flatlands; Middlehorough to Newtown; Rusdorp to Jamaica; and the ancient name of Breukelen became Brooklyn, and Vlissengen was changed to Flushing.

The code adopted as aforesaid has generally obtained the appellation of the " Duke's Laws," original manuscript copies of which are still preserved in some of the town clerk's offices. They were designed to operate in a newly settled country and among a population composed of emigrants from different nations, accustomed to hold various and perhaps entirely opposite opinions upon law and government. That the numerous provisions of this code should prove satisfactory to all, was not in the nature of the case to be expected, yet all things considered, it was probably as just and reasonable as any which at that time existed in the neighboring colonies. Indeed, it is strongly to be inferred, from their similarity in many respects, that the latter contributed essentially to the former, and that the colony of New York drew largely from the legal codes of Massachusetts and Connecticut. Be this as it may, many imperfections were soon discovered to exist, and it became necessary to introduce a number of new provisions, to render the whole not only more acceptable to the people, but more adapted to the condition of the province.

The important revolution which had been effected in the country by the conquest of the English, was, on the whole, highly flattering to the hopes and aspirations of the colony.

The English towns which had been subject to the Dutch rejoiced at the change of affairs resulting from the conquest, as they were thereby absolved from obedience to a government which they despised; and the other English towns equally exulted at the prospect of being relieved from the constant jealousy and ambition of a foreign power in their neighborhood. The eastern towns on Long Island, notwithstanding, would greatly have preferred to continue their former alliance with Connecticut, and therefore they submitted, with general reluctance, to the separation. Some attempts were made to retain their connection, and they were renewed on more than one occasion thereafter.

The English towns, as well those which had been settled under the Dutch as those associated with Connecticut, were authorized, from the proclamation of the commissioners at the conquest, to expect that they should be admitted to the ordinary privileges and immunities of British subjects, to participate in the government, and have a voice in choosing representatives to a general assembly, with power to make laws for the government of the colony. How great, then, must have been their astonishment, as well as disappointment, when on the promulgation of the Duke's laws at the convention held at Hempstead, they found themselves deceived in their reasonable anticipations, and that by the very government which had inspired them with hopes of enjoying very many civil and political advantages, of which they had before been deprived. It cannot, therefore, excite much surprise that the people should feel indignant at the servile submission of their deputies, contained in their address to the Duke of York.

The boundaries of the several towns having been definitely settled by the convention of 1665, at Hempstead, it was strongly insisted by the governor, that new patents should be taken out by those who had formerly been under the Dutch, and more especially was it required of those who had never had any patent, or charter whatever, as was the case of all the towns in the East Riding of Yorkshire. The fees for granting these executive parchments under the great seal of the province were a perquisite of the governor, and the aggregate amount of all that were issued was not a matter in those times to be lightly regarded.

Individuals, also, who had purchased large tracts of land from the natives, were required to obtain patents of confirmation for the better establishing their titles thereto.

The capture of New Netherlands being made in a manner and under circumstances hardly warranted by the established law of nations, or in accordance with the principles of justice, it might be expected that the authorities of Holland would improve any fair opportunity which presented, of re-possessing themselves of the country, thus most unreasonably and illegally obtained. Information which reached New York, that an attempt would probably be made to recapture the province, occasioned the governor, on the 22nd of June, 1665, to recommend to the inhabitants of Long Island to put themselves in a position of defense against " a threatened invasion by the States of the United Provinces."

The cause of alarm proved groundless, and the affairs of the colony continued for some years to move on harmoniously and prosperously. Efforts were successfully made for the more perfect administration of justice in every part of the country. Among other Important measures for the promotion of order, a high sheriff was commissioned for the whole of Yorkshire, and a deputy for each riding, with the requisite number of justices in each town. Of these the high sheriff and deputies were appointed annually, but the justices held for an Indefinite period, and at the pleasure of the governor. In 1666, the office of deputy was abolished, and in 1683 that of high sheriff was discontinued, and a sheriff afterwards appointed for each county.

These laws authorized the several towns annually, on the first or second day of April, to elect a constable; at first eight, and by a subsequent amendment four, overseers; who were the assessors of the town, and with the constable were empowered to make regulations respecting matters which concerned the police and good government of the town. The constable and overseers were required annually to appoint two of the overseers to make the rate for building and repairing the church, for the maintenance of the minister, and for the support of the poor.

From the overseers, the constable selected the jurors who attended the courts of sessions and assize.

The principal courts established by these laws were the town court, the court of sessions, and the court of assize.

The town court was composed of the constable and, by an amendment of the original law, two overseers, and had cognizance of all causes of debt and trespass under five pounds. The justice of the peace was authorized, but not required, to preside at this court.

The court of sessions was established in each riding, and was to be held twice a year. It was composed of the justices of the peace of the several towns in the riding, each of whom was at first allowed £20 a year, which, in 1666, was altered into an allowance for their expenses.

The court had jurisdiction of all criminal causes, and of all civil causes over £5, arising in the riding. Causes were tried in this court in civil cases, and in criminal cases not capital, by a jury of seven men, and the verdict was determined by the voice of a majority; but in capital cases the jury consisted of twelve men, and they were required to be unanimous.

The judgments of this court for sums under £20, were final; from such as were for more than that sum, the parties might appeal to the court of assize.

The members of the council, the secretary of the colony, and the high sheriff were respectively authorized to sit with the justices of the court of sessions; and when neither of them was present, the sheriff was required to preside. The court of sessions also took the proof of wills in the respective ridings.

The court of assize was composed of the governor, council, and magistrates of the several towns, and was held once a year in the city of New York. It heard appeals from the sessions and other inferior courts.

Suits for demands above £20 might be commenced in this court on the warrant of the governor; so that it had original as well as appellate jurisdiction, and was a court of equity as well as common law.

The Duke's laws making no provision for a general assembly, the people had no voice in the government; but the governor had unlimited power, executive, legislative, and judicial. He was commander-in-chief; all public officers were appointed by him, and most of them held their offices at his pleasure. With the advice of his council, he could make what laws he pleased, and could repeal them, even against the opinion or consent of the council.

Some of the amendments to the original code purport to have been made at the court of assize, of which the justices of the several towns formed a part. This was not a legislative, but a judicial body; and the power of the justices with regard to legislation was probably like that of the parliament of France before the revolution, merely to register the edicts made by the governor and council.

So far as they were permitted to interfere, the indulgence was calculated, if not intended, to lessen the responsibility of the governor without diminishing his power.

It is certain that their presence or concurrence was not necessary, and that the act imposing duties and establishing an excise, and many other important acts, were adopted by the governor in council, and not at the court of assize. The people never considered the justices as their representatives, and censured the acts made at the court of assize as much as others. The governor presided in the court of assize, which, by appeal, had the control of all inferior tribunals. The judgments and decrees of this court were probably such as the governor dictated; his assistants not being colleagues, but merely advisers, who held their authority under him, and were dependent on him.

In this court the governor united the character of both judge and legislator. He interpreted his own acts, and not only pronounced what the law was, but what it should be.

Notwithstanding the disappointment experienced by a large portion of the inhabitants of the English towns, in default of a representative government, the executive was enabled to allay, in great measure, the feelings of discontent on that score, by the caution and moderation which distinguished his administration; although, in consequence of the extensive powers he possessed, it might have been easy for him to have wielded an almost despotic authority. He appears, however, to have been uninfluenced by the love of power, and, as is believed, voluntarily relinquished the reins of government in 1668, leaving his secretary, Matthias Nicoll, behind.

Colonel Nicoll is supposed to have left the country about the first of September, 1668, and was succeeded in the administration of the government the same year by Colonel Francis Lovelace, of whom it may be said that he might possibly have been respected in some other situation, but was by no means fitted to satisfy the expectations of any party. This resulted in a great measure from his remarkable indecision of character, and his exerting very little, if any, means to conciliate those whom he was sent to govern. His continuance in the province was not characterized by any extraordinary public measure, if we except several very extravagant grants of land, and his purchasing the soil of Staten Island from the native Indian proprietors, which last was the most distinguished act of his administration. And whatever of discontent was engendered during the time of his immediate predecessor, continued unabated, and concentrated upon his head the almost unanimous ill will of the people.

Smith, in his History of New York, supposes that the court of assize had not been established till the time of Governor Lovelace. This is a great mistake. It was established by Nicoll in the code he had compiled for the government of the colony, and published in the assembly at Hempstead, March 1, 1665. In the fall of the same year, on the last three days in September and the second, third, and fourth days in October, a general court of assize was holden at New York, composed of Richard Nicoll, the governor, the members of the council, and the justices of the three ridings of Yorkshire, on Long Island and Staten Island.

The number of justices who attended this court rendered it a grievance. In the act of 1684, passed for its repeal, it is alleged that it had " become a great charge and expense to the province; and by reason of the great number, not so fit and capable to hear and determine matters and causes of a civil nature, usually brought to the said court;" and it was for that reason abolished.

The last court of assize held under Sir Edmund Andros, October 6, 1680, was composed of the governor, five councilors, the mayor of New York, five aldermen, and seventeen justices of the peace.

The charges of the several towns and counties under the Duke of York were defrayed by a direct tax on the persons and estates, real and personal, of the inhabitants, according to an estimate made by the constable and overseers of the several towns, in conformity with certain rules prescribed by law. The rate for the public or county charge in each riding was fixed by the governor and council, by the amount of its estimate. A penny in the pound was usually sufficient for the purpose. A tax was collected by the constables, and paid over to such persons in the several towns as were entitled to it on the warrant of the high sheriff. The town charges were fixed by the constable and overseers, and levied by the same estimate. Governor Lovelace in 1670, and Governor Dongan in 1686 or 1687, both attempted to raise money for colony purposes, by their own authority; but the attempt met with so much opposition, that it could not be carried into effect.

The colony charges were paid out of the moneys arising from duties imposed by the governor and council on exports and imports. In the fall of 1664, Governor Nicoll established a tariff of duties on goods exported to the Netherlands; and shortly after on other goods, exported and imported.

From the origin of the colony, each town was required to support its own poor; the money for the purpose to be raised by those who from time to time adjusted the contingent expenses of the different counties. By the Duke's laws the constable and overseers were required to take charge of the poor. In 1747 the several towns in Suffolk were authorized to choose overseers of the poor, and soon after some other counties were empowered to do the same. By the act of November ii, 1692, the power of taking the proof of wills, and of granting letters testamentary and of administration, was vested in the governor, or a delegate to be appointed by him. In 1778, and not before, the legislature ordered surrogates to be appointed by the governor and council of appointments, in every county; which is still continued, except that the power is now vested in the governor and senate. The courts of sessions, which by the Duke's laws were to be held in each riding, and afterwards in each county, continued to be held with great regularity afterwards.

The records of this court, as originally constituted, and as reorganized by the act of 1683, are still to be found in the clerks' offices of Kings, Queens, and Suffolk. In Kings, there is a regular series of them, from 1669 to 1711. From these records, it appears to have been a common practice for the secretary of the colony, a member of the council, or the high sheriff, to sit and act in court with the justices. In the record of the court held at Gravesend, December 13, 1671, Matthias Nicoll, the secretary, is styled president of the court. This court was held at Gravesend from its origin till 1685, when it was removed to Flatbush by virtue of an act of the colonial legislature. There is also in the clerk's office of King's County, copies of most of the acts of the first assembly, passed in 1682 and 1684, with one or more acts passed by the second assembly in 1685.

The people on Long Island considered some of the laws established by the original code, as arbitrary and oppressive; and they deemed some that were made by Colonel Lovelace, who commenced his administration in May, 1667, as still more exceptionable — wherefore they came to a determination to represent their grievances to the governor and council, and to pray for redress thereof.

On October 9, 1669, the towns of Hempstead, Jamaica, Oyster Bay, Flushing, Newtown, Gravesend, Westchester, and East Chester, severally petitioned for redress in like manner.

They enumerated the defects in the existing laws which they wished to be remedied, stated the provisions which they wished to be adopted, remonstrated against the restrictions which the governor had imposed on trade; and reprobated, as the greatest of their grievances, the exclusion of the people from any share in legislation.

In their petitions they refer to the proclamation issued to the people of Long Island and others, by the commissioners, on their first landing at Gravesend, before the surrender of the colony, promising that they " should enjoy all such privileges as his Majesty's other subjects in America enjoyed;" the most important of which they allege is a participation in the power of making the laws, by which they are to be governed, " by such deputies as shall be yearly chosen by the freeholders of every town and parish:" and they claimed a fulfilment of that promise.

They also complain of it as a grievance, that any acts should be made by the governor under pretense of his secret instructions; and pray " to be informed what is required of them by virtue of the commission granted by his Royal Highness the Duke of York."

The governor and council received the petitions, granted some of their minor requests, but in the most important cases refused any redress.

The town of Southampton was purchased and settled under the authority of the Earl of Stirling while he held the island, which circumstance the people of that town supposed exempted them from the necessity of taking out a patent for their lands from the governor, as was required of other towns by the laws of 1665, and neglected to do it; in consequence of which the governor and council, at the court of assize, October 8, 1670, declared the titles to lands in that town invalid, unless a patent was obtained for them within a limited time.

By another act passed at the same time, a levy or contribution was ordered to be made in the several towns on Long Island, to repair the fort at New York.

The governor had also imposed duties on goods imported and exported according to his pleasure for the support of government, and was now attempting to raise money by direct tax for other purposes without the consent of the people.

Several of the towns were alarmed at the precedent about to be established, as dangerous to their liberties, and determined to resist it.

' The want of a general assembly was felt as a great grievance from the first establishment of the Duke's government; the inhabitants considered themselves in great measure disfranchised, and therefore little better than slaves, liable at all times to suffer by the arbitrary exactions of the government; in short, that the whole system was only a tyranny in disguise, which, under the color of prerogative, might at any time trample upon the most sacred rights of the people, under the plausible pretense of upholding the authority of government and supporting the dignity of the crown; against all which alarming encroachments the people possessed no constitutional security or any mode of redress, should petition and remonstrance fail, short of open and direct opposition to the government itself. The governor, it has been seen, possessed the sole appointing power; and united in himself all the attributes of despotic authority, which he might any time, and frequently did, exercise in the most arbitrary manner. This concentration of power in the hands of a single individual might well alarm the timid, and awaken the most serious jealousies and discontents among the entire population of the colony, which was, in fact, the case. Difficulties continued to exist after the establishment of the assembly, by the influence which the governors possessed, and their sometimes refusing their sanction to laws the most salutary and indispensable for the public security.

It was evidently the object of many governors to control, as far as possible, the public revenues, and to fill their own pockets at the expense of the people; and there are not wanting instances of their having accumulated large fortunes in a surprisingly short period by acts of oppression and peculation.

The governor could suspend the members of the council and appoint others, subject to the king's approbation; he had a negative on the acts passed by the assembly and council; he had power to summon, prorogue, or dissolve the assembly; and with consent of the council, who were in general sufficiently submissive, could dispose of the public lands, and disburse the public money raised for the support of government.

For some years the public revenue went into the hands of a receiver general, who was appointed by the crown, and was not accountable to the assembly. The acts for raising revenue for the support of government were continued for a series of years without any appropriation; and the council exercised a concurrent power over revenue bills, as in other cases.

This mode of managing the revenue was liable to great abuse. An indefinite support enabled the governor to dispense with the assembly, and rendered him in a great measure independent of them during that period; and the omission of specific appropriations enabled the governor to fix the salaries of all public officers, to dispose of the public moneys as he pleased, gave him the entire power over the civil list, and led to misapplication and embezzlement.

The English colonists on Long Island brought with them the doctrine that taxation and representation were inseparable — that the power of disposing of his own money was the birthright of every British subject, and one of the elementary principles of British liberty, — and that taxes could only be imposed with the consent of the people, by their representatives in a general assembly.

They had for some years paid a direct tax of a penny in the pound to defray the public charges of the several towns and counties, of which they had not complained.

The towns of Southold, Southampton, and Easthampton, in a joint meeting by their delegates at Southold, agreed to contribute to the repairing of the fort, " if they might have the privileges that other of his majesty's subjects in these parts have and do enjoy," alluding to the governments of New England.

On June 24, 1672, the town of Easthampton, to whom the proceedings of the delegates were communicated, approved of the decision of the deputies, and agreed to comply with the order, " if the privileges may be obtained, but not otherwise." The towns of Huntington, Flushing, Hempstead, and Jamaica, by the votes of their respective town meetings, refused to comply with the order, and communicated the reasons of their refusal in writing to their respective constables and overseers, to whom the order was sent.

The people of Huntington assigned this among other reasons for their refusal, viz: "because they were deprived of the liberties of Englishmen;" Intimating that they deemed it a violation of their constitutional rights, that their money should be taken from them without their consent, by their representatives in a general assembly.

The people of Jamaica, in justification of their refusal, stated that they considered themselves already sufficiently burdened by the enhanced price which they paid for their goods, in consequence of the duties which the governor had imposed on them, in addition to a penny in the pound, which they paid towards the public charges; and that a compliance with the order would be contrary to the king's instructions, which forbid any law to be enforced on the country that was contrary to the laws of the nation; meaning, that no law for taking their money out of their pockets without their consent by their representatives, was consistent with the British constitution. " That on the same principle that this order was imposed, they might be required to maintain the garrison, and whatever else we know not, till there be no end; but If it may appear to us that it is the king's absolute order to impose the said burdens and disprivilege us, contrary to his former good Intentions and instructions, and contrary to the liberties his majesty's subjects enjoy in his territories and dominions, we shall, with patience, rest under the said burdens until address be made to the king for relief."

The votes of Flushing and Hempstead have not been discovered, but there is no doubt they were to the like effect. The constables of Flushing, Hempstead, and Jamaica laid the resolutions of their respective towns before the ensuing court of sessions of the north riding held at Jamaica; but it seems that the court did not act on them. They then laid them before the court of sessions of the west riding, which met the next week, December 21, 1670, at Gravesend. That court, under the influence of the secretary of the colony, who presided, and a member of the council, after examining the writings containing the proceedings of the said towns, adjudged " That the said papers were in themselves scandalous, illegal, and seditious; tending only to disaffect all the peaceable and well-meaning subjects of his Majesty in these his royal Highness's territories and dominions." And the court further ordered " That the said papers should be presented to the governor in council, for them to proceed on as they shall conceive will best tend to the suppression of false suggestions and jealousies in the minds of peaceable and well-meaning subjects in alienating them from their duty and obedience to the laws."

Agreeable to this illegal order, the papers were presented to Governor Lovelace, and were by him and his council adjudged to the flames, and ordered to be publicly burned before the townhouse of the city, at the next mayor's court to be held there.

It was this sage and humane Governor Lovelace, who, (as Smith, in his History of New Jersey informs us,) in 1668 wrote to Sir Robert Carr, then in authority there, that the best method to keep the people in order was " to lay such taxes upon them as may not give them liberty to entertain any other thoughts hut how they shall discharge them."

A man of such a temper, with such despotic principles, was sure to draw down upon him the public indignation, and would have experienced the consequences of it in a very exemplary manner, had not his administration been cut short by an event as sudden as it was extraordinary and unexpected. His estate here was attached soon after for a debt of £7,000, due to his principal, the Duke of York. The country which had now been nine years governed by the Duke of York's deputies, and experienced in very full measure the ill effects of ignorance and indiscretion in the conduct of its rulers, came once more under the government of their ancient masters, the Dutch.

NEW YORK RECAPTURED BY THE DUTCH

There is a chasm in our history from 1672 to 1674, which English writers have manifested little anxiety to supply, for during this period, and in a manner more extraordinary than the conquest by the English in 1664, the whole of New Netherlands came under the control of the States General. The war waged by Charles II. and Lewis XIV., of France, against Holland, in 1672, having been commenced and prosecuted under the most frivolous pretenses, induced an apprehension, although slight, that an attempt might possibly be made upon this province, it being at that time destitute of any considerable means of defense against a powerful naval force. Orders were accordingly transmitted to Governor Lovelace to place New York in as strong a position for defense as could be. Fort James was thereupon immediately entrusted to Captain John Manning, and pecuniary contributions were earnestly solicited from the towns on Long Island (as has been seen) for repairing and increasing the fortifications. Measures were also taken for the security of Albany, and a small fort was recommended to be erected at some suitable place upon the banks of the North River.

It seems that the Hollanders did not fail, on the commencement of hostilities with England, to send a fleet to the American coast, under the command of two well-known officers, Jacob Binkes, and Cornells Evertsen, assisted by three captains of the Dutch army, Anthony Colve, Nicholas Boes, and Abraham Frederick Van Zye. This force had been sent to the West Indies to destroy as far as possible the English and French trade in that quarter. In the course of the expedition they captured one hundred and twenty sail of English and French merchant vessels, which they dispatched to Europe, and which arrived safe at Cadiz.

The commanders of the Dutch squadrons, highly elated with their success, concluded to extend their operations to New York. They accordingly united their forces, consisting of twelve men-of-war, and meeting with no obstacle, arrived safe at Sandy Hook, July 28, 1672, sailed up the bay, and with the first fair wind, stood for the city, where on the 30th they formed a line-of-battle off the present site of the Battery. They had received very different accounts of the condition of the fort, and the ability of the garrison to defend itself, which probably caused some hesitation in the minds of the commanders of the squadrons before taking their position; but many of the Dutch of Staten Island had been on board while the ships lay off that island, and informed their countrymen of the true state of things, which induced them to make an attempt at capture without further delay, the governor (Lovelace) and many of the principal men being absent from the city.

Captain Manning went on board, and demanding the reason of this extraordinary visit, was told that they intended to take the place, claiming it as a Dutch province, and surely the claim was in many respects a plausible one, it having been quite unceremoniously taken from them by the English in 1664. Manning asked for time to make suitable preparations for defense, for which one half hour only was conceded, when a broadside was fired from the ships, whereupon guns were fired from the fort, which, says an eye witness, " shot the General's ship through and through." One man was killed in the fort, and although the contest lasted about four hours, little damage was done the garrison. The ammunition being expended, no further effort at defense could be made, and a surrender was made by Manning's order. The gates being opened, the Dutch soldiers marched in. The English soldiers were required to lay down their arms, and go on board the ships, Captain Manning being politely allowed to wear his sword, as a token of his gallantry; but his house was plundered, as well as that of the governor, and Captain Deleval's, a person high in confidence of the government. The conquerors were so elated with their success that they immediately dispatched a messenger to Holland with the news.

A proclamation was issued, establishing a new order of things; the people took the oath of allegiance, and a small expedition being sent to Albany, that place surrendered unconditionally.

A most singular mistake seems to have existed till lately, in relation to the conduct of Captain Manning, it having been asserted that the garrison voluntarily surrendered without opposition or a gun being fired, he being guilty not only of cowardice, but treachery not much better than treason. This is the language of the historian. Smith, and is followed by Holmes in his valuable American Annals, by Dunlap and by Bancroft. Smith even gives the proceedings of a court martial in which charges were exhibited against the commandant of the fort, to which it is alleged he pleaded guilty, and being convicted, received the punishment awarded him. If the facts above stated be true, he was wholly without blame, and well deserves our sympathy, as an innocent and injured man.

The commanders of the forces immediately appointed Captain Anthony Colve governor of the colony, who at once set himself about reinstating the Dutch government.

The commission issued by the Dutch commanders is sufficient in its novelty and importance to occupy a place in the history of that eventful period, a copy of which is here given:

" The Honourable and awful council of War, for their High Mightinesses the States General of the United Netherlands, and his Serene Highness the Prince of Orange, over a squadron of ships now at anchor in Hudson's River, in New Netherlands — To all those who shall see or hear these, Greeting. As it is necessary to appoint a fit and able person, to carry the chief command over this conquest of New Netherlands, with all its appendences and dependencies, from Cape Hinlopen on the south side of the South or Delaware Bay, and fifteen miles more southerly, with the said Bay and South River included; so as they were formerly possessed by the Directors of the city of Amsterdam, and after by the English Government, in the name and right of the Duke of York; and further from the said Cape Hinlopen, along the Great Ocean to the east end of Long Island, and Shelter Island; and from thence westward to the middle of the Sound, to a town called Greenwich, on the main, and to run landward in, northerly, provided that such line shall not come within ten miles of the North River, conformable to a provincial treaty made in 1650, and ratified by the States General, Feb. 23, 1656, and Jan. 23, 1664, with all lands, islands, rivers, lakes, kills, creeks, fresh and salt waters, fortresses, cities, towns and plantations, therein comprehended. So it is, that we being sufficiently assured of the capacity of Anthony Colve, captain of a company of Foot, in the service of their High Mightinesses the States General of the United Netherlands and his Serene Highness the Prince of Orange, &c. by virtue of our commission, granted to us by thier before mentioned High Mightinesses and his Highness, have appointed and qualified, as we do by these presents appoint and qualify the said Captain Anthony Colve, to govern and rule these lands with the appendices and dependencies thereof, as Governor General; to protect them from all invasions of enemies as he shall judge most necessary; hereby charging all high and low officers, justices and majestrates, and others in authority, soldiers, burghers and all inhabitants of this land, to acknowledge, honor, respect and obey, the said Anthony Colve as Governor General; for such we judge necessary for the service of the country, waiting the approbation of our Principals. Thus done at Fort William Hendrick, the 12th day of August, 1673." (Signed)

" Jacob Benkes, Cornelius Evertse, Jun."

Ebeling, the Dutch historian, says, that the civil officers of the city were convened immediately, who received the conquerors with joy, and had their commissions continued by the new government. Lovelace had permission to return to England, where, it seems, he was received with much disapprobation, and severely censured for the loss of a province which, it must be confessed, he had very inadequate means of protecting: for it must be recollected that the towns of Long Island, containing at that time a large portion of the population, had generally refused their aid towards increasing the defenses of the city. The fort was miserably constructed, had only forty-six small cannon, and was garrisoned by only one company of regular soldiers, commanded by Captain Manning. The Dutch squadron anchored off Staten Island; some communications passed between the ships and the fort, the result of which, as has been seen, was an unconditional surrender of the latter to the invaders.

The city was now denominated New Orange, and the fort William Hendrick, the name and title of the Stadt Holder. On the 14th of August, 1673, the new governor issued his proclamation, directing and requiring each of the Long Island towns to send two deputies to the city, with full powers to make their submission to the States General and the Prince of Orange, on behalf of their constituents.

The Dutch towns, and others settled under the Dutch authority, submitted without opposition; while the remaining towns, at first, paid some attention to the governor's orders, but afterwards declined, with a full determination to seek protection from their ancient ally, Connecticut, as they had done previously in 1664. The following letter from the authorities of that colony, was addressed to the commanders of the Dutch fleet, as soon as its arrival at New York was communicated to them:

"Hartford, Aug. 17th, 1673. " Sir: — Although we have heard of your actions at Yorke, yet because the chief trust of these parts did reside in other hands, from whom you have too suddenly surprised it, we made it our business to attend, what was devolved upon ourselves that way nextly, yet we, understanding you content not yourselves with what you have already taken, but demand submission of the people, his Majesty's subjects, seated on Long Island, eastward beyond Oysterbay; and have seized a vessel of Mr. Sillick's, one of our people, near one of our harbors; we have therefore sent Mr. James Richards, and Mr. William Roswell, to know your further intentions; and we must let you know that we and our confederates, the United Colonies of New England, are, by our Royal Sovereign, Charles II., made keepers of his subjects' liberties in these parts, and do hope to acquit ourselves in that trust, through the assistance of Almighty God, for the preservation of his Majesty's Colonies in New England. Which is all, at the present, represented to you, from the Governor and General Assembly of the Colony of Connecticut. Signed, per order per me,

" John Allyn, Sect'y."

To this letter was sent the following reply:

" In Fort William Hendrick, Aug. 24, 1673. " Sir: — To answer your letter of the 17th August, which was delivered unto us, we say, that we are sent forth by the High and Mighty Lords, the States Gen'll of the United Netherlands, and his Serene Highness the Lord Prince of Orrange, to doe all manner of dammage unto the enemyes of the said High and Mighty Lords, both by water and by land, from which cause we being come heere into Hudson's River, have brought the land and forts within the same, under our obedience, and in regard the villages lying to the eastward of Oysterbay did belong to this government, soe it is, that to prevent all inconvienceys we have cited the same to give the oath of fidelity, in which if they remain defective, we are resolved to force them with the armes, likewise allso we shall not be afraid to goe against those that shall seeke to maintaine the said villages in thier injustis: concerning the vessel that is taken by us close by your havens, thier is no other consideration but that it was taken from o' enemyes; wherefore it appears very strange before us, that we should be objected against conserning It: wee doe well believe that those that are set for keepers of his Majesty of England's subjects will quitt themselves as ought to doe for the preservation of the colonyes in New England; however we shall not for that depart from o'r firme resolutions. We conceive we have herewith answered yo'r letter. Thus don in the place as above. By order of the command'r and counsell of War."

" A. Bayard, Secretary."

October 1, 1673, Governor Colve sent William Knyff and Anthony Malypart to the English towns, requiring them to take the oath of allegiance. Oyster Bay, it seems, complied, while Huntington and Brookhaven offered to sign an agreement to be faithful to the Dutch government, but refusing to take any oath that should bind them to take up arms against the King of Great Britain, their lawful sovereign.

The three eastern towns in particular declined any compromise, and sent deputies forthwith to Connecticut, to solicit that colony to receive them under her jurisdiction, and to furnish them with necessary aid against the Dutch, should they attempt to enforce their demands; and on the 9th of October, 1673, the general court of Connecticut, referred their application to a committee, consisting of the governor, assistants, and two others; and authorized them, with the concurrence of the colonies of Massachusetts and Plymouth, to grant their request, and to do what should be considered most advantageous for the benefit of both parties.

The committee having agreed to take them under their jurisdiction, erected the three towns of Easthampton, Southampton, and Southold into a county, established a county court, appointed judges and such other civil and military officers as they deemed expedient, and sent a military force for their assistance and protection.

October 25, the governor sent William Knyff and Nicholas Voss to the towns of Huntington and Brookhaven; and, to induce the inhabitants to comply with his wishes, promised them liberty of conscience, security of property, and the choice of their officers, in the same manner as had been enjoyed in the Dutch towns, and also consented that the oath of allegiance should be modified so as to accommodate their scruples on that subject.

Huntington and Brookhaven consented to the wishes of the governor on condition that none but the magistrates should take the oath required. This was promptly conceded, and those towns submitted to the Dutch authority.

October 30, the governor dispatched Cornelius Steenwyck, first councillor, and two others, to the eastern towns, to persuade them to comply upon the like terms, having just confiscated the shares of Constant Sylvester and Thomas Middleton, in Shelter Island (they being British subjects, residing at Barbados) and sold the same to Captain Nathaniel Sylvester, taking his bond for the payment of £500; the island being then known as Sylvester's Island. The party sent upon this expedition sailed down the Sound and stopped at that island, where they fell in with Samuel Wyllis and Captain

Winthrop, who had been sent there by Connecticut, to carry the aforesaid resolutions into effect. The Dutch commissioners also visited Southold, and found the people there assembled in arms. They offered to receive their submission in writing, and to accept of the oath of allegiance from the magistrates only. The people of that town, however, refused submission, and the commissioners were obliged to return without effecting the object of their mission.

The governor afterwards undertook to reduce the said three eastern towns by force; whereupon Connecticut sent Major Treat with sufficient assistance to repel the attempt. The Dutch were too few in numbers to ensure success, and, after endeavoring in vain to effect the principal object in view, landed at Shelter Island, compelled Mr. Sylvester to pay the amount of his bond, and returned safely with the money to New Orange. Mr. Trumbull says that the " Dutch threatened the eastern towns with fire and sword unless they would submit and swear allegiance to the States General, but were repelled by the troops sent from Connecticut." In this expedition Major Treat obtained much credit for his skill and bravery, and the General Court of Connecticut returned him public thanks for his conduct in defending that colony, and the towns upon Long Island, against the Dutch. It should be remembered that Connecticut had, on the 26th of November, 1673, formally declared war against this people, and made liberal preparations to commence extensive operations in the ensuing spring. This gave the people of New Orange no inconsiderable alarm, and on the 27th of March, 1674, the Dutch Governor ordered all vessels to be removed to a particular place, lest, he says, they should hinder the defense of the city; and likewise made provision for transporting the inhabitants of the neighboring villages to a place of safety, in case of an attack. But another revolution in the political condition of the province was destined to follow, and this second epoch of Dutch power, was terminated by the treaty of Westminster, February 19, 1674, by the terms of which England was to receive New Netherlands in exchange for Surinam. The sixth article of this treaty stipulated, " that whatever lands , towns, forts, &c, had been reciprocally taken since the beginning of the war, should be restored to their former possessors" New York was accordingly restored to the English, October 31, 1674, Captain Colve having administered the government fourteen months and eighteen days. The news of peace had, indeed, suspended hostilities sometime before, but no person being on the spot authorized to accept a surrender of the province, the English government was not fully re-instated till the date last mentioned.

The people of Southold, Southampton, and Easthampton, were in reality little more disposed to submit to the Duke's government, than to that of the Dutch, and consequently used every possible effort to prevent it by sending delegates to Connecticut to solicit their continuance under that colony. On the 14th of May, 1674, the General Court at Hartford took their application into consideration, and finally consented that they might retain their political relation as before, and enjoy the same privileges as other towns within their jurisdiction, so far as it was in their power to grant or secure the same. The court also appointed, or, rather, re-appointed Captain John Youngs, Captain John Howell, and Mr. John Mulford judges of the county, and authorized " Samuel Wylys, John Talcott, and the secretary, Mr. Allyn, or any two of them, to go over to the Island, to order and settle the affairs of the people there, and to establish such military officers among them as they should judge to be necessary."

June 13, 1674. — Easthampton appointed a committee, who should, in connection with Southampton and Southold, humbly petition the king to permit them to remain under the jurisdiction of Connecticut, and they continued thus attached, when the colony of New York was finally restored to the agent of the Duke of York in the month of October, 1674.

RESTORATION OF THE DUKE'S GOVERNMENT

On the 29th of June, 1674, his Royal Highness, the Duke of York, to remove all doubts respecting the validity of his title, obtained from his brother, Charles II., a new patent for the same territory which had been conveyed to him in 1664, and July 22, 1674, commissioned Major (afterwards Sir Edmund) Andros, to be governor of all his possessions in America. He was also commissioned to raise 100 men as a garrison for the fort, now again called Fort James, and New Orange became once more New York. This commission of the governor bears date two days only subsequent to the renewal of the patent, a proof that his qualifications were known, and his appointment previously determined upon by his Royal Highness. The patent confirmed the power formerly conferred, of framing all such ordinances as the duke or his assigns should think fit, with a right however, of appeal to the king and council. No trade could be carried on without the duke's assent, and he could impose such duties as he thought proper. The new governor arrived here October 31, 1674, and having received a formal surrender of the province, issued a declaration to the effect following:

" it hath pleased his Majesty and his Royal Highness, to send me with authority to receive this place and government from the Dutch, and to continue in the command thereof, under his Royal Highness, who hath not only taken care for our future safety and defense, but also given me his commands for securing the rights and properties of the inhabitants, and that I should endeavor, by all fitting means, the good and welfare of this province and dependencies under his government, that I may not be wanting in anything that may conduce thereunto, and for the saving of the trouble and charge of any coming hither for the satisfying themselves in such doubts as might arise concerning their rights and properties upon this change of government, and wholly to settle the minds of all in general, I have thought fit to publish and declare, that all former grants and privileges or concessions heretofore granted, and all estates legally possessed by any under his Royal Highness before the late Dutch government, as also all legal judicial proceedings during that government anterior to my arrival in these parts, are hereby confirmed, and the possessors, by virtue thereof, to remain in quiet possession of their rights. — it is hereby further declared, that the known book of laws formerly established, and in force, under his Royal Highness' government, is now again confirmed by his Royal Highness, the which are to be observed and practiced; together with the manner and time of holding courts therein mentioned as heretofore, and all magistrates and civil officers belonging thereunto, to be chosen and established accordingly."

He also sent a special messenger to the three eastern towns of Long Island, requiring them to take the oath of allegiance and return to the government of New York. The inhabitants not only hesitated to comply, but sent a memorial to the governor, in which, among other things mentioned, they set forth, that through the aid furnished them by the kindness of Connecticut, they had theretofore repelled the Dutch; that they had joined that colony, and put themselves under that government, which had appointed their civil and military officers; that they had become bound by oath to that colony, and could not dissolve the connection without its approbation.

November 17, 1674. — The people of the town of Southold, in town meeting, declared themselves to be under the government of his Majesty's colony of Connecticut, and that they would use all lawful means to continue so. The town of Easthampton likewise instructed their deputies, (who were appointed to consult with the other towns what course they should take) to see that all lawful endeavors should be put forth, to the utmost, for their continuance under Connecticut.

November 18, 1674. — The governor and council ordered another messenger to be sent to the three resisting towns, demanding in the most peremptory manner that the former overseers and constables should be restored to their places, "under the penalty of being declared rebels; " and they ordered John Mulford, John Howell, and John Youngs, who had signed the aforesaid memorial, to appear and answer forthwith before the council on the like penalty. Thus the solicitude and endeavors of these towns to remain in connection with their friends across the Sound, proved unavailing, and they were reluctantly obliged to succumb to the demands of the governor of New York.

Sir Edmund pursued the same arbitrary course that his predecessors had done, and showed himself both selfish and tyrannical. Immediately on assuming the government a court martial was ordered to try Captain Manning for what was termed his treacherous and cowardly surrender of Fort James to the Dutch forces the preceding year. The articles exhibited were. In substance, that the accused, on the 28th of July, 1673, being apprised of the enemy's approach, took no measures for defense, and even refused the assistance that was offered. That while the fleet was anchored under Staten Island he had held communication with it — that he suffered them to moor under the fort, forbidding a gun to be fired on pain of death. That he allowed the enemy to land without opposition, and treacherously caused the gates of the fort to be opened to the enemy, thereby cowardly and basely surrendering the garrison, without even requiring conditions of capitulation. The accused had, it seems, visited England, and returned for the purpose of a trial and punishment on the spot where the crime, if any, was committed. The trial, which in the end turned out a mere mockery of form, was postponed till February, 1675, when he was found guilty of cowardice only, and on the 5th of the month this noted individual (who had been high sheriff of Yorkshire on Long Island in 1671, and been entrusted also with the defense of the province which was alleged to have been betrayed) was " ordered to be brought to the public place before the City Hall, there to have his sword broken over his head, and from that time forth rendered incapable of wearing another, or from serving his Majesty in any public employ, or place of benefit and trust within this government."

The infliction of so slight a punishment (if, Indeed, it deserves the name) where (if guilty) death was evidently so well merited, was probably the result of a previous arrangement between his Royal Highness and his pliant deputy, and furnishes no satisfactory proof of the merciful temper of the latter, for subsequent experience fully showed that mercy was not an element in his composition, but that like the infamous Jeffreys (who in 1680 was solicitor to this same duke) he was the constant object of hate and detestation.

It is somewhat extraordinary that so much uncertainty and contradiction should exist in relation to the taking of the fort, and the behavior of Captain Manning — for if some accounts be true he was deserving of high applause for his bravery; but if the facts be as insisted upon by others, he had most undoubtedly forfeited his life. It is hard to say that he was accountable for the dilapidated condition of the fort, or its want of the means of defense, and how he could have been guilty at all is strange, or how, if deserving of punishment, he should have escaped with one so inadequate to the crime charged upon him.

The same inconsistency exists in the amount of force which he had to oppose, the accounts differing very much; according to some there were twelve, to some sixteen and to others twenty ships, besides several prizes which had been captured on the cruise. At any rate, it seems the fort held out four hours against this force, and then only struck its flag for want of means to continue the fight, for the last cartridge had been used. Of the subsequent career of Captain Manning we have no satisfactory account. Binkes it seems fell in 1677 at the capture of Tobago, and Evertsen reposes at Middleburgh in the island of Walchesen, where as late as 1818 an oration was delivered in honor of his memory, and funds were raised to restore the tomb which covers his ashes.

November 26, 1674, Andros suspended a term of the court of sessions in the east riding of Yorkshire, and ordered the towns of Huntington and Brookhaven to have their business for that term transacted at the ensuing court of sessions at Jamaica, in the north riding, because the three eastern towns had not returned the accounts of the constables and overseers of those towns, according to his orders; and in April, 1681, he in the most arbitrary manner summoned Isaac Piatt, Epenetus Piatt, Samuel Titus, Jonas Wood, and Thomas Wicks, inhabitants of Huntington, to New York; and caused them to be imprisoned without trial, and without being chargeable with any legal offence, but, as is supposed, merely for having attended a meeting of delegates of the several towns, convened for the purpose of contriving the means of procuring a redress of grievances. But this circumstance took place near the close of his administration, as he appears to have left the country, in

May, 1682, when the administration of public affairs devolved upon the Hon. Anthony Brockholst, senior member and president of the council. In 1686 he was again sent to America and held the government of New England about three years, exhibiting, however, his usual despotism, when, on news of the revolution in England being received, he was seized by the populace and thrown into prison, where he was detained some time. On his liberation Andros returned to England in 1699, was governor of the island of Guernsey from 1704 to 1706, and died in London, February, 1714, at the age of eighty-two. History has condemned him as a tyrant, and Oldmixon in 1741 said he was as mean in character as fortune. Smith says he knew no law but the will of his master, and like the infamous Jeffreys, was fitted to execute the despotic projects of James II. His wife died in Boston, February 7, 1688, and was buried with great pomp, the hearse being drawn by six horses, and torches carried in the procession. His father. Amice Andros, was bailiff of Ireland from 1660 till his death, April 7, 1664, and his son. Sir Edmund, filled the office from the time till August of the same year. Major General Brock, who fell at Queenston in October, 1812, was a descendant of this family.

At a special court of assize, June 29, 1681, the grand jury presented the want of a general assembly as an insupportable grievance, and one which ought to be redressed; and the court appointed Captain John Youngs, high sheriff of Long Island, a gentleman of family and education, and of known ability, to draft a petition upon the subject to the Duke of York. One was accordingly drawn, approved and transmitted, and appears to have been favorably received, for instructions were soon after forwarded to the new governor, to summon a general assembly on his arrival in the colony. All parties (says the elegant Bancroft,) joined in entreating for the people a share in legislation. The Duke of York was at the same time solicited by those about him to sell the territory. He demanded the advice of one who always advised honestly; and no sooner had the father of Pennsylvania (after a visit to New York,) transmitted an account of the reforms which the province required, than without delay, Thomas Dongan, a papist, came over as governor, with instructions to convoke a free legislature. He was commissioned September 30, 1682, and arrived August 25, 1683, having landed on the east end of Long Island. He soon after issued orders to the sheriffs to convene the freeholders of the province, in their several towns, to elect deputies to meet him in a general assembly. At length, then, after long and unwearied efforts, on the 17th of October, 1683, about sixty years from the time the island of Manhattan was first occupied by civilized people, and thirty years after the popular demand therefor, the representatives of the people met, and their self-established charter of liberties gave New York a place by the side of Virginia and Massachusetts. And thus, by the persuasions of a Quaker (once so odious) did a bigoted Roman Catholic prince give orders to a papistical governor, to introduce a popular assembly, elected by the people themselves, who had before no share in the government — an event similar in principle, and of nearly equal importance to that glorious independence which their descendants procured for themselves in less than a century after.

Dongan's commission was, it seems, renewed by King James II., June 10, 1686, but his instructions, which are very full and minute, bear date previously by May 29, 1686, and are referred to in the commission.

The first colonial legislature, consisting of the governor, council and seventeen members chosen by the people, assembled in the city of New York, October 17, 1683, and elected Matthias Nicoll their speaker. It continued to be held till the 3rd of November following; and declared, among other things, that, as a fundamental principle, the supreme authority under the duke should forever thereafter reside in a governor, council, and the people met in general assembly. At this time the three ridings upon Long Island were abolished, the province was divided into shires or counties, and names were given to each. The number of these was twelve, viz: New York, Ulster, Albany, Dutchess, Westchester, Orange, Richmond, Kings, Queens, Suffolk, Duke's and Cornwall. The great and all important result of this enlightened assembly, was the adoption of a bill of rights, or charter of liberties and privileges. Courts of justice were established, some of the more objectionable of the Duke's laws repealed or amended, and such new ones passed as were most imperiously required. It was also recommended, that a general assembly should ever after be held in the province, triennially at least, which should be sole judge of the qualifications of its own members, and be free from all arrest in civil cases, eundo, morando et redeundo. A court was established in every town, to be held on the first Wednesday of every month — a court of sessions in each county to be held annually; for Kings County, at Gravesend; for Queens, at Jamaica; and for Suffolk, at Southold and Southampton alternately; and a court of general jurisdiction, called a court of oyer and terminer and general jail delivery, to be held in the city and county of New York twice a year, and once a year in each of the other counties. The governor and council constituted, ex officio, a court of chancery, which should be esteemed and considered the supreme court of the province, and from which appeals lay to the king.

This assembly held another session in October, 1684, at which they abolished the court of assize, made further alterations in the Duke's laws, and enacted several new ones. A new assembly was summoned in September, 1685, which met at New York the ensuing October, and chose William Pinhorne their speaker. This assembly passed several acts; among which was an act of November 4, 1685, for regulating the proceedings of monthly courts throughout the province, by which the jurisdiction was extended to £5, and an act of November 7, 1685, for removing the court of sessions from Gravesend to Flatbush. But there is no evidence that this assembly ever met again, or that any other was summoned, (except one by Leisler during his usurpation,) until the arrival of a governor under William and Mary, in 1691. Charles II. died February 16, 1685, and his brother, the Duke of York, proprietary of this province, succeeded him as James II. As he seemed determined to have as little to do with parliaments as possible, so it is highly probable that he had secretly forbidden his governor here to convene any more assemblies, and was determined that in future the colony should be governed by his instructions alone. Dongan, whose commission was renewed in 1686, was directed, among other things, to allow of no printing press in the colony, and being at the same time deprived of the assembly, New York was thereby reduced to the condition of a conquered province; and there were now here 4,000 foot, 300 horse, and a company of dragoons, to keep the people in the most servile subjection, and to repress effectually any commotions, which the new state of things was so well calculated to produce. Andros, who had been appointed in 1686 governor of all New England, during pleasure, was now, by a new commission, reinstated in this colony and New Jersey; and an order in council was read in New York, July 28, 1688, directing Colonel Dongan to deliver the seal of the province to Sir Edmund, who shortly after revisited the colony, and resumed the administration of public affairs. On the 25th of August, new commissions were issued to the civil officers who had been appointed for Kings and Queens counties. On his return to Massachusetts, to which his authority likewise extended, the administration here was conducted by Colonel Francis Nicholson, the lieutenant governor, and the council. This man had also been an officer in the British army, and was, if possible, more obnoxious than even Andros himself, especially to the people of Long Island. Colonel Dongan, after his release from office, retired to his possessions upon Staten Island, where he remained till the spring of 1691, if not longer, when he left the country. Ebeling affirms that he returned to his native country of Ireland, where he finally succeeded to the earldom of Limerick, and is believed to have been killed in some engagement in that country. Governor Dongan left no descendants, nor is it known that he was ever married. Two brothers, John and Walter, accompanied him to this country, and to the latter he devised his large domain upon Staten Island, which included nearly all of the present town of Castleton. He married Ruth, daughter of Colonel Richard Floyd, of Brookhaven, by whom he had issue Richard, Thomas, and Ruth; the former of whom married Cornelia Shanks, and had issue Thomas, Walter, Ruth, and Sarah; of whom Walter, born January 2, 1763, is still living on a part of the ancient manor, having a wife and several children. The said Thomas, son of the first Walter, lived upon Staten Island, was raised to the rank of colonel in the British army, and placed in command of a regiment stationed there, where he fell at the head of his troops August 22, 1777, in an engagement with the Americans under Colonel Ogden.

As may well be supposed, the public rejoicing was ardent and sincere, at the abdication of James II., December 23, 1688, and the succession to the throne of his daughter Mary and her husband, William, Prince of Orange, February 16, 1689. The news was received at Boston in April, 1689, when the person of Andros was seized by an indignant people and thrown into prison, where he was detained until they heard from England.

The news of the proceedings in Boston prompted certain persons in New York, whose zeal or ambition was too impatient of delay to await the changes which would necessarily have succeeded the revolution in England, to wrest the government out of the hands of Nicholson, the lieutenant governor.

On May 31, Captain Jacob Leisler put himself at the head of the party, seized the fort, and kept possession of it. On June 3, he was joined by the other captains of the militia, with their companies. They immediately issued a proclamation, stating that their intention in seizing the fort was to keep it for King William; and that they would surrender it to the governor who should be appointed by him. Nicholson immediately retired aboard a vessel, and returned to England. On June 12, Leisler and his friends wrote to the several towns on Long Island, inviting them to send two men from each county to meet the deputies of the other counties at New York, on the 26th instant, to form a committee of safety; and also to send two men from each town to assist in guarding the fort.

It is supposed that Kings and Queens counties complied with the request, although there was a powerful opposition in the latter to the measure.

The several towns in Suffolk met by their deputies at Southampton, June 20, when a majority of them refused to send deputies to New York; and immediately opened a negotiation with Connecticut, and made another unsuccessful effort to put themselves under the jurisdiction of that colony, the laws and Institutions of which were more congenial with their ideas of good government than those of any other royal province.

Most or all of the other counties, it is supposed, sent deputies to New York.

The committee of safety, which convened at New York, had, June 8, 1689, given the superintendence of affairs to Leisler, which he managed according to their advice till the ensuing fall. He was of an eager, headlong temper, of narrow capacity, whose opposition to Popery, and the ill treatment he had received from Andros, seemed to point him out as a suitable leader in a religious and political controversy. Being possessed of small qualifications for so important a station, he was under the influence of others, and particularly of his son-in-law Milbourne, a man of more talent, but of less discretion. The inhabitants of the two western counties of Long Island acquiesced, but Suffolk sought again to renew her union with Connecticut, in which, being unsuccessful, they remained neutral and inactive, during Leisler's administration. In the meantime, a letter of July 29, 1689, was received from the English ministry, addressed to Francis Nicholson, or in his absence, to such as, for the time being, take care for preserving the peace and administering the laws, in their Majesties' province of New York in America, and authorizing Nicholson " to take upon him the chief command, and to appoint for his assistance as many of the principal freeholders and inhabitants as he should think fit," and to do everything appertaining to the laws and customs of New York, until further orders. This letter was received in December, 1689, and in the absence of Colonel Nicholson, Leisler chose to consider the orders as addressed to himself, and assumed the title and powers of a lieutenant governor. He selected a council, commissioned public officers in the several counties, and required an entire submission to his authority. He assembled the committee of safety to aid him by their advice, and also to give greater weight and confidence to his measures. In the spring of 1690, a general assembly was summoned, probably to obtain the means of defending the frontiers, which met at New York, April 24, and elected John Spratt, speaker. Two deputies from Connecticut were admitted to assist by their counsel, but nothing of great Importance was done at this meeting, except the adoption of a few necessary regulations for the temporary government of the province, and it was prorogued to the first of September. No members attended the assembly either from Suffolk, Albany, or Ulster, while one from New York and one from Queens refused to serve, thus reducing the number of delegates to ten. During this period the towns in Suffolk held meetings to consult about the course which it would be proper to take, without coming to any definite conclusion.

The summons received by them, March 15, 1690, for the election of assemblymen they had refused to obey, although Huntington was half inclined, on the score of expediency, to recognize the authority of Leisler. The people of Easthampton on the 3rd of May, peremptorily resolved not to submit, but to continue as they were, but on the 9th of September following, they consented " that certain moneys, formerly raised for the public service, might be paid to Leisler, or to his order."

The people of Hempstead, Jamaica, and Flushing convened on the 7th of November, 1690, and remonstrated in very severe language, to his Majesty the King of England, against the tyrannical usurpations of Leisler and his accomplices, wherein they represent that his son-in-law, Milbourne, had once been convicted of a crime deserving of death, the nature of which is not mentioned.

On the arrival of news, April, 1689, conveying intelligence of the accession of William and Mary, Leisler lost no time in proclaiming them King and Queen at the fort, and proceeding from thence to the city hall, repeated the proclamation by sound of trumpet, to the enthusiastic and rejoicing multitude. He also dispatched a messenger to England, giving an account of his proceedings, which at first seem to have been favorably received by their

Majesties. January 1, 1690, he issued a warrant to have Andrew Gibb, clerk of Queens County, before him, for refusing to deliver the papers of his office to Daniel Denton, the new clerk, whom he had appointed, and he issued orders to the sheriff of the same county to secure Colonel Dongan, late governor, in his own house, and to bring Colonel Thomas Willet, Captain Thomas Hicks, Daniel Whitehead, and Edward Antill, Esqs., before the council, for declining to acknowledge his authority. February 21, he ordered Colonel Dongan, Stephen Van Cortland, Anthony Brockholst and Mathew Plowman, Esqs., to be seized and brought before him. August 9, he issued a proclamation requiring the assembly to meet at New York, the first of September ensuing, to which day they were prorogued. August 11, after reciting that Nathaniel Piersall, elected to the assembly from Queens, and Wilhelmus Beekman from New York, had refused to serve at the meeting in April, he ordered those counties to elect others to meet at the ensuing September session. It seems, however, that the opposition to his measures in Queens County had not been quelled by the means heretofore used, and accordingly, October 18, 1690, he ordered Major Milbourne " to take what force he could raise, to suppress it; " and October 26, he suspended the court of oyer and terminer, about to sit in Kings County, " until Long Island should he reduced to obedience." On the 30th of October, after stating that a rebellion existed in Queens County, he issued orders to Samuel Staats, and Captain Thomas Williams, to " suppress it." He likewise directed Williams and Samuel Edsall to go to Flushing Bay, examine the vessels there and see that none were employed in " a way prejudicial to his interest."

January 30, 1691, Captain Richard Ingolsby arrived at New York with his company and demanded possession of the fort, which Leisler refused, thus adding a new subject of contention to the already overexcited state of public feeling, and in this unhappy condition the colony remained until the usurpation of Leisler was terminated by the arrival of Governor Henry Slaughter, March 19, 1691. It seems Leisler acknowledged him as governor, but persisted nevertheless in retaining the fort, thereby violating his former professions of loyalty and zeal for King William, forfeiting all claims of merit for his services, and incurring not only the reproach of the people, but the more severe penalty of usurpation. He had taken upon himself the direction of affairs at a time and under circumstances, requiring all the address, knowledge, and firmness of a veteran statesman, and he brought to the task the mere ordinary experience of a merchant, desirous of the good of the province and the Protestant succession.

Leisler and his son-in-law, Milbourne, were afterwards tried by a special commission, consisting of Sir Thomas Robinson, Colonel William Smith, and others, which found the accused guilty of high treason, and sentenced them to death. The warrant for their execution was made out by the concurring advice of the assembly and council; yet Slaughter hesitated to order their execution, and wrote to the English ministry for direction of the subject. That he disapproved of so terrible a sentence, for a political offence which he could not but deem, in a great measure, venial, is most probable; but on the 16th of May, 1691, in a moment of intoxication, into which he had been designedly betrayed for the purpose, he signed the fatal order; and before he recovered his senses, the unfortunate prisoners were in eternity.

The populace were greatly affected at the melancholy result, and would have been gratified with the escape of the sufferers. The son of Leisler afterwards preferred a complaint against the governor, which, being referred to the Lords of Trade, they reported, March 11, 1692, " that they were humbly of opinion, Jacob Leisler and Jacob Milbourne, deceased, were condemned, and had suffered according to law." November 12, 1694, on like application the British parliament reversed the attainder of Leisler and Milbourne, and, in compassion for their families, restored their estates, and the assembly, by recommendation of his Majesty, voted £1000, to be raised by tax on the colony, for the relief of the widow and children of Leisler.

Leisler, says Mr. Sparks, when arraigned, exhibited his wonted directness of character in rejecting the authority of the court thus constituted. He said " he was not holden to plead to the indictment, until the power be determined whereby such things have been acted." But the insolent mockery of justice proceeded, and he and Milbourne were condemned to death as rebels and traitors; rebels to the laws, whose dignity Leisler had to the last so nobly asserted in his own person; traitors to the king, whose standard he was the first to rear among his subjects here. The customary confiscation of property and attainder of blood, which is part of the English law of high treason, followed. They were executed at the lower end of what is now the park, where the spray of the fountain has succeeded the blood stain of the martyrs.

" Why must you die? " said Leisler to his son-in-law; "you have been but as a servant, doing my will, and as a dying man, I declare before God, that what I have done was for King William and Queen Mary, the defense of the Protestant religion, and the good of the country."

For every offence he asked pardon of God, and next, of all persons offended; prayed that malice might be buried in the grave, and forgave the most inveterate of his enemies.

The widow of Milbourne, and daughter of Leisler, afterwards married Abraham Goveneul, Esq., who had been secretary to Leisler, and speaker of the assembly in 1701. Leisler appears to have acted with an honest endeavor to promote the public welfare, and although somewhat imprudent, yet his loyalty to his sovereign ought not to be questioned, and justice requires that his name be rescued from obliquy and disgrace so long resting upon it.

The royal commission to Governor Slaughter, of January 9, 1689, constituted the foundation of the colonial government, which was consequent upon the revolution in England and continued as then settled, with some slight changes, till the more glorious revolution of 1776.

The executive power was vested in the governor; the legislative in the governor, council, and general assembly, periodically elected, subject to approval of the king, to whom all laws were required to be submitted within three months after their passage. The council consisted, at first, of seven members, which was afterwards increased to twelve, and they received their appointment from his Majesty. The assembly was composed of deputies, chosen by the freeholders of each county, the number being regulated by law. The term of service was indefinite till 1743, when it became limited to seven years.

Among the first acts of Slaughter's administration, was that of May 6, 1691, "for Settling, Quieting, and Confirming unto the Cities, Towns, Manors and Freeholders within this Province, their several Grants, Patents and Rights respectively;" and another for quieting and settling the public disorders, which had long prevailed, to the destruction of confidence and disregard for private right. These acts gave much satisfaction, and removed the doubts which had been entertained by many, and led them to conclude that the governor was influenced by a proper zeal for the interests of the province. But alas! the hopes entertained of a long and prosperous administration were suddenly prostrated by the unexpected death of his excellency, on the 23rd of July, 1691, only four months and as many days from the time of his arrival at New York. His body was deposited in the vault of the Stuyvesant family. The governor is, however, described by the historian Smith, as licentious in his morals, avaricious and poor, and as having been probably sent over, as others had previously been, to gratify some powerful relative or friend, by affording him a chance for making money out of the people. It was at first generally supposed that he had been clandestinely destroyed by poison, but a thorough post mortem examination removed all reasonable grounds of suspicion in that respect.

The legislature had in 1683 passed a declaration of rights, in which it was enacted, " that no person or persons which profess faith in God by Jesus Christ, shall at any time be any wayes molested, punished, disquieted, or called in question for any difference of opinion, or matter of religious concernment who do not actually disturbe the civille peace of the province, but all and every such may at all times fully enjoy his or their judgments or consciences in matters of religion."

This clause is creditable to the legislature of that period, and to the correct and liberal ideas of Governor Dongan. It was in a manner annulled by the legislature in 1691, who declared that nothing therein contained, should extend to give liberty to any Roman Catholic to exercise their manner of worship. The same illiberality was likewise manifested toward Quakers, they being considered and treated as heretics, not worthy of being tolerated among these self-styled Christians.

On his death, the council conferred the chief authority upon the Hon. Richard Ingolsby, (at that time also captain of an independent company,) who held the trust till the arrival of the new governor, Colonel Benjamin Fletcher, August 30, 1692. Of this gentleman history affords no very flattering account, for although he was a good soldier, he is represented at the same time, as passionate, avaricious, and arbitrary; and a bigot to his own mode of faith (that of the Established Church of England) . Consequently he was soon on bad terms with the assembly. He became, also, in a short time, very generally unpopular with the people. He evidently consulted his own pecuniary interest, more than the happiness and prosperity of those he was sent to govern, and fell almost of course, into the hands of the aristocratic party, whose principles he adopted. Piracies at this period were extensively practiced upon the coast, and the governor was suspected of countenancing them, from motives best known to himself, but which others did not fail to conjecture abundantly. One of the first acts of his government was the establishment of a public fair or market, every Thursday at Jamaica, for the sale and exchange of cattle, horses, grain, and other articles; and provision for holding two fairs annually in Queens and Suffolk, and one in Kings.

April 10, 1693, the name of Long Island was changed to the Island of Nassau, — an alteration which arose from political vanity, and was neither popular, nor generally adopted. The act, although it is believed never explicitly repealed, was suffered to become obsolete by disuse. The words of this act are as follows:

" BE it enacted by the Governor, and Council, and Representatives, convened in General Assembly, and by the Authority of the same, That the Island commonly called and known by the Name of Long-Island, shall from henceforth be called the Island of Nassau; and that after the Publication hereof, all their Majesties loving Subjects are hereby required, in all Grants, Patents, Deeds, Conveyances, Bargains of Sale, Bills, Bonds, Records, and other Instruments in Writing, that shall hereafter be made, granted, conveyed, bargained, sold, and executed, for or concerning the said Island, or any Part or Place, within the same, or in any County thereof, to call and denominate the said Island in all such Deeds and Escripts, as aforesaid, the Island of Nassau; any Thing contained in any former Act to the Contrary hereof in any wise notwithstanding."

This administration, whatever faults it possessed, presents one redeeming feature at least, which justly entitles it to lasting honor. It was at this period that a Press was for the first time set up in the city of New York, an institution which had been expressly discountenanced by its predecessors, and positively forbidden by his Majesty King James II., the lawful proprietor and pretended patron of the colony. The owner of this Press was William Bradford, who came here from Philadelphia, and was made government printer to the province, which office he held from 1693 to May 23, 1752, a period of almost sixty years, when he died at the great age of ninety-two years. The first book from Mr. Bradford's press was a small folio volume of the colony laws, a copy of which would now be considered by us as a great curiosity, yet it is quite doubtful if one could be found. The first newspaper published between Philadelphia and Boston, was begun by him October 16, 1725, entitled The New York Gazette. In 1728 he erected a paper manufactory at Elizabethtown, N. J., certainly the first in that province, and probably the earliest in America.

By an act of May 6, 1691, the courts of common pleas and general sessions were distinctly organized in the several counties. On pretense of producing uniformity in the language and literature, as well as the religion of the province, composed of a heterogeneous mixture of Dutch and English, the governor brought into the assembly a bill for the settlement of ministers, throughout the colony, such as should be approved of by himself, as the event showed, and for levying a tax upon the inhabitants for the building of churches.

The assembly, after much debate, agreed that ministers should be settled in certain parishes, but left the choice to the people. The act passed in September, 1693, for settling and maintaining a ministry, made no allusion to any sect or denomination, though secretly and purposely intended by the governor and his partizans, as afterwards appeared, to favor Episcopalians only. This, then, was the first step towards the introduction of a religious order, which, at this day, forms so respectable a portion of our immense population. This statute was confined, in terms, to the city of New York, and to the counties of Richmond, Westchester, and Queens, by the provisions of which, £100 was to be raised by tax upon the city, £100 in Westchester, £120 in Queens, and £40 in Richmond. It is pretty evident from the limiting the operation of this act to a few counties, apparently most friendly to the object aimed at, that it was intended as an experiment.

The assembly was composed almost entirely of dissenters, and could not. Itis believed, have suspected the covert design of those who originated a measure the purpose of which, a few years after, and during the administration of Lord Cornbury, was so clearly developed, by acts not only arbitrary, but odious and disgraceful. As much opposition was manifested by the public to this act, on account of the inexplicitness of the language, and its liability to be construed in favor of the denomination to which his excellency was known to be zealously attached, the assembly. In 1695, resolved, by way of explanation, that its benefits extended to the dissenting Protestant clergy. In common with others. But that which had remained a problem was now solved; for the governor rejected that interpretation, and declared that it applied solely to the Episcopal clergy, who, as may well be supposed, did not fail thereafter to engross all the advantages of it, up to the close of the American Revolution. There being comparatively very few Episcopal families in Queens County, the raising of money, by tax, for the support of ministers of that church, whose doctrines and ceremonies were held both erroneous and ridiculous, by a vast majority of those who would be compelled to pay it, was very properly considered as an imposition and a grievance of no ordinary magnitude. But the executive fiat had gone forth, and the people were obliged to endure, as best they might, what they had not the power to hinder or avoid.

Sir Richard Coote, Earl of Bellomont, was the successor of Governor Fletcher. He was appointed in 1695, and commissioned June 18, 1697, but delaying his voyage until after the peace of Ryswick, and then being blown off the American coast to Barbados, he did not reach New York till the 2nd of April, 1698. He brought with him as lieutenant governor, John Nanfan, Esq., whom he called his cousin. His wife, whom he married under twelve years old, accompanied him. The governor lived scarcely three years from the time of his arrival, dying the 15th of March, 1701, universally regretted, and was buried under the chapel of the fort, from whence the body was afterwards removed to St. Paul's Church. At the death of this nobleman, the ancient animosities of the rival factions were revived with the utmost zeal and fury. Colonel Nicholas Bayard had procured addresses, to be sent to the king, to the parliament, and to Lord Cornbury, charging Lieutenant Governor Nanfan, the chief justice, and the assembly, with public plunder, oppression, and even bribery. The party in power, conscious that their rule would be short, determined to bring Bayard to trial before the arrival of the new governor. A court of oyer and terminer was therefore immediately erected for his trial, consisting of three justices, and it assembled February 19, 1702. Broughton, the attorney general, was so opposed to the whole proceeding, that he not only refused to prosecute the prisoner, but even to be present on the occasion. The accused was defended by Messrs. Emot and Nicoll. When the jury was called, some of them were objected to, for having declared, " that if Bayard's neck was made of gold, he should he hanged." The indictment charged the prisoner, with falsely, maliciously, advisedly, rebelliously and traitorously using divers Indirect practices and endeavors to procure mutiny and desertion among the soldiers in the fort, and drawing numbers of them to sign false and scandalous libels against his Majesty's government. Many objections were urged against the proceedings, which were of course of no avail with his prejudiced judges. On this trial, Samuel Clowes, a respectable lawyer of the city, who afterwards lived and died in the village of Jamaica, L. I., was examined as a witness, by which it appears that he was decidedly in favor of the measures pursued by Colonel Bayard. After the most violent and one-sided charge by the chief justice to the jury, urging the conviction of the prisoner, he was found guilty. A motion in arrest of judgment was also overruled, and the unhappy man sentenced to be drawn upon an hurdle to the place of execution, there to be hanged by the neck, to be cut down alive, his bowels taken out, his privy members cut off, and burnt before his face; his head cut off, and his body to be divided into four quarters, and placed at the disposal of the king. This terrible fate was, however, avoided; the prisoner was released, on the arrival of Lord Cornbury, and reinstated in all " honor and estate " as If no such trial had taken place, while Atwood, the chief justice, and Weaver, the solicitor general, were obliged to leave the province, to escape the popular rage. The act of May 12, 1699, " for vacating, breaking and annulling" several extravagant grants made by his Immediate predecessor, to his party favorites and the vestry and wardens of Trinity Church, was one of the most popular measures of his brief administration. Piracies continued to exist to an alarming extent, in the American seas, and the inhabitants of some of the colonies were suspected of favoring the marauders. To suppress these disorders was the avowed purpose of the king in selecting a person of the exalted rank, resolution, and integrity of the Earl of Bellomont; and it must be acknowledged that his vigilance did much to repress the lawless career of these freebooters, and led eventually to the apprehension of Kidd, the most noted sea robber of the age.

Of the profligate and unprincipled character of Governor Fletcher there can be but one opinion among those who examine his motives and reflect upon his conduct, from the beginning to the close of his administration. This is made more evident from the representations of his successor. Lord Bellomont, in May, 1698, complains to the Council of Trade and Plantations that his predecessor had countenanced and protected pirates, who, he says, were fitted out either at New York or Rhode Island. That ships engaged in this wicked business were commissioned by the governor, and that he received large bribes for protecting them. That the notorious pirate, Captain Tew, was received and caressed by him. That he received a present of a piratical vessel, which he sold to Colonel Heathcote for £800, besides receiving presents for his lady and daughter. That he charged £40 a man for protection issued by him to the crews of piratical vessels, and gratifications to Mr. Nicoll, his broker. In his letter of May 3, 1699, he complains of Fletcher's extravagant grants, and among others, one to Colonel Smith, upon Long Island, which he had been assured by the attorney general, was fifty miles long, and the whole breadth of the island. In his letter of May 18, 1698, Lord Bellomont says that Mr. Nicoll was suspected of favoring pirates and was accordingly dismissed from the council, whose opinion was that he ought to answer for his offence. Mr. Nicoll thereupon gave £2000 security for his appearance in England when demanded. He admits him to be a man of good sense and knowledge in the law, but that he had been a great instrument and continuer of many corrupt and unjust practices. In a letter of June 22, 1698, he charges him with being industrious in making cabals and encouraging discontents in the colony, and fears he shall be obliged to send him home a prisoner, on account of his dealings with pirates, and for the quiet of the government. One Raynor, he says was seized as a pirate, on the east end of Long Island, by Sheriff Hobart, and discharged by Fletcher, without consulting the attorney general, although a matter of so much consequence to his Majesty's crown and dignity. A parcel of pirates, he says, were taken at Boston, among whom was Joseph Bradish, a native of Cambridge in that colony. They came to the east end of Long Island and sunk their ship of about 400 tons between that and Block Island. He sends affidavits of Syman Bonare (a Jew), of Captain Mulford, Cornelius Schellinger, and Lieutenant Pierson, with whom Bradish had deposited £942 19s. 3d., and a bag of jewelsfound to be counterfeit.

This Pierson, he says, was at that time a man of fair character, a man of substance, and member of the assembly.

On the 19th of May, 1701, Lieutenant Governor Nanfan assumed the government, but in less than twelve months thereafter was superseded by the new governor, Edward Hyde, more commonly called Lord Cornbury, who reached New York May 3, 1702. He was the only son of Henry, second Earl of Clarendon, and grandson of Lord Chancellor Clarendon, prime minister to Charles II., and historical writer of distinguished reputation. Henry succeeded his father in the earldom December 19, 1674, and married Theodosia, daughter of Arthur Lord Capel, who was beheaded for his loyalty to Charles I., March 9, 1649.

The governor was brother to the Queen of James II., and first cousin to Queen Anne, who succeeded to the throne of her father in March, 1702. Having been among the first to desert the army of King James, William, his successor, chose to make him some return for his loyalty to him, by appointing him to this colony, which he did not however reach till after the death of his patron, (whose decease took place March 8, 1701,) and his cousin, Anne, was seated upon the throne of England.

Lord Cornbury, during his administration of the affairs of New York and New Jersey, (which were now united,) by his avaricious and despotic conduct, rendered himself not only odious but despicable. It would seem that his sense of justice was as weak as his bigotry was uncontrollable, a position which is capable of complete illustration, by numerous acts of his administration. As he came here in the most indigent circumstances, hunted out of England by a host of hungry creditors, some of whom had been ruined by his profligacy, he was bent on getting as much money as he could squeeze out of the purses of an insulted people. His talents were little superior to any of his predecessors, while in his zeal for the established church of England he was surpassed by none.

In him was exemplified the fact, that an ardent zeal for a particular church is no certain indication of honor or integrity, a position which at first view may appear inconsistent, and a solecism in ethics. In 1708 the assemblies of New York and New Jersey, no longer willing to submit to his tyranny, sent a formal complaint to the Queen, who, in consequence, soon after removed him from office. This nobleman, says an able writer, whose character and principles were equally detestable, had been appointed to this office by the influence of his high connections, and not on account of any fitness for the situation; so true is the observation that the colonies had never been looked upon, in any other light, than that of an hospital, where the favorites of the minority might remain until they had recovered their broken fortunes, and oftentimes they served as asylums from their creditors. He hated the Presbyterians, and in the same degree became a staunch supporter of the established church. He therefore embraced every opportunity, legal or otherwise, to persecute the one, and favor and promote the other.

An interesting example of the severe instructions given to Lord Cornbury by Queen Anne, which he was only too eager to carry out, is herewith appended. The extract is taken from the collections of the New Jersey Historical Society. New York and New Jersey were at this time (1702) united into one province of which he was governor:

" Forasmuch as great inconveniences may arise by the liberty of printing in our province, you are to provide, by all necessary orders, that no person keep any press for printing, nor that any books, pamphlets, or other matters whatsoever, be printed without your especial leave and license first obtained."

Of the bad character generally ascribed to this representative of royalty, the following instance of his bigotry and persecution may be cited in corroboration.

A great mortality prevailed in the city of New York in the summer of 1702, which has since been designated as " the time of the great sickness," and in consequence of which, the governor and council removed therefrom and took refuge in Jamaica, a place both near and convenient of access.

The parsonage house of the Presbyterian Church had been then lately built, and was one of the best private residences in the place, and occupied by the Rev. John Hubbard. The possession of this dwelling was politely tendered by the minister to his excellency, the former subjecting himself and family thereby to considerable inconvenience.

In return for this generous, and (as it happened) misplaced confidence, in one whom he had reason to believe merited the character of a gentleman, at least, his excellency, instead of surrendering the premises to the former occupant, most perfidiously gave possession thereof to the Episcopal clergyman, who, it is to be regretted (for his own sake at least) seems to have felt no delicacy in countenancing an act so dishonorable to all concerned. But this was not the worst; the governor even authorized the sheriff and his subordinates to seize upon the church edifice also, as well as the glebe, and appropriate the same to the exclusive use of the Episcopal party, who were at this time a small minority of the people there. This wanton and most illegal proceeding led to a series of contentions and litigations, which agitated and distressed the community for a quarter of a century. " Indeed (says the Rev. Dr. Spencer) many of the principal people were harassed with severe persecutions, heavy fines, and long imprisonment, for assuming their just rights; and others fled out of the province to avoid the rage of Episcopal cruelty."

In addition to this, the same governor. In 1707, caused two Presbyterian ministers to be imprisoned for preaching without his license. One of these, the Rev. Francis McKennie, who had been refused a license by him to preach in one of the churches of the city, held forth in a private house in Pearl Street, and also baptized a child, for which acts he was tried before a civil tribunal and was compelled, although acquitted by the court, to pay a heavy amount in costs. It Is, however, but charitable to believe that few of the Episcopal party approved of or countenanced such acts of Intolerance and persecution. For in these gross outrages upon religious liberty, the governor lost his aim, and they served only to Increase the odium under which he fell, and finally sunk. He was a bankrupt in reputation and fortune at home, and as no man took more pains to make himself despised, so few men were in this respect more entirely successful.

The place made vacant by the removal of Lord Cornbury was supplied December 18, 1708, by the appointment of John, Lord Lovelace, Baron of Hurly, whose administration was rendered extremely brief by his sudden death on the 6th of May following. The people had formed high expectations from the change, and the short experience they had had of his excellency. To express their high respect for his memory, the assembly, on the 10th of June, 1709, ordered £500 to be presented to his widow, and other tokens of condolence were shown to the unfortunate lady, bereaved of her natural protector among strangers, in a distant land. In this unexpected emergency, the command again fell upon Ingolsby, who being displaced within a year thereafter, the station was occupied by Gerardus Beekman, the senior member and president of the council, till June 10, when the new governor, Colonel Robert Hunter, arrived, bringing with him nearly three thousand emigrants from the Palatinate of Germany. These unhappy individuals having been reduced to great Indigence and distress by the perpetual wars in their own country, solicited in person the charity of the British Queen, who, it seems, sympathized in their misfortunes, and contributed to their removal to America. Many more of the same nation arrived shortly after, and located in different parts of the country. " The Queen's liberality (says Smith) was not more beneficial to them than serviceable to the colony." These respectable people were of the Lutheran religion, and by their aid the first German Lutheran church was erected in New York, on the spot where Grace Church now stands. It was burned down in 1776, at the same time with Trinity

Church, and a great many other buildings. The administration of Colonel Hunter commenced most inauspiciously for himself, he being almost immediately involved in a controversy with the assembly, to terminate which he put in exercise the power of prorogation, and dissolved that body, November 25, 1710, with the following laconic speech:

" Gentlemen: — I have waited with great patience, hoping that at last some temper might have been found, by means of which, her Majesty's government here might have found its necessary support, and some other matters, earnestly recommended to you by her, might have met with returns in some measure proportioned to so matchless goodness; but being disappointed in my hopes, the season far advanced, and many of your members gone home, I have thought fit to prorogue you to the first day of March next: and you are prorogued accordingly. — By which time second thoughts and better acquaintance may, perhaps, create a better disposition.

" Robert Hunter."

It was during his administration that a military expedition was undertaken against the French in Canada, but it proved abortive, after a very considerable waste of time and money.

An act was passed November 2, 1717, for destroying foxes and wildcats upon Long Island, which had become at this time not only numerous, but greatly Injurious to the farmers.

Her Majesty Queen Anne died August 12, 1714, and was succeeded by George I., of the Royal House of Brunswick. January 21, 1719, Governor Hunter announced that his health and private affairs demanded his return to Europe, and accordingly he took leave of the colony on the 31st of July, 1719, and the Hon. Peter Schuyler, senior member of the council, entered on the duties of the executive office, which he performed acceptably to the people. The Hon. William Burnet arrived with the commission of governor of New York and New Jersey, September 17, 1720. He was the eldest son of the venerable and learned Gilbert Burnet, Bishop of Sarum, and was born at the Hague, in March, 1688; being named William, in compliment to the (then) Stadtholder, the Prince of Orange, who was his godfather. His means had been entirely dissipated in the great South-Sea scheme, and the office of governor of New York was intended to repair, in some measure, his ruined fortunes. In the assembly of 1721, and mainly, as is supposed, through his influence, a curious bill was introduced, with the more singular title of "An act against denying the divinity of our Savior Jesus Christ, the doctrine of the blessed Trinity, the truth of the Holy Scriptures; and spreading atheistical hooks; " but the good sense of the assembly led them immediately to reject the bill.

On the 17th of June, 1726, an act was passed, entitled, "An act to prevent the setting on fire or burning the old grass on Hempstead Plains," which, says the preamble of the act, " is frequently set on fire by several of the inhabitants, through folly and the gratification of their own wanton tempers and humors." Those named in the bill to aid in extinguishing fires, were James Jackson, William Cornwell, Nathaniel Seaman, Benjamin Seaman, Obadiah Valentine, Thomas Williams, Peter Titus, Henry Willis, John Pratt, Nathaniel Townsend, Jeremiah Robbins, Thomas Powell, Samuel Jackson, Thomas Seaman, John Mott, John Mott, Jr., John Whitson, John Birdsail, John Tredwell, Jr., James Burtis, and Caleb Carman; all of whom were then residents of the town of Hempstead.

Burnet was afterwards appointed governor of Massachusetts and New Hampshire, and reached Boston in July, 1728, where he died the 7th of September, 1729. During his administration of the government of New York, on the 16th of October, 1725, the first newspaper in the city, entitled The New York Gazette, was commenced by William Bradford (who had been some years printer to the colony), which was two years before the death of King George I., which took place June 11, 1727. Governor Burnet was possessed of many agreeable qualities; his conversation was the delight of literary men, and his library was considered the richest private collection at that period in America. There is no doubt but that he was a gentleman of superior talents and attainments. His wife, Miss Van Horn of New York, was a lady of great personal accomplishments, and belonged to one of the most ancient and respectable families. His son, William, married Anne, daughter of the Hon. James De Lancey.

John Montgomery, Esq., was the next governor, and entered upon his duties, April 14, 1728. He was by birth a Scotchman, had been bred a soldier, and lately held the office of groom of the bed-chamber of his Majesty George II. while Prince of Wales. He was a gentleman of mild temper, and fond of retirement. Two days after his arrival the common council of the city presented him a congratulatory address in a gold box. No very important acts of a public nature marked his short administration, and he died, much regretted, July 1, 1731. On his decease the chief command of the province devolved upon Rip Van Dam, Esq., the oldest of the council and an eminent merchant of the city. He, however, passively permitted the encroachments of the French, and -during his administration they erected a fort at Crown Point, commanding Lake Champlain, which was within the acknowledged limits of the colony of New York. He relinquished his post, of course, on the arrival of Colonel William Cosby, August 1, 1732. This gentleman was as much distinguished for his folly and imprudence as his predecessor was for prudence and good sense, and soon found himself involved in difficulties that placed him in direct collision with the people he was sent to govern.

John Peter Zenger at this time published a weekly journal in the city. He was a bold and energetic man, and his taking sides with Van Dam led to an imprisonment of the printer, caused, as alleged by his persecutors, by his extreme insolence and abuse. The trial of Zenger, for a libel, appears to have been published by himself soon after, in 1735; entitled, "A Brief Narrative of the Case and Trial of John Peter Zenger, Printer, of the New York Weekly Journal for a Libel." In this affair, the new chief justice, De Lancey, took a very strong part against the defendant, but with all effort the grand jury refused to find a bill. The council then interfered, and ordered Zenger's newspaper to be burned by the common hangman. Zenger was arrested, thrown into jail, and denied pen, ink, and paper. He was brought to trial upon an information filed by the attorney general. The accused was assisted by his council, James Alexander and William Smith, who manifested a laudable firmness and independence in his defense; in consequence of which an order was passed by the bench, excluding these gentlemen from any further practice in the court. The friends of Zenger secretly procured the services of the venerable Andrew Hamilton, then about eighty years old, from Philadelphia, a distinguished barrister of that day, and occupying the highest rank in his profession. He was an ardent friend of liberty, and possessed a powerful and graceful eloquence, which, in connection with his advanced age, secured him the respect and admiration of those who differed with him in opinion. His argument upon this occasion was of the highest order, and proved completely successful. The trial took place in the supreme court of New York, August 4, 1735, before Chief Justice De Lancey, and was managed, on the part of the people, by Bradley, attorney general of the province. The trial was a tedious one, and when the cause was submitted to the jury, they almost instantly returned a verdict of not guilty, which was received by the populace with shouts of applause. Mr. Hamilton was conducted from the hall to a splendid entertainment, and the whole city renewed the compliment at his departure next day, he entering a barge near the fort, under a salute of cannon. The common council presented him the freedom of the city, in a gold box, on which the arms of the city were engraved, encircled by an inscription in Latin. He had been speaker of the Pennsylvania Assembly, which he resigned, on account of age and infirmities, in 1739, and died in 1741. " In the administration of Governor Cosby," says the historian Smith, " there was something to admire and much to condemn." No governor commenced his administration with better prospects and greater popularity, yet none endeavored less to retain the confidence and respect of the people. With high opinions of prerogative, and being decidedly hostile to free and equal legislation, he became at length odious to the colony, and was finally deserted and opposed by many who had been his best friends. He died the 7th of March, 1736, and the direction of public affairs devolved upon George Clarke, Esq., as lieutenant governor, although he was violently opposed by the personal friends of Rip Van Dam, who, they thought, as the oldest of the council, was best entitled to supply the vacancy. But Mr. Clarke was afterwards confirmed in the office by the commission of the king. It was during the administration of Governor Clarke that the act was passed, on the

16th of December, 1737, for lowering the interest of money upon loans, to seven per cent., as the high and excessive usury before taken, it was said, had been found by experience to be a very great discouragement of trade. It was also in his time that the memorable conspiracy was discovered, called the " Negro Plot," which, it was supposed, had for its object the destruction of the city of New York by fire. This was in the year 1741.

The first fire broke out the 18th of March, in his Majesty's house, at Fort George, which, with the chapel, and some other buildings, was consumed. Fires continued to happen daily, and were at first supposed to be accidental, but at length such disclosures and confessions were made, that prosecutions were set on foot. A number of people of color were committed to jail as incendiaries, kept in dungeons for some months, and finally condemned to be hanged. Daniel Horsmanden, Esq., who died at Flatbush, September 28, 1778, aged eighty-eight years, was recorder of the city at the time and published an account of the trials in 1744 in which he says, " many people had such terrible apprehensions on the subject, that several negroes, some of whom had assisted to put out the fires, were met and imprisoned; and when once there, were continued in confinement, because the magistrates could not spare time to examine them." During this dreadful consternation, more than one hundred and fifty negroes were imprisoned, of whom eleven were burned, eighteen hanged, seventy-one transported, and the remainder pardoned, or discharged for want of proof. Four white persons were also hanged either as principals or accessories. At this gloomy period, the population of the city was twelve thousand, of whom one-sixth part were slaves; a strange comment, surely, upon the professions of those who had left Europe for the sole purpose of enjoying perfect freedom in America. Most of the slaves were Africans by birth, who had been violently torn from their native land and reduced to servitude. Their spirits were not yet entirely subdued; and a race which, at this day, is remarkable for Implicit obedience and quiet submission, were at the time alluded to, rude, boisterous, and vicious, and had in their number many restless and daring spirits, whose influence was justly feared by the white population. The panic occasioned by the first disclosures of a plot being formed, was very great, and the court immediately summoned all the lawyers in the city, to consult upon the measures most proper to be adopted in such an emergency. There were seven of them, besides the attorney general; namely, Murray, Alexander, Smith, Chambers, Nicoll, Lodge, and Jamison. Two of these, Alexander and Smith, notwithstanding their exclusion from the bar in the case of Zenger, appear to have been restored, as they took a very active part in the prosecution of the negroes and others supposed to have been concerned in the plot.

A jury was allowed in these trials, although, by a law of the colony, negroes might be tried for any offences in a summary way; but as the testimony of slaves could only be used against each other, the unfortunate persons accused were deprived of the benefit of any such evidence. The prisoners severally and solemnly protested their innocence, and called upon God to bear witness thereto.

Governor Clarke, it must be admitted, studied his own interest; for he retired from office with a fortune of £100,000 sterling; surely, no inconsiderable sum in that day. He was born near Bath, England, in 1680, of an ancient family, and in 1703 married Miss Ann Hyde, of the house of Hyde, in the county Palatine of Chester. He was sent over here to mend his broken fortunes, during the reign of Queen Anne, and being a man of genius and good manners, exerted himself to make friends, and was successful. One of his daughters married Samuel Clowes, a lawyer of some reputation at Jamaica, Long Island, whose grave may be seen in the Episcopal churchyard of that place, where he was interred by the side of his father, of the same name.

George Clinton, who had been an admiral of the British navy, was commissioned governor; and, arriving September 22, 1743, put an end to the administration of Governor Clarke. He was the son of Francis Clinton, Earl of Lincoln, of an ancient and honorable family in Somersetshire, England, and was bred to the sea. His wife was an heiress of the elder branch of the house of Hyde, in the county of Chester, and his son. Sir Henry Clinton, was a commander of the British forces here in 1776. Governor Clinton was received with great joy by the people, because they were desirous of a change; but they were quite as well pleased to be entirely rid of him a few years after. He possessed few of the qualities which the hopes of the community had ascribed to him; was constitutionally indolent, and fond of Indulgence in wine, which, on many occasions, wholly unfitted him to discharge. In a proper manner, the responsible duties of his office. He had, it appears, a private residence at Flushing, where he resided a part of the summer. His administration of ten years was turbulent and unhappy, and he became involved in a violent controversy with the assembly, to which he was Instigated, Itis believed, by Chief Justice De Lancey, the ruling demagogue of that period, to whom, as a man of more experience and ability, the governor, in great measure, confided the direction of affairs. The most terrible murders and devastations were at this time enacted by the French and Indians, upon the inhabitants in the neighborhood of Saratoga.

In September, 1746, the governor held a council with the Six Nations at Albany, for the purpose of securing their friendly alliance, and thereby counteracting the intrigues of the French in Canada. It deserves to be noticed as somewhat remarkable, that notwithstanding the public discontents, more laws were passed and more valuable improvements made in the internal police of the province, during the administration of Governor Clinton, than of any one that had preceded it. He retired from the office here in 1753, and was afterwards made Governor of Greenwich Hospital, where he died in 1763. Like most of his predecessors, he continued, while here, to amass the peoples' money for himself, taking £80,000 with him to Europe. His successor was the amiable and much to be lamented Sir Danvers Osborne, who arrived October 6, 1753, and was received, as he deserved to be, with every demonstration of public respect and rejoicing. This worthy individual had lately lost his wife, on whom he doted with fond affection, and whose death produced, in a mind like his, great depression of spirits, amounting almost to melancholy. His friends had hoped that a change of scene, together with the novelty of the voyage, and the occupation of a new employment, might help to divert his attention and dispel the load of grief which weighed upon his heart. In this expectation his friends were doomed to be disappointed, for on the fifth day after his arrival, he committed violence upon himself, and was found suspended by his handkerchief, from the garden fence of Mr. Murray, near the place of the present Bowling Green. A paper was found on a table in his bedroom, upon which was written with his hand: " Quem deus vult perdere, prius dementat." He had the reputation of being a man of good sense, of great modesty, and of courteous behavior. He had once been a member of the British parliament, and the lady whose premature death he so much lamented was a sister of the Earl of Halifax.

On his decease the administration of affairs fell upon Chief Justice James De Lancey, the prominent leader of the former administration, and a man of the most unscrupulous ambition. He was now (September, 1753) both chief justice and lieutenant governor, the former of which offices, he had held for some time; and although it is said he was but little versed in jurisprudence when created a judge, yet, that by exemplary industry and perseverance, he became in the end a learned and profound lawyer, and appeared for the time he administered the government, to have the confidence of the assembly, while at the same time he preserved harmony in the province. At the great congress held at Albany, June 4, 1754, he was the only person that opposed the plan devised by Dr. Franklin for a union of the colonies, and which was substantially adopted, July 4, 1754. Although not then put in operation, it probably formed the germ of that independence, which twenty-two years after was so happily accomplished.

Mr. De Lancey continued at the head of the government until the arrival of Admiral Sir Charles Hardy, September 2, 1755. This gentleman was a distinguished officer of the British navy, for which he was in all respects better fitted; and therefore his appointment as governor here scarcely diminished the power of Mr. De Lancey, since the governor, being greatly ignorant of civil affairs, and entirely unacquainted with the necessities of the colony, put himself into his hands, and was guided mainly by his councils.

It was during this year that preparations were made for a war in America, between the English and French.

The governor was promoted to the rank of rear admiral of the blue, with a command in the projected expedition against Louisburgh, and, therefore, left the entire administration of affairs in the hands of Mr. De Lancey. In July, 1758, the British under Colonel Bradstreet captured Fort Frontenac, besides several armed vessels on the St. Lawrence. The New York troops consisted of two detachments; one commanded by Lieutenant Colonel Charles Clinton, containing 440 men, under Captains Ogden of Westchester, Dubois of New York, Bladgley of Dutchess, and Daniel Wright of Queens; the second was commanded by Lieutenant Colonel Isaac Corsa of Queens, and Major Nathaniel Woodhull of Suffolk, with 668 men, under Captain Elias Hand of Suffolk and Richard Hewlett of Queens.

The Hon. James De Lancey was found by one of his children, July 30, 1760, expiring, as he sat in his study, and was buried with great ceremony next day in the middle aisle of Trinity Church. He was the son of Stephen, a French emigrant, and born in 1693. The act of incorporation of Kings (now Columbia) College was signed by him in 1754. He possessed the faculty of conciliating the powerful and of intimidating others into a submission to his will. His sister Susan married Admiral Sir Peter Warren, of the British navy. His daughter, Anne, married the Hon. Thomas Jones, a colonial judge of New York, and accompanied him to England in 1783. His son, Oliver De Lancey, was an adjutant general in the British army and lost a large estate by his loyalty. He died at Beverly, England, October 27, 1785, aged sixty-eight. His daughter, Susanna, married Sir William Draper, whose fame must be as lasting as the eloquence of Junius. We append herewith a note of the marriage:

" By the Honorable CADWALLADER GOLDEN, ESQUIRE,

His Majesty's Lieutenant Governor, and Commander-in-Chief of the Province of New-York, and the Territories depending thereon in America. " To any Protestant Minister of the Gospel. " Whereas, There is a mutual purpose of marriage between Sir William Draper, Knight of the Bath, of the one party, and Miss Susanna De Lancey, daughter of the Honorable Oliver De Lancey, Esquire, of the other party, for which they have desired my License, and have given Bond, upon condition, that neither of them have any lawful Let, Impediment of Pre-Contract, Affinity, or Consanguinity, to hinder their being joined in the Holy Bands of Matrimony: — These are therefore to authorize and empower you, to join the said Sir William Draper and Susanna De Lancey in the Holy Bands of Matrimony, and them to pronounce man and wife.

" Given under my Hand, and the Prerogative Seal of the Province of New-York, at Fort George, in the City of New-York, the Tenth day of October, in the Tenth Year of the Reign of our Sovereign Lord, George the Third, by the Grace of God, of Great Britain, France, and Ireland, King, Defender of the Faith, &c, Annoq: Domini, 1770. CADWALLADER COLDEN."

" By his Honor's Command, Go. Banyar, D. Sec'ry."

On the back of this license, which is printed with blanks for names and dates, and at one corner, is written, in a fair, round hand,

" The within named couple were married by me, Octo. the 13th, 1770. Sam'l AUCHMUTY."

On the sudden death of Mr. De Lancey in 1760, the burden of the administration devolved upon Cadwallader Colden, Esq., he being the senior member and president of the council. He soon after received the commission of lieutenant governor, being then at the age of seventy-three years. This gentleman, a celebrated physician, botanist, and astronomer, was a native of Scotland, and graduated at Edinburgh in 1705. Allured by the fame of Penn's colony, he came to America in 1708. Governor Hunter was so well pleased with him that he became his warm friend, and offered him his patronage if he would come to New York. He consequently settled here in 1718, and was the first person that filled the office of surveyor general in this colony. On the arrival of Governor Burnet he was made one of the council, and rose afterwards to the head of the board, thus succeeding to the administration of the government in the absence of the governor. He owned a large tract of land in Orange County, and afterwards purchased a farm at Flushing in Queen's County, which he named " Spring Hill," to which he retired from the cares and perplexities of office, and where he died on the 21st of September, 1776.

The death of King George II. occurred October 25, 1760.

Mr. Colden was relieved from the duties of the office for one year, commencing October 26, 1761, by the arrival of Robert Monkton, Esq., who had been appointed governor of the province; but being the next year placed at the head of an expedition against Martinique, he left the government again to Mr. Colden, with an agreement, it is said, to divide with him the salary and perquisites of the office.

In 1762 an act was passed for erecting a lighthouse at Sandy Hook, this being the first built in this portion of the United States.

Sir Henry Moore was commissioned governor of New York in 1765, at the very time when the attempt was first made to impose stamp paper upon the people, which gave rise to a spirit of opposition, and a jealousy of their rulers that was never afterwards allayed, and ended only in the final establishment of independence. He, however, managed with so much discretion, as to avoid any very considerable difficulties till his death, which happened at Fort George, September 11, 1769, and his body was interred in the chancel of Trinity Church, New York. The funeral ceremony took place in the evening, boys carrying lighted flambeaux and the church being illuminated. His communications to the assembly were characterized by good sense and brevity; and in enforcing the odious requirements of the parent country, he did not suffer his zeal for the crown to urge him into indiscreet controversies with the people among whom he lived, and whose respect and esteem he appeared anxious to preserve. At the termination of his administration, the supreme court of the colony consisted of the following named judges, — Daniel Horsmanden, chief justice, and David Jones, William Smith, and Robert R. Livingston, judges. The salary of the first was three hundred pounds, and that of the others two hundred each. On the death of Sir Henry Moore the duties of lieutenant governor again fell upon Mr. Colden, and continued so till the 18th of November, 1770; when John, Lord Dunmore, the new governor, arrived. He was less avaricious than some of his predecessors; for when the assembly, on the 17th of January, 1771, voted him two thousand pounds as a salary for the ensuing year, he refused it, and returned a message, saying, " that the king had appointed him a salary out of his treasury, and he wished this allowance omitted." The object of this refusal was not so very disinterested as it might at first appear, as it was intended to keep the governor independent of the people, and to raise moneys for the support of the government by the imposition of taxes upon the colonists. His lordship finally removed to Virginia, where he was made governor, and his place was supplied by William Tryon, Esq., as governor, who arrived the 8th of July, 1771

Governor Dunmore was, in 1775, obliged to abdicate the government of Virginia, and take refuge on board of a man-of-war. He manifested his resentment, as well as the badness of his heart, by acting the part of a corsair and plunderer. He also caused the conflagration of Norfolk, January 1, 1776. In 1786 he was appointed governor of Bermuda, and died in England in 1809. His wife was Lady Charlotte Stewart, daughter of the Earl of Galloway.

Governor Tryon commenced his administration at a time of great excitement, and it required the greatest degree of prudence to steer clear of the most serious difficulties with the people. Yet he managed with such discretion as to preserve the good will of the Inhabitants till the period when all regular government was dissolved in the elements of revolution. On the 2nd of September, 1773, he laid the first stone of the New York Hospital, which was then far beyond the settled portion of the city. Before it was completed, an accidental fire consumed the interior, and retarded the work for a considerable time. On the 29th of December, 1773, the governor's house at the fort (now the Battery) was also destroyed by fire.

himself and wife escaping with great difficulty, while one of his female servants was burned to death. The great seal of the province was afterwards raked from the ashes, entirely uninjured. The governor left the colony April 8, 1774, after the honor of a public festival and ball. Addresses of friendship were likewise presented to him from many public and corporate bodies; and Kings College, in which a law professorship (being the second of the kind within the British dominions) had been established by him, conferred upon him the honorary degree of Doctor of Laws.

Governor Tryon returned once more, in 1775, doubtless at the instance of the ministry, but did not again meet the assembly, that body having adjourned, April 3, 1775, to meet no more.

It is lamentable that a person evidently possessing so many amiable qualities, and having a reputation for kindness and humanity, should, from his zeal for monarchy or resentment towards his opponents, have forfeited so entirely the good opinion of all his American friends, and Incurred all the odium due to the most consummate villainy, by conduct so atrocious and disgraceful as he afterwards exhibited. For he almost seemed to have changed his nature, and to have enjoyed a sort of demoniac pleasure in burning and plundering villages and towns, as a means of distressing the inhabitants.

With Governor Tryon terminated the rule of colonial governors, and with him expired also the name of colony, and subjects of a foreign power. The territory was organized into a state, and Its citizens joined heart and hand with their political brethren of the other provinces, in every measure calculated to free them from oppression, and to establish a free and Independent government. On the 4th of July, 1776, was published, by the representatives of an enlightened and free people, that Declaration which has been, with great propriety, denominated the Charter of American Liberty. Tryon was continued as nominal governor under British rule till March, 1780, when he was succeeded by General James Robertson, who was followed by Sir Guy Carlton, commander-in-chief of the British army in America, as the successor of Sir Henry Clinton. Tryon had been governor of North Carolina, from whence he was transferred to New York, 1771. He died in London, February 27, 1788.

The whole history of the colonial government sufficiently demonstrates, that Itis in vain to expect a patriotic devotion to the public welfare, and the happiness of the people, from rulers unconnected with the country by the strong ties of personal feeling, and a kindred Interest in the prosperity of its citizens; and that a subserviency to the crown, and a disregard of the welfare of the country, are vices which seem to be Inherent in the nature of all colonial governments. At the adoption of the constitution of New York, in 1777, the state was divided into fourteen counties, those on Long Island remaining as they had been established in 1683.

HISTORICAL REMINISCENCES OF INTERESTING CIRCUMSTANCES AND EVENTS,

Preceding and Attending THE Occupation of Long Island by the British During the Revolutionary War.

The permanent establishment of an annual assembly under the administration of Governor Slaughter in 1691, may properly be considered as the first regular approach toward free government in the colony of New York. The representatives of the people, when assembled, claimed and exercised the right of being themselves the exclusive judges of the qualifications and fitness of their own members; a principle, in their opinion, essential to the purity and independence of this branch of the legislature.

The executive, it has been seen, possessed large powers, and sometimes used them in a selfish and arbitrary manner. He could, of his own head, suspend a member of the council without assigning any cause whatever, and appoint another in his stead; he had a negative on all acts passed by the assembly and council; could summon, prorogue or dissolve the house of representatives at pleasure; appoint almost all public officers, and by and with the consent of his council, could establish courts of justice, dispose of the public lands, and disburse all moneys raised for the support of government. This prerogative of using the people's money at discretion, could hardly fail of being often and greatly abused, and frequent misapplication and embezzlement were the necessary consequences. This extraordinary exercise of power led to an application to Queen Anne in 1706, after which, authority was given to the assembly for the appointment, by them, of a treasurer, who should thereafter receive and disburse, under their authority, all moneys raised for public purposes. Under this very important arrangement, the assembly, in 1709, assumed the general control of the finances, by making specific appropriations; and in 1711 resolved to allow of no alteration in revenue bills by the council, who claimed to have a right over the subject, saying, "that the power of the council flowed from the pleasure of the prince, personified by the commission of the governor, but that the power of the assembly, in relation to taxes, flowed from the choice of the people, who could not be divested of their money without their consent." In 1737 it was resolved to continue the revenue only for a year, and in answer to the executive who demanded an indefinite support, they said, " we will not put it in the power of a governor to misapply them, or continue the revenue for any longer term than one year" And in 1741, on a renewal of his demand, the assembly said, " that the course he recommended had formerly been pursued, and had led to the misapplication and embezzlement of the public money; that the practice of providing public supplies, by annual grants, and the receipt and payment of the public moneys by their own treasurer, with appropriations to specific purposes, was the only method to correct the evil."

In 1747, the assembly, in reply to Governor Clinton upon this same matter, said, " we cannot answer it to our constituents to pass any bill for raising money on them, and leave it to be disposed of at the will and pleasure of a governor." This species of altercation between the executive and assembly, continued to vex the colony till September 24, 1756, when Governor Hardy informed them, " he had received instructions, allowing him to assent to their temporary bills for the support of government." The difficulties on this subject most undoubtedly had their origin in the disposition always manifested by the mother country, to exercise an unlimited control over the colony, and a resolute determination in the people's immediate representatives, never to submit to it but by compulsion. The British government claiming, most absurdly, to have planted and sustained the colony in its infancy, were not at all willing to relax their supremacy, now that it had attained a rank in wealth and power, which enabled-its citizens to contribute a share to her necessities. It was reasonably concluded by the people, that an almost entire monopoly of the trade and commerce of the province, was of itself more than paramount to anything which England had ever done to advance its interest and prosperity. And it began to be an opinion entertained by many very intelligent persons, at the conclusion of peace in 1763, that the colony was pretty competent to manage its own affairs, independently of foreign dictation, yet they were nevertheless willing, on account of the advantages resulting from a close political connection with England, to allow her the exclusive right of regulating foreign trade and navigation. The disposition, on the part of any of the American colonies, to prescribe limits to the universal supremacy of Britain, led to the exercise, on her part, of measures so despotic and unjust, that passive submission or instant resistance became the only alternative. The nature and tenure of the governor's office, made it both his duty and interest to maintain the policy of the parent government, and to withhold his assent to all laws which he thought infringed upon his own or the king's prerogatives, while the assembly were equally disposed to maintain what they considered absolutely essential to their own and the people's constitutional rights and liberties. This difference in opinion and practice gave rise to frequent prorogations and dissolutions, to coerce the assembly, if possible, into compliance with the wishes of the executive, or punish a contempt of them; and the whole subsequent course of colonial administration was a perpetual conflict, sometimes silent, but constant, between the encroachments of power on one side, and the spirit of liberty to prevent or defeat them, on the other. The struggle was, however, productive of one highly important result; it induced the people to investigate their rights, and to appreciate their intrinsic value, which led eventually to the assertion and attainment of their national independence.

The outbreak of the Revolution suspended the administration of Governor Tryon in October, 1775; and until the adoption of the state constitution in 1777, the civil affairs of the colony were administered by a provincial congress or convention, aided and strengthened by town and county committees, composed of the best and most intelligent inhabitants. Patriotism supplied the place of authority, and gave to the resolutions and recommendations of those bodies the force of law. The sentiment that taxation and representation were, or ought to be, inseparable, was the basis upon which the colonies resisted the pretensions of England; and to maintain this cardinal principle the colonies united, when, on the 4th of July, 1776, they declared themselves free and independent states.

The consequences of a long, arduous and bloody contest were not entirely unforeseen, but could not be avoided, and it became an indispensable duty to prepare for the worst. The exposed situation of Long Island, having nearly 300 miles of shore, and vulnerable at numerous points, unavoidably occasioned a diversity of opinion among Its inhabitants, as to the expediency of resistance or submission; it was a struggle between the love of liberty, and the dread of losing everything, life included, by an opposition, honestly thought by many to be hopeless. Motives of personal safety, and the preservation of their property, would necessarily induce many either to remain inactive, or join with the ranks of the opposition. Others, and those not inconsiderable in number, were desirous for the opportunity of rioting upon the property of their neighbors, thereby benefiting themselves, without the liability to punishment. And it so happened that more frequent and daring outrages, upon persons and property, were practiced by our own citizens, than by many who had come three thousand miles to force our submission to the tyranny of a foreign master. The engagement of the 27th of August, 1776, was followed by an abandonment of Long Island to the enemy, and the town and county committees in many instances, either through fear or necessity, were induced to repudiate all legislative authority exercised by the provincial and continental congresses. The inhabitants who continued on the island were compelled to subscribe the oath of fidelity to the king. General Howe had immediately, on landing at Gravesend, issued a proclamation, promising security of person and property to those who should remain peaceably upon their farms. This island became, therefore, at once a conquered territory, forts being erected, and garrisons established in different places. Martial law prevailed, the army became a sanctuary for criminals of every grade, and means the most despicable were resorted to, for increasing the numerical force of the enemy. Those inhabitants who had theretofore taken an active part as officers of militia and committee men, deemed it most imprudent to remain and consequently took refuge within the American lines, leaving the greater part of their property exposed to the ravages of an unprincipled foe. The British commanders were exorbitant and arbitrary in their exactions, requiring the more peaceable and unoffending inhabitants to perform every species of personal service, to labor upon the forts, to go with their teams on foraging parties, and to transport cannon, ammunition, provision, and baggage, from one place to another, at the option of every petty officer. The enemy took possession of the best rooms in their houses, and obliged the owners to provide them accommodations and support for men and horses. The property of those who had fled from their homes, and especially those engaged in the American service, was particularly the object of rapine, and in very many instances the damages were immense. Woods and fences were lavishly used for fuel and in any other way which served the purposes of those stationed in the neighborhood, as well as for the garrisons of Brooklyn and New York. Churches and places for religious worship were desecrated for any objects which suited the convenience of the enemy, except those of the Episcopalians, which were, it seems, scrupulously regarded, doubtless in pursuance of governmental instructions, their members (upon Long Island) being in general in the interests of England.

When the British army invaded Long Island in 1776, many persons who belonged to the island and had joined the British forces on Staten Island, landed with the invading army. Those royalists were ordered to wear red rags in their hats, as badges of friendship, to distinguish them from the rebels. The red rag men proceeded with the army in every direction, giving information against every person whom they disliked, and causing them to be plundered, imprisoned and tormented at their pleasure. Those red rag informers continued as instruments of cruelty and terror to the peaceful citizens, whom the chances of war had placed within their power, until their wanton acts of baseness brought a few of them into the clutches of Cunningham the provost marshal, when the badge was disgraced.

This wretched individual, so notorious for his unfeeling barbarity in the exercise of his office of provost marshal in the city of New York while it was in possession of the enemy, was executed for forgery in London, August 10, 1791. The day preceding the tragical event he wrote and signed the following confession, quite a curiosity in the annals of retributive justice:

" I, William Cunningham, was born in Dublin-Barracks, in the year 1738. My father was trumpeter in the Blue Dragoons; and at the age of eight years I was placed with an officer as his servant, in which station I continued until I was sixteen, and being a great proficient in horsemanship, was taken as an assistant to the riding master of the troop, and in the year 1761 was made sergeant of dragoons; but the peace coming the year following, I was disbanded. Being bred to no profession, I took up with a woman who kept a gin shop, in a blind alley, near the Cole Quay; but the house being searched for stolen goods, and my doxy taken to Newgate, I thought it most prudent to decamp; accordingly I set off for the north, and arrived at Drogheda, where, in a few months after, I married the daughter of an excise-man, by whom I had three sons.

" About the year 1772, we removed to Newery, where I commenced the profession of scaw-banker, which is that of enticing mechanics and country people to ship themselves for America, on promise of great advantage, and then artfully getting ah indenture upon them, in consequence of which, on their arrival in America they were sold, or obliged to serve a term of years for their passage. I embarked at Newery in the ship Needham, for New York, and arrived at that port the fourth day of August, 1774, with some indented servants I kidnapped in Ireland; but they were liberated in New York, on account of the bad usage they received from me during the passage. In that city I used the profession of breaking the horses, and teaching ladies and gentlemen to ride; but, rendering myself obnoxious to the citizens, in their infant struggle for freedom, I was obliged to fly on board the Asia man-of-war, and from thence to Boston, where my own opposition to the measures pursued by the Americans, in support of their rights, was the first thing that recommended me to the notice of General Gage; and when the war commenced, I was appointed Provost-Marshal to the royal army, which placed me in a situation to wreak my vengeance on the Americans. I shudder to think of the murders I have been accessory to, both with and without orders from the government, especially while in New York, during which time there were more than two thousand prisoners starved in the different churches, by stopping their rations, which I sold.

" There were also two hundred and seventy-five American prisoners and obnoxious persons executed, out of all which number there were only about one dozen public executions, which chiefly consisted of British and Hessian deserters. The mode for private executions was thus conducted: A guard was dispatched from the Provost, about half-past twelve at night, to the barrack street, and the neighborhood of the upper barracks, to order the people to shut their window shutters, and put out their lights, forbidding them, at the same time, to presume to look out of their windows and doors on pain of death, after which the unfortunate prisoners were conducted, gagged, just behind the upper barracks, and hung without ceremony, and there buried by the black pioneer of the Provost.

" At the end of the war I returned to England with the army, and settled in Wales, as being a cheaper place of living than in any of the populous cities; but being at length persuaded to go to London, I entered so warmly into the dissipations of that capital, that I soon found my circumstances much embarrassed, to relieve which I mortgaged my half pay to an army agent; but that being soon expended, I forged a draft for three hundred pounds sterling on the Board of Ordnance, but being detected in presenting it for acceptance, I was apprehended, tried and convicted, and for that offence am here to suffer an ignominious death.

" I beg the prayers of all good Christians, and also pardon and forgiveness of God for the many horrid murders I have been accessory to.

" Wm. Cunningham."

Shortly after the British army landed on Long Island in 1776, General Howe ordered that every inhabitant who desired favor, should attend at headquarters and receive a certificate of protection. Many obeyed as friends, and many from fear; but the greatest number remained at home. Everyone who attended at headquarters was ordered to mount a red rag in his hat. When those persons who remained at home found out that there was magic in a red rag, they all mounted the badge; negroes, boys, old and young, wore red rags. These badges of submission soon produced a scarcity of the needful article, and then, forsooth, the red petticoats suffered. Many were torn into shreds for hat-bands, and those who wore them were held in derision by the British, and called the petticoat gentry.

Many of the Presbyterian and Dutch churches were taken possession of without hesitation, some of them being converted into apartments for riding schools, store houses, garrisons, and hospitals, while others, as at Huntington, Babylon, and Foster's Meadows, were torn down, and their materials employed in the construction of barracks, stables, and for other purposes.

The tory inhabitants, whether natives or refugees, were the constant dread of those on the other side, who had anything to lose, or who had, by their patriotism, rendered themselves obnoxious to their despicable malice. Even the more inoffensive, who remained at home with their suffering families, were often harassed, and perpetually exposed to the predatory disposition of the worst men, and could hardly be said to have anything which they could call their own. In some instances the lives of peaceable citizens were sacrificed in the most unprovoked and wanton manner, disgraceful even to barbarians, because they would not discover their money and other valuables to the robbers.

An appalling Instance of this happened in the village of Jerusalem, when Parmenas Jackson, a wealthy and respectable farmer of that place, was robbed and murdered in the most brutal manner. Lloyd's Neck was then a British garrison, commanded by Colonel Gabriel G. Ludlow, of Queens County. One of the soldiers stationed there, named John Degraw, had a sister who lived as a servant in the family of Mr. Jackson, and who, Itis supposed, Informed her brother of her master's being in possession of a considerable amount of money. On the night of the 10th of January, 1781, the family were aroused by the entrance of Degraw and six other ruffians, who demanded of Mr. Jackson his money; and upon his declining their request, began the work of death by cutting him in a terrible manner, over his head, arms, &c. Not obtaining what they wished from him, they commenced a like inhuman attack upon Thomas Birdsall, an aged man, the father-in-law of the former — upon which, his wife, to save the life of her husband, agreed to point the robbers to the place of deposit. The money, to the amount of $3000 in gold and silver, together with divers articles of apparel and furniture, was carried off. On their departure, information of the facts was conveyed, as soon as possible, to the commanding officer at Lloyd's Neck, who thereupon posted a guard on the only passage leading to the Neck, when the robbers soon came up and were secured with their booty. The property was of course restored to the family, and the villains sent on shipboard for trial at New York. As the vessel neared the dock, Elgar, the worst of the gang, sprang overboard and was drowned. Degraw died in prison, and the others are said to have been sent to the mines on the Spanish Main or to Honduras.

Mr. Jackson survived till January 19, 1781, when he expired at the age of thirty-seven. His widow subsequently married James Downing and was the mother of Coe S. Downing, Esq., of Brooklyn.

Most parts of the island, and particularly along the Sound, suffered greatly from depredations of little bands of piratical plunderers, designated " whaleboat men," from the fact of their craft resembling those used in whaling along shore. With these they would make frequent descents, under cover of night, attack detached houses, rifle the inhabitants of their money, plate, and other valuables, and availing themselves of the speed of their boats, reach their lurking places among the islands of the Sound, or upon the main shore, before any effectual means could be taken to intercept them. Indeed, so great was the apprehension of those sudden attacks, that many of the inhabitants had their doors and windows protected by iron bars; and it became usual for people to pass the night in the woods and other secret places, to avoid personal violence. On the 24th of October, 1782, the dwelling owned by John Burtis, at the head of Cow Bay, was attacked about midnight by a gang of these marauders, who had first robbed the store of James Burr, a few rods off, and killed the owner, whose position they ascertained by his voice, having, by their devices, called him from his bed. David Jarvis, an apprentice to Mr. Burtis, saw the robbers by the light of their own fire, and shot at them from the windows of the house. Mrs. Burtis, with admirable courage, employed herself in loading the guns, of which they had several, while Jarvis fired upon the gang as often as opportunity offered. They succeeded in beating off the robbers, with the loss of their leader, Captain Martin, and the wounding of several others, indicated by traces of blood found next day, in their path to the boats. The dwelling in which this courageous defense was made, is now the residence of Dr. George B. Purdy. They killed. May 13, 1783, a young man named Benjamin Mitchill, son of John Mitchill, upon Cow Neck, wholly without provocation, and at the same time cruelly maltreated his parents. Two years after one of the robbers named Jackson, who was hanged at St. John, confessed the murder of Mitchill. He had, it seems, once lived in the family and was, of course, well acquainted with the premises.

To recount any considerable proportion of the insults and injuries sustained by the people of Long Island during the tedious septennial contest, would require more space than can well be afforded, even were we in possession of the requisite information on the subject. A few, only, of a more aggravated character, are found in the public journals of that eventful period, the whigs of that day having no press nearer than Dutchess County, while the tories could boast of a Rivington and a Gaine in the city of New York, ready at all times to suppress or extenuate the base conduct of their allies, and to misrepresent and exaggerate the doings of the whigs.

Brooklyn had a full share of the military operations during the revolutionary war; and was for a long time in the possession of the British army. It is covered with remains of fortifications, thrown up at different times by the Americans and English for defense against each other. In the southern portion of this town was fought the most sanguinary part of the battle of Long Island, August 27, 1776. On the retreat of the American army within their lines, and the attempt of a portion of them to ford the mill-pond at Gowanus, nearly a whole regiment of young men from Maryland were cut off.

Many events connected with this battle, and of the revolutionary contest, are fast sinking into oblivion, and the compiler has thought proper to give the following piece of history, not with an idea that he can immortalize any event which he relates, but with a hope that his efforts will call forth some nobler pen to do justice to the memories of the almost forgotten heroes of those hard-fought and arduous contests. In the battle aforesaid, part of the British army marched down a lane, or road, leading from the Brush tavern to Gowanus, pursuing the Americans. Several American riflemen, in order to be more secure, and the more effectually to succeed in their designs, posted themselves in the high trees near the road. One of them, name not known, shot at and killed the English Major Grant; in this he passed unobserved. Again he loaded his deadly rifle, and fired; another English officer fell. Being then discovered, a platoon was ordered to advance and fire into the tree; this order was immediately executed, and the unfortunate rifleman fell dead to the ground. After the battle was over, the two British officers were buried in a field near the place, their graves fenced in with posts and rails, and here their remains still rest. But, for " an example to the rebels," the American rifleman was refused the rites of sepulture, and his body lay exposed on the ground till the flesh was decayed, and torn off the bones by the fowls of the air. After a considerable length of time, and during a heavy gale of wind, a large tree was uprooted; in the cavity formed thereby, some friend to the Americans, notwithstanding the prohibition of the English, deposited the soldier's skeleton, to mingle in peace with its kindred earth.

The following miscellaneous selections from old newspapers, journals of the provincial congress, committee of safety, and other authentic sources, are deemed of sufficient importance to occupy a few pages in this portion of our history:

"At a meeting of the inhabitants of the town of Eas tHampton in the county of Suffolk, legally moved by the Trustees of the town June 19, 1774. Eleazer Miller, Esq., Moderator.

" 1. Voted: That we will to the utmost of our ability, assist, and in a lawful manner defend the immunities of British America; that we will cooperate with our brethren in this colony, in such measures as shall from time to time appear to us most proper, and the best adapted to save us from the burthens we fear, and in a measure already feel, from the principles adopted by the British parliament, respecting the town of Boston in particular, and the British colonies in North America in general.

" 2. Voted: That a non-importation agreement through the colonies is the most likely means to free us from the present and further troubles.

" 3. Voted: That John Chatfield, Esq., Colonel Abraham Gardiner, Burnet Miller, Stephen Hedges, Thomas Wickham, Esq., John Gardiner, Esq., and Capt. David Mulford, be a standing committee for keeping up a correspondence with the city of New York, and the towns of this colony, and if there is occasion, with other colonies; and that they transmit a copy of these votes to the committee of correspondence for the city of New York. Voted unanimously, not one contrary vote.

" Burnet Miller, Town Clerk."

"July 14, 1775. — The N. Y. Committee of Safety stated to John Sloss Hobart, Esq., that they had information of the shipping of provisions by George Youngs and his son, of Huntington, and by Capt. Brush and one Conklin, in such manner as they must inevitably serve to supply Gen. Gage's fleet and army at Boston."

" At a town meeting, held in Smithtown, August 9th, 1774, it was resolved, and we do fully declare ourselves ready to enter into any public measures that shall be agreed upon by a general congress; and that Solomon Smith, Daniel Smith, and Thomas Tredwell be a committee for said town, to act in conjunction with committees of the other towns in this county, to correspond with the committee of New York; and the said committee is fully empowered to choose a delegate to represent this county at the general congress; and that said committee do all that shall be necessary in defense of our just rights and liberties against the unconstitutional acts of the British ministry and parliament, until another committee be appointed."

"July 22nd, 1775. — Thomas Wickham, member of the provincial congress from Suffolk, produced a certificate from John Chatfield of East Hampton, showing that every male inhabitant of the town, capable of bearing arms, had joined an association for resisting the measures of Great Britain; and on the 5th July following, the people of that town represent to congress, that they have not less than 2000 cattle, and 3 or 4000 sheep on Montauk, exposed to the enemy, and requesting that troops should be stationed there for protection."

" Congress August 5, 1775, permitted John Foster, of South Hampton, to ship a cargo of livestock to the West Indies, to be exchanged for military stores."

"Aug. 6th, 1775. — Congress is informed by Mr. Robert Hempstead, of Southold, that thirteen sail, eight of which are supposed to be ships of war, were seen cruising between Montauk and Fisher's Island, and finally anchored off Oyster Ponds. He states that the people there are destitute of powder, and prays that measures may be taken to afford them a supply."

"Aug. 11th, 1775. — Congress are informed by letter, dated the 3rd, from Thomas Helme of Brookhaven, chairman of the committee of safety of that town, that Parson James Lyon, Benjamin Floyd, Doctor Gilbert Smith, Joseph Denton, Richard Floyd and John Baylis, Inn-keeper, had, from the beginning, taken every method in their power to seduce the ignorant, and counteract every measure recommended for the redress of grievances; damning all congresses and committees, and wishing them in hell. They had also been suspected of furnishing the vessels of the enemy with provisions."

""Aug. 18th, 1775— Congress recommends the removal of the cattle and sheep, from Gardiner's and Plumb Islands, and about this time General Gage's fleet and army took from Gardiner's and Fisher's Islands, 86 cattle, and between 2 and 3000 sheep."

"Aug. 22nd, 1775. — William Smith, Esq., chairman of the Suffolk county committee (met for the purpose of concerted measures to remove the stock from Gardiner's and Plumb Islands) in his letter of that date says, an officer of the ministerial fleet Col. Abijah Willard informed Col. Gardiner that they should come again with a force sufficient to take the stock from Long Island, that there were three cutters at the east end of the island cruising, and the stock there in danger of falling into the hands of the enemy."

"Aug. 27th, 1775. — General Wooster, writing from Oyster Ponds, recommends to the provincial congress, to keep a good guard over Queens county, as he supposed the enemy designed to get stock from that part of the island."

"Sept. 14, 1775. — Letter written to congress by Richard Woodhull and Samuel Thompson of Brookhaven, asking instructions in relation to the mode of appointing the non-commissioned officers in the militia."

The inhabitants of Queens County had carried their opposition to the revolution so far, as to refuse to send deputies to the provincial congress, and declared themselves neutral in the struggle; it had therefore become necessary to disarm them, and at the same time to arrest the most odious. Arms were indeed so scarce that congress was justified in taking those in the hands of tories, that they might be used in aid of, instead of hostility to, independence.

An officer sent on this business writes to the Committee of Safety September 25, 1775, as follows:

" I have endeavored, in the towns of Jamaica and Hempstead, to carry the resolutions of congress into effect, but without the assistance of a battalion, I shall not be able to do it. The people conceal all their arms that are of any value. Many declare they will sooner lose their lives than give up their arms, and that they would blow any man's brains out who should attempt to take them away. Some persons are so hardy and daring as to go into the houses of those who are friendly, and take away their arms by force, which they have received from the clerk of the county. That Gov. Colden sent his servant around to some of the leading people advising them to arm and defend themselves. That Capt. Hewlett of Hempstead said he had his company together on the Monday before, and that had the battalion appeared, they should have warmed their sides. Whereupon the committee appointed Samuel Verplank, Thomas Smith, David Clarkson, John Vanderbilt and Benjamin Kissam, to proceed to Queens County, and use every prudent measure to collect arms in said county; also to report the names of such as oppose the measures of the Continental or provincial congresses, or the Committee of Safety of the county."

It should be remarked that in all cases where arms were taken from the tories, they were appraised and paid for out of the treasury of the colony.

A letter is received by the provincial congress, October 12, 1775, from the committee of Great Neck, and Cow Neck, in Queens County, consisting of Daniel Kissam, Henry Stocker, William Thorne, Benjamin Sands, William Cornwell, John Cornwell, John Mitchill, Senator John Burtis, Simon Sands, Martin Schenck, Daniel W. Kissam, Peter Onderdonck, Adrian Onderdonck, and Thomas Dodge, complaining that they shall be unable to pursue proper measures for their common safety, while considered as part of the township of Hempstead, and therefore they resolved no further to be considered a part of that township, during the pending controversy, than is consistent with peace, liberty, and safety, but to consider themselves as an entire, separate, and independent beat or district, so long as the general conduct of the people of Hempstead is inimical to freedom.

At a meeting of the several committees of the first regiment of Suffolk County, held at Smithtown, October 24, 1775, of which William Smith was chairman, the following persons were present:

Jesse Brush, Thomas Wicks, Gilbert Potter, Stephen Kelsey, John Squires, Stephen Ketcham, Timothy Ketcham, Henry Scudder, Thomas Brush, Jun., Israel Wood, and Ebenezer Piatt, of Huntington; — Daniel Tillotson, Thomas Tredwell, Jeffrey Smith, Philetus Smith, Job Smith, Jacob Mills, Edmund Smith, Jun., Epenetus Smith, and Samuel Phillips of Smithtown; William Smith, and Jonah Hulse, of St. George's Manor; Josiah Smith, of

Moriches; Samuel Thompson, William Brewster, John Woodhull, Daniel Roe, Noah Hallock, Jonathan Baker, and Richard Woodhull, of Brookhaven.

The committee, among other matters transacted at this meeting, elected the said Jeffrey Smith, first major, and Jesse Brush, second major.

In a New York newspaper of January 27, 1776, is the following article:

" On Tuesday last, 700 Jersey militia and 300 of the Jersey regulars, under Col. Heard, entered Queens county to disarm those who opposed American liberty; and although they have repeatedly declared their resolution of defending their arms at the risk of their lives, yet such is the badness of their cause, (which no doubt rendered them cowards,) that they were disarmed without opposition; and the generality of them have sworn to abide by the measures of the congress. Two young men brought seventeen prisoners into Hempstead with their arms; and a boy of twelve years of age demanded a pair of pistols of a man who had threatened to shoot the first person that attempted to disarm him, but with fear and trembling delivered his pistols to the boy, who brought them away in triumph."

In provincial congress, February 19, 1776:

" The petition of William Cock and Thomas Cock of Oyster Bay, in Queens county, was read and filed, in the words following, to wit: — ' The petition of William and Thomas Cock humbly sheweth, that we, your petitioners, are inhabitants of said county, and that at the last election of deputies for the provincial congress we opposed the election of deputies for said county; since which we are convinced of our error, and think it was absolutely necessary that there should be a representation of said county. And your petitioners did not oppose the choice of said deputies from any desire or inclination of injuring this country, but owing entirely to error of judgment. And your petitioners are ready to obey all orders and recommendations of the continental and provincial congresses. Your petitioners therefore desire that your honorable body will take our case into consideration, and grant us such relief in the premises as to you shall seem meet. (Signed)

' William Cock, ' Thomas Cock.' " On hearing the said petition read, and upon due consideration thereof, and considering that any former resolves of this congress against the delinquents of Queens county were only intended to convince them of their error, and bring them to a just sense of their duty to the public: Ordered, that the said petitioners be restored to the state and condition in which they were before the passing of the said resolves, during their good behavior. A true copy from the minutes.

" Robert Benson, Secretary."

"Feb. 9, 1776. — Letter received from Isaac Thompson, chairman of the Islip committee, stating that Benajah Strong had been chosen captain, Jeremiah Terry, and Samuel Oakley, first and second lieutenants, and Annin

Mowbray, ensign; and desiring that commissions might be sent to those gentlemen."

"Letter, Feb. 15th, 1776, from Doctor Samuel Thompson, of Brookhaven, by order of the committee of Suffolk county, inclosing drafts of Setauket and Stony Brook harbors, made by himself, including also a description of the beaches and lands between them, with their length and distances. He then proceeds to recommend the erection of a small fort, on the beach, running off from Mount Misery Point, with six or eight guns, some of which should be nine or twelve pounders; and at Stony Brook, two six or nine pounders, placed on the high bank, overlooking the harbor. He concludes by expressing a wish that a capable gunsmith should be sent to them."

" A map of the east end of Long Island is also communicated by Thomas Youngs, chairman of the committee at Sag Harbor."

"March 4, 1776. — A resolution passed the provincial congress directing the committees of East and South Hampton to station suitable persons, at proper places for observing the approach of a fleet — the British army being then about to leave Boston, as was supposed."

"March 6, 1776. — Maj. Gen'l Lee informs congress that he had ordered Col. Ward to secure the whole body of tories in Long Island, saying, that when the enemy is at our doors, forms must be dispensed with."

" A letter is received from Thomas Wicks, chairman of the Huntington committee, communicating the intelligence that a fleet of thirty square-rigged vessels had been seen in the Sound."

" Letter received, dated April 10, 1776, from the Rev. Samuel Buell of Easthampton, stating that a fleet had been discovered, supposed to be Wallis's fleet, and soliciting that a regiment or two should be stationed at the east end of the island."

"May 10, 1776. — Henry Dawkins, Isaac Ketcham, Isaac Youngs, Townsend Hewlett, and Israel Youngs were apprehended in Huntington, upon a charge of counterfeiting the provincial currency, and of which they were subsequently convicted and imprisoned."

"May 20, 1776. — Richard Hewlett, Stephen Hewlett, Thomas Cornwell, James Smith, and Isaac Denton, of Hempstead, reported as active and bitter enemies to the country, the last of whom had been detected, with his vessel in the South Bay, supplying the British with provisions."

"May 27, 1776. — A letter was received from John Lawrence, chairman of the committee of Newtown, stating that John Moore, junr. had been complained of for insulting the united colonies, by hoisting a large flag on his ground, in imitation of a king's standard, and that he had been apprehended and would be sent to them, under the care of Captain Abraham Remsen, for further examination, together with the flag."

The provincial convention had on the 10th of August, 1776, received " Information that the Inhabitants of Kings County had determined not to oppose the enemy; whereupon, a committee was appointed to repair there, and If such was the fact, to secure the disaffected, to remove or destroy the stock of grain, and. If they should judge necessary, to lay the whole country waste." This committee consisted of William Duer, Colonel Remsen, Mr. Hobart and Colonel DeWitt.

"Aug. 24, 1776. — in provincial convention, ordered, that Brig. Gen. Woodhull, or in his absence Lieut. Col. Potter, march without delay one half the western regiment of Suffolk county, with five days' provision. Into the western parts of Queens county; that the officers of Queens order out their whole militia, with their troop of horse, and use all possible diligence to prevent the stock and other provisions, falling into the hands of the enemy, by removing or killing them. That all the horses, horned cattle, and sheep, south of the ridge, be forthwith removed to the east of Hempstead Plains, and the people were in like manner requested to remove their grain to such places, that it might be burnt if necessary, without endangering buildings."

"Sept. 11, 1776. — Brig. Gen. Oliver Delancey, then at Jamaica, in pursuance of an order from his excellency, Gen. Howe, directed all the fat cattle and sheep in Suffolk county, to be drove to that place, where the owners would receive certificates of their weight and be paid for them, except such as belonged to those who were in actual rebellion, which must be forced from them.

" This same officer, a few days previous, issued a proclamation from Jamaica, in which he stated that he was authorized to raise a brigade of provincials, solely for the defense of Long Island, and promising that any persons of good character, raising a company of seventy men, should have commissions, and they and their men be paid, as other officers and soldiers in British pay."

After the disastrous defeat of our army at Brooklyn, August 27, 1776, Long Island fell into the hands of the British. Thereupon the following address was presented to Governor Tryon, by the people of Queens County, October 21, 1776:

" To his Excellency, Wm. Tryon, Esq., Capt. General, and Governor of the Province of New York, and the territories thereon depending, in America; Chancellor and Vice-Admiral of the same, &c., &c., &c.:

" May it please your Excellency: — We, the freeholders and inhabitants of Queens county, are happy once again to address your Excellency in the capital of the Province. We heartily congratulate you on your return which we consider as the earnest of farther success, and hope ere long the whole province will feel the blessing of your Excellency's upright administration.

"Anxiously do we look forward to the time, when the disobedient shall return to their duty, and the ravages of war cease to desolate this once flourishing country. That we may be restored to the King's most gracious protection, torn from us by the hand of violence; and quicken others by our example to embrace the repeated invitations of his Majesty's commissioners, we have resolved on and subscribed a dutiful representation and petition, setting forth to them our loyal disposition, and praying that the country be declared at the King's peace.

"We entreat your Excellency to present our petition; and rely on your known humanity and benevolence for the exertion of your influence in behalf of the well affected county of Queens, that it may again in the bosom of peace enjoy the royal favor under your Excellency's paternal care and attention.

"Signed by desire of, and in behalf of 1294 freeholders and inhabitants, by David Colden."

The Governor's Answer

"New York, Nov. 12, 1776. "Sir:

" In compliance with the request in the address presented to me by you, in behalf of the inhabitants of Queens county, I immediately after my return from headquarters waited on Lord Howe, one of the King's commissioners for restoring peace to his Majesty's colonies, and presented to his Lordship the very dutiful and loyal petition and representation of the said inhabitants, who was pleased to say, ' He would take the earliest opportunity of communicating with Gen. Howe on the occasion.'

" This public testimony from the inhabitants of Queens county, of their unshaken loyalty to our most gracious sovereign, and of their zealous attachment to the British constitution, is particularly agreeable to me, and entitles them to my best endeavors for a speedy accomplishment of their wishes; the season and the expediency of the granting whereof are safely and happily committed to the wisdom and direction of his Majesty's commissioners. " I am, with regard, Sir, " Your most obedient servant,

" Wm. Tryon.

" David Colden, Esq., of Queens Co."

"Aug. 14, 1776. — The convention orders Elizabeth Hicks, of Rockaway, to be confined in the jail of Queens county, until she should disclose from whence she received a certain letter, which had passed through her hands to the sheriff of said county."

Extract of a letter from Governor Tryon to Lord George Germaine, December 24, 1776:

" On the 10th Instant I reviewed the militia of Queens county, at Hempstead, when eight hundred and twenty men were mustered; and on Thursday following, I saw the Suffolk militia at Brookhaven, where eight hundred men appeared; to all of whom, as well as to the militia of Queens county, I had in my presence an oath of allegiance and fidelity administered. A very large majority of the inhabitants of Queens county have indeed steadfastly maintained their loyal principles, as have small districts in Suffolk county. Three companies, I learned, had been raised out of Suffolk county for the rebel army, most of whom, I was made to understand, would quit the service if they could get home. While on Long Island, I gave certificates to near three thousand men, who signed the declaration presented by the king's commissioner's proclamation of the 30th of November last. Large bodies of the people have already taken the benefit of the grace therein offered them."

In retaliation for the burning of Danbury and Ridgefield in Connecticut, by General Tryon and the wretches under his command, April 26, 1777, (in which affair Generals Wooster, Silliman, and Arnold acted with great bravery, the former being mortally wounded and the latter having his horse shot under him,) a few soldiers from New Haven went on a predatory excursion to Long Island. A quantity of provisions had been collected at Sag Harbor by the British forces stationed there, to destroy which was the object of this expedition. The enterprise was one of the most spirited and successful of that eventful period.

General Parsons conceived it possible to surprise the place, and confided the execution of the project to Lieutenant Colonel Meigs, who, accordingly, embarked from New Haven, May 21, 1777, with two hundred and thirty-four men in thirteen whaleboats. He proceeded directly to Guilford but, on account of the roughness of the sea, could not cross the Sound till the 23rd; on which day, at one o'clock in the afternoon, he left Guilford with one hundred and seventy men, under the convoy of two armed sloops, and arrived at Southold about six o'clock. The enemy's troops on this part of the island had marched for New York two or three days before, but it was reported that there was a party at Sag Harbor on the south branch of the island about fifteen miles distant. Colonel Meigs ordered the whaleboats to be transported over the land to the bay, between the north and south branches of the island, where one hundred and thirty men embarked, and at twelve o'clock at night arrived safely on the other side of the bay within four miles of Sag Harbor. Here the boats were secured in a wood, under a guard, and the remainder of the detachment marched quickly to the harbor, where they arrived at two o'clock in the morning, in the greatest order, attacking the outpost with fixed bayonets, and proceeding directly to the shipping at the wharf, which they found unprepared for defense. The alarm was given, and an armed schooner with twelve guns and seventy men began to fire upon them at the distance of one hundred and fifty yards. This fire continued three-quarters of an hour, but did not prevent the troops from executing their design with the greatest intrepidity and effect. Twelve brigs and sloops, one of which was an armed vessel of twelve guns, and one hundred and twenty tons of hay, corn, oats, ten hogsheads of rum, and a large quantity of merchandise, were entirely destroyed. Six of the enemy were killed and ninety taken prisoners. Not one of Colonel Meig's men was either killed or wounded. He returned to Guilford at two o'clock in the afternoon, having been absent only twenty-five hours; and in that time had transported his troops by land and water full ninety miles, and completed his undertaking with the most entire success. On the report of this matter to the commander-in-chief, he addressed the following letter to General Parsons:

" Head-quarters, Middlebrook, May 29th, 1777. Dear Sir: — I am just now favored with your letter of the 25th by Major Humphrey. The intelligence communicated by it is truly interesting and agreeable. And now I shall take occasion not only to give you my hearty approbation of your conduct in planning the expedition to Long Island, but to return my sincere thanks to Lieutenant Col. Meigs, and all the officers and men engaged in it. This enterprise, so fortunate in the execution, will greatly distress the enemy in the important and essential article of forage, and reflects much honor upon those who performed It. I shall ever be happy to reward merit when in my power, and therefore wish you to inquire for a vacant ensigncy in some of the regiments for Sergeant Gennings, to which you will promote him, advising me of the same and the time. I am. Sir, &c,

" G. Washington."

The successful result of this expedition was considered at the time of such importance, and the conductor of it so deserving of high approbation, that congress forthwith directed a sword to be presented to Colonel Meigs, as a manifestation of their sense of the prudence, activity, enterprise, and valor with which the undertaking had been executed, and the commander-in-chief published the affair with expressions of his applause in general orders.

Brookhaven, as well as other towns, was the scene of some interesting events, and no inconsiderable number of robberies and other acts of violence were perpetrated by the enemy, the tories being distinguished in particular for abusing all who preferred the good of their country in the pending contest.

In the early part of 1777, a body of tory troops, under the command of Colonel Richard Hewlett, of Hempstead, took possession, as was the common practice with the royal forces, of the Presbyterian church at Setauket, and converted it into a garrison, by surrounding it with a picket and other means of defense. Large guns were fixed so as to be discharged from the upper windows; the burying ground was also occupied, the monuments thrown down, and most of the graves leveled with the earth.

For the purpose of capturing the force encamped here, Colonel Parsons, with 150 picked men, embarked on the 14th of August, 1777, from Black Rock, Conn., in a sloop and six whaleboats, with a competent number of muskets and a brass six-pounder. They landed before daybreak next morning, at Crane Neck Bend, about three miles from Setauket, and leaving their boats with a sufficient guard, marched as quietly as possible to a place in the neighborhood of the garrison. A flag of truce was immediately dispatched to the commander, demanding an instant surrender to them, which being promptly refused, the firing commenced on both sides, and was continued for some time with great spirit, but without doing much injury to either side. News having now arrived from the boats, that several British ships had been discovered coming down the Sound, by which the company might be intercepted on their return if delayed too long. Colonel Parsons prudently ordered his men to repair forthwith to the place of their debarkation, and the whole party arrived safely at Black Rock the same evening, with a few of the enemy's horses, and a quantity of military stores. The persons engaged in this affair were volunteers from Colonel Webb's regiment, among whom were the late Captain Caleb Brewster, a native of Setauket, and Mr. (now Rev.) Zachariah Greene, the present minister of the Presbyterian church at that place, where he was installed pastor in about twenty years from the time he thus aided in an attempt to rescue the church from the possession of the enemy — a circumstance in itself somewhat extraordinary and entirely unexpected. Mr. Greene is now in his ninetieth year.

" Mr. Greene was the father-in-law of the author. For further particulars of him see biography of Thompson." Editor.

"N. Y. Gazette, March 31, 1777. — On Thursday last, Thomas Willet, sheriff of Queens county, accompanied by a number of gentlemen, waited upon his excellency Governor Tryon, with an address expressive of their warm attachment, and regret at his leaving the country; hoping he may be restored to health, and again return to govern a loyal and grateful people in dignity and happiness. To which his excellency made a respectful answer; as he did also to addresses from the ministers, elders and deacons of the Reformed Dutch Church, and the rector and inhabitants of the Church of England in New York."

"Same, Sept. 1, 1777. — 'Whereas, I, Benjamin Carpenter, of Jamaica, butcher, did, on the 22nd of August last, violently assault and beat Joseph French, Esq., one of his Majesty's justices for Queens county, at a time when his hands were held, and did otherwise greatly abuse him in the execution of his office; I do therefore in this public manner declare, that I am sorry for what has happened, and most humbly beg forgiveness. I do further declare, that I will of my own accord, cause this my acknowledgment to be inserted for two weeks successively, in the public newspapers of the city of New York; that I will, at the head of each company of militia of said county, at their next muster, read this my acknowledgment; and I will immediately pay into the hands of the churchwardens of the town of Jamaica, the sum of five pounds currency, for the use of the poor of said town.

' Benjamin Carpenter.' "

"New York Gazette, February 16, 1778. — At 2 o'clock last Thursday morning, a party of twelve rebels seized at Coram, in Suffolk county, two wagons loaded with dry goods, the property of Obadiah Wright of

177

Southampton. These marauders had been several days on the island, visited most parts, and committed many robberies, especially at the house of Col. Floyd, Setauket, which they robbed of goods and cash to a considerable amount, also the communion plate presented by Queen Anne to Caroline Church, Setauket; and took some property of Mr. Dunbar, who rides down the island occasionally, and happened to lodge in the house that night."

"New York Mercury, March 10, 1778. — Moses Sawyer, who formerly lived at Shelter Island, came over from the main a few days since, and robbed the farm of William Nicoll, Esq., at said island, of no bushels of wheat; and carried off grain belonging to Thomas Dering."

"April 16, 1778. — Last Saturday night fifteen men of Col. Meig's regiment, under Lieut. Lay, crossed from Horse Neck, to Long Island, and cut two sloops out of Hempstead Harbor, bound to New York. One was deeply laden with wood, the other with vegetables, which they brought safe to Horse Neck and unloaded."

" Rivington' s Gazette, July 3, 1779. — On Tuesday last a party of refugees from Long Island crossed to Westchester and brought off with the assistance of the guard ship below City Island, 50 milch cows, 12 horses and 150 sheep, which they drove to Jamaica Plains."

In 1779 Major-General Silliman was appointed by the governor and council of Connecticut, superintendent of the coast of Fairfield. In the month of May, Sir Henry Clinton directed a small company of refugees to cross the Sound in a whaleboat from Lloyd's Neck, and, if possible, to take him prisoner. One of them was an inhabitant of Newtown, Conn., named Glover, a carpenter who had previously been in the employ of the general, and having been some time at the house, was perfectly acquainted with the safest and easiest modes of access to it. The crew consisted of nine — one was left in the boat, and eight came to the house about midnight. The family were awakened by a violent assault upon the door. The general sprang from bed, raised a musket and approached the door. As he passed by the window, he saw the men, and at once comprehended their design. He attempted to fire, but his musket only flashed. At that instant the assailants broke through the window and seized him, exclaiming that he was their prisoner, and that he must go with them. At his request they permitted him to dress, and having plundered him of a fusee, a pair of pistols, a sword, and a few other articles of small value, proceeded with expedition to the shore, which they reached about two o'clock, and immediately embarked for Long Island. As they approached the shore of Lloyd's Neck, Colonel Simcoe, the commanding officer, who was waiting for them, exclaimed, " Have you got him? " They answered, "Yes." "Have you lost any men?" "No." " That is well, your Sillimans are not worth a man, nor your Washingtons." General Silliman's eldest son was taken with him. The prisoners were ordered to the guard-house. The general asked whether this was the manner they treated prisoners of his rank. The adjutant replied, " We do not consider you in the same light as we should a continental general." " How, then," said the general, " will you view me when an exchange shall be proposed? " " I understand you," said the officer, and withdrew. These questions, probably, saved the general from the indignity of being confined in a guard-house. Soon after, he and his son were conducted in a carriage to New York under an escort of dragoons and on his arrival a large body of people assembled to see him. A friend advised him to withdraw to avoid insult, and very kindly conducted him to good lodgings. Here he remained for some time, when he was ordered to Flatbush, At that time there was no prisoner in the possession of the Americans whom the British would accept for the general, and after some consideration it was determined to procure one. The person selected was the Hon. Thomas Jones of Fort Neck, Long Island, a justice of the supreme court of the province of New York; and Captain Daniel Hawley of Newfield (now Bridgeport) undertook to accomplish the design. On the 4th of November, 1779, about twenty-five volunteers, under the command of Captains Hawley, Lockwood, and Jones, and Lieutenants Jackson and Bishop, set off from Newfield Harbor. They crossed the Sound that evening, arrived at Stony Brook near Smithtown, and marched to Mr. Jones' residence, where they arrived on the 6th, about nine o'clock in the evening, the whole distance being fifty-two miles. There was a ball in the house, and the noise of music and dancing prevented the approach of the adventurers being heard. Captain Hawley knocked at the door, and perceiving that nobody heard him, forced it, and found Judge Jones standing in the entry. He instantly told him he was his prisoner, and immediately conducted him off, together with a young man named Thomas Hewlett. A guard of soldiers was posted at a small distance from their road. When they came near the spot, Judge Jones hemmed very loud, and was forbidden by Captain Hawley to repeat the sound. He, however, did repeat it; but being told by his conductor that another repetition would be followed by fatal consequences, he desisted. On their way they were obliged to lodge in a forest through the day. The third night they reached their boat, having taken two prisoners more, crossed the Sound, and arrived safe at Black Rock on the 8th, except six men, who being in the rear, were overtaken and captured by the light horse. As soon as Mrs. Silliman heard of the judge's arrival, she sent him an invitation to breakfast, which he accepted. And during several days that he remained at her house, she used every means in her power to make his situation agreeable. But although few ladies could contribute more effectually to such a purpose, the judge was distant, reserved, and sullen. From this place he was ordered to Middletown. It was a long time before the British would consent to an exchange; but in May, 1780, they agreed that if one Washburn, a refugee of notoriously bad character, could be included in the exchange as a kind of makeweight, they would release General Silliman for Judge Jones, and his son for Mr. Hewlett. The vessel which conveyed him met another employed to transport General Silliman to his own house on the Sound. The two gentlemen having dined together, proceeded immediately to their respective places of destination. The general's return was welcomed with demonstrations of joy by all the surrounding country; but Judge Jones was doomed to further suffering; for, having taken a very decided stand in favor of royalty, his estate at Fort Neck was forfeited by his attainder, and on the approach of peace he departed for England, where he ended his days — an exile from his friends and country.

"June 16, 1780. — James Robertson, a British officer, styling himself Captain General and Governor-in-Chief in and over the province of New York, issued a proclamation to the inhabitants of Long Island, requiring them to furnish a sufficiency of wood for the barrack-yard in New York, of which Kings county should supply 1500 cords; Queens, 4500 — and the western part of Suffolk (including Huntington, Islip, Smithtown and Brookhaven) 3000; to be cut, and carted to the nearest landings, by the 15th of August ensuing. The inhabitants of Southold, and South and East Hampton, were particularly ordered to cut upon the woodlands of William Smith and William Floyd, of Suffolk county (two notorious rebels) in those parts nearest to the landing at Mastick Neck: 3000 cords to be ready on the landing, by the first of September, for which they were to receive ten shillings a cord. The proclamation further encourages the farmers to cut and cure as much grass as the season would permit."

"New York Gazette, June 17, 1780. — Three days ago, Captain William Dickson, commander of one of the New York volunteer companies, was unfortunately drowned while bathing in a pond at Success, in the neighborhood of Jamaica, Long Island, whither the corpse was brought and interred on Monday evening, attended by Major Small and the officers of the regiment of Royal Highland Emigrants stationed there."

"New York Gazette, June 19, 1780. — Last Saturday, three boats going from New York to Huntington, were attacked near Butler's Point (Dosoris) by two rebel boats from Connecticut, which they beat off, after exchanging several shots; but one of the boats, not sailing so well as the others, was run on shore and burnt."

"Same. — Last Sunday evening was married at the seat of Gen. Skinner, near Jamaica, Capt. Meredith, 70th Reg't, to Miss Gertrude, third daughter of Brig. Gen. Skinner, a young lady whose mental and personal accomplishments promise the most permanent felicity."

"Same, July 17, 1780. — We hear from Setauket, that last Friday night a party of rebels surrounded the dwelling house of Doctor Punderson, took him prisoner, and carried him to Connecticut; and on that night the same party took Mr. William Jayne, Jun. The rebels told Mrs. Punderson that they had taken the doctor to exchange for John Smith, and Mr. Jayne for William

Phillips, who were taken at Smithtown, at the widow Blydenburgh's, on a trading party."

"New York Gazette, July 27, 1780. — Mr. Gaine: Sir — As the account of the capture of the crew belonging to the rebel privateer sloop Revenue, published in your paper of the 10th instant, is wrong in several particulars, you will please insert the following: — Thirteen of the militia of loyal Queens County, commanded by Ensign Elijah Wood, namely, Joseph Mott, John Mott, Joseph Raynor, Elijah Raynor, Ezekiel Raynor, Reuben Pine, Benjamin Palmer, Abel Southard (who was wounded) , Richard Green, Amos Shaw, Isaac Smith, Joseph Smith, William R. Smith, assembled, and after a skirmish of six hours, took ten of the rebels prisoners, together with their boat. Ensign Wood was then reinforced by twenty-six more, namely Lieutenant McKain, an officer on half-pay, Israel Smith, Stephen Powell, William Johnson, Samuel Johnson, Abraham Simonson, Joshua Pettit, William Pettit, James Pettit, Morris Green, William Pearsail, James Denton, James Southard, Elijah Cornell, Reuben Jackson, Benjamin Cornell, Elijah Handy, Uriah Seaman, Barnabas Smith, David Pine, Michael Demott (a trooper), Joseph Dorlon, and Alexander Dunlap."

"Same, August 7, 1780. — About five o'clock last Friday morning, an account was brought to Rockaway that two rebel boats were at Hog Island, and had taken a schooner in Jamaica Bay; in consequence of which. Captain Charles Hicks, of the militia of that place, mustered his company, and with a few volunteers in two boats, went in quest of them. At four the next morning he sent a flag of truce, to inform the rebels that if they would surrender prisoners, they should have good quarters, which they refused, and a smart action ensued; but seeing they could not escape, agreed to the terms offered by Captain Hicks. The prisoners amounted to twenty-eight, and among them a clergyman. Several grape-shot went through Captain Hicks' jacket; but nobody killed."

"New York Gazette, June 4, 1781. — A number of whaleboats got into the South Bay, near Islip, from Connecticut, and took off one vessel and plundered some others. They also robbed several people on shore. This induced a royal party of militia to follow the crews of the boats down to Canoe Place, where they surprised them, killed one, wounded another, and made the whole party prisoners, with four boats and thirty stand of arms; a part of the pirates were subsequently confined in a sugar-house in New York.

Onderdonk's Rev. Incidents of Queens Co. " The whaleboatmen were Americans (many of them refugees from Long Island) living on the Connecticut shore, who had commissions from the Governors of New York and Connecticut to cruise in the Sound against British vessels; and it required no great stretch of conscience to go on land and plunder indiscriminately Whig and Loyalist, under pretense of carrying off British goods. The whaleboat warfare at length degenerated into downright robbery. The whaleboats were sharp at each end, the sheathing often not over half an inch thick, and so light as to be easily carried on men's shoulders, either to be hid in the bushes or re-launched in the South Bay. Some were thirty-two feet long, and impelled by from eight to twenty oars, and would shoot ahead of an ordinary boat with great velocity, and leave their pursuers far behind. They were always on the lookout, and in a calm would row out of their lurking places, and board market boats, or even cut off the detached vessels of a convoy. Another more honorable employment of whaleboats was to carry off distinguished Loyalists, so as to exchange them for Whig prisoners."

"New York Gazette, Aug. 13, 1781. — On the night of the 4th inst. the crew of a rebel whaleboat from New Jersey landed near Flatlands on Long Island, and robbed the house of Col. Jeromus Lott of about six hundred pounds, and carried off with them two of his slaves. They also robbed the house of Captain Lott of a considerable amount of specie."

" Last Thursday night, eight rebel whaleboats made their appearance at Flushing Bay, and landed a few men; but as they did not like the appearance of things, they speedily embarked."

"New York Journal, Sept. 29, 1782. — On Saturday last two men were detected in transporting some forces to Long Island near Flushing; they were sent to Killingworth and committed to gaol, and about the same time thirty sail of shipping were seen under Long Island taking in wood."

In the fall of 1782, and about the time the provisional articles of the treaty of peace were signed, Colonel Thompson (afterwards Sir Benjamin Thompson, Count Rumford), who commanded the troops at Huntington, without any assignable purpose, except that of filling his own pockets, by affording the ground of a claim on the British treasury for the expenses, caused a fort to be erected in the center of the public burying-place, overlooking that village, against the entreaties and remonstrances of the inhabitants, and even compelled them to assist in pulling down the Presbyterian Church, to furnish materials for the building of the fort.

In April, 1783, Sir Guy Carlton instituted a board of commissioners for the purpose of adjusting such demands against the British army as had not been settled. The accounts of the people of the town of Huntington alone, for property taken from them for the use of the army, which were supported by receipts of British officers, or by other evidence, which were prepared to be laid before the board, amounted to £7,249, 9s, 6d, and these accounts were not supposed to comprise one fourth part of the property which was taken from them without compensation. These accounts were sent to New York to be laid before the board of commissioners, but they sailed for England without attending to them, and the people from whom the property was filched were left without redress. If the other towns on the island (says Mr. Wood) suffered half so much in proportion as Huntington, the loss

182

sustained by Long Island alone, during the war, exceeded half a million of dollars.

"Independent Gazette, Dec. 13, 1783. — On Monday last the glorious event of peace was celebrated by the whig inhabitants of Queens County at Jamaica. At sunrise a volley was fired by the continental troops stationed in town, and the thirteen stripes were displayed on a liberty pole, which had been erected for the purpose. At four o'clock a number of gentlemen of the county and officers of the army who were in the neighborhood, sat down to an elegant dinner, attended by the music of a most excellent band, formerly belonging to the line of this state. After drinking thirteen toasts, the gentlemen marched in column thirteen abreast, in procession through the village, preceded by the music, and saluting the colors as they passed. In the evening every house in the village, and several miles around, was most brilliantly illuminated, and a ball given to the ladies concluded the whole. It was pleasing to view the different expressions of joy and gratitude apparent in every countenance on the occasion. In short, the whole was conducted with the greatest harmony, and gave universal satisfaction. An address was likewise agreed upon, to his Excellency George Clinton, governor of the state, and signed by Francis Lewis, John Sands, Richard Thorne, Joseph Robinson, Prior Townsend, Abraham Skinner, Benjamin Coe, Robert Furman, and James Burling.

" His excellency thereupon returned an answer in which he thanked them for their respectful address, and concluded by saying, ' You have now abundant opportunities, which I have the highest confidence you will cheerfully embrace, of manifesting your patriotism, by a firm attachment to our excellent constitution, and a steady support of good government, domestic tranquility, and the national justice and honor."

October 22, 1779, an act was passed, entitled "An act for the forfeiture and sale of the estates of persons who had adhered to the enemy, and for declaring the sovereignty of the state, in respect to all property within it" And another act confirming forfeitures, and authorizing the governor to appoint commissioners for the sale of the estates which had been confiscated was passed, May 12, 1784. Those of Long Island subjected to the penalty of attainder, were George Duncan Ludlow, his brother, Gabriel G. Ludlow, Daniel Kissam, Senator Thomas Jones, Henry Lloyd, David Golden, John Rapelje, Richard Floyd, George Muirson, and Parker Wickham, all of whom left the state and most of whom retired to some part of the British dominions.

In conclusion, we may be permitted to say that as much as the people of Long Island had suffered from the oppression and cruelty of their invaders, they were not permitted to taste the sweets of liberty, until it was in some degree embittered by the unkindness of their friends, as circumstances of that period fully prove. It was their unhappy lot, resulting principally from their geographical position, to be abandoned, in a great measure, by their country, and fall of course into the power of the enemy, from whom they could expect no quarter, much less protection, unless by entire acquiescence in their wishes. It was their misfortune and not their fault, that they were not within the American lines. They had been disarmed and were now in subjection to the enemy. Instead of being employed in the field against them. Yet an act was passed March 17, 1783, by which those of Long Island, as in other places, who should be prosecuted for damages to the property of others, which had even been committed under military orders, were prohibited from pleading that matter in justification, or giving it in evidence under the general issue, to prevent or diminish a recovery. By the act of May 6, 1784, a tax to raise £100,000 was levied upon the southern district, to be appropriated as a compensation to other parts of the state; the former not having been in a condition to take an active part in the war against the common enemy. Both these last acts were obviously flagrant violations of the doctrine of equal rights and the immutable principles of justice, partial and oppressive in their operation, and fully prove that an abuse of power is almost always consequent upon the possession of it; and is not confined to those only, who, in every age and nation, have been stigmatised as the enemies of free government.

SOME FURTHER MATTERS
OF CURIOSITY AND INTEREST

EXTRACTED FROM THE JOURNAL OF THE NEW YORK PROVINCIAL CONGRESS.

Joseph French of Jamaica, and Thomas Hicks of Hempstead, having been ordered by a resolution of the provincial congress to attend in their places as deputies from Queens County, decline to do so. The answer of the former to the secretary, is as follows:

" Jamaica, June 26, 1775. "Sir: Yours of the 22nd instant, came safe to hand. In answer to which I must acquaint you that I have made it my rule in life, never to accept any office or place of trust, unless I could acquit myself with honor. Some time ago we had an election at Jamaica, to send Members to Congress, and it was carried in the negative. These same men have acquainted me, if I attend in Congress I do not represent them, but the minority. As, for my part, I have signed the Association in New-York, and expect to abide by the consequences."

Who this Mr. French was has not been satisfactorily ascertained, yet it is quite certain that he was a man of some note, though his patriotism was afterwards doubted. He knew the general unwillingness of the people to take sides against the mother country, and therefore pretended that he could not assume authority not conferred upon him by his constituents. He is said to have been a retired sea captain and was one of the king's justices; and lived in the home now Walter Nichols' at Jamaica, and went to England at the Peace.

Mr. Hicks in his letter of June 27, 1775, admits having received a notice to serve as a deputy, or to assign his reasons for his neglect. He states the disagreement among the people of Hempstead on the subject of sending deputies, and considers that his attendance would not be a fair expression of their wishes, which it appears were opposed to sending any representative at all. Also that the bad state of his health obliged him to avoid New York as much as possible in the summer, from the long experience of the bad effects of the city air at that season. " The people," he says, " are much inclined to remain peaceable and quiet; and he had therefore declined taking his seat in Congress, persuaded of the impropriety and injustice of transacting business of so much consequence, for people who disavowed his authority."

It may be mentioned that Governor Tryon was very popular with the people of Queens County, and he had exerted himself both by proclamation, and going personally among them, to attach them to the government, and lead them to oppose, as much as possible, the growing disposition in other parts of the country for emancipation, and the establishment of independence.

The following letter was received from Thomas Helme, chairman of the Brookhaven Committee, dated Augusts, 1775:

"Gentlemen: As well-wishers to our country, we cannot any longer delay giving you an account of the conduct of sundry persons within the limits of this committee — Parson James Lyon, rector of the Episcopal Church at Setauket, Benjamin Floyd, Doct. Gilbert Smith, Joseph Denton, Richard Floyd, and John Bayles, innkeeper. These persons have from the beginning taken every method in their power to seduce the ignorant about them, and to counteract every measure that has been recommended for the redress of grievances. They damn all Congresses and committees, wishing they were in hell. They have declared that they will furnish, and it is suspected they have furnished, the men-of-war and cutters with provisions. Such conduct, we think, is insufferable, and desire that you would be pleased to direct such measures as you shall think proper to suppress it."

A letter written by Burnet Miller, Esq., chairman of the committee of South and East Hampton, of July 5, 1775, says that the people there are much exposed to the ravages of their unnatural enemy, in regard to their stock on Montauk, where any number may land at pleasure. That their stock is large, not less than 2000 neat cattle, and 3000 or 4000 sheep, which, if taken, would greatly distress them, and give support to the enemy. He requests that troops of which their company might form a part should be stationed at Montauk, until some matter of more importance shall call them away. He also suggests that whaleboats might be employed in rendering aid to other places in the vicinity, they having a number of them, which were of no use at that season.

Robert Hempstead, Esq., of Southold, informs Congress August 7, 1775, that the situation of things there, required their immediate assistance, as a large number of vessels had been seen the day before, between Montauk and Fisher's Island, which were hourly expected to land at Oyster Ponds, or some other place. That being destitute of powder, they would be unable to make defense. He desires that their case may be taken into consideration, and ways and means provided for their immediate supply. Lieutenant Norton had informed him that his company from Brookhaven were many of them destitute of powder, and some of them even of arms.

Colonel Phineas Fanning, in a letter from the same place, of August 8, 1775, says, that on his way there he met an express informing him, that during the morning the ministerial fleet of thirteen sail of square rigged vessels (seven of which were ships) arrived from the west end of Fisher's Island, and came to anchor off Gardiner's Island Point, where they then lay. That at 5 o'clock, in the afternoon, a boat attacked Rufus Tuthill, while landing fifty sheep from Plum Island, and drove him from his boat, which they took with twenty of his sheep; that the officers of the militia in that neighborhood were ordered to Oyster Ponds, as it was feared a descent would either be made there, or some other place in the vicinity. Rufus Tuthill was a warm whig and was imprisoned in 1778, with his townsmen Thomas Youngs, Jared Landon, John Brown, and Storrs Lester. He however lived to the advanced age of ninety-seven years, at Oyster Ponds, where he died December 11, 1843.

Colonel Fanning was a man of education, having graduated at Yale College, in 1769, and as respectable for his bravery and patriotism, as his cousin Edmund Fanning, the son-in-law and secretary of Governor Tryon, and afterwards lieutenant governor of Nova Scotia, was for his toryism and unnatural treatment of his countrymen. There were at this time few who had more sincere friendship for the country, or few who suffered more in their property from the common enemy in consequence of it. He informs Congress in a letter of August 22, 1775, that directions had been given for taking the stock from Gardiner's and Plum Islands; but that much concern was felt in consequence of the troops on the east end of the island being ordered away, whereby they should be left defenseless. That three cutters were there cruising at the east end, and the stock on Montauk, Shelter Island, and Oyster Pond Point was in the utmost danger of falling into the hands of the enemy, besides the constant alarms and expense the people would be exposed to, unless they should be allowed a number of men to secure those parts from depredations; that Colonel Gardiner, of Plum Island, had informed him that Colonel Willard, of the ministerial fleet, said they should come again, with a force sufficient to take the stock from Long Island.

Brigadier General Wooster, then upon the east end of the island, in a letter from Oyster Ponds,' of August 27, 1775, informs the President of the convention that the " Kingfisher " (an enemy's vessel) had gone up the Sound with several small cutters, reconnoitering the north side of the Island, and the next day there followed two topsail vessels, supposed to be transports, as they fired two signal guns when they went through the Race. He recommends a good guard to be kept over Queens County, as he imagined the enemy designed to get stock from Huntington, Lloyd's Neck, and Flushing.

It may be well to mention in this place, that General David Wooster was born at Stratford, Conn., in 1711, educated at Yale College, where he graduated in 1738, was a captain in the expedition against Louisburgh in 1745, and in 1756 was raised to the command of a brigade in the French War. He commanded the troops sent to guard New York, where it was expected, that a part of the British army, which came over in 1775, would land. He had the command in Canada after the death of General Montgomery, and returning home in the summer of 1776, was appointed first Major General of the Militia of Connecticut. He was mortally wounded in a skirmish with the British troops, at the time of their incursion to Danbury, April 26, 1777, and died the 2nd of May following, at the age of sixty-six. He was a brave and good officer, an ardent patriot, and in his various public and private relations sustained a character distinguished for integrity, benevolence, and virtue.

On the 25th of September, 1775, Information was received by the Committee of Safety, from Colonel Abraham Skinner (afterwards first clerk of Queens County, under the constitution) that the persons sent to Jamaica for the purpose had collected a few arms, but apprehended that they would meet with opposition, and requested to have a battalion sent up from New York to their assistance.

The committee, however, deferred sending a battalion to Queens County, until they should have advice from Major Williams, and the gentlemen sent up there; and they ordered Mr. Benson, one of the secretaries, to proceed to Jamaica, to ascertain the true state of affairs there. They were subsequently informed by Major Williams by a letter of the same date, that he had endeavored in the towns of Jamaica and Hempstead, but in vain, to carry the resolutions of Congress into effect; for, said he, the people conceal their arms that are of any value, and many declare they will sooner lose their lives than give them up; that they would blow any man's brains out who should attempt to take them away. That Governor Colden sent his servant round to some of the leading people, advising them to arm and defend themselves. That Captain Hewlett of Hempstead said he had his company together on the Monday before and, had the battalion appeared, they should have warmed their sides.

The committee thereupon appointed Samuel Verplank, Thomas Smith, David Clarkson, John Vanderbilt, and Benjamin Kissam, to proceed to Queens County, and use every prudent measure to collect arms; and to report the names of those who should oppose them. December 13, 1775, an affidavit of Samuel Nostrand and Isaac Losee was read, informing the Congress that on the 30th of November, preceding, they were at the house of John Nostrand of Hempstead, who told them that there was a great quantity of powder at Captain Richard Hewlett's, Rockaway, which came from on board the "Asia," man-of-war, with ball, small arms and some cannons etc. They were, also, so informed by Isaac Denton, Jun., who declared that he would fight against the country, while he could see a damned whig left.

Whereupon it was ordered that Captain Benjamin Whitehead, Charles Arden, Joseph French, Esq., and Johannes Polhemus of Jamaica, Nathaniel Moore, John Moore, Sen., Captain Samuel Hallet, John Moore, Jun., William Wyman, John Shoals, and Jeromus Rapelje of Newtown, John Willet of Flushing, Justice Gilbert Van Wyck, Daniel Kissam, Esq., Captain Jacob Mott, Thomas Cornell, Gabriel G. Ludlow, Richard Hewlett, Captain Charles Hicks, Dr. Samuel Martin, and Justice Samuel Clowes of Hempstead, Justice Thomas Smith, Justice John Hewlett, George Weeks, Dr. David Brooks, and Justice John Townsend, being charged as principal men among the disaffected in said county, do attend this Congress on the 19th inst. to give satisfaction in the premises.

The said persons not appearing, Congress on the 21st of December, 1775, among other things, " resolved that the delinquents be and hereby are entirely put out of the protection of Congress; that all friendly and commercial intercourse between them and the other Inhabitants of the colony be Interdicted, until the further order of Congress or the committee of safety, and that the names of such delinquents be printed and dispersed in said county.

William Smith, Esq., of Suffolk County, Informs Congress by letter of November 2, 1775, that Nathan Woodhull and Edmund Smith, Jun., had declined the offices of first and second major, of the First Regiment, and that Jeffrey Smith and Jesse Brush had been nominated for said offices.

In committee of safety, January 4, 1776, Thomas Place and Gabriel Van Cott, of Queens County, by their petition say, that they are extremely sorry and sincerely repent of, having voted against electing delegates at the last election, saying they were misled by the artful insinuations of designing men. The like was received on the 16th from Captain Jacob Mott, Jackson Mott, and Seaman Weeks, all of whom pledge their future attachment to the country.

A letter was received in Provincial Convention, August 1, 1776, from George Townsend, Esq., chairman of the committee of Queens County, dated July 31st, enclosing a copy of the declaration issued by Richard, Viscount Howe, and Sir William Howe, attested by Governor Tryon, and certified as a true copy, and subscribed by Thomas Willet, sheriff of Queens County. 'Whereupon it was resolved that said Willet be taken into custody to answer for his conduct. Being brought to the bar of the convention on the 6th of August, he admitted the paper to have been signed by him, but that he had not then seen the Declaration of Independence by Congress — that he held the commission of sheriff under Governor Tryon, and thought it having been published by Congress, there could be no harm in his publishing it also. That the more public it was the better. But the convention ordered him to be committed. Note. — The original declaration above mentioned was acknowledged by Miss Elizabeth Hicks, of Rockaway, to have been received by her, and handed by her to one Joshua Mills. She was ordered to be arrested and kept in close custody till she should discover, on oath, from whom she received the paper. What was the result, does not appear from the journals of the convention.

In March, 1776, Captain Isaac Sears, (commonly called King Sears,) a person of great activity and courage, and truly devoted to the Interest of his country, was sent into Queens County, by order of General Charles Lee, in behalf of the Provincial Congress, to require an oath of fidelity from the disaffected portion of the people. As the oath administered on this occasion may seem a curiosity to some, a copy of it is here given:

" I, A. B., do here, in the presence of Almighty God, most religiously, solemnly and devoutly swear, that I will not, during the present contest, convey any intelligence, directly or indirectly, to any of the Ministerial Troops, or Navy of Great Britain, or to any wicked instrument of tyranny; and that if I should become acquainted with any such treasonable practices, in others, I will give notice of it to the Provincial Congress. I do likewise swear by the same Almighty and Tremendous God, that I will not, by any action, conversation or hint, endeavor to intimidate or dissuade other men, from embarking in the cause of their country and liberty; or to check the ardor of those who are already engaged. I do further pledge myself, as I hope for eternal salvation, to abide by, and strictly observe all the regulations and laws of the Continental Congress, so help me God."

It seems that his instructions were to offer the test to certain persons of whom a list of names was furnished to Captain Sears; that the refusal of any to sign It, must be considered an avowal of their hostile Intentions; those persons were to be secured and sent up, as irreclaimable enemies to their country. Richard Hewlett to have no conditions offered to him, but be .secured without ceremony.

It may be remarked that Captain Sears was distinguished for his many daring exploits during the revolution; that after peace he entered into mercantile business in Boston, with Paschal N. Smith, who it is believed married his sister; but meeting with disappointment, he sailed in a vessel of his own, for the purpose of retrieving his fortune, and died in the Island of Java, in indigent circumstances.

A letter from John Lawrence, Esq., chairman of the committee, of Newtown, dated May 27, 1776, acquaints the Congress, that the inhabitants had complained of John Moore, Jun., for a fresh insult offered to the United Colonies by hoisting a large flag, or suffering the same to be hoisted on his ground, in imitation of a King's standard — the committee ordered him to be taken into custody, and brought before them; and having given no sufficient satisfaction they thought proper to have him conducted to the board under the care of Captain Abraham Remsen, for further examination.

A letter from John Lloyd, Jun., to the Hon. John Sloss Hobart, is referred to the Congress, in which his advice is asked whether he may safely dispose of the stock upon Lloyd's Neck, belonging to his uncle Henry Lloyd, who being a royalist, was then under the censure of the public. The stock if left there must inevitably fall into the hands of the enemy, should they land in that part of the island. What disposition was made of the application does not appear.

Mr. John Foster of Southampton acquaints Congress February 8, 1776, that he had engaged a quantity of tow cloth, as he had been requested, for which he gave two and two pence, to two and three pence a yard, and asks to be informed whether he shall purchase any more at that price or not.

A letter from Isaac Thompson, Esq., chairman of the Islip committee, of February 9, 1776, Informs Congress that the precinct had unanimously chosen Benajah Strong, Captain; Jeremiah Terry and Samuel Oakley, as first and second lieutenants, and Annin Mobray, ensign; and desires that commissions may be granted, which he says will very much tend to unite the people of the precinct.

A letter received from William Smith, Esq., chairman of the Suffolk County Committee, of January 24, 1776, containing a return of minute and artillery officers, and praying that some of them may be furnished with arms; also that such number of continental troops may be stationed there as the Congress may judge necessary. The following is the list of the officers, chosen and approved by the committee. Josiah Smith, colonel; John Hulburt, second colonel; Isaac Reeve, first major; Jonathan Baker, second major; Isaac Overton, adjutant; Ebenezer Dayton, second master; William Rogers, captain of artillery; John Franks, captain lieutenant; Jeremiah Rogers, first lieutenant; Thomas Baker, second lieutenant; and John Tuthill, lieutenant fireworker.

The following letter was received from certain tories of Queens County, viz.:

Jamaica, L. I., April 13, 1776. " Gentlemen: We, the subscribers, inhabitants of the township of Jamaica, in Queens County on Long Island, beg leave to acquaint you that we have heretofore been disarmed by order of the Continental Congress, which we quietly and peaceably submitted to, as not having it in our intention to act contrary to their regulations, or the resolves of your Congress: notwithstanding which we have been lately plundered of our cattle and effects, which have been publicly sold at vendue for half the value, in consequence of an order issued by Capt. Abraham Bailey in this township, for not appearing in arms and answering to our names, when it is well known we have been deprived of our arms, and thereby disqualified from any such service; besides which it appears to us quite contrary to a late resolve of the Continental Congress, We therefore request it as a favour that you will be pleased to take this matter into your serious consideration, and if the treatment we have received does not proceed from any order or direction of yours, that you will give us such relief as you may think necessary, and oblige your respectful humble servants, Nathaniel Mills, Jabez Woodruff, Joshua Mills, John Lamberson, Nicholas Ludlam, Joseph Oldfield, Samuel Mills, John Remsen, Jacob Dean, Dirck (his X mark) Bargin, Peter Mills, Abraham Colyer."

May 11, 1776, Thomas Woolley of Great Neck was ordered by the Congress to be imprisoned in Queens County Jail, for contumaciously refusing to appear in arms, in the company commanded by Captain Sands.

The Rev. Samuel Buell of Easthampton, in his letter of April 10, 1776, writes to the Congress from Huntington as follows: " After cordial salutation, these Inform that I left Easthampton on Monday morning, after nine o'clock.

No farther discoveries were made of the fleets mentioned in the committee's letter, unless that a considerable number of shipping made a harbor at Fisher's Island, Lord's day evening. There I suppose, were what we call Wallis's fleet. Those seen at sea on Sunday afternoon, perhaps were from the West Indies or Boston. By their clustering in together and frequent firing. It seems they were collecting in their scattered fleet. We, sir, at the east end of Long Island are certainly much exposed to ravages and plundering, by the hand of violence. Whether we do not greatly need a regiment or two at the east end, must be submitted to your superior wisdom."

A letter from Thomas Wicks of Huntington, of April 8, 1776, informs Congress that intelligence was received that a fleet of thirty sail of square-rigged vessels had been seen off between Crane and Eaton's Neck — that their motions would be watched and their intention when discovered announced to Congress. He says " we are mustering our Militia and shall do the best in our power."

The like information is received from Burnet Miller of Easthampton, who adds that the vessels had fired cannon by spells all the afternoon, for the purposes as he supposes of keeping them together, the fog being very thick.

A letter was received from Lieutenant Colonel Benjamin Birdsall, detailing the unpatriotic conduct of certain persons in the southeast part of Queens County, and enclosing the copy of a song, publicly and frequently sung with joy and jollity, in which he says they drink damnation to the Congress.

On the 15th of February, 1776, a letter was sent to the Congress by Samuel Thompson, one of the committee of Brookhaven, accompanied by a map or draft of the north coast of the town and the harbor of Setauket and Stony Brook. He observes that from Oyster Pond Point to Setauket there is no harbor that a vessel of any considerable burden can get into, in a distance of more than 50 miles; and recommends that a small fort be built on the beach running off from Mount Misery Point, defended by not less than 6 or 8 guns, some of them 9- or 12-pounders. Also that Stony Brook would need two 6- or 9-pounders placed on the high cleft. He says, " we are much in want of a gunsmith to fix the guns and make bayonets. — There are numbers amongst us that have no guns, nor could they buy them if they had money."

Thomas Hicks, Esq., in a letter from Little Neck, of May 28, 1776, says: "I received yesterday an extract from the minutes of Congress, by which I am ordered to attend and take my seat, or show the cause of my neglect. The ill state of my health, and the extreme weakness of my constitution render me utterly incapable of performing the duty of a deputy. This I hope will be considered by the Congress as a sufficient apology for my non-attendance."

A proclamation from Major General DeLancey, of September 1, 1776, is received, saying that he is ordered by his Excellency the Honorable William Howe, General and Commander-in-chief of all his Majesty's forces in North

America, from Nova Scotia to the Floridas, to state that on the application of the County of Suffolk, he is willing to accept of the submission of the inhabitants and promise them protection, on their laying down their arms, taking the oath of allegiance, disclaiming the order of Congress, and totally refusing obedience to them, obeying the legal authority of government and in all places of worship to pray for the King and royal family, as was usual before the present unprovoked rebellion.

A letter from the commissioners for detecting conspiracies was received in Congress, giving Information under date of June 18, 1777, that a number of the people called Quakers had lately been to Long Island without permission, to attend their annual meeting at Flushing — that as soon as the commissioners had information of it, they issued the necessary orders to have them apprehended, and had several detained as prisoners in Poughkeepsie. The Quakers averred that they attended said meeting solely for religious purposes and had not the least intermeddled in political matters, but the commissioners had no evidence on that point — there being upwards of twenty in that predicament, the commissioners thought it a matter of too much importance to determine without communicating with the council of safety for advice and directions.

General Silliman, in a letter of June 16, 1777, from Fairfield, informs John Sloss Hobart, Esq., that a boat was then lying at Norwall, belonging to Shubael Smith of Huntington, which he formerly used as a ferryboat between Huntington and Norwall — that she was a neat and valuable boat, and as the owner had joined the enemy, the boat ought to be seized for the benefit of the state of New York, and recommends that proper measures be taken to have her immediately secured.

Extract from a letter of Ebenezer Dayton, dated Bethany, Conn., October, 1776, to the President of the convention, in which he says:

" Sir: — I removed from Brookhaven with my family in September last, leaving valuable possessions, and am now both ready and desirous to obey any commands the convention may please to lay upon me, to the best of my skill and ability, in any department they may please to occupy me. I have had the boldness and vanity to recommend the sending one or more ranging companies upon Long Island. I have thought much of the plan, and am convinced it would be a very essential service, in many respects, to the State; and I am fully convinced that the same is practicable while the weather is warm, and that there is a sufficient extent of woods, swamps, plains, and faithful friends, &c., on Long Island, to shelter and secrete companies of rangers from the eye and injury of any enemy able to harm them, even upon the supposition that half the British troops and tories in America should be employed in search of them. That they might always have it in their power to make a safe retreat from the land or send off prisoners or important news, by going over with small light boats. They would be able to do much execution by surprise, being industriously moving from place to place, making unexpected attacks in unexpected places, depending upon surprise as the soul of their enterprises, to take an unlikely course, and always take the advantage of night, and always have a place of rendezvous agreed upon, to be able to embody, in case of being on any occasion obliged to separate or disperse.

" If the convention should judge proper to send rangers upon Long Island, I would be glad to have the command of a company of them — though my abilities are but small, yet the great advantage I have had of knowing the geography of the Island and its inhabitants with their several political principles, has rendered me more capable to conduct the operations of such a company than a man of the greatest abilities who has not had such advantages. I hope an unfeigned desire to promote my country's good, will induce the convention to excuse my boldness in troubling them with reading this and the enclosed outline of a favorite plan of my own invention."

John Chatfield, chairman of the committee of Easthampton, informs the committee of safety, March ii, 1776, that the ship " Sally," belonging to Samuel Franklin of New York, taken by the British and sent for Boston, drove on shore at Montauk in a gale of wind; and that Charles Smith, mate of the " Asia," man-of-war, three passengers, and ten seamen of the " Asia," were sent under guard to New York, conducted by Lieutenant John Foster, with all letters and papers that were found on board.

ADDITIONAL REVOLUTIONARY INCIDENTS.

ORIGINALLY COMMUNICATED TO THE EDITOR OF THE NAVAL MAGAZINE, BY GENERAL JEREMIAH JOHNSON.

The enterprising whaleboat privateersmen of our country deserve notice, although their acts of robbery are censurable. Captains Adam Hyler and William Marriner of New Brunswick annoyed the British troops so much, that an armed force was sent to that place to destroy their boats. The object was effected, but the cost was more than it was worth. New boats were immediately built.

Hyler and Marriner cruised between Egg Harbor and Staten Island. Hyler took several ships, and levied contributions on the New York fishermen, on the fishing banks. He frequently visited Long Island. He took a Hessian major at night, April, 1781, from the house of Michael Bergen, at Gowanus, when his soldiers were encamped near the house. He surprised and took a sergeant's guard at Canarsie, June, 1781, from the house of their captain, Schenck. The guards were at supper, and their muskets standing in the hall, when Hyler entered with his men. He seized the arms, and, after jesting with the guard, he borrowed the silver spoons for his family; took a few other articles with all the muskets, and made one prisoner. He sent the guard to report themselves to Colonel Axtell, and returned to New Jersey.

Captain Hyler also paid a visit to Colonel Lott at Flatlands, August, 1781. The colonel was known to be rich; his money and his person were the objects desired. He was surprised in his house at night, and taken. His cupboard was searched for money, and some silver found; and, on further search, two bags supposed to contain guineas were discovered. These, with the silver, the colonel, and two of his negroes were embarked and taken to New Brunswick. In the morning, on the passage up the Raritan, the captain and crew agreed to count and divide the guineas. The bags were opened, when, to the mortification of the crew, they were found to contain only halfpennies belonging to the church of Flatlands; and the colonel also discovered that his guineas were safe at home. The crew were disappointed in their Scotch prize. They, however, determined to make the most of the adventure; they took the colonel and his negroes to New Brunswick, where they compelled him to ransom them, and then permitted him to return home, on parole. Captain Hyler also, with two boats, took a corvette of twenty guns, about nine o'clock at night, in Coney Island Bay. The ship lay at anchor, bound for Halifax, to complete her crew. The night was dark; one of the boats, with muffled oars, was rowed up close under the stern of the ship, when the officers were to be seen at a game of cards in the cabin, and no watch on deck. The spy-boat then fell astern to her consort, and reported; when orders were passed to board. The boats were rowed up silently — the ship boarded instantly on both sides — and not a man was injured. The officers were confined in the cabin, and the crew below. The captain ordered the officers and crew to be taken out of the ship, well fettered, and placed in the whaleboats. Afterwards a few articles were taken from the ship, and she was set on fire; when Captain Hyler left her, with his prisoners for New Brunswick. My Informant, one of the men who took the ship, stated, that the captain of the corvette wept as they were crossing the bay, and reproached himself for permitting one of his Majesty's ships to be surprised and taken "by two d — d eggshells"; and he added, that there were $40,000 on board the burning vessel, which Captain Hyler and his crew deserved for their gallant enterprise. The booty, however, was lost.

After the notorious refugee Lippencott had barbarously murdered Captain Huddy at Sandy Hook, General Washington was very anxious to have the murderer secured. He had been demanded from the British general, and his surrender refused. Retaliation was decided upon by General Washington. Young Argill was to be the innocent victim to atone for the death of Captain Huddy. He was saved by the mediation of the Queen of France. Captain Hyler was determined to take Lippencott. On inquiry, he found that he resided in a well-known house in Broad Street, New York. With a boat-load of men dressed and equipped like a man-of-war press gang, he left the Kills after dark, and arrived at Whitehall about nine o'clock. Here he left his boat in charge of three men, and then passed to the residence of Lippencott, where he inquired for him, and found he was absent, and gone to a cock-pit. Captain Hyler thus failed in the object of his pursuit and visit to the city. He returned to his boat with his press gang, and left Whitehall; but finding a sloop laying at anchor off the Battery, from the West Indies, laden with rum, he took the vessel, cut her cable, set her sails, and with a north-east wind sailed to Elizabethtown Point, and before daylight had landed from her, and secured forty hogsheads of rum. He then burned the sloop to prevent her recapture. Captain Hyler died at New Brunswick, N, J., in 1782.

Captain Marriner resided many years at Harlem, and on Ward's Island after the war. He died by a fall from his wagon near Harlem bridge, 1814, aged eighty-five years. He was a man of eccentric character, witty and ingenious, and abounding in anecdotes; but he had his faults. He had been taken by the British, was on parole in Kings County, and quartered with Rem Van Pelt, of New Utrecht. The prisoners, among the officers, had the liberty of the four southern towns of the county. Many of them frequented Dr. Van Buren's tavern in Flatbush, Here our captain's sarcastic wit, in conversation with Major Moncrieffe, of the British army, led to abusive language from the major to the prisoner. After some time, Marriner was exchanged, when he determined to capture Major Moncrieffe, Colonel Matthews (the mayor of New York) , Colonel Axtell, and Mr. Bache, who all resided in Flatbush, and were noted and abusive tories, and obnoxious to the American officers. For the purpose of carrying his designs into execution, he repaired to New

Brunswick, and procured a whaleboat. This he manned with a crew of well-armed volunteers, with whom he proceeded to New Utrecht, and landed on the beach at Bath about half past nine o'clock of a fine moonlight night, June 13, 1778. Leaving two men in charge of the boat, with the rest of the crew he marched unmolested to Flatbush church, where he divided his men into four squads, assigning a house to each; each party or squad was provided with a heavy post, to break in the doors. All was silent in the village. Captain Marriner selected the house of George Martense, where his friend, the major, quartered, for himself; the other parties proceeded to their assigned houses. Time was given to each squad to arrive at Its destination, and it was agreed, that when Marriner struck his door, the others were to break in theirs, and repair to the church with their prisoners. The doors were broken at the same time. Marriner found the major behind a large chimney in the garret, where he had hidden himself, and where he surrendered. In presence of his landlady, who lit the way for Marriner. The major was permitted to take his small clothes in his hand, and thus was marched to the church, where the parties assembled. Major Moncrieffe and Mr. Theophylact Bache were taken, but Axtell and Matthews escaped. The parties marched with their prisoners unmolested to their boat, and returned safe to New Brunswick. After Captain Marriner's visit to Flatbush, four inhabitants of New Utrecht were taken separately, and separately imprisoned in the Provost in New York, on suspicion of having been connected with Marriner in his enterprise, viz: Colonel Van Brunt, his brother Adrian Van Brunt, Rem Van Pelt, and his brother Art Van Pelt. Captain Marriner also paid Simon Cortelyou of New Utrecht a visit, November, 1778; and took him to New Brunswick, as a return for this uncivil conduct to the American prisoners. He took his tankard, and several articles, also, which he neglected to return.

When Colonel Van Brunt was taken by the officer of the guard, he requested permission to get a clean shirt to take with him, when he also put a few guineas into his pocket. On the morning after their confinement, the deputy of Cunningham visited the prisoners, to give them the usual breakfast when Colonel Van Brunt gave the keeper a guinea, and requested him to send a cup of coffee and toast, for his breakfast. The coffee and toast were brought in by the keeper's wife, to whom he also gave a guinea, and requested her to supply his neighbors with their breakfasts and dinners. When she brought in the colonel's dinner, he heard from his neighbors. In the evening she brought in his tea, when he requested her to permit him to see his fellow-prisoners, which she persuaded her husband to allow, for another guinea, and they had an interview that night.

Although they suspected the reason of their imprisonment, still they did not know why they were confined separately. At this interview, they agreed to deny all knowledge of Captain Marriner's visit. The next morning they were examined, separately, before the mayor. Colonel Axtell, and a number of officers, in reference to Marriner's visit. They adhered to their previous agreement, and, there being no proof against them, were discharged, with an abundance of rebel blessings. Thus, they narrowly escaped the tails of Cunningham's cats.

It may be added that Rem Van Pelt died at New Utrecht, L. I., aged nearly ninety-one years, March 18, 1829. His father was Peter, a farmer in the town, who with his sons were imprisoned in the Provost, where they suffered, under the iron hand of the notorious Cunningham, all that his heartless cruelty could inflict.

Colonel Axtell, who commanded Kings County, after Marriner's visit, feared that he might be caught napping. To leave his command, did not comport with his honor; and, for his safety, he immediately ordered two of his dragoons to his house, who were relieved weekly. He also ordered a strong militia guard to be kept in Flatbush, which was relieved daily; as he had no great confidence in these militia, he compelled his regiment to raise a company of men, at their expense, which were named the Nassau Blues. This company was stationed at Flatbush, and commanded by Captain Frederick Depeyster, late of the city of New York, deceased, a nephew of the colonel. Colonel Robinson, who for a time commanded Queens County, resided at Jamaica, and considered himself safe under the protection of two dragoons, and of the troops usually stationed there. From the taking of Long Island and New York in 1776, to the evacuation, martial law prevailed within the British possessions in this state. All offences of a military character, or wherein military persons were implicated, were decided by courts martial. It rarely happened, however, that officers or soldiers were punished for crimes or injuries toward the inhabitants.

The Connecticut whaleboats rendered Long Island Sound very unsafe to the British, except to strong armed vessels. The whaleboats visited certain positions along the Sound, whenever they pleased, and carried on a trade with New York, for dry goods, &c., to a great amount.

The enterprising and predatory warfare of the American whaleboat men alarmed the royalists greatly. They considered themselves unsafe, unless they were surrounded by an armed force; and many of the British officers, who were residing on Long Island, left their quarters, and repaired to Brooklyn or New York.

The ferries between Brooklyn and New York were under the surveillance of a military guard. All the inhabitants were compelled to obtain passports for themselves and their families, by name, to cross the ferries; and every market boat, with her hands, was licensed, to come to the city. Nor was this all. Every farmer, or person, who wished to take any goods from New York, was compelled to take a bill of the goods to the police office, in the city, for a permit to take the same from the city.

Every permit cost two shillings. The passports to cross the ferries, and the licenses of the market boats, were renewed and paid for every year. In this manner favorites were provided for. During the war, a continual trade was carried on between favored individuals of the British, and treacherous Americans. The Sound whaleboat men, usually, were the protectors and carriers of the goods for the owners. These London traders were permitted to take any quantity of goods from the city, for sale, while a farmer had to give an account of the number and requirements of his family.

A Major Stockton, who murdered a miller named Amberman, at Foster's Meadow, without justifiable cause or provocation, was tried for the crime at Bedford, before a court martial. The culprit was acquitted for want of surgical evidence that Amberman died of the wound inflicted by him. James Hedger, of Flushing, was murdered in his house by six soldiers of the Fifty-fourth Regiment, who also plundered the house. Five of them were subsequently tried, and two of them. Tench and Porter, were hanged upon land late of Francis Skillman. Some soldiers had killed one of Captain Suydam's cattle, of Bedford, three of whom were shot by him, while they were skinning it. Two other persons were killed in Bushwick, three in Newtown, one at the Half-way House, and others at Jamaica and Flushing.

In the year 1777, a police court was established in the city of New York, under Mayor Matthews, and in 1780 another for Long Island, under Judge Ludlow, at Jamaica. These courts decided, in a summary manner, controversies between the inhabitants.

In the month of March, 1779, flour and bread stuffs were very nearly exhausted in the British store houses at New York. There was no good flour: and the Hessians, who were in Brooklyn, drew damaged oat meal instead of bread; this meal, baked in cakes, was unfit for use; and the writer has seen them cast to the swine, which would not eat them. The soldiers were mutinous. All the grain possessed by the farmers was estimated and placed under requisition. The timely arrival of a few victualing ships relieved the scarcity, and saved the British from a surrender to the Americans to escape starvation. If the Hessians at this time received bread which the hogs refused, what may we suppose to have been the quality of that given to the prisoners? in 1777 the continental paper money had depreciated so much that it was of little value, and it was contrived to borrow money for the use of the army from the whigs of Long Island. Perfect secrecy was preserved in these transactions; and before the year 1782, loans to a large amount were obtained. Major Hendrick Wyckoff crossed the Sound frequently, and was concealed at the house of Peter Onderdonk at Cow Neck; from thence he came to the house of his father at New Lots, and by his means a large amount of money was procured, and safely conveyed to headquarters at Poughkeepsie.

It was also decided that exchanges should be effected of confidential officers, who were to be agents in these transactions; and Colonel William

Ellison, who was taken at Fort Montgomery, was fixed upon as the first gentleman who was to receive a loan. He was exchanged early in November, and carried with him about $2000 in gold to Governor Clinton, for the use of the country; and a simple receipt given for the money.

I was in New York (says General Johnson) on the 25th of November, 1783 (the day of the evacuation of the city) and at the Provost, or city prison, about ten o'clock in the morning, when an American guard relieved the British guard at that place. The latter joined a detachment of British troops, then on parade in Broadway, which wheeled on the right, into platoons, and marched down Broadway to the Battery, where they embarked in boats, and went on board of the shipping lying at anchor in the North River.

About eleven o'clock I saw General Washington and suite, at the head of a detachment of American troops, march down Pearl Street to the Battery; on their arrival they expected to set the American stripes on the flag-staff, but they found the halyards unrove, and the staff slushed. The departing salute was fired; and, before the last gun, the American flag waved in the wind at the top of the staff, over the heads of freemen — an American sailor having managed to climb the staff with an halyard, which he rove and descended; when the colors were hoisted to the tree top amid the huzzas of thousands of spectators. The sailor received his hat crown half full of silver pieces for the service; while this last act of the British caused feelings of unmingled disgust in all who were present.

BATTLE OF BROOKLYN OR LONG ISLAND.

August, 1776.

This battle was the first of a series of disasters to the American arms under Washington, which continued throughout the campaign, until the battles of Trenton and Princeton closed the conflicts of the succeeding winter.

After the evacuation of Boston, in the spring of 1776, by the British troops. New York was considered by the home government as the next place of attack — a city where the whole invading force could be concentrated at once — whose bay would allow the whole navy of England to ride in comparative security. A division of the invading army, proceeding from Canada under Burgoyne (then already in preparation), was to unite with another division from the city of New York ascending the Hudson, and thus divide the northern and New England states, as well as separate in a measure the southern colonies from the confederacy.

This plan had been arranged by Lord George Germaine, in council, at Whitehall. It was well arranged and well devised; but it was far more grand in theory than it proved to be in practice. Still it was evident that they had made an extraordinary effort, in hopes of terminating the war at a single blow. New York being situated near the center of the colonial sea-board, and readily accessible from the ocean, was selected by the enemy as a principal point, and the most advantageous position, for their future operations. In the month of June, 1776, the first division of the invading army destined to attack New York arrived at Staten Island. In July arrived also another portion of the grand armament under Lord Howe, consisting of eight ships of the line, over thirty frigates, and between one and two hundred troop and victualling transports. Never before nor since was congregated so vast a fleet of ships of war in the harbor of New York. Think of it now, reader; after the arrival of Commodore Hotham, to add to the fleet of Lord Howe, there were in our bay and its immediate vicinity a dozen ships of the line, something like forty frigates and sloops of war, and about three hundred vessels laden with troops and the necessary provisions, all to accommodate twenty-four thousand English, Hessians and Waldeckers, in their attack upon the city of New York! Sometime in August, say near the middle, the first detachment of the royal army landed at Gravesend and New Utrecht. Being well received by the inhabitants, a large proportion of whom had remained firm to the royal cause, a few days later the main body landed from the ships, and the English standard floated in triumph over a portion of Long Island.

Several regiments of Hessian infantry were expected to arrive shortly, when the army would be swelled to the number of 35,000 combatants of the best troops of Europe, all abundantly supplied with arms and ammunition, and manifesting an extreme ardor for the service of their king. The plan was first to get possession of New York, which was deemed of most essential importance. Then if General Carleton, after having passed the lakes of

Canada, could penetrate to the banks of the Hudson, and descend the river, at the same time that General Howe should ascend it, their junction would have the immediate effect of interrupting all communication between the provinces of New England on the left bank, and those of the middle and south upon the right. While General Howe was seconded in his invasion of New York by the twelve or thirteen thousand men coming from Canada under Governor Carleton, General Clinton was to operate in the provinces of the south and to attack Charleston. The American troops being thus divided, and their generals surprised, and pressed on so many sides at once, it was not doubted but that the British arms would soon obtain a complete triumph. But in executing this design they had counted too much on an admirable concurrence of a great number of parts, and had not taken into account the difficulties of the winds and the seasons. Admiral Howe did not arrive until after Clinton's expedition of Charleston had totally miscarried. The army of Canada was entirely interrupted at the lakes. It was still, however, confidently expected that General Howe would be able to make a decisive campaign. To resist this Impending storm. Congress had ordained the construction of rafts, gunboats, galleys and floating batteries, for the defense of the port of New York and the mouth of the Hudson. They had also decreed that 13,000 of the provincial militia should join the army of Washington, who, being seasonably apprised of the danger of New York, had made a movement into that quarter; they also directed the organization of a corps of 10,000 men, destined to serve as a reserve in the provinces of the center. All the weakest posts had been carefully entrenched and furnished with artillery. A strong detachment occupied Long Island to prevent the English from landing there, or to repulse them if they should effect a debarkation. But the army of Congress was very far from having the necessary means to support the burden of so terrible a war. It wanted arms, and it was wasted by disease. The reiterated instances of the commander-in-chief had drawn into his camp the militia of the neighboring provinces, and some regular regiments from Maryland, Pennsylvania, and New England, which had swelled his army to the number of 27,000 men; but a fourth of these troops was composed of invalids, and scarcely was another fourth furnished with arms. The American army, such as it was, occupied the positions most suitable to cover the menaced points. The corps which had been stationed on Long Island was commanded by Major General Greene, who, in consequence of sickness, was afterwards succeeded by General Putnam. The main body of the army encamped on the island of New York, which, it appeared, was destined to receive the first blows of the English.

The Americans, anticipating the probable invasion of Long Island, had fortified Brooklyn before the arrival of the British at Staten Island. A line of entrenchment was formed from a ditch near the late Toll House of the Bridge Company at the Navy Yard, to Fort Green, then called Fort Putnam, and from thence to Freek's mill pond. A strong work was erected on the lands of Johannis Debevoise and of Van Brunt; a redoubt was thrown up on Boerum's Hill, opposite Brower's mill, and another on the land of John Johnson, west of Fort Green. Ponkiesberg, since called Fort Swift (near the railroad tunnel), was fortified and a fort built upon the land of Mr. Hicks on Brooklyn Heights.

" We append herewith a letter from General Jeremiah Johnson, Brooklyn's well known historian to the Long Island Star, regarding the fortifications of the Americans before the battle, and of the British afterwards."

Editor.

" Mr. Editor: — The writer deems it proper to place before his fellow-citizens a brief sketch of the works of defense constructed by the Americans, for the defense of Brooklyn, in the year 1776, and also the works of defense constructed by the British, in the years 1781 and 1782.

" In the year 1775 the hill now called Fort Green belonged to John Cowenhoven, Senior, to his son, Rem Cowenhoven, and to Casper Wooster. The place was then woodland, and named Cowenhoven's woods.

" In May, 1776, the Americans determined to fortify Brooklyn, when the woodland on the hill was cut down, and a fort was built on the hill, which was named Fort Putnam. An entrenchment was dug from the ditch, where the tannery now is, to Fort Putnam. From the westerly side of the fort an entrenchment was dug across the old Jamaica Road to the mill pond of Adolphus Brower. About midway between Fort Putnam and the Jamaica Road, and joining the entrenchment, a redoubt was built on the land of John Johnson. A fort was constructed on the land of Johannis Debevoise and Rutger Van Brunt, between the Jamaica Road and Brower's mill pond. This fort was named Fort Green. A small redoubt was built on the land of Nicholas Boerum opposite to Brower's mill-dam. A small fort was built on Cobble Hill, and a fort was constructed on the west side of the ferry, along the margin of the hill, upon the land of Jacob Hicks and others. This fort was named Fort Sterling. Such were the American works of defense in Brooklyn, on the 27th day of August, 1776.

" The first ground broken by the British in Brooklyn was done on the night of the 28th of August, 1776, upon the land of George Debevoise, on the highest part of his land, where an entrenchment was made on the night aforesaid, and in the morning a firing from two field pieces was opened upon Fort Putnam, but no man was injured by the guns. The ruins of this entrenchment remained unlevelled fifteen years ago.

"After the 30th of August, 1776, the British had peaceable possession of Brooklyn; and in the months of October and November following, the American lines were demolished.

" In the year 1781 the fortune of the war had changed, and the British commenced to fortify the hill now named Fort Green; and in November,

1782, a very strong fortress was finished on said hill. This British Fort was rebuilt in the years 1813 and 1814, and then named Fort Green.

"In the years 1781-2, the British also built a large strong fortress on the Heights, where Fort Sterling had been; and in the spring and summer of the year 1782 a strong line of entrenchment was made from the hill of Rem A. Remsen, along the high land of John Rapelje, crossing the present line of Sands street, near Jay street, and thence over the highest land at Washington street to the Jamaica road, and across the same to the large fort upon the Heights.

" Such were the British works of defense in Brooklyn, on the 25th day of November, 1783.

" Jeremiah Johnson."

July 5, 1847.

In addition to the defenses of Brooklyn in 1776 a *chevaux de frise* was sunk in the main channel of the river below New York. The troops of both divisions of the British army were landed on Staten Island after their arrival in the bay, to recruit their strength and prepare for the coming conflict. It was not till the 226. of August that a landing on Long Island was made by them at New Utrecht. Here they were joined by many royalists from the neighborhood, who probably acted the infamous part of informers and guides to the enemy.

Two feeble detachments guarded Governor's Island and the point of Paulus Hook. The militia of the province, commanded by the American general, Clinton, were posted upon the banks of the Sound, where they occupied the two Chesters, East and West, and New Rochelle. For it was to be feared that the enemy, landing in force upon the north shore of the Sound, might penetrate to Kingsbridge, and thus entirely lock up all the American troops on the island of New York. Lord Howe made some overtures of peace upon terms of submission to the royal clemency, which, resulting in nothing, decided the British general to attack Long Island. " Accordingly," says Botta, " on the twenty-second of August, the fleet approached the Narrows; all the troops found an easy and secure landing place between the villages of Gravesend and New Utrecht, where they debarked without meeting any resistance on the part of the Americans. A great part of the American army, under the command of General Putnam, encamped at Brooklyn in a part of the island Itself which forms a sort of peninsula. He had strongly fortified the entrance of it with moats and entrenchments; his left wing rested upon the Wallabout Bay, and his right was covered by a marsh contiguous to Gowanus Cove. Behind him he had Governor's Island, and the arm of the sea which separates Long Island from the Island of New York, and which gave him a direct communication with the city, where the other part of the army was stationed under Washington himself. The commander-in-chief, perceiving the battle was approaching, continually exhorted his men to keep their ranks, and summon all their courage; he reminded them that in their valor rested the only hope that remained to American liberty; that upon their resistance depended the preservation or the pillage of their property by barbarians; that they were about to combat in defense of their parents, their wives, and their children, from the outrages of a licentious soldiery; that the eyes of America were fixed upon her champions, and expected, from their success on this day, either safety or total destruction."

The English, having effected their landing, marched rapidly forward. The two armies were separated by a chain of hills, covered with woods, called the heights, and which, running from west to east, divide the island into two parts. They are only practicable upon three points; one of which is near the Narrows, the road leading to that of the center passes the village of Flatbush, and the third is approached, far to the right, by the route of another village called Flatlands. Upon the summit of the hills is found a road, which follows the length of the range, and leads from Bedford to Jamaica, which is intersected by the road last described; these ways are all interrupted by precipices, and by excessively difficult and narrow defiles.

The American general, wishing to arrest the enemy upon these heights, had carefully furnished them with troops; so that, if all had done their duty, the English would not have been able to force the passages without extreme difficulty and danger. The posts were so frequent upon the road from Bedford to Jamaica, that it was easy to transmit, from one of these points to the other, the most prompt intelligence of what passed upon the three routes.

It now becomes necessary to state the position of the American troops on the evening preceding, and the morning of the disastrous battle of Long Island — the most disastrous of all to the Americans during the whole revolution, except that of Camden, in South Carolina, where Gates was defeated.

Dusk had fallen on the evening of the 26th of August, 1776. The outposts of the American army extended southerly along Brooklyn Heights, beyond Gowanus Bay; and easterly to the Wallabout, or Walleboght, where now lies the Navy Yard. A range of fortifications had been thrown up across this peninsula, behind which, their rear protected by the East River, lay some ten or fifteen thousand troops under the command of General Putnam.

Along Gowanus Heights lay two or three regiments of Maryland and Delaware riflemen and Pennsylvanian musketeers, to guard against the approach of the enemy over the heights. Alas! had the result of the day's battle which succeeded their taking this position depended upon them, no retreat would have been necessary; but it was not to rest upon them, severely as they were handled by the enemy.

The Jamaica road, leading into Brooklyn, as it led in a measure through the defiles, was the most Important of all passes. Strange as it may seem, it was not guarded, as it should have been, on the night of the 26th August. A great deal of blame has been attached to different officers for the proceedings of that night; but a close examination of the subject shows that it was the fault chiefly of the subaltern in command that night, in not guarding the Jamaica and Flatbush roads. Colonel Miles, with his battalion, was to guard the road of Flatlands, and to scour it continually with his scouts, as well as that of Jamaica, in order to reconnoiter the movements of the enemy. Meanwhile the British army pressed forward, its left wing being to the north and its right to the south; the village of Flatbush was found in its center. The Hessians, commanded by General Heister, formed the main body; the English, under Major General Grant, the left; and other corps, conducted by General Clinton and the two lords, Percy and Cornwallis, composed the right. In this wing the British generals had placed their principal hope of success; they directed it upon Flatlands. Their plan was that while the corps of General Grant and the Hessians of General Heister should disquiet the enemy upon the first two defiles, the left wing, taking a circuit, should march through Flatlands, and endeavor to seize the point of intersection of this road with that of Jamaica; and then rapidly descending into the plain which extends at the foot of the heights upon the other side, should fall upon the Americans in flank and rear. The English hoped that, as this post was most distant from the center of the army, the advanced guard would be found more feeble there, and perhaps more negligent; finally, they calculated that, in all events, the Americans would not be able to defend it against a force so superior. This right wing of the English was the most numerous, and entirely composed of select troops.

On the evening of the 26th of August, General Clinton commanded the vanguard, which consisted of light infantry; Lord Percy the center, where were found the grenadiers, the artillery, and the cavalry; and Cornwallis the rear-guard, followed by the baggage, some regiments of infantry and of heavy artillery; all this part of the English army put itself in motion with admirable order and silence, and leaving Flatlands traversed the country called New Lots. Colonel Miles, who this night performed his service with little exactness, did not perceive the approach of the enemy; so that two hours before day the English were already within a half mile of the road to Jamaica, upon the heights. Then General Clinton halted, and prepared himself for the attack. He had met one of the enemy's patrols, and made him prisoner. General Sullivan, who commanded all the troops in advance of the camp of Brooklyn, had no advice of what passed in this quarter. He neglected to send out fresh scouts; perhaps he supposed the English would direct their principal efforts against his right wing, as being the nearest to them.

General Clinton, learning from his prisoners that the road to Jamaica was not guarded, hastened to avail himself of the circumstance, and occupied it by a rapid movement. Without loss of time he immediately bore to his left towards Bedford, and seized an important defile, which the American generals had left unguarded. From this moment the success of the day was decided in favor of the English. Lord Percy came up with his corps, and the entire column descended by the village of Bedford from the heights into the plain, which lay between the hills and the camp of the Americans. During this time General Grant, in order to amuse the enemy, and divert his attention from the events which took place upon the route of Flatlands, endeavored to disquiet him upon his right; accordingly, as if he intended to force the defile which led to it, he had put himself in motion about midnight, and had attacked the militia of New York and of Pennsylvania, who guarded it. They at first gave ground; but General Parsons being arrived, and having occupied an eminence, he renewed the combat, and maintained his position till Brigadier General Lord Stirling came to his assistance with fifteen hundred men. The action became extremely animated, and fortune favored neither the one side nor the other. The Hessians, on their part, had attacked the center at break of day; and the Americans, commanded by General Sullivan in person, valiantly sustained their efforts. At the same time the English ships, after having made several movements, opened a very brisk cannonade against a battery established in the little island of Red Hook, upon the right flank of the Americans who combated against General Grant. This also was a diversion, the object of which was to prevent them from attending to what passed in the center, and on the left. The Americans defended themselves, however, with extreme gallantry, ignorant that so much valor was exerted in vain, since victory was already in the hands of the enemy. General Clinton, being descended into the plain, fell upon the left flank of the center, which was engaged with the Hessians. He had previously detached a small corps, in order to intercept the Americans.

As soon as the appearance of the English light infantry apprized them of their danger, they sounded the retreat, and retired in good order towards their camp, bringing off their artillery. But they soon fell in with the party of the royal troops which had occupied the ground in their rear, and who now charged them with, fury; they were compelled to throw themselves into the neighboring woods, where they met again with the Hessians, who repulsed them upon the English; and thus the Americans were driven several times by the one against the other with great loss. They continued for some time in this desperate situation, till at length several regiments, animated by an heroic valor, opened their way through the midst of the enemy, and gained the camp of General Putnam; others escaped through the woods. The inequality of the ground, the great number of positions which it offered, and the disorder which prevailed throughout the line were the cause that for several hours divers partial combats were maintained, in which many of the Americans fell.

Their left wing and center being discomfited, the English, desirous of a complete victory, made a rapid movement against the rear of the right wing, which, in ignorance of the misfortune which had befallen the other corps, was engaged with General Grant. Finally, having received the intelligence, they retired. But, encountering the English, who cut off their retreat, a part of the soldiers took shelter in the woods; others endeavored to make their way through the marshes of Gowanus Cove; but here many were drowned in the waters or perished in the mud; a very small number only escaped the hot pursuit of the victors, and reached the camp in safety. The total loss of the Americans, in this battle, was estimated at more than three thousand men, in killed, wounded, and prisoners. Among the last were found General Sullivan and Brigadier General Lord Stirling. Almost the entire regiment of Maryland, consisting of young men of the best families in that province, was cut to pieces. Six pieces of cannon fell into the power of the victors. The loss of the English was very inconsiderable; in killed, wounded, and prisoners, it did not amount to four hundred men.

The enemy encamped in front of the American lines; and on the succeeding night broke ground within six hundred yards of a redoubt on the left, threw up a breastwork on the Wallabout heights, upon the Debevoise farm, commenced firing on Fort Putnam, and reconnoitered the American forces. The Americans were here prepared to receive them; and orders issued to the men to reserve their fire till they could see the eyes of the enemy. A few of the British officers reconnoitered the position, and one, on coming too near, was shot by William Van Cott of Bushwick. (Captain Rutgers, brother of the late Colonel Rutgers, fell, August 26.) Several other British troops were killed and the column, which had incautiously advanced, fell back beyond the range of the American fire. In this critical state of the American army on Long Island — in front, a numerous and victorious enemy, with a formidable train of artillery; the fleet indicating an intention of forcing a passage up the East River; the troops lying without shelter from heavy rains, fatigued and dispirited — General Washington determined to withdraw the army from the Island. This difficult movement was effected with great skill and judgment, and with complete success. The retreat was to have commenced at eight o'clock. In the evening of the 29th; but a strong north-east wind and a rapid tide caused a delay of several hours; a south-west wind springing up at eleven, essentially facilitated the passage from the Island to the city; and a thick fog hanging over Long Island toward morning concealed all movements from the enemy, who were so near that the sound of their pick-axes and shovels was distinctly heard by the Americans. General Washington, as far as possible, inspected everything; from the commencement of the action on the morning of the 27th till the troops were safely across the river he never closed his eyes and was almost constantly on horseback.

Within the American lines at Brooklyn, during the Revolution, lived John Rapelje; who, being suspected of disaffection to the American cause, had been sent by the whigs to the interior of Connecticut. His wife remained in possession of the house, and probably felt more hostile to the party who had deprived her of her husband, than she would have done had he been permitted to remain at home. The house was near the shore whence General Washington embarked in his memorable retreat from Long Island, in August, 1776. She obtained early knowledge of this movement the night it took place, and herself saw the first detachment push off. Thinking it a good opportunity to be revenged upon those who, she believed, had deeply injured her family, she resolved to inform the British of what was taking place among their enemies. She had no one to send, however, with the information, but a black servant; and accordingly dispatched him, with orders to communicate the intelligence to the first British officer he could find. The black succeeded in passing the American sentinels, and made his way to the neighboring camp; but, unluckily for the success of his mission, came to a part of the encampment where the Germans were stationed, and was stopped by a soldier who did not understand English, and to whom, consequently, he could not communicate the message. He was committed, therefore, to the guard, as a suspicious person, and kept until morning; when an officer, visiting the post, examined him, and was informed of what had taken place during the night. The alarm was immediately given, but it was too late — Washington and his troops were all safely landed on the opposite shore.

After this, the British and their allies, the tories and refugees, had possession of Long Island; and many distressing scenes occurred, which were never made public, and can therefore never be known. The whigs who had been at all active in behalf of independence, were exiled from their homes, and their dwellings were objects of indiscriminate plunder. Such as could be taken were incarcerated in the churches of New Utrecht and Flatlands; while royalists, by wearing a red badge in their hats, were protected and encouraged. It is believed that had Lord Howe availed himself of the advantage he possessed by passing his ships up the river between Brooklyn and New York, the whole American army must have been almost inevitably captured or annihilated. General Washington saw but too plainly the policy which might have been pursued, and wisely resolved rather to abandon the island, than attempt to retain it at the risk of sacrificing his army.

The unfortunate issue of the battle of Long Island is doubtless to be ascribed, in part, to the illness of General Greene. He had superintended the erection of the works, and become thoroughly acquainted with the ground. In the hope of his recovery, Washington deferred sending over a successor till the urgency of affairs made it absolutely necessary; and then General Putnam took the command, without any previous knowledge of the posts which had been fortified beyond the lines, or of the places by which the enemy could make their approach; nor had he time to acquire this knowledge before the action. The consequence was, that, although he was the commander on the day of the battle, he never went beyond the lines at

Brooklyn; and could give no other orders than for sending out troops to meet the enemy at different points. The following is a letter to Congress, describing the events of the day, by Colonel Harrison, secretary to the commander-in-chief.

" New York, 8 o'clock P. M. 27 Aug. 1776.

" Sir: — I this minute returned from our lines on Long Island, where I left his excellency the General. From him I have it in command to inform Congress, that yesterday he went there, and continued till evening, when, from the enemy's having landed a considerable part of their forces, and from many of their movements, there was reason to apprehend they would make in a little time a general attack. As they would have a wood to pass through, before they could approach the lines, it was thought expedient to place a number of men there, on the different roads leading from where they were stationed, in order to harass and annoy them in their march. This being done, early this morning a smart engagement ensued between the enemy and our detachments, which, being unequal to the force they had to contend with, have sustained a considerable loss; at least many of our men are missing. Among those that have not returned are General Sullivan and Lord Stirling. The enemy's loss is not known certainly; but we are told by such of our troops as were in the engagement, and have come in, that they had many killed and wounded. Our party brought off a lieutenant, sergeant, and corporal, with twenty privates, prisoners.

" While these detachments were engaged, a column of the enemy descended from the woods, and marched towards the center of our lines with a design to make an impression, but were repulsed. This evening they appeared very numerous about the skirts of the woods, where they have pitched several tents; and his excellency inclines to think they mean to attack, and force us from our lines by way of regular approaches, rather than in any other manner. To-day five ships of the line came up towards the town, where they seemed desirous of getting, as they tried a long time against an unfavorable wind; and, on my return this evening, I found a deserter from the twenty-third regiment, who informed me that they design, as soon as the wind will permit them to come up, to give us a severe cannonade, and to silence our batteries if possible. I have the honor to be, in great haste. Sir, your most obedient.

" Robert H. Harrison."

As the two generals, who commanded in the engagement, were taken prisoners, no detailed official account of the action was reported to the commander-in-chief. The following letter from Lord Stirling, and extracts from General Sullivan's, contain a few particulars not hitherto published. Lord Stirling was a prisoner on board Lord Howe's ship when he wrote.

Lord Stirling to General Washington

"Eagle, 29 August, 1776. " My Dear General: — I have now an opportunity of informing you of what has happened to me since I had the pleasure of seeing you. About three o'clock in the morning of the 27th, I was called up, and informed by General Putnam that the enemy were advancing by the road from Flatbush to the Red Lion, and he ordered me to march with two regiments nearest at hand to meet them. These happened to be Haslet's and Smallwood's, with which I accordingly marched, and was on the road to the Narrows just as the daylight began to appear. We proceeded to within about half a mile of the Red Lion, and there met Colonel Atlee with his regiment, who informed me that the enemy were in sight; indeed, I then saw their front between us and the Red Lion, I desired Colonel Atlee to place his regiment on the left of the road, and to wait their coming up; while I went to form the two regiments I had brought with me, along a ridge from the road up to a piece of wood on the top of the hill. This was done instantly on very advantageous ground.

" Our opponents advanced, and were fired upon in the road by Atlee's regiment, who, after two or three rounds, retreated to the wood on my left, and there formed. By this time Kichline's riflemen arrived; part of them I placed along a hedge under the front of the hill, and the rest in the front of the wood. The troops opposed to me were two brigades of four regiments each, under the command of General Grant; who advanced their light troops to within one hundred and fifty yards of our right front, and took possession of an orchard there, and some hedges, which extended towards our left. This brought on an exchange of fire between those troops and our riflemen, which continued for about two hours, and then ceased by those light troops retiring to their main body. In the meantime Captain Carpenter brought up two field pieces, which were placed on the side of the hill, so as to command the road, and the only approach for some hundred yards. On the part of General Grant there were two field pieces. One howitzer advanced to within three hundred yards of the front of our right, and a like detachment of artillery to the front of our left. On a rising ground, at about six hundred yards' distance, one of their brigades formed in two lines opposite to our right, and the other extended in one line to the top of the hills, in the front of our left.

" In this position we stood, cannonading each other till near 11 o'clock; when I found that General Howe, with the main body of the army, was between me and our lines; and I saw that the only chance of escaping being all made prisoners, was, to pass the creek near the Yellow Mills; and, in order to render this the more practicable, I found it absolutely necessary to attack the body of troops commanded by Lord Cornwallis, posted at the house near the Upper Mills. This I instantly did, with about half of Smallwood's regiment; first ordering all other troops to make the best of their way through the creek. We continued the attack for a considerable time, the men having been rallied, and the attack renewed, five or six several times; and we were on the point of driving Lord Cornwallis from his station; but large reinforcements arriving, rendered it Impossible to do more than provide for safety. I endeavored to get in between that house and Fort Box; but, on attempting it, I found a considerable body of troops in my front, and several in pursuit of me on the right and left, and a constant firing on me. I Immediately turned the point of a hill, which covered me from their fire, and was soon out of the reach of my pursuers. I found that it would be in vain to attempt to make my escape, and therefore went to surrender myself to General de Heister, commander-in-chief of the Hessians. Wm. Stirling."

General Sullivan to the President of Congress

" Whitemarsh, N. J., 25 October, 1777. " I know it has been generally reported that I commanded on Long Island when action happened there. This is by no means true. General Putnam had taken the command from me four days before the action. Lord Stirling commanded the main body within the lines. I was to have commanded under General Putnam within the lines. I was uneasy about a road, through which I had often foretold that the enemy would come, but could not persuade others to be of my opinion. I went to the hill near Flatbush to reconnoiter, and with a picket of four hundred men was surrounded by the enemy, who had advanced by the very road I had foretold, and which I had paid horsemen fifty dollars for patrolling by night, while I had the command, as I had no foot for the purpose.

" What resistance I made with these four hundred men against the British army, I leave to the officers who were with me to declare. Let it suffice for me to say, that the opposition of the small party lasted from half past nine to twelve o'clock.

" The reason of so few troops being on Long Island, was because it was generally supposed that the enemy's landing there was a feint, to draw our troops thither, that they might the more easily possess themselves of New York. I often urged, both by word and writing, that, as the enemy had doubtless both these objects in view, they would first try for Long Island, which commanded the other; and then New York, which was completely commanded by it, would fall of course. But in this I was unhappy enough to differ from almost every officer in the army till the event proved my conjectures were just. John Sullivan."

The following extract of a letter from General Wm. Smallwood, afterwards governor of Maryland, to the Hon. Matthew Tilghman, president of the convention of that state, contains some particulars not noticed in the preceding account of the battle of Long Island.

"Headquarters, October 12, 1778. " Sir: — Through your hands I must beg leave to address the honorable convention of Maryland, and confess, not without an apprehension that I have incurred their displeasure for having omitted writing when on our march from Maryland for New York, and since our arrival here; nor shall I in a pointed manner urge anything in my defense, but leave them at large, to condemn or excuse me, upon a presumption, that should they condemn, they will at least pardon, and judge me perhaps less culpable, when they reflect in the first instance, on the exertions necessary to procure baggage wagons, provisions and house room for 750 men, marched the whole distance, in a body, generally from 15 to 20 miles per day, as the several stages made.it necessary; and in the latter, I trust they will give some indulgence for this neglect, for since our arrival at New York, it had been the fate of this corps, to be generally stationed at advanced posts, and to act as a covering party, which must unavoidably expose troops to extraordinary duty and hazard, not to mention the extraordinary vigilance and attention, in the commandant of such a party, in disposing in the best manner, and having it regularly supplied; for here the commanders of regiments, exclusive of their military duty, are often obliged to exert themselves in the departments of commissary, and quartermaster general, and even directors of their regimental hospitals.

" Perhaps it may not be improper to give a short detail of occurrences upon our march to Long Island and since that period.

"The enemy from the 21st to the 27th of August, were landing their troops on the lower part of Long Island, where they pitched a large encampment, and our, and their advanced parties were daily skirmishing at long shot, in which neither party suffered much. On the 26th the Maryland and Delaware troops, which composed part of Lord Stirling's brigade were ordered over. Colonel Haslet and his Lieutenant Colonel Hare, and myself, were detained on the trial of Lieutenant Colonel Zedwitz, and though I waited on General Washington, and urged the necessity of attending our troops, yet he refused to discharge us, alleging there was a necessity for the trials coming on, and that no other field officers could be then had.

" After our dismission from the court martial, it was too late to get over, but pushing over early the next morning, found our regiments engaged, Lord Stirling having marched them off before day, to take possession of the woods and difficult passes, between our lines and the enemy's encampment, but the enemy overnight had stole a march on our generals, having got through those passes, met and surrounded our troops on the plain grounds, within two miles of our lines. Lord Stirling drew up his brigade on an advantageous rising ground, where he was attacked by two brigades in front, headed by the Generals Cornwallis and Grant, and in his rear the enemy's main body stood ready drawn up to support their own parties, and intercept the retreat of ours; this excellent disposition and their superior numbers ought to have taught our generals, there was no time to be lost, in securing their retreat; which might at first have been effected, had the troops formed into a heavy column and pushed their retreat; but the longer this was delayed, it became the more dangerous, as they were then landing more troops in front of the ships. Our brigade kept their ground for several hours, and in general behaved well,

213

having received some heavy fires from the artillery and musketry of the enemy, whom they repulsed several times, but their attacks were neither so lasting or vigorous, as was expected, owing as it was imagined to their being certain of making the whole brigade prisoners of war; for by this time, they had so secured the passes on the way to our lines (seeing our parties were not supported from thence, which indeed our numbers would not admit of) that there was no possibility of retreating that way. Between the place of action and our lines there lay a large marsh, and deep creek, not above 80 yards across at the mouth, toward the head of which there was a mill and bridge, across which a certain Colonel Ward from New England, who is charged with having acted a bashful part that day, passed over with his regiment, and then burnt them down, tho' under cover of our cannon, which would have checked the enemy's pursuit at any time, otherwise this bridge might have afforded a secure retreat; there then remained no other prospect but to surrender or attempt to retreat over this marsh and creek at the mouth, where no person had ever been known to cross. In the interim I applied to General Washington for some regiments to march out to support and cover their retreat, which he urged would be attended with too great risk to the party of the lines; he immediately sent for and ordered me to march down a New England regiment, and Captain Thomas' company, which had just come over from York, to the mouth of the creek, opposite where the brigade was drawn up, and ordered two field pieces down, to support and cover their retreat, should they make a push that way. Soon after our march, they began to retreat, and for a small time the fire was very heavy on both sides, till our troops came to the marsh, where they were obliged to break their order and escape as quick as they could to the edge of the creek, under a brisk fire, notwithstanding which they brought off 28 prisoners.

" The enemy taking advantage of a commanding ground, kept up a continual fire from four field pieces, which were well served and directed, and a heavy column advancing on the marsh, must have cut our people off, their guns being wet and muddy, not one of them could have fired; but having drawn up the musketry and disposed of some riflemen conveniently, ordered to fire on them when they came within shot; however the latter began their fire too soon, being at 200 yards distance, which notwithstanding had the desired effect, for the enemy Immediately retreated to the fast land, where they continued parading within 600 yards, till our troops were brought over; most of those who swam over, and others who attempted to cross before the covering party got down, lost their arms and accoutrements in the mud and creek, and some fellows their lives, particularly two of the Delaware, one of Astley's Pennsylvania, and two Hessian prisoners were drowned.

" Thomas' men contributed much in bringing over this party — have enclosed a list of the killed and missing, amounting to 256, officers Included. It has been said the enemy during the action also attacked our lines, but this was a mistake; not knowing the ground, one of their columns advanced within long shot, without knowing they were so near, and upon our artillery and part of the musketry's firing on them, they retreated.

"The 28th, during a very hard rain, there was an alarm that the enemy had advanced to attack our lines, which alarmed the troops much, but was without foundation. The 29th, it was found by a council of war that our fortifications were not tenable, and it was therefore judged expedient that the army should retreat from the island that night; to effect which, notwithstanding the Maryland troops had had but one day's respite, and many other troops had been many days clear of any detail duty, they were ordered on the advanced part of Fort Putnam, within 250 yards of the enemy's approaches and, joined with two Pennsylvania regiments on the left, were to remain and cover the retreat of the army, which was happily completed under cover of a thick fog and a southwest wind, both which favored our retreat, otherwise the fear, disorder and confusion of some of the eastern troops, must have retarded and discovered our retreat and subjected numbers to be cut off.

" After remaining two days in New York, our next station was at Harlem, nine miles above, at an advanced post opposite to Montresor's and Bahama's Islands, which in a few days the enemy got possession of without opposition, from the former of which we dally discoursed with them, being within 200 yards and only a small creek between.

" I am very respectfully, your obt. and very humble servant, W. Smallwood."

The following additional facts in relation to the retreat of the American army to New York, will close our account of this memorable engagement, of the 27th August, 1776:

" On the morning of the 29th of August, 1776, a council of officers was held at the quarters of Washington, in the city of New York. Those assembled to take part in the deliberations, introduced by the commander-in-chief, were Putnam, Parsons, Mifflin, McDougal, Spencer, Scott, Wadsworth, and Fellows. It was decided that there was no way of preserving the army then within the lines at Brooklyn, but by bringing them off. To attempt this was a most dangerous and hazardous experiment. The East River, at its narrowest part, was near half a mile wide, and the enemies' vessels of war lay both above and below the places of embarkation; while within a hundred yards of the entrenchments on Long Island, a victorious army, supplied with every facility and means of attack, had broke ground, preparatory to storming the earthen ramparts which protected the Americans.

" Near ten thousand troops were, in the face of all these difficulties, to be taken over this river, with all their ammunition and stores, or else in a few days they would be forced into a surrender. Let the reader think for a few moments calmly over this matter, as if it were to happen even at this day.

Suppose that ten thousand American militia were pent up in Brooklyn, and behind them an overwhelming force, separated only by a few earthen redoubts, armed with everything needful for attack: beyond Corlaer's Hook lay several frigates and vessels of war, and below Governor's Island a number of still heavier ships belonging to the same enemy: no steamboats, no ferryboats crossing, and on the New York side only a few scows and sloops, Instead of the endless shipping you now see lying in the East River! Would it not seem a desperate undertaking to bring over ten thousand men in the face of such difficulties? Yet it was done in 1776 by Washington — done when the thing looked still drearier than we have supposed. If Washington had performed nothing else during the revolution but accomplishing this feat, it would have ranked him among the great military commanders of the age.

" Washington, in this masterly retreat, concealed his movements and intentions completely. It was given in evidence before a committee of the House of Lords after Burgoyne's defeat, that the American leaders always concealed their real movements, whilst in the British camp it seemed as if the proceedings of their council of officers were known as soon as they had dissolved. Not an officer in the lines, except the general officers, had the least idea that a retreat was intended; but all expected that a defense was to be made, which, placed in the most favorable point of view, was doubtful as to its security.

" Throughout the 28th and 29th the weather was bad in the extreme, and rained heavily. On the 29th, all the boats, scows and vessels of every kind and nature that were capable of crossing the East River, were collected on the New York side as privately as possible. Boats were drawn on rollers, in many instances from the North to the East River, to prevent observation from the men-of-war that lay in the bay below the city.

" All day during the 29th, a constant skirmishing was kept up between the two lines. The situation of the Americans was unpleasant in the extreme. They had no tents, and their rations were pickled pork and biscuit; but they had no fire to cook the former, and a two days' soaking to the best of troops is uncomfortable. Yet the brave fellows murmured not. They swallowed their daily gill of rum with a toast to ' the good cause, and better luck next battle! ' "

" It was 10 o'clock on the night of the 29th of August, 1776, that Washington himself took his station on the ferry stairs, (where now is the Fulton ferry,) to superintend the embarkation. Calm, cool, and composed, he issued his orders. The artillery and baggage were first brought down and placed on board the heavy barges, with all the stores and ammunition. This occupied several hours. Recollect, reader, it was done within gun shot of twenty thousand of the best troops in the world. Next followed the embarkation of the troops, the nearest regiments from right to left marching down to the ferry, and the troops in the lines gradually moving down to the stations occupied by the regiments embarked. The sentries were left in their

216

usual stations, to deceive the enemy, with orders not to move from their position till a certain hour, when they would all be called in, and a special boat or boats left for their embarkation.

" For two days after the battle many stragglers reached the American camp, having concealed themselves in the woods. General Parsons escaped in this way the day after the fight.

" Day broke drearily in the east, yet still several regiments remained to be embarked. Fortunately a heavy mist rose, that completely enveloped the American lines, and by seven o'clock the last boats had left the shore.

The sun broke out in full glory as the last of the troops reached New York, showing on the opposite side the foe, who had thus, by the skill and perseverance of Washington, been deprived of the capture of ten thousand men that Howe considered certain within his grasp. Heaven smiled on our cause! — Heaven was with us! "

HISTORY OF THE PRISON-SHIPS

There are no great circumstances connected with the annals of the American Revolution, so perfectly calculated to harrow up the feelings in their recollection, after the lapse of more than half a century, as those terrible scenes of affliction, to which many of the best and bravest spirits were subjected in that eventful period, and who, with virtuous desperation, sacrificed their lives in a manner most terrible and appalling, that by pestilence and starvation. Doubtless, a very small proportion of the sufferings actually experienced have ever met the light; and only a part of what is known can find a place in this work, as it would require a volume to do the subject adequate justice.

In 1776, and for six years next following, there were stationed at the Wallabout, near Brooklyn, several condemned hulks, used for the reception and confinement of American seamen taken prisoners by the British. For many of the facts in connection with this exciting subject, we are indebted to a communication made by General Jeremiah Johnson, to the editors of the Naval Magazine, for September, 1836, and to statements made to the world at different times, by individuals who had been incarcerated in those loathsome store-houses of disease and death. From journals published in New York at the close of the war, it appears that eleven thousand five hundred American prisoners had died on board the prison-ships. Although the number is very great, still, if the number who perished had been less, the commissary of naval prisoners, David Sproat, Esq., and his deputy, had it in their power, by an official return, to give the true number exchanged, escaped, and dead. Such a return has never appeared in the United States. This man returned to America after the war, and resided in Philadelphia, but died in Scotland. He could not have been ignorant of the statements published here on this interesting subject. We may therefore infer, that about that number perished in the prison-ships. A large transport, named the " Whitby," was the first prison-ship anchored in the Wallabout. She was moored near " Remsen's Mill," about the 20th of October, 1776, and was then crowded with prisoners. Many landsmen were prisoners on board this vessel; she was said to be the most sickly of all the prison-ships. Bad provisions, bad water, and scanted rations were dealt to the prisoners. No medical men attended the sick. Disease reigned unrelieved, and hundreds died from pestilence, or were starved, on board this floating prison. Indeed, the sand beach between a ravine of the hill and Mr. Remsen's dock became filled with graves in the course of two months; and before the 1st of May, 1777, the ravine alluded to was itself occupied in the same way. In the month of May of that year two large ships were anchored in the Wallabout, when the prisoners were transferred from the " Whitby " to them. These vessels were also very sickly, from the causes before stated. Although many prisoners were sent on board of them, and none exchanged, death made room for all.

On a Sunday afternoon, about the middle of October, 1777, one of the prison-ships was burned; the prisoners, except a few, who, it was said, were burned in the vessel, were removed to the remaining ship. It was reported, at the time, that the prisoners had fired their prison; which, if true, proves that they preferred death, even by fire, to the lingering sufferings of pestilence and starvation. In the month of March, 1780, the remaining prison-ship was burned at night; when the prisoners were removed from her to the ships then wintering in the Wallabout. In the month of April, 1780, the old " Jersey " was moored in the Wallabout, and all the prisoners (except the sick) were transferred to her. The sick were carried to two hospital ships, named the " Hope " and the " Falmouth," anchored near each other, about two hundred yards east from the " Jersey." These ships remained in the Wallabout until New York was evacuated by the British. The " Jersey " was the receiving ship — the others, truly, the ships of Death! it has been generally thought that all the prisoners died on board of the " Jersey." This is not true; many may have died on board of her, who were not reported as sick; but all the men who were placed on the sick list were removed to the hospital ships, from which they were usually taken, sewed up in a blanket, to their long home.

The " Jersey " was originally a British ship of the line. She was rated and registered as a sixty-four gun ship, but had usually mounted seventy-four guns. At the commencement of the American Revolution, being an old vessel, and proving to be much decayed, she was entirely dismantled, and soon after was moored in the East River, at New York, and converted into a store-ship. In the year 1780, she was fitted as a prison-ship, and was used for that purpose during the war. Fears being very naturally felt that the destructive contagion by which so many of her unfortunate inmates had been swept away,

might spread to the shore, she was, in consequence, removed, and moored, with chain cables, at the Wallabout, a solitary and unfrequented place on the shore of Long Island. She had been dismantled, and her rudder unhung. Her only spars were the bowsprit, a derrick for taking in supplies of water, &c., and a flag-staff at the stern. Her port holes had all been closed and strongly fastened, and two tier of small holes cut through her sides. These holes were about ten feet apart, each being about twenty inches square, and guarded by two strong bars of iron, crossing it at right angles; thus leaving four contracted spaces, which admitted light by day, and served as breathing holes at night.

After the hospital ships were brought into the Wallabout, it was reported that the sick were attended by physicians; few, very few, however, recovered. It was no uncommon thing to see five or six dead bodies brought on shore in a single morning; when a small excavation would be made at the foot of the hill, the bodies be cast in, and a man with a shovel would cover them by shoveling sand down the hill upon them. Many were buried in a ravine on the hill; some on the farm. The whole shore, from Rennie's Point to Mr. Remsen's dooryard, was a place of graves; as were also the slope of the hill near the house, the shore from Mr. Remsen's barn along the mill-pond to Rapelje's farm, and the sandy island, between the flood-gates and the mill dam; while a few were buried on the shore, the east side of the Wallabout. Thus did Death reign here, from 1776 until the peace. The whole Wallabout was a sickly place during the war. The atmosphere seemed to be charged with foul air, from the prison-ships, and with the effluvia of the dead bodies, washed out of their graves by the tides. We have ourselves examined many of the skulls lying on the shore; from the teeth, they appear to be the remains of men in the prime of life. A singularly daring and successful escape was effected from the " Jersey," about four o'clock one afternoon, in December, 1780. The best boat of the ship had returned from New York, and was left fastened at the gangway, with the oars on board. It was stormy; the wind blew from the north-east, and the tide ran flood. A watch-word was given, and a number of prisoners placed themselves between the ship's waist and the sentinel; at this juncture four eastern captains got on board the boat, which was cast off by their friends. The boat passed close under the bows of the ship, and was a considerable distance from her, before the sentinel on the forecastle gave the alarm and fired at her. The boat passed Hell Gate, and arrived safe in Connecticut next morning.

The Rev. Thomas Andros, late pastor of the church in Berkeley, Mass., who was himself a prisoner on board the old " Jersey," prison-ship, remarks (in The Old Jersey Captive), as follows:

" This was an old sixty-four gun ship, which, through age, had become unfit for further actual service. She was stripped of every spar and all her rigging. After a battle with a French fleet, her lion figure-head was taken away to repair another ship; no appearance of ornament was left, and nothing remained but an old, unsightly, rotten hulk. Her dark and filthy external appearance perfectly corresponded with the death and despair that reigned within, and nothing could be more foreign from truth than to paint her with colors flying, or any circumstance or appendage to please the eye. She was moored about three-quarters of a mile to the eastward of Brooklyn ferry, near a tide-mill on the Long Island shore.

The nearest distance to land was about twenty rods. And doubtless no other ship in the British navy ever proved the means of the destruction of so many human beings. It is computed that not less than eleven thousand American seamen perished in her. But after it was known that it was next to certain death to confine a prisoner here, the inhumanity and wickedness of doing it was about the same as if he had been taken into the city and deliberately shot in some public square. But as if mercy had fled from the earth, here we were doomed to dwell. And never while I was on board, did any Howard or angel of pity appear to inquire into, or alleviate our woes.

Once or twice, by the order of a stranger on the quarter deck, a bag of apples was hurled promiscuously into the midst of hundreds of prisoners crowded together, as thick as they could stand, and life and limbs were endangered by the scramble. This, instead of compassion, was a cruel sport. When I saw it about to commence, I fled to the most distant part of the ship.

" On the commencement of the first evening, we were driven down to darkness between decks, secured by iron gratings, and an armed soldiery. And a scene of horror, which baffles all description, presented itself. On every side, wretched, desponding shapes of men could be seen. Around the well-room an armed guard were forcing up the prisoners to the winches, to clear the ship of water, and prevent her sinking, and little else could be heard but a roar of mutual execrations, reproaches, and insults. During this operation there was a small dim light admitted below, but it served to make darkness more visible, and horror more terrific. In my reflections I said, this must be a complete image and anticipation of Hell. Milton's description of the dark world rushed upon my mind: —

" Sights of woe, regions of sorrow, doleful Shades, where peace and rest can never dwell."

" If there was any principle among the prisoners that could not be shaken, it was the love of their country. I knew no one to be seduced into the British service. They attempted to force one of our prize brig's crew into the navy, but he chose rather to die, than perform any duty, and was again restored to the prison ship.

" When I first became an inmate of this abode of suffering, despair, and death, there were about four hundred prisoners on board, but in a short time they amounted to twelve hundred. And in proportion to our numbers, the mortality increased.

" All the most deadly diseases were pressed into the service of the king of terrors, but his prime ministers were dysentery, small pox, and yellow fever. There were two hospital ships, ' Hunter ' and ' Scorpion,' near to the old ' Jersey,' but these were soon so crowded with the sick, that they could receive no more. The consequence was that the diseased and the healthy were mingled together in the main ship. In a short time we had two hundred or more sick and dying, lodged in the fore part of the lower gun deck, where all the prisoners were confined at night. Utter derangement was a common symptom of yellow fever, and to Increase the horror of the darkness that shrouded us (for we were allowed no light between decks) the voice of warning would be heard, ' take heed to yourselves. There is a mad man stalking through the ship with a knife in his hand.' I sometimes found the man a corpse in the morning, by whose side I laid myself down at night. At another time he would become deranged, and attempt in darkness to rise, and stumble over the bodies that everywhere covered the deck. In this case I had to hold him in his place by main strength. In spite of my efforts he would sometimes rise, and then I had to close in with him, trip up his heels, and lay him again upon the deck. While so many were sick with raging fever there was a loud cry for water, but none could be had except on the upper deck, and but one allowed to ascend at a time. The suffering then from the rage of thirst during the night was very great. Nor was it at all times safe to attempt to go up. Provoked by the continual cry for leave to ascend, when there was already one on deck, the sentry would push them back with his bayonet. By one of these thrusts, which was more spiteful and violent than common, I had a narrow escape of my life. In the morning the hatch-ways were thrown open, and we were allowed to ascend, all at once, and remain on the upper deck during the day. But the first object that met our view in the morning was an appalling spectacle. A boat loaded with dead bodies, conveying them to the Long Island shore, where they were very slightly covered with sand. I sometimes used to stand and count the number of times the shovel was filled with sand, to cover a dead body. And certain I am that a few high tides or torrents of rain, must have disinterred them. And had they not been removed, I should suppose the shore, even now, would be covered with huge piles of the bones of American seamen. There were, probably, four hundred on board, who had never had the small pox, — some, perhaps, might have been saved by inoculation.

" But humanity was wanting to try even this experiment. Let our disease be what it would, we were abandoned to our fate. Now and then an American physician was brought in as a captive, but if he could obtain his parole he left the ship. Nor could we much blame him for this; for his own death was next to certain, and his success in saving others by medicine in our situation was small. I remember only two American physicians who tarried on board a few days. No English physician, or any one from the city, ever, to my knowledge, came near us. There were thirteen of the crew to which I belonged, but in a short time all died, but three or four.

The most healthy and vigorous were first seized with the fever, and died in a few hours. For them there seemed to be no mercy. My constitution was less muscular and plethoric, and I escaped the fever longer than any of the thirteen, except one, and the first onset was less violent."

Andros was allowed to go on shore for water, and so escaped, hiding by day and travelling by night, till he reached Sag Harbor, whence he crossed to Connecticut.

Mr. John Manley, who was confined on board one of the ships, gives the following account, viz:

" During three months' confinement in the summer of 1781, and one of the ' eight hundred and fifty souls ' that it contained, half-starved for bread and famished for water, consequently drove to desperation, frequent daring attempts to escape were made. I witnessed several of them, and they generally ended tragically. They were always undertaken in the night, after wrenching or filing the bars of the port-holes (she was an old sixty-four). Having been on board several weeks, and goaded to death in various ways, four of us concluded to run the hazard. We set to work and got the bars off, and waited impatiently for a dark night; we lay in front of Mr. Remsen's door, inside of the pierhead, and not more than twenty yards distant. There were two guard sloops, one on our bow and the other off our quarter, a short distance from us. ' The dark night ' came — the first two were lowered quietly into the water — the third made some rumbling, I was the fourth that descended, but had not struck off from the vessel before the guards were alarmed, and fired upon us. The alarm became general, and I was immediately hauled on board. They manned their boats, and with their lights and implements of death, were quick in pursuit of the unfortunates, cursing and swearing, and bellowing and firing. It was awful to witness this scene of blood. It lasted about one hour — all on board trembling for our shipmates. These desperadoes returned to their different vessels, rejoicing that they killed three of the d — d rebels."

The number that perished on board these ships, is said to be more than 10,000, as the writer. Captain Thomas Dring, feelingly observes — " thousands there suffered and died, whose names have never been known to their countrymen. They died where no eye could witness their fortitude, no tongue describe their sufferings, or praise their devotion to their country."

" For years, the very name of the old ' Jersey,' seemed to strike a terror to the hearts of those whose necessities required to venture upon the ocean; the mortality which prevailed on board her was well known throughout the country; and to be confined within her dungeons, was considered equal to a sentence of death, from which but little hope of escape remained."

The first day. — After getting on board, he describes the prisoners as being a motley crew of wretches, with tattered garments and pallid visages, shrunken and decayed, who but a short time before had breathed the pure breezes of the ocean, " or danced lightly in the flower-scented air of the meadow and the hill; and had from thence been hurried into the pent-up air of a crowded prison-ship, pregnant with putrid fever, foul with deadly contagion; here to linger out the tedious and weary day, the disturbed and anxious night; to count over the days and weeks and months of a wearying and degrading captivity, unvaried but by new scenes of painful suffering, and new inflictions of remorseless cruelty; their brightest hope and their daily prayer, that death would not long delay to release them from their torments."

" During the night, in addition to my other sufferings, I had been tormented with what I supposed to be vermin; and on coming upon deck, I found that a black silk handkerchief, which I wore around my neck, was completely spotted with them. Although this had often been mentioned as one of the miseries of the place, yet as I had never before been in a situation to witness anything of the kind, the sight made me shudder; as I knew, at once, that so long as I should remain on board, these loathsome creatures would be my constant companions and unceasing tormentors.

" During my confinement in the summer of 1782, the average number of prisoners on board the ' Jersey ' was about one thousand. They were composed of the crews of all nations, with whom the English were at war — but far the greater number were Americans.

" The ' Jersey ' at length became so crowded, and the mortality on board so increased, that room could not be found on board the hospital ships for their reception."

Such was the condition and treatment of the sick, that few ever came out alive. Everything belonging to the dying and the dead was claimed by the nurses, and was generally secured at the first opportunity.

The following is extracted from a communication of Alexander Coffin, Jun., in answer to some inquiries in relation to the sufferings of the prison-ships, on board of which he was confined.

" The first time I was on board the ' Jersey,' prisonship, was in 1782. I was taken in a letter of marque from Baltimore, bound for Havana, by the king's frigate Ceres, on board of which we were treated in a most shameful and barbarous manner by her commander. From that ship we were put on board the ' Champion,' of twenty-four guns, brought into this port, and from her sent on board the ' Jersey,' prison-ship, where I found about 1,100 American prisoners; amongst them several of my own townsmen, and all the prisoners in a most deplorable situation.

" I soon found that every spark of humanity had fled the breasts of the British officers, who had charge of that floating receptacle of human misery; and that nothing but abuse and insult was to be expected; for the mildest language made use of to the prisoners was, You damn'd Yankee; and the most common, You damn'd rebellions Yankee rascals. This language at length became so familiar to our ears, however insulting it was at first, that we took no more notice of it than we did of the whistling of the wind, passing over our heads. Many of the prisoners, during the severity of winter, had scarcely clothes sufficient to cover their nakedness, and but very few enough to keep them warm: to remedy those inconveniences we were obliged to keep below, and either get into our hammocks or keep in constant motion, without which precautions we must have perished. But to cap the climax of infamy, we were fed (if fed it might be called) with provisions not fit for any human being to make use of; putrid beef and pork, and worm-eaten bread, condemned on board their ships of war, were sent on board the 'Jersey' to feed the prisoners; water sent from this city in a schooner called (emphatically) the ' Relief '! — water, which I affirm, without the fear of refutation, was worse than I ever had, or ever saw, on a three years' voyage to the East Indies; water, the scent of which would have discomposed the olfactory nerves of a Hottentot; while within a cable's length of the ship, on

Long Island, there was running before our eyes, as though intended to tantalize us, as fine, pure, and wholesome water as any man would wish to drink. The question will be very naturally asked, why, if good water was so near at hand, it was not procured for us instead of bringing it at considerable expense and trouble from the city? it is impossible for anyone, but those who had the direction of the business, to answer that question satisfactorily; but the object in bringing the water from New York, was to me, and the rest of the prisoners, as self-evident as the plain and simple fact that two and two make four: because the effects that water had on the prisoners could not be concealed, and were a damning proof why it was filled in New York. On the upper gun deck of the ' Jersey,' hogs were kept in pens, by those officers who had charge of her, for their own use; they were sometimes fed with bran; the prisoners, whenever they could get an opportunity undiscovered by the sentries, would, with their tin pots, scoop the bran from the troughs and eat it (after boiling, when there was fire in the galley, which was not always the case) with seemingly as good an appetite as the hogs themselves.

" The second and last time I was on board the prisonship, was in February and March, 1783, just before peace took place. I was taken in a brig from Providence, R. L, off the capes of Virginia, by the ' Fair American,' privateer of this port, commanded and officered principally with refugees; though it is doing Capt. Burton but bare justice to declare, that he treated us civilly, and with much more humanity than I had before experienced from Hawkins, commander of the British king's ship ' Ceres,' whose inveterate hatred of Americans was never exceeded by any man living. The only hard treatment on board the ' Fair American ' was being kept in irons the whole time: but that was a precautionary measure on the part of her commander; there being so many prisoners on board, who doubtless would have availed themselves of any opportunity that might have offered, to have risen upon the privateer. We were brought within the Hook by her, and sent up to the city in a pilot-boat. We had our irons knocked off at the Crane-wharf, and from thence we were sent on board the ' Jersey,' in the schooner ' Relief,' before mentioned. On my arrival again on board the ' Jersey,' which I had left but a few months before, I found more prisoners than I had left, though but very few of my former fellow prisoners: some of them had got away, but the greater part had paid the debt of 'nature, and their bones, with others, are the objects of your present solicitude and patriotic exertions,

" There being so many prisoners on board the ' Jersey,' and others daily arriving, two or three hundred of us were sent on board the ' John ' transport, which they had converted into a prison-ship, and where the treatment we received was much worse than on board the ' Jersey.' We were subjected to every insult, every injury, and every abuse that the fertile genius of the British officers could invent and inflict. For more than a month we were obliged to eat our scanty allowance, bad as it was, without cooking, as no fire was allowed us; and I verily believe this was the means of hastening many out of existence. One circumstance I think deserves particular notice, as it was a most singular one: A young man of the name of Bird, a native of Boston or its neighborhood, was one evening, with others, playing at cards to pass away the time. At about ten o'clock I retired with my cousin to our hammock; we had but just got asleep when we were called by one of the card party, who requested us to turn out, for that Bird was dying; we did turn out, and went to where he lay, and found him in the agonies of death; and in about fifteen or twenty minutes he was a corpse. It was mentioned to the sentry at the gangway that one of the prisoners was dead, and the body was soon hurried on deck. The impression Bird's death made on our minds is still fresh in my recollection: that he was poisoned we had no doubt, as his body swelled considerably, and two hours before, he was to all appearance, as well as any of us. Many, shortly after, went off in the same manner, and amongst them my cousin, Oliver C. Coffin. I did but just escape the same fate: I was taken ill before I left the prison-ship, and my legs began to swell; but being exchanged or rather being bought off, I made out to reach my father's house, in a most deplorable situation. I was attended in my sickness by a noted tory physician, Dr. Tupper, who declared to my mother, that nothing could have saved my life but having, as he expressed it, a constitution of iron; for that he knew of nothing that could have affected me in the manner in which I was affected but poison of some kind or other.is it possible then, after all these facts, for any person to form any other opinion than that there was a premeditated, organized system pursued to destroy men whom they dare not meet openly and manfully as enemies, in that base, inhuman and cowardly manner. It is an old adage, and a very true one, that the brave are generous, and the coward savage and cruel; and it was never more completely exemplified than in the conduct of the British officers in this country during the revolution. Their cruelties here and in India have become proverbial. Let it not be said in extenuation, that those cruel deeds were necessary to repress the spirit of revolt, for every man of common sense knows that cruelties exercised towards revolters, unless they can be completely subdued, only tend to irritate and urge them on to a more determined and desperate resistance. We acknowledge we were revolters, but our revolt was legitimate; we revolted against oppression, against a government that had revolted (if I may be allowed to use the expression) against its own subjects, and violated the most sacred of all duties towards its people — the duty of defending and protecting their constitutional rights and privileges, which had been left them as a legacy by their brave ancestors, who had fought and bled to obtain them, in common with Englishmen.

" There are other facts which, perhaps, are not generally known to the American people, that I shall mention. One is, that a man of the name of Gavot, a native of Rhode Island, died, as was supposed, and was sewed up in his hammock, and in the evening carried upon deck, to be taken with others who were dead, and those who might die during the night, on shore to be interred (in their mode of interring). During the night it rained pretty hard: in the morning, when they were loading the boat with the dead, one hammock was observed, by one of the English «seamen, to move; he spoke to the officer, and told him that he believed the man in that hammock, (pointing to it) was not dead. ' in with him' said the officer; 'if he is not dead, he soon will be'; but the honest tar, more humane than his officer, swore he never would bury a man alive, and with his knife ripped open the hammock, when behold! the man was really alive. What was the cause of this man's reanimation, is a question for doctors to decide: it was at the time supposed, that the rain during the night had caused the reaction of the animal functions, which were suspended, but not totally annihilated. This same man, Gavot, went afterwards in the same flag with me to Rhode Island. Capt. Shubael Worth of Hudson was master of the flag, and will bear testimony to the same fact.

" Another fact is, that although there were seldom less than 1,000 prisoners constantly on board the ' Jersey ' — new ones coming about as fast as others died, or were exchanged (which, by the bye, was seldom) — I never, in the two different times that I was on board, knew of but one prisoner entering on board a British ship of war, though the boats from the fleet were frequently there, and the English officers were endeavoring to persuade them to enter; but their persuasion and offers were invariably treated with contempt, and even by men who pretty well knew they should die where they were. These were the men whose bones have so long been bleaching on the shores of the Wallabout; these were the patriots who preferred death in its most horrible shape, to the disgrace and infamy of fighting the battles of a base and barbarous enemy, against the liberties of their country; these were the patriots whose names suffer no diminution by a comparison with the heroes and patriots of antiquity!

Shall Americans, then — shall we, the survivors of that glorious revolution refuse the humble tributes of respect and veneration due to the memories of those heroes, and the common rites of sepulture to all that remains of them that is mortal? Forbid it, heaven! let it not be said that Americans are ungrateful — that they have received a legacy, and that the heroes who lost their lives in assisting to obtain it, because dead, are not to be remembered."

In addition to the above we have the testimony of an aged gentleman, who says he was an officer on board of the United States frigate " Confederacy," captured by two English frigates. Being at the time sick, he was put on board one of the hulks in the Wallabout that served as an hospital for convalescents, but was as soon as somewhat restored, transferred to the old " Jersey," to make room for others more helpless. Here he experienced all the sufferings, and witnessed the horrors described by Andros, for five months. The confinement in so crowded a place, the pestilential air, the putrid and damaged food given to the prisoners (procured by the commissaries for little or nothing, and charged to the English government at the prices of the best provisions) soon produced a fever, under which this young man suffered, without medicine or attendance, until nature, too strong for even such enemies, restored him to a species of health, again to be prostrated by the same causes. He says he never saw given to the prisoners one ounce of wholesome food. The loathsome beef they prepared by pressing, and then threw it with damaged bread, into the kettle, skimming off the previous tenants of this poisonous food as they rose to the top of the vessel.

That these commissaries became rich, and reveled in luxuries, hearing the groans of their victims daily, and seeing the bodies of those who were relieved from torture by death, carried by boat-loads to be half buried in the sands of the Wallabout. The testimony proving these atrocities, cannot be doubted. Yet, in answer to the remonstrances of Washington, Admiral Arbuthnot denied the charge altogether.

The old prison-ship was sunk after the Revolution and now remains under water, off the present Navy Yard. But a few years since, part of her hull was seen above water at low tide.

In the year 1803, a correspondence was set on foot between the different military associations, masonic societies, and others in New York, the object of which was to pay funeral honors to the remains of these most unfortunate martyrs of American liberty. Nothing effectual was, however, accomplished till 1808, when the Tammany Society, composed (as it then was) of many Revolutionary patriots, took the lead in this holy work. It was proposed to collect the bones of the deceased tenants of the prison-ships, enclose them in a permanent vault, and to erect an enduring monument, emblematic of the noble design, which should be alike respectful to the dead, and creditable to the living.

The corner stone of this monument was laid April 13, 1808, upon land near the Navy Yard at Brooklyn, generously contributed for the purpose by John Jackson, Esquire.

The entombment took place May 26, 1808, and was considered in all its aspects, as one of the most splendid and imposing spectacles ever witnessed in this country.

Thirteen capacious coffins, filled with the bones of deceased American citizens and soldiers, made a principal feature in this sublime and mournful exhibition, to each of which was assigned, as pall bearers, eight Revolutionary patriots, making in all one hundred and four.

The number of individuals in the august procession was immense. It started from the park, in New York, traversed the principal streets of the city, and reached the East River, where thirteen large open boats were ready to transport the thirteen Tammanial Tribes (each having, also, one of the coffins, with its pall-bearers and appropriate standard) to the shores of Brooklyn.

The corporation of the city of New York, Governor Tompkins, Lieutenant-Governor Broome, and other officers of distinction, passed over in another boat. All the other bodies, civil, military, and naval, crossed in barges, prepared for the occasion by the committee of arrangements, while fleets of small boats covered the surface of the river, from the Battery to Corlear's Hook, filled with those anxious to join in the melancholy duty of paying the last homage of respect to the long-neglected remains of their countrymen. The weather was fine, and the surface of the waters was almost hidden, beneath the infinite variety of craft, and foamed with the lashing of many thousand oars. Itis supposed that more than 30,000 persons male and female, thronged the heights near the place of sepulture.

The Rev. Ralph Willlston addressed the throne of Heaven, in a very eloquent and solemn manner, after which a beautiful and appropriate oration was delivered, by the late Dr. Benjamin De Witt.

Indeed, the whole ceremony was a highly exciting, yet heartrending, scene to the many thousand sympathizing bosoms, then and there assembled.

Nearly twenty hogsheads of bones, in the whole, were collected, and deposited in one common grave.

Notwithstanding all that took place on the momentous occasion above mentioned, yet candor and truth compel us to state, that the long talked of monument, to the memory of these venerated martyrs to liberty, has never been erected, and that, but for the patriotic solicitude and care of Benjamin Romaine, Esq., of New York, now deceased, the imperfect and perishable structure, raised at the time of interment, would, ere this, have ceased to point the stranger to the hallowed spot, where these consecrated relics now repose.

Several patriotic citizens of Brooklyn, among whom may be mentioned the Hon. Cyrus P. Smith, have long since endeavored to awaken the public pride and sympathy on the subject, and it is to be hoped, for the honor of the present generation, that something may be done, worthy of themselves, and deserving the sincere and lasting gratitude of posterity.

A BRIEF ACCOUNT OF THE CIRCUMSTANCES ATTENDING THE DESTRUCTION OF THE SHIPS " BRISTOL " AND " MEXICO," ON THE SOUTH SHORE OF LONG ISLAND, IN THE YEARS 1836 AND '37.

The awful catastrophe of these ill-fated vessels, and the consequent loss of life, are among the most melancholy events in the annals of Long Island. Since the wreck of the British sloop of war " Sylph," off Southampton, in the winter of 1815, no similar accident had occurred upon our shores, involving the sacrifice of human life to any very considerable extent.

The " Bristol " was an American ship, nearly new, this being her second voyage, and commanded by Captain McKown, a gentleman long and favorably known as an able, prudent, and experienced shipmaster. The cargo consisted of crockery, railroad iron, and coal, besides an assortment of dry goods. She had on board a crew of sixteen, including officers, and about one hundred passengers, chiefly emigrants from Ireland.

The voyage was commenced at Liverpool, October 16, 1836, and after a pleasant passage across the Atlantic, she made the highlands of New Jersey on the night of November 20th, and exhibited the usual signals for a pilot, but without success. At one o'clock, on the morning of the 21st, it began to blow severely, and the captain endeavored to stand out to sea, but the violence of the gale forced the ship more toward the shore, and about four o'clock she grounded upon Far Rockaway shoals, a few miles westward of the Marine Pavilion, it being on Sunday, November 21. The following night was extremely dark, and the sea rose so high, as to make a clear breach over the ship. The greatest danger was now apparent, and the passengers were advised to go below, as the place of greater safety. The tempest increasing, a tremendous wave struck the vessel about midships, carrying away her bulwarks, boats, and everything movable upon the deck.

The hatches were forced open by the concussion, and the hold was, of course, instantly filled with water, drowning most of the passengers below decks.

From the dying, however, not a sound was heard, so instantaneous and complete was the work of death. Parents and children, husbands and wives, relatives and friends, met, in the same moment, a common fate; thus perished, in an instant of time, between 60 and 70 souls, of different ages, almost within sight of the port of their destination.

Although the vessel lay within half a mile of the land, yet owing to the heavy sea, no relief could be afforded by the people now assembled on the beach. At daylight, on the 2nd, the scene which presented itself may be more easily imagined than described. The wretched and suffering passengers and crew that yet survived, were clinging to the shrouds, and to every other part of the ship which promised the least hope of safety. In this dreadful state of almost hopeless despair, they remained through the succeeding day, although the shore was thronged with anxious spectators, ready to afford any possible assistance to the exhausted and perishing sufferers. But the gale continuing with unabated fury, no aid could be given; the surf ran mountains high, so as sometimes to exclude the hull of the vessel from the view of those on the land.

In the meantime, the ship struck against the hard beach with such terrible force as to break her in two, when the foremast, which had not been cut away, went by the board. The miserable passengers continued thus a part of the following night, exposed to the spray of the sea, to the most intense cold, and the absolute certainty of perishing by starvation also.

About midnight the wind somewhat abated, and by almost superhuman efforts, and at the imminent risk of life, a boat manned by resolute and experienced seamen from the shore reached the vessel twice, landing the surviving females, and a portion of the crew, safely on the beach. The captain resolutely refused to go on shore, until the survivors were safe, and was the last person who left the wreck. The ship went to pieces soon after, her stern post being the only part of her visible the next day.

About half the bodies of those drowned, were driven upon the shore, and were decently interred by the public authorities.

Mrs. Hogan, her daughters, Miss Hogan and Mrs. Donnelly with her two children and nurse, and a few other women and children, were among those saved, but Mr. Arthur Donnelly, the husband, was lost. He had twice yielded his place to others, saying he would not leave the wreck while a female or child remained on board. In a third attempt made to reach the vessel, the boat was swamped, which deterred the hands from any further trial. Mr. Donnelly, with the two Messrs. Carletons, the remainder of the passengers and the crew, sought safety in the rigging of the foremast. This soon failed them and out of 20 persons upon it, Mr. Briscoe only was saved, having accidentally caught hold of the rigging of the bowsprit, and thus drifted ashore.

Scarcely had the public mind recovered from the painful excitement occasioned by the preceding event, when another disastrous shipwreck occurred, attended with still more awful and aggravated circumstances.

The American barque " Mexico," of 300 tons, was also from the port of Liverpool, commanded by Captain Charles Winslow, her cargo consisting of crockery, railroad iron, and coal, which had been taken in alongside the " Bristol." She sailed, however, seven days later, leaving Liverpool, October 23, 1836, with a crew of twelve men, including the captain, and one hundred and twelve steerage passengers, the greater portion of whom were Irish emigrants. After a most disagreeable and boisterous passage of sixty-nine days, at the most inclement season of the year, the vessel arrived off Sandy Hook, on Saturday night, December 31, about eleven o'clock, and lay to, on discovering the light upon the Highlands of New Jersey. On the morning of the following day, she bore up for the Hook, making the usual signals of distress, and also for a pilot. None, however, made their appearance, and the captain being apprehensive of rough weather, stood out to sea, under the most discouraging and distressing circumstances. The voyage had thus far been unusually long and tedious; the passengers had generally exhausted their stores of provisions, and had for some time been allowed one biscuit a day each from the ship, a quantity barely sufficient to sustain life. To which were added all the direful apprehensions of still more protracted suffering, from the want of a pilot, and the danger of attempting at that season of the year, to enter the harbor without one.

The weather was cold in the extreme, attended by a violent tempest of snow. On Monday, the captain again approached the Hook, and also signalized for a pilot, in which he was equally unsuccessful. With an anxiety not to be described, he was compelled, amid the intense severity of the weather, and the almost unspeakable suffering of his crew, to keep away from the land during the remainder of the day and ensuing night. On Tuesday morning, five o'clock, after the most terrible buffeting with the waves, the crew and passengers being nearly perished with the cold, the vessel having drifted toward shore, struck the beach at Hempstead south, within about ten miles of the wreck of the " Bristol."

The thermometer was now below zero, and there was a high surf breaking on the shore. The main and mizzen masts were immediately cut away; the rudder was torn off, by collision with the bottom; the water was rising in the hold, and the spray, which dashed incessantly over the vessel, was instantly converted into ice. The wretched and despairing passengers, driven from below by the accumulation of water, and without any means whatever of shelter or protection from the cold, crowded together upon the forward deck, exposed every moment either to be washed overboard or frozen to death, as everything around them was encrusted in ice.

Some secured their money and other valuables about their bodies, and each clung with death-like tenacity to those they held most dear. In this extremity of despair, when scarce a ray of hope remained, men, women, and children, from the sire to the lisping infant, embraced each other, and with what feeble power remained, tried in vain to encourage and support each other.

In this horrible condition they remained, till secured by death from further agony; and husbands, wives, and children were afterwards found, congealed together in one frozen mass. It was, in all respects, a scene of terror which language is incapable of depicting, and which the most fertile imagination only can conceive.

On the morning of the 3rd of January, Raynor R. Smith and a few others, crossing the south bay upon the ice, dragging their boat with them, arrived at the beach, a distance of several miles, determined if possible to afford some sort of relief to the suffering victims, but they soon found that any attempt to reach the vessel in the [then] state of the surf, would only be to sacrifice their own lives, to no valuable purpose.

The miserable strangers, yet clinging to the mass of ice which the vessel presented, poured forth their supplications and cries for assistance, in a manner which could hardly fail to melt the stoutest heart. The heroic Smith and his valiant crew were wrought up to the highest pitch, and finally resolved that a trial at least should be made. The boat was accordingly launched from the shore, and in the utmost peril of being filled or upset, was able to reach the bowsprit of the vessel, when the captain, four passengers and three of the crew, who were upon the bowsprit, dropped into the boat, and were conveyed with great difficulty to the beach. But the danger which had been incurred — the state of the tide — the extreme cold, and the approach of night, deterred the crew from attempting again to reach the vessel. Turning their backs upon the horrible scene, they made the best of their way home across the bay, aiding and supporting, as best they could, those they had rescued. But what must have been the feelings of persons on board, when they saw those from whom alone any relief was to be expected, departing from their sight, can only be conceived; their agonizing breasts must have been filled with tenfold horror. Thus, on that fated night, perished, in the most awful manner, 116 human beings, 3000 miles from their homes, and within a few miles of the port for which they set out.

Death, in its most appalling form, came to their relief, and their cries of anguish and despair were soon hushed in eternal silence.

Seventy days had elapsed since leaving their native country, and on the shores which they sought with so much anxiety, they found a watery grave.

" Thus perished, one by one, that pilgrim crowd,
The silver-hair'd, the beautiful, the young;
Some were found wrapp'd, as in a crystal shroud
Of waves congeal'd, that tomb'd them where they clung.
Some on the sand the sounding breakers fling,
Link'd in affection's agonized embrace;
And to the gazer's eye the warm tears spring.
As he beheld two babes — a group of grace, |
Lock'd in each other's arms, and pillow'd face to face."

A majority of the passengers were children and youth of both sexes, as appeared from a list made by the collector at Liverpool — the oldest passenger on board being fifty-two, and the youngest less than two years old. About sixty bodies were finally recovered from the waves, and interred, with very appropriate solemnities, in a common grave, amid an immense concourse of citizens of Queens County, at Near-Rockaway, on the 11th day of January, 1837, and a suitable discourse was delivered by the Rev. William

M. Carmichael, D. D., of Hempstead. The bodies of those previously saved from the " Bristol " were finally deposited at the same place, where a handsome marble monument was erected October 26, 1840.

" They rest in earth, the sea's recovered prey,
No tempests now their dreamless sleep assail;
But when to friends and kindred, far away,
Some quivering lip shall tell the dismal tale.
From many a home will burst the voice of wail;
But when it ceases and the tear-drop laves
No more, shall gratitude prevail,
Yearnings of love towards those beyond the waves,
Who bore, with solemn rites, these exiles to their graves."

Several citizens of New York, duly sensible of the highly meritorious services of Raynor R. Smith, on the above occasion, caused a silver cup, with a suitable device and inscription, to be presented him; the ceremony of which was performed by the late William P. Hawes, Esq., March 25, 1837.

The Inscription

" Presented to Raynor R. Smith, of Hempstead South, L. I., by a number of his fellow citizens, of the fifth ward, of the city of New York, as a token of regard for his noble daring, performed at the peril of his life, in saving eight persons, from the wreck of the fated Mexico, on the 2d of January, 1837"

OF THE AWFUL CONFLAGRATION OF THE STEAMER "LEXINGTON," IN LONG ISLAND SOUND, JAN. 13, 1840.

The steamboat " Lexington," Captain George Child, left New York for Stonington, Conn., late in the afternoon of January 13, 1840, with a great number of passengers, and a large quantity of cotton in bales, with other merchandise, on deck.

At seven o'clock in the evening, when she was about opposite Eaton's Neck, L. I., and nearly in the middle of the Sound, going at the rate of twelve miles an hour, the cotton near the smoke pipe was discovered to be on fire, and the wind blowing fresh, all endeavors to extinguish the flames were found Ineffectual, and the boat was headed for Long Island. But the tiller ropes were soon burnt off, which rendered the vessel unmanageable.

The alarm and consternation were now so great, and the consequent confusion so universal, that the boats, three in number, besides the life boat, were no sooner lifted out, and let down into the water, than they were swamped by the crowd and the rapid motion of the vessel.

The engine also gave way, and the boat, which had now become unmanageable, was drifted about at the mercy of wind and tide, while the fire was sweeping over her, in the most terrific manner imaginable.

The fire being amid-ships, cut off necessarily, all communication from stem to stern, where the passengers were collected, bewailing their awful condition, not knowing the fate of their friends, and fully aware that to remain longer on board, was certain destruction, the flames spreading with terrible rapidity, and involving the whole vessel in one sheet of fire.

The lurid light of the blazing wreck shone far over the cold and heavy waste of waters, showing with fearful distinctness the dreadful scene. The greater number, therefore, threw themselves into the sea, laying hold of any floating body within their reach, while others, not so fortunate, were instantly drowned. Some who hesitated to precipitate themselves into the water, clung to some portion of the burning wreck, in the hope of prolonging for a few moments their miserable existence.

The night was cold in the extreme, and the surrounding darkness was rendered more terrific, by the glare of the burning mass. The cries of distress, mingled with the deepest supplications for relief, were such as cannot be described — the anguish of hopeless despair. The captain, it is believed, was suffocated in the wheel house, at an early stage of the fire, and out of the whole number on board, four only were saved, while one hundred and twenty men, women, and children were lost. The following is the report of Captain Comstock, of the steamer " Statesman," who was dispatched on the occasion, from New York.

"Steamer Statesman, Friday night, Jan. 17, 1840.

" We are now returning to New York, having searched the shore of Long Island from Huntington to Fresh Pond landing, a distance, taking into consideration the depths of the bays and Inlets, of nearly ninety miles, every rod of which I think has been thoroughly examined by those on board the boat with me, and others on shore who came down by land. We have been enabled to regain, however, only five bodies.

" One is identified as being that of Mr. Stephen Waterbury, of the firm of Mead and Waterbury, of New York. On another was found a memorandum book, with the name of Philo Upson, of South Egremont, Mass.; one a little boy, probably three or four years old.

" From the appearance of others, they are probably deck hands of the boat.

" We have thirty packages of baggage, and the life boat of the Lexington. These, with the bodies, we are now conveying to New York. From Crane Neck to Old Man's landing, twelve or fifteen miles east, including the deep bays adjacent, is covered with pieces of the wreck, among which I noticed her name upon the siding, nearly in full length, large pieces of her guards, and portions of almost every part of the boat, all of which is mostly burned to a coal. We found one of her quarter boats, from which three of the bodies now in our possession, were taken; she is very slightly damaged.

" The boat is at a place called Miller's Landing, and here we learned that a man had come ashore on a bale of cotton, alive, fifteen miles to the eastward of this place, to which I immediately repaired. Here I could effect no landing, owing to the large quantities of ice drifted in by the stormy northerly wind. We, however, crowded the steamboat in near enough to the shore to converse with persons drawn to the beach by our signals, and from them learned the fact that Mr. David Crowley, second mate of the Lexington, had drifted ashore upon a bale of cotton on Wednesday night at 9 o'clock, after being forty-eight hours exposed to the severity of the weather — after which, he made his way through large quantities of ice, and swam before gaining the beach, and then walked three-quarters of a mile to a house — his hands are little frozen — his feet and legs considerably so — he is not able, however, to be moved for the present; this I have been told by a person who saw him this day; it appears next to an impossibility, considering the severity of the weather, but it is undoubtedly true. Since leaving New York, we have had severe cold weather, and the ice completely blocked up the shores. The northerly winds kept driving the ice to leeward, and everything floating very light would naturally be buried beneath this constant accumulation of ice. In consequence of this, I think we have been prevented from procuring many bodies that, in very moderate weather, could have been seen.

" I left New York in the steamer ' Statesman,' on Wednesday, A. M., since which time, up to the moment of our leaving the scene of sorrow — which the shores that we have visited presented — no time has been lost in doing all that lay in our power to search the greatest possible track of beach, vainly hoping to save alive someone clinging to an thing within their power; and also to regain all the bodies possible, for the purpose of rendering to surviving relations the only consolation left them in this painful separation from their departed friends. I feel myself obligated to Capt. Peck for his unceasing efforts to enter with his boat every bay or creek where the least hope was entertained of accomplishing the object of our undertaking. To Mr. Christopher Townsend, and Mr. Dexter Bingham, Jr., I feel partially indebted for their valuable services in assisting me in my difficult, and many Instances, dangerous undertaking in effecting a landing. Messrs. Henry Ide, James McKenna, W. Bercher, T. Donelly, and C. Homan joined the boat at Bridgeport on Wednesday night, and have been essentially useful to-day, in collecting the baggage and things together for embarkation, while I was otherwise engaged, for which I feel greatly indebted — also to Mr. Samuel Yeaton, who joined us at Long Island.

" I saw Capt. Manchester at Southport on Wednesday night, who perfectly corroborates Capt. Hilliard's statements, which shows how collected each must have been in their perilous situation.

" We left Crane Neck, for New York, at half past 5 P. M. Arrived at New York at 9 A. M., after a passage of fifteen and a half hours — came fifty miles through the ice. Respectfully yours,

" Joseph J. Comstock."

After the return of the " Statesman," an inquest was convened, to investigate the matter of the burning of the " Lexington," and to decide upon the cause of the death of those brought in the " Statesman." The bodies mentioned above were identified, and given over to their friends; two bodies, supposed to be deck hands, were recognized as Benjamin Ladeu, twenty-seven or twenty-eight years old, without family, and Silas Thornburn, aged about twenty, belonging to Providence. The bodies of both were much burned in their faces and necks; as was also the child, mentioned above. They were frozen perfectly stiff, and covered with Ice.

On board of the steamer, in charge of young Harnden, a man of much promise, who attended the express car, were $18,000 in specie; and from one to three thousand dollars in eastern funds, which had been purchased by brokers, for remittance to Boston.

Mr. Hamden's agent, who prosecuted a search in the Sound, wrote to Mr. Harnden, mentioned the discovery of the body of Mr. Osgood, and says:

" Much baggage continues to drift ashore. It is painful to state, that not even the terrible circumstances under which it was thrown adrift, can guard it from plunder. Mounted men have been placed upon duty, who ride constantly up and down the beach. The Transportation Company, to whom the boat belonged, has addressed a letter to Mr. Wilsie, the Wreck Master, at Old Field Point, authorizing him to employ a sufficient number of hands to search the shore for property and bodies, the living and the dead, and to act himself, in conjunction with Mr. John G. Morse and William Kennedy, who went from this city to assist. He is requested also to send to the office, 22 Broadway, an accurate description of the bodies and baggage."

Mr. Samuel Hutchinson says, in a letter dated Riverhead, January 16;

" I first learned that a boat had been seen on fire in the Sound, at Smithtown on last Monday evening, and when I arrived at Setauket, I learned that the lifeboat had come on shore there, without any body in or attached to her. She had a coat in her, by which it appeared from letters in the pocket, that the owner was a Mr. or Captain Manchester. After I had been home two or three hours, about 7 ½ o'clock, a young man came to my father's in a very exhausted condition, having just floated ashore opposite the house, on a bale of cotton, on which he had been for two days and nights. His fingers and both feet were frozen as stiff as marble, and he was without coat or hat. His name is David Crowley, and he lives at Providence, and was second mate of the Lexington.

" We have taken the best care we could of him, by immersing his feet and hands in cool and lukewarm water. We had to cut off his boots. I have sent the doctor to him this morning. We succeeded in softening all the frosted parts, but his feet are very much swollen this morning, and what the result will be, is somewhat doubtful."

Mr. John Wilsie, wreck master at Setauket, and George K. Hubbs, Esq., of Smithtown, with great promptness and zeal, stationed a line of guards for fifteen miles, along the north shore of Long Island, for the purpose of taking charge of such bodies and property, as might drift on shore. About thirty trunks and chests were found in the vicinity of Old Field Point, but nothing was heard of Harnden's express car, which, as it contained an iron chest, sunk to the bottom.

In this chest were $10,000 in gold and $20,000 in bank notes. The bodies of H. C. Craig and Charles Bracket of New York, William A. Green of Providence, and D. Green of Philadelphia, went on shore near Stony Brook, L. I. Fifteen thousand dollars, in bank notes, were found on the body of Wm. A. Green.

The following is as full a list of the officers, passengers, and crew of the " Lexington," as could be obtained:

Passengers. — Capt. Chester Hilliard of Norwich, the only passenger saved; Isaac Davis of Boston; John Corey of Roxboro', Mass.; Charles W. Woolsey, John Brown, and Abraham Howard, firm of Howard & Merry, Boston; J. Porter Felt, Jr. of Salem; H. C. Craig, firm of Maitland, Kennedy & Co. N. Y. (body found); Alphonso Mason of Gloucester, Mass., surveyor of the port; Charles Bracket, clerk to N. Bracket, N. Y. (body found); Robt. Blake of Wrentham, Mass., President of Wrentham Bank; Mr. Fowler of New York; Wm. A. Green, firm of Allen & Green, Providence (body found);

Samuel Henry, firm of A. & S. Henry, Manchester, England; R. W. Dow, firm of Dow & Co., N. Y.; Charles H. Phelps of Stonington; the widow of Henry A. Winslow, firm of Winslow & Co., New York; John Winslow of Providence; Wm. Winslow, ditto., father of the above. The three last mentioned persons were returning to Providence, with the corpse of H. A. Winslow, who died in New York, a few days previous.

Rev. Charles Follen, D. D., of Boston, late Professor of German Literature of Harvard University; Adolphus Harnden, superintendent of Harnden's Express. He had in charge $20,000 in specie for the Merchant's Bank, Boston; and from forty to fifty thousand dollars in bank notes; Thomas White of Boston, firm of Sands & White; Capt. J. D. Carver of Plymouth, Mass., of the barque Brontes; Mr. Pierce of Portland, mate of the Brontes; Miss Sophia T. Wheeler, daughter of Robt. Wheeler, Stonington, Conn.; Capt. E. J. Kimball; Capt. B. T. Foster, late of the John Gilpin. These captains had recently returned after several years' absence, and were on their way to visit their families at the east.

Mr. Everett of Boston, returning from the burial of a brother, who died in N. Y. the previous week; Royal T. Church of Baltimore; Richard Picket of Newburyport; Mr. Ballard of New York; Capt. Theophilus Smith, Dartmouth, Mass.; Charles S. Noyes, clerk to C. B. Babcock, and Albert E. Harding, firm of Harding & Co. N. Y.; Henry J. Finn, comedian, he was a native of Virginia, his family resided at Newport, R. I.; Charles L. Eberle, of the theatre; Mrs. Rusell Jarvis of New York, and her two children, one about 12 and the other about 8 years of age, Mrs. Jarvis was a daughter of Thomas Cordis of Boston; Capt. John G. Low, agent for the Boston underwriters, husband of the niece of Mr. Cordis; John Lemist, treasurer of the Boston India Rubber Co. Roxbury, uncle to Mrs. Jarvis, John W. Kerle, and Mr. Weston, firm of Weston & Pendexter, of Baltimore; John G. Brown, firm of Shall & Brown, N. Orleans; Stephen Waterbury, firm of Mead & Waterbury, N. Y. (body found), and E. B. Patten, of New York; J. A. Leach, Nathaniel Hobart, and Mr. Stuyvesant of Boston; N. F. Dyer of Pittsburg, formerly of Braintree; John Brown, a colored man; H. C. Bradford, from Kingston, Jam.; Chas. Lee of Barre; Jonathan Linfield, Stoughton, Me.; Philo Upson, Egremont, Mass. (body found); Mr. Van Cott, Stonington, Conn.; Capt. Mattison; Robert Williams, or Wilson, of Cold Spring, N. Y.; David M'Farlane, mate of the brig Clarion; James Walker and John Gorden, seamen, of Cambridgeport, from brig Raymond; Wm. H. Wilson, grocer, of Williamsburg, L. I., late of Worcester, Mass.; Patrick McKenna, No. 7 Monroe St., N. Y., clerk with Donnelly & Hyatt; George Benson Smith, recently of Brooklyn; Elias Brown, Jr. of Stonington, nephew of Silas E. Burrows, Esq.; Mr. Lawrence, firm of Kelly & Lawrence, New York; Charles Bosworth, schoolmaster of Royalton, Vt., from 37 Franklin St.; David Green of Philadelphia, agent of the Minot (Me.) Shoe Manufacturing Company (body found); William Nichols, colored, steward of steamboat Massachusetts; Dr. Joshua Johnson of Philadelphia; Thomas James, tailor, of New York, formerly of Boston; James Ray, 2nd mate of barque Bohemia, Kennebunk; Mary Russell of Stonington, Ct.; Jonathan G. Davenport, Middletown, N. J.; Mrs. Lydia Bates, wife of James Bates of Abington, Mass., and their two children, Lydia C. Bates and Jacob C. Bates (body of the boy found). The body of Mrs. Bates was found Sept. 13, 1840, on the shore at Smithtown, L. I.

John Walker, whose parents reside at Cambridgeport; George W. Walker; John Martin, and his son

Gilbert Martin, recently from England; William ,

an English boy; William Cowen, aged 21, New York City; Benjamin D. Holmes, copper-smith, and William Dexter of Boston; George O. Swan, son of Judge Swan of Columbus, Ohio. He was on his way to join the law school at Cambridge, Mass.; John Ricker, Monroe, Me.

Boat's Company. — Capt. Geo. Childs, commander; Jesse Comstock, clerk; H. P. Newman, steward; E. Thurbur, first mate; David Crowley, second mate, saved, after being 48 hours on a bale of cotton; Stephen Manchester, pilot, (saved); John Hoyt, baggage master; Mr. Walker, barkeeper; Cortland Hemsted, chief engineer (body found); Wm. Quimby, 2nd do.; Martin Johnson, wheelman; R. B. Schulz, Geo. Baum, Benj. Cox, and Chas. B. Smith (saved), firemen; Chas. Williams, Ben Laddie, C. Humber, Joel Lawrence, three others, and a boy, deck hands; Job Sands (body found), Dan'l Aldridge, Mr. Gilbert, Oliver Howell, King Cade, Jos. Rostin, John H. Tab, E. Parkson, John Masson, Solomon Askons, Isaac Putnam, colored waiters; Susan C. Hulcumb, chambermaid, colored; Joseph Robinson, cook, do.; Oliver Howell, second do., do.; Robert Peters, do.; Henry Reed and another, coal heavers.

Number of passengers ascertained 91
Number of officers and crew 39
Total 130

OF BILLS OF CREDIT, AND
COLONIAL AND CONTINENTAL MONEY.

For the good part of a century after the first settlements in this country by Europeans, the people were dependent upon foreign countries for everything in the shape of metallic money, and with the exception of the seawan of the Indians, called also wampum, which was pretty extensively used as the medium of domestic exchange, the inhabitants were, in cases of emergency, driven to the issuing of what were generally denominated bills of credit, large sums of which were provided for by the local governments, as the public necessities required.

A full and correct account of the descriptions and amount of this species of circulating medium, would, if well executed, prove highly interesting and curious; suffice it to say, that paper money, of some kind or other, has constituted the greatest portion of the currency in this country, from the latter part of the eighteenth century, to the present time. While connected with the parent country, money, to a large amount, was issued from time to time in the shape of bills of credit, for the final redemption of which, the faith of the colony was pledged.

These bills, says Mr. Pitkin, were called in by taxes, payable at different times, and were not only made receivable in the payment of those taxes, and of all duties payable to government, but were even a tender in payment of private demands, until prohibited by act of parliament.

After the Revolution of 1688, England was engaged in almost perpetual war with France, and as France was until 1763 in possession of Canada, of course the colonies were engaged with the mother country. The first of these wars continued from 1689 to 1697, and it was for the purpose of paying off her soldiers, on their return from an expedition to Canada in 1690, that Massachusetts made the first emission of paper money. In 1714, they emitted a bank (as it was called) of £50,000, and as they were the first in America to issue this kind of money, so they went beyond all others in the amount of their issues. The first emission in Rhode Island was £5,000, in 1710, to be received for colony dues, and pass current in all payments for five years. The reasons for the emission were the scarcity of specie and the debts contracted by the expedition against Annapolis Royal. These bills of credit were often loaned out to individuals, or as specie could not often be had the interest was made payable in hemp, flax, and other articles. The principal was called in instalments of one-fifth, or one-fifteenth annually, so as to render it easy for the borrowers. The bills of one colony generally passed in the neighboring colonies as their own bills did, depending entirely upon the faith of the colony for their redemption.

In 1720 an order of council was made in England forbidding any emissions by the colonies without the royal assent.

The emissions of paper money were generally opposed by the merchants and business men, and the more intelligent part of the community. They were generally advocated by the multitude, who were indebted and distressed in pecuniary circumstances, as a measure of relief. It was an easy way of paying old debts. And members of the General Assembly would often be inclined to favor the emissions, not only from the desire of popularity, but from the less honorable motive of pecuniary interest. Pretenses were never wanting. The colony was in debt; the fort was out of repair, or a new gaol or court house was to be built. And when the specie had been driven away by the increase of paper money, the " scarcity of silver " was a fresh excuse for further issues. And each new issue only involved the people, as a whole, in greater difficulties.

As specie could not be had for the purpose, new bills were issued from time to time, for the redemption of the former, and various means resorted to, to sustain their credit, but, without an adequate specie basis, legislative enactments could not avail, the bills being of unequal values in different states. They were even, when first issued, of less worth than specie; in New England they were valued at six shillings for a silver dollar, in New York at eight shillings, and in Pennsylvania at seven shillings and sixpence; hence arose the different currencies in those provinces, which exist even to the present day. It depreciated very rapidly, till forty-five shillings came to be of the value of one dollar, at which it stood many years, and was denominated old tenor (old tender). In this, accounts were kept and contracts made. The standard value, therefore, came to be called lawful money, by way of distinction to bills of credit, which were constantly fluctuating.

The mode of liquidating the public demands, and satisfying the claims of private creditors, was imitated in many instances by the other provinces, and, among the rest, New York. In 1745, Massachusetts alone issued bills to the amount of between two and three millions of pounds, lawful money; and in three years after, by depreciation, £1100 of these bills was only worth, or equal to, £100 sterling. Great Britain paid to that colony £180,000 sterling, for expenses incurred by her in the expedition against Louisburgh, in the last mentioned year; with which she redeemed her bills, at the rate of fifty shillings per ounce of silver.

When the troubles of the Revolution commenced, congress, having no other resources for revenue, resorted to the system of paper money, and the provinces did the same to a large amount. In 1775, congress issued bills of credit to the amount of $3,000,000; and, to force their circulation and prevent their return for redemption, made them, by resolution, a lawful tender, and declared a refusal to receive them, an extinguishment of the debt for which they were offered in payment.

They appointed twenty-eight citizens of Philadelphia to sign and number the bills: the names of two being necessary to every bill. Each person was allowed, out of the continental treasury, one dollar and one-third for each and every thousand bills signed and numbered by him.

But to administer these paper funds, joint treasurers were appointed at a salary of five hundred dollars; the number of inhabitants of all ages, including negroes and mulattoes, in each colony, to be taken as a ratio in order to levy the ways and means of paying bills when presented at the treasury. They were taken for taxes; and in order to keep up their credit, the treasurers were directed, when they happened to receive silver or gold, to advertise their readiness to pay the same for continental bills to all persons requiring an exchange.

In November of the same year, three millions came out in bills of various value, one-third, one-half, and two thirds of a dollar, and from one dollar to eighty. The colonies were called upon to sink proportionally a sum of three millions. In fixing the proportion for redeeming that amount, Virginia was rated highest, and stood charged with $496,000; Massachusetts, $434,000; Pennsylvania, $372,000; Maryland, $310,000; Connecticut, North Carolina, South Carolina, and New York were each rated at $248,000.

By the foregoing scale we find the relative wealth, by congressional estimation, of these colonies, at the beginning of the war, seventy years ago. It is worthy of remark, that the State of New York, the capital of which was then unoccupied by the enemy, is placed at little more than half of Massachusetts, while Boston was in the actual possession of the enemy.

On a subsequent recommendation of a new tax, (when the city of New York was held by the British) , congress assessed the State of New York at one-fourth of Virginia and Massachusetts, and at a less sum than New Jersey. The city of New York, at that period, being a place of small dimensions and moderate commerce.

This was a sort of forced loan, and congress declared January 11, 1776, that "whoever should refuse to receive in payment continental bills, should be declared and treated as enemies to their country, and be precluded from intercourse with its inhabitants."

" Till the amount," says Mr. Jefferson, " exceeded $9,000,000, the bills passed at their nominal value, after which the depreciation was great." This continental money formed almost the entire circulating medium of the country during the Revolution, and accounts were kept in it, but the specie value was also generally entered as follows: — " 1779, June 5 — to cash paid Reuben Dean, for a screw for a state seal — cont. £9, law. £0 16s. 4d."; which is as eleven to one.

August 30, 1775, the provincial congress of New York ordered an emission of bills to the amount of £45,000, in sums from ten to half a dollar; and March 5, 1776, they ordered $137,000 more. August 13, 1776, they again resolved to issue bills of credit, for $500,000, in sums from one shilling to ten dollars. In the same congress. May 28, 1776, it was resolved that Thomas

Harriot had violated the resolutions of congress, in refusing to receive continental bills in payment, and that he be held up to the public as an enemy to his country. It seems he was afterwards imprisoned for the like offence.

January 14, 1777, the continental congress declared, that bills of credit issued by their authority, ought to pass current in all payments, &c., and they recommended the state legislatures to make them a lawful tender; that a refusal to receive them should work a forfeiture of the debt, and that persons so conducting, ought to be declared enemies to the liberties of the United States.

Congress further " Resolved, that if any person shall hereafter be so lost to all virtue and regard for his country, as to refuse to receive the bills in payment, or obstruct and discourage the currency or circulation thereof, and shall be duly convicted by the committee of safety of the district, such person shall be deemed, published, and treated as an enemy of the country, and precluded from all trade or intercourse with the inhabitants of these colonies."

On the 26th of December, 1776, General Washington was authorized to arrest and confine those who rejected the continental currency, and return their names to the authorities of the states in which they resided. The council of safety of Pennsylvania was invited to take most vigorous and speedy steps for punishing all such as refused the bills, and the general was directed to give aid to the council: meantime Virginia and the other states were besought to furnish all the gold and silver they could procure, and take paper in exchange.

The years 1776 and 1777 proved as unpropitious to the paper credit as the preceding; and very strong measures were resorted to for the purpose of fixing a value on the currency; of compelling the people to receive as substance a mere shadow; of putting the stamp of reality on a fiction: measures certainly at variance with justice and expediency, and which operated on the people with the harshness of despotism. The resolutions which followed will show the bad temper of the great men at the head of affairs, and their forgetfulness of the rights of their constituents.

On the 3rd of December, 1777, congress recommended the respective states to enact laws, requiring persons possessed of bills of credit (struck under the sanction and authority of the King of Great Britain), forthwith to deliver them in exchange for continental money: and those not so delivered, to be thenceforth utterly irredeemable.

Such pernicious legislation could result in nothing but ruin to the confiding patriot, while it enabled the unprincipled to discharge their debts at an enormous discount. This fact soon became evident, and to a degree so alarming, that congress besought the states to repeal their iniquitous tender laws, which had been so pressingly recommended a few months before.

The Hon. John Sloss Hobart reported to the congress of New York, that the bills issued by them, then circulating, and not on interest, amounted, August 2, 1777, to £1,060,110, or $2,650,275.

In 1780 they were worth only one-half, and continued to fall, till $500 and even more of these bills were required to buy a pound of tea, and $1000 to pay for a pair of boots. The next year they entirely stopped, except at one hundred for one, under the funding system established by the national government.

The consequence of the constant fluctuation and depreciation of these bills, a greater part of those outstanding, was absorbed by speculators, who vainly expected they would eventually be redeemed at par. During the war, every device was resorted to by the enemy to destroy their credit, and counterfeiting was carried on to a wonderful extent.

Out of several hundred millions. Issued by the continental and the different provincial congresses, probably more than one hundred millions are still held by public bodies and by individuals, which are entirely worthless, except as matters of curiosity. This is the more to be regretted, Inasmuch as losses often fell upon the honest patriot and worn-out soldier. But, with all its faults, the system was not only indispensable, but unavoidable, and answered the purpose of carrying the country triumphantly through the long and bloody conflict, to the establishment of its independence. Yet it is now evident, that it might and ought to have been redeemed, at the value given for it by the holder, and paid either in money or in public lands, which the creditors would gladly have received.

When the Constitution went into operation, Alexander Hamilton, secretary of the treasury, added to the domestic debt the claims held by several states against the national exchequer, to the amount of twenty-one million five hundred thousand dollars, and then funded the whole by putting a part on interest at six per cent., postponing a part, without interest, for ten years, then to bear six per cent; and the remainder on immediate interest at three per cent. The arrears of six years' interest being added, with some other unsettled claims, made the whole debt amount to ninety-four millions of dollars.

In 1778 the whole amount of gold and silver received into the treasury of the United States was $78,660, and in 1779, $73,000; so that the whole machinery of government was carried on, for two entire years (as far as concerned the agency of specie), with only $151,666.

This handful of coin, which, in gold, would weigh only seven hundred pounds, and might be put into a wheelbarrow, was all that came in to the public chest for two years; and therefore we may be less surprised at the government being so chary of it as to refuse General Washington's demand of a small share, to pay a part of the bounty to enlisted soldiers. In denying which they declared that the precious metals must be kept for the commissaries of prisoners, to be used where paper would not pass.

Paper money continued the chief instrument in the hands of government. The press was kept in perpetual motion. Printers who labored at it obtained an exemption from militia duty. Ragged and torn notes were replaced, and bills of every denomination were issued by millions. But congress had no alternative. One source of revenue only was at their command, the emission of bills of credit. The very necessity of the case forced them sometimes to abuse it; for even in its depreciated condition, paper money offered facilities so attractive that those at the head of affairs, always intending to pay them, were glad to find the people willing, at the current exchange, to receive that which could be so easily supplied.

" Who," said a member (during a debate upon this subject) , " will consent to load his constituents with taxes, when we can send to our printer for a wagon load of money, and pay for the whole with a quire of paper?" And with wagon loads thus cheaply obtained, they carried on the campaigns of 1778 and 1779, keeping an army of thirty or forty thousand men in the field, issuing paper to the amount of sixty-three millions for the former year, and seventy-two millions for the latter.

Thus, with an active press, and commissioners hired by the day to sign the bills, ways and means were found to defray the expenses of government in a war with the most powerful nation on the globe.

The whole amount of such money issued during the war, was not far from three hundred millions of dollars, of which the government in various ways cancelled, from time to time, about one-third; so that the maximum of circulation, at no period, exceeded two hundred millions. Nor did it reach that sum, until its depreciation had compelled congress to take it in, and pay it out, at the rate of forty paper dollars for one in specie.

Mr. Hamilton, as secretary of the treasury, on the 9th of January, 1790, made a long and able report to congress on the subject of preserving the public credit, in which he advocated the redemption of continental bills, premising that the public credit was a matter of the highest importance to the honor and prosperity of the United States, and could only be supported by good faith and a punctual performance of contracts.

The debt of the United States, said he, was the price of liberty; the faith of America had been repeatedly pledged for it, and with solemnities that give peculiar force to the obligation. To justify and preserve public confidence; to promote the increasing respectability of the American name; to answer the calls of justice; to sustain landed property to its true value; to furnish new resources both to agriculture and commerce; to cement more closely the union of the states; to add to their security against foreign attack; to establish public order on the basis of an upright and liberal policy, are the great and valuable ends to be secured by a proper and adequate provision for the support of public credit. The nature of the contract, upon the face of the bills, is, that the public will pay to the holder the sum therein expressed, and it was from this circumstance that the bills were ever received or circulated as money.

The bills thus issued may be better understood from the following description.

On each bill was stamped a rudely printed emblem, with a Latin motto, twenty in number. Those devices and pithy sentences are said to have been composed by Doctor Franklin and Charles Thomson, aided by others of the continental congress.

On the small bills of one-third, one-half, and two thirds of a dollar, " Fugio " was the Latin motto, and in English, " Mind your business."

Decorated with these fine maxims, congress sent forth this cheap defense of the nation, with a recommendation to the legislatures of the states not only to make the bills a lawful tender in payment of public and private debts, but in case of refusal to receive them, to declare such refusal an extinguishment of the debt.

The circulation of this currency came to an end. The bills of the individual states had generally become so worthless, that congress would not receive them into its treasury, but congressional bills were kept in circulation at a great discount until May, 1781, when they fell to five hundred, and subsequently to one thousand paper dollars for one of silver, when they ceased as a currency. Two hundred millions lost all their value, and were laid aside.

The annihilation was so complete, that barbers' shops were papered, in jest, with the bills; and sailors, on returning from their cruise, being paid off in bundles of this money, had suits of clothes made of it, with characteristic lightheartedness turning their loss into a frolic, by parading through the streets in decayed finery, which in better days, had passed for thousands of dollars!

The continental money, however, endured for nearly six years, was a prodigy of revenue, of exceeding mysterious and magical agency, and when it failed the loss was divided into such fractional parts during the five or six years' circulation of its millions that it was laid aside, not only unpaid and unhonored, but even unwept. The people were tired of the variation in constant value, and felt how ridiculous was a currency that required five hundred dollars in paper to pay for a breakfast that could be bought for a silver half-dollar. It carried no regret with it, and seems doomed to sleep in silence, unfriended and unsung; unless, indeed, an attempt be occasionally made to awaken sympathy for some public creditor, who may have taken it at the rate of five hundred to one, from some heartless speculator who obtained it at a depreciation still more extravagant.

THE PERSECUTIONS OF THE QUAKERS

Whether the seventy with which the Quakers were formerly treated in this province, should be ascribed to the temper and prejudices of the age, or to the bigotry of particular sects or of individuals, it is not necessary to discuss; yet some account of any unjustifiable outrages, upon the rights of conscience and the liberty of speech, is a necessary duty of the historian.

The expectation of enjoying in this country greater freedom of opinion and speech, than they could enjoy in their native land, induced many worthy persons with their families, to risk the dangers of a voyage over the Atlantic, and the privations incident to a settlement in a new and distant country. Little could they have anticipated so soon being made objects of abuse and intolerance, by those who had transported themselves here for the same purpose, the enjoyment of religious freedom.

That many of the disciples of Fox were imprudent and fanatical, is undoubted; but the treatment they received from the puritans of New England, particularly corporeal punishment, could not be justified upon any principle of propriety, law, or justice.

" it has often been remarked," says the Rev. Mr. Upham, in his Life of Sir Henry Fane, " that our fathers were guilty of great Inconsistency in persecuting the followers of Mrs. Hutchinson, the Quakers, and others, inasmuch as they settled the country in order to screen themselves from persecution. They are often reproached, as having contended manfully for the rights of conscience, when they were themselves sufferers, and, as then turning against others, and violating their rights of conscience, as soon as they had the power and the opportunity to do it.

" But the remark and the reproach are founded in error. It was for religious liberty, in a peculiar sense, that our fathers contended, and they were faithful to the cause as they understood it. The true principle of religious liberty, in its wide and full comprehension, had never dawned upon their minds, and was never maintained by them."

In 1640, the court at Plymouth ordered, that, if any should bring into that jurisdiction a Quaker, rantor, or other notorious heretic, he should, upon the order of a magistrate, return such person to the place from whence he came, upon the penalty of twenty-five shillings for every week such person should remain there after warning.

In 1652, it was enacted, that no Quaker should be entertained within that government, under the penalty of £5 for every default, or whipping. In 1657, the court of Massachusetts imposed a fine of £100 on any bringing a Quaker into that jurisdiction; and a Quaker returning, after being sent away, to have one of his ears cut off; for a second offence, to lose the other ear. Every Quaker woman so returning, to be severely whipped, and for a third offence, to have her tongue bored through with a hot iron.

These harsh measures served in some Instances to provoke even the Quaker to acts approaching Insanity. Humphrey Norton, of whom it is hard to say whether he was most fool or knave, addressed an Insulting epistle to the governor, filled with the most virulent terms of reproach of which language is capable; and another to John Alden, a magistrate, equally abusive, both of which bear date at Rhode Island, April 16, 1658, and are curiosities in their way.

But the laws already made, proving ineffectual, it was resolved to substitute, in some cases, even the punishment of death.

October 19, 1659, William Robinson, Marmaduke Stevenson, and Mary Dyer, who had returned from banishment, were tried and committed. The two former were executed October 27, 1659; the last was reprieved, but returning again the next year, was hanged June 1, 1660.

William Leddra, who had been whipped and banished, was again offered his liberty, upon condition of not returning, which he declined, and was executed March 14, 1660.

In the colonies of Connecticut and New Haven, the enactments were less severe, and no one suffered death there for heresy. Holden, Copeland, and Rouse, had their ears cut off at Boston, September 6, 1658. Witches, Quakers, and Baptists seem to have been almost equally obnoxious to punishment in the eastern provinces.

The Rev. George Burroughs was executed for witchcraft in August, 1692, and about twenty others suffered on the like charge.

In this province the Quakers were treated with great severity. On the 8th of January, 1658, a written answer was received by the governor and council, from John Tilton, late clerk of Gravesend, to the complaint of the sheriff there, that he gave lodgings to a Quaker woman.

In council, January 10, 1658 — present, the director-general, Petrus Stuyvesant, the Hon. Nicasius de Sille, and Pieter Tonneman — the conclusion of the attorney-general versus John Tilton, for lodging a banished Quaker woman, was read, with the written answer of John Tilton, and after it was examined, the following sentence was pronounced:

" Whereas John Tilton, residing at S. Gravesend, now under arrest, has dared to provide a Quaker woman with lodging, who was banished out of the New Netherlands; so, too, some other persons of her adherents, belonging to the abominable sect of the Quakers, which is directly contrary to the orders and placards of the Director-General and Council of New Netherlands, and therefore, as an example for others, ought to be severely punished: however, having taken in consideration the supplication of the arrested Tilton, in which he declares that the aforesaid Quaker woman came to his house with other neighbors during his absence, and further reflected on his former conduct, so it is, that the Director-General in New Netherlands, doing justice in the name of the high and mighty Lords the

States General of the United Netherlands, and the noble Directors of the privileged West Indian Company, condemn the aforesaid John Tilton in an amende of £12 Flanders, with the costs and mises of justice, to be applied, one-third in behalf of the Attorney-General, one-third in behalf of the Sheriff of Gravesend, and the remaining third part as it ought to be."

From the first appearance of the Quakers in the jurisdiction, it seems to have been the determination of Governor Stuyvesant to prevent, by every possible means, the dissemination of opinions which he was pleased to denominate " seditious, heretical, and abominable "; and the whole sect was always spoken of with the utmost contempt and with the most opprobrious epithets. Among the first that fell under his displeasure, was Hodgson (or Hadson). He came over in August, 1657, on board the vessel called the " Woodhouse," Captain Robert Fowler. He was charged with holding conventicles, and proceeding toward Hempstead, he was seized by order of Richard Gildersleeve, a magistrate there, and committed to prison. Information being sent to the city, a guard was ordered to bring him before the governor and council. Two women, who had entertained him, were also taken; one of whom had a young child. These were put into a cart; and Hodgson being fastened behind it, was dragged through woods by night to the city, and thrust into the dungeon of Fort Amsterdam. On being brought out next day, he was examined, condemned, and sentenced to two years' hard labor at a wheelbarrow, with a negro, or to pay a fine of 600 guilders. With the latter alternative he was either unable or unwilling to comply, and was again confined, without permission to see or converse with any one. Being afterwards chained to a wheelbarrow, and commanded to work, he refused to do so, and was, by order of the court, beaten by a negro with a tarred rope till he fainted: the punishment was continued, at intervals, to one hundred lashes, with the same result. After having been for some months confined, and frequently scourged as before, he was liberated, at the solicitations of the governor's sister, and banished from the province. Upon the Dutch records, the case of Henry Townsend is alluded to, who, on the 15th of September, 1657, was condemned in an amende of £8 Flanders, or else to depart the province within six weeks, upon the penalty of corporeal punishment, for having called together conventicles. Being a person of great worth and consideration with the people of Flushing, where he had previously resided, they assembled, and addressed a remonstrance to the governor, dated December 27, 1657, of which the following is a copy:

" Right Honorable:

" You have been pleased to send up unto us a certain prohibition or command that wee should not relieve or enterteine any of those people called Quakers, because they are supposed to bee by some, seducers of the people. For our parte we cannot condemn them in this case, neither can wee stretch out our handes against them, to punish, bannish or persecute them, for out of Christ, God is consuming fire, and itis a fearfull thing to fall into the hands of the living God. Wee desire therefore in this case not to judge, least we be judged, neither to condem least wee bee condemd, but rather let every man stand or fall to his own malster. Wee are commande by the law to doe good unto all men, especially to those of the household of faith. And though for the present, wee seeme to be Insensible of the law and the lawgiver, yet when death and the law assault us. If we have an advocate to seeke who shall pleade for us in this case of conscience betwixt God and our own soules, the powers of this world can neither assist us, neither excuse us, for If God justifye, who can condem, and if God condem, there is none can justifye. And for those jealousies and suspicions which some have of them, that they are destructive unto magistracy and minlsterye (this) cannot bee for the magistrate hath the sword in his hand and the minister hath the sword in his hand, as witnesse those tew great examples which all magistrates and ministers are to follow (Moses) and Christ whom God raised up malnetalned and defended against all the enemies both of flesh and spirit; and therefore that which is of God will stand, and that which is of man will come to noething. And as the Lorde hath taught Moses or the civil power to give an outward liberty in the state by the law written in his heart, for the good of all, and can truely judge who is good, who is evil, who is true and who is false, and can pass definitive sentence of life or death against that man which rises up against the fundamentall law of the States General. Soe he hath made his ministers a saver of life unto life, and a saver of death unto death. The law of love, peace and liberty in the state extending to Jewes, Turkes, and Egyptians, as they are considered the sonnes of Adam, which is the glory of the outward State of Holland, soe love, peace and liberty, extending to all in Christ Jesus, condems hatred, warre and bondage. And because our Saviour saith it is impossible but that offences will come, but woe be unto him by whom they Cometh; our desire is not to offend one of his little ones, in whatever forme or name or title he appeares in, whether presbyterian, independent, baptist, or quaker, but shall be glad to see any thing of God in any of them, desiring to doe unto all, as wee desire that all men should do unto us, which is the true law both of church and state. For our Saviour saith, this is the law and the prophets. Therefore, if any of these said persons come in love unto us, we cannot in conscience lay violent hands upon them, but give them free egresse and regresse unto our towne and houses, as God shall persuade our consciences. And in this we are true subjects both of church and state, for wee are bounde by the law of God and man to do good unto all men, and evil to noe man. And this is according to the Pattent and charter of our towne, given unto us in the name of the States Generall, which wee are not willing to infringe and violate, but shall houlde our pattent, and shall remaine your humble subjects the Inhabitants of Vlissingh. Written this 27th of Dec. 1657, by me,"

" Edward Hart. Clerk,"

251

To this dignified and spirited document are subscribed the names of thirty of the principal inhabitants of the town, including Henry and John Townsend of Jamaica, (or Rusdorp). It was presented next day in person by Tobias Feake, sheriff, one of the signers. The governor was highly Incensed, and ordered his attorney-general, Nicasius de Sille, immediately to arrest him. Farrington and Noble, two of the magistrates, signers also, were taken and Imprisoned. Hart admitted writing the paper, saying he was requested to do so, as containing the sentiments of the village meeting, at the house of Michael Milnor. He was, therefore, imprisoned. On the 29th of December, 1657, the magistrates of Rusdorp informed the governor that the Quakers and their adherents were lodged, and entertained, and unrelentingly corresponded in said village, at the house of Henry Townsend; who, they say, formerly convocated a conventicle of the Quakers, and assisted in It, for which he had been condemned on the 15th of September, 1657, in an amende of £8 Flanders, that had not as yet been paid. He was thereupon cited to appear, January 8, 1658. John Townsend, who had also been summoned January 10, on being asked if he had gone with Hart to persuade Farrington to sign the remonstrance, answered that he had been at Flushing, and visited Farrington as an old acquaintance; and that he had also been at Gravesend, but not in company with the banished female Quaker. The court having suspicions of his favoring the Quakers, he was ordered to find bail for £12, to appear when summoned.

On the same day, Noble and Farrington were brought up, and made a verbal confession of being seduced and inveigled by Feake, and promising to conduct with more prudence in future, were discharged on paying costs. The trials which followed, may well be considered as a perfect mockery of judicial proceedings, and a burlesque on the administration of justice — inflated language, mixed with barbarous Latin, unmeaning technicalities, and affected ceremony, are manifest at every step, and can produce in the mind of the reader only disgust. This feeling is increased by the fact that the accused were denied the privilege of counsel, or even of defending themselves.

On the 15th of January, 1658, Henry Townsend was again brought before the council, and the farce ended by the attorney-general declaring, " that as the prisoner had before, and now again, trespassed and treated with contempt the placards of the director general and council in New Netherlands, in lodging quakers, which he unconditionally confessed, he should, therefore, be condemned in an amende of £100 Flanders, as an example for other transgressors and contumelious offenders, of the good order and placards of the director general and council in New Netherlands, and so to remain arrested till the said amende be paid, besides the costs and mises of justice." On the 28th, Sheriff Feake was brought from prison, and "though (says the record) he confessed that he had received an order of the director general not to admit in the aforesaid village, any of that heretical and abominable sect, called quakers, or procure them lodgings, yet did so in the face of the placards; and, what was worse, was a leader in composing a seditious and detestable chartable, delivered by him and signed by himself and his accomplices, wherein they justify the abominable sect of the quakers, who treat with contempt all political and ecclesiastical authority, and undermine the foundations of all government and religion, maintaining and absolutely concluding that all sects, and principally the aforesaid heretical and abominable sect of quakers, shall or ought to be tolerated, which is directly contrary to the aforesaid orders and placards of the director general and council; whereas he ought to have maintained and observed the execution of the aforesaid orders and placards in conformity to his oath, as he was in duty bound, as a subaltern officer of the director general and as sheriff of the aforesaid village of Flissingen." He was, therefore, degraded from his office, and sentenced to be banished or pay an amende of two hundred guilders. On the 26th of March, 1658, the governor, in order to prevent as much as possible the consequences of Quaker influence among the people, resolved to change the municipal government of the town of Flushing; and therefore, after formally pardoning the town for its mutinous orders and resolutions, says, " In future I shall appoint a sheriff, acquainted not only with the English and Dutch language, but with Dutch practical law; and that in future there shall be chosen seven of the most reasonable and respectable of the inhabitants, to be called tribunes and townsmen; and whom the sheriff and magistrates shall consult in all cases; and that a tax of twelve stivers per-morgen is laid on the inhabitants for the support of an orthodox minister; and such as do not sign a written submission to the same in six weeks, may dispose of their property at their pleasure, and leave the soil of this government."

On the council records of January 8, 1661, it is stated that the governor addressed the people of Jamaica, informing them that he had received their petition for a minister to baptize some of their children; and their information that Quakers and other sects held private conventicles. He tells them that he had dispatched his deputy sheriff, Resolve Waldron, and one of his clerks, Nicholas Bayard, to take notice thereof, and requiring the inhabitants to give exact information where and in what house such unlawful conventicles were kept; what persons had exercised therein; what men or women had been present; who called the meeting, and of all the circumstances appertaining thereunto. In consequence of this inquisitorial espionage of the governor's deputy, and the fact that Everit and Denton, two of the magistrates of Jamaica, had furnished the names of twelve persons, including Henry and John Townsend, and their wives, who had countenanced the Quakers, Henry Townsend was a third time dragged to the city, and again incarcerated in the dungeons of Fort Amsterdam. On the day following, he and Samuel Spicer, who had also given entertainment to a Quaker at his mother's house in

Gravesend, were brought from their loathsome prison. It was proved by witnesses procured for the occasion, that Townsend had given lodging to a Quaker, and besides notifying his neighbors, had even allowed them to preach at his house and in his presence; also, that Spicer was present, both at the meeting at Jamaica and Gravesend, and procured lodging for the Quaker at his mother's house. They were accordingly condemned in an amende of six hundred guilders each, in conformity to the placard respecting conventicles, and to be imprisoned until the said amende be paid; and further, that the said Henry Townsend be banished out of the province, for an example to others. The widow Spicer, mother of Samuel, was also arrested, accused, and condemned in an amende of £15 Flanders. The said Henry Townsend having ingenuously acknowledged that he lodged in his house some other friends who are called Quakers, and had a meeting of friends at his house, at which one of them spoke, concluding by saying that they might squander and devour his estate and manacle his person, but that his soul was his God's, and his opinions his own; whereupon he was again condemned, and sentenced with much formality. These acts of violence were more particularly frequent from 1647 to 1664, during the administration of Stuyvesant, who was a zealous and intolerant member of the Dutch Calvinistic Church, and disposed to execute the instructions accompanying his commission with the most extraordinary rigor. His official oath required " the maintenance of the Reformed Religion in conformity to the word and the decrees of the synod of Dordrecht, and not to tolerate in public any other sect." By an ordinance made in 1656, any one preaching doctrines other than those authorized by the synod was fineable one hundred, and every one attending thereon twenty-five, guilders. In the spirit of this provision, the governor, in 1656, imprisoned some Lutherans, and in 1658 banished a clergyman of that church. He was reproved for the former by the Dutch West India Company, who directed him to permit the free exercise of their religion to all persons within their own houses; and though commended for the latter, was instructed to use moderate measures in future. Against the Quakers, who had, by their peaceful and prudent conduct, made many converts in some of the western towns of the island, particularly at Jamaica and Flushing, the temper of the governor was violent and revengeful. Orders in writing or placards, were issued to the town authorities forbidding them to entertain members of this odious sect; and the ordinance of 1662 provided, that besides the reformed religion, no conventicles should be holden in houses, barns, ships, woods, or fields, under the penalty of fifty guilders for each person, man, woman, or child attending for the first offence, double for the second; quadruple for the third; and arbitrary correction for every other. The importation of seditious and seducing books, and the lodging of persons arriving in the province without reporting themselves and taking the oath of allegiance, subjected the offenders to severe penalties. These, with some other causes of discontent, rendered the government very unpopular; and it is probable, that, had not the province been conquered in 1664 by a foreign power, a revolution would have, in a very short time, been effected by the inhabitants themselves, either with or without the aid of the other colonies.

Materials upon the subject of the Quaker persecutions are both abundant and authentic; yet want of space will necessarily restrict our inquiries within narrow limits, and confine us to a few cases of more than ordinary severity. The most prominent individuals against whom these atrocities were committed were Robert Hodgson, Edward Farrington, William Bowne, William Noble, Edward Feake, Henry Townsend, John Townsend, Edward Hart, John Bowne, Samuel Spicer, and John Tilton. Of Hodgson little more is known than that he was a worthy man, and highly esteemed by the Friends for his intelligence and zeal in defense of civil and religious liberty. The cruel treatment he received from the government drove him from the province, after the termination of his sufferings and imprisonment. Spicer and Tilton, and probably Farrington, came with Baxter and Hubbard to Gravesend in 1643, accompanied by the Lady Moody, from Massachusetts. William Bowne came about the same time to Gravesend, and was a magistrate there in 1657. He afterwards removed, with his family and a few other Quakers, to New Jersey, where they made a purchase, embracing the present county of Middlesex and part of Monmouth. John and Henry Townsend, with their brother Richard, emigrated, it is believed, from Lynn Regis, in Norfolkshire, England, to Saugus (now Lynn), Massachusetts, a little previous to 1640, and soon after arrived in the New Netherlands. John Bowne, and his father Thomas Bowne, were among the earliest and most venerable inhabitants of Flushing. They embraced, with zeal, the opinions and principles of George Fox, and were, on this account, marked out by the minions of arbitrary power, as fit subjects of unceasing persecution. It has been mentioned in a former part of this work, that John Bowne was, in 1663, transported to Holland for his supposed heretical opinions, for which act the governor was severely reprimanded by the West India Company, whose servant he was.

On the 5th of October, 1662, John Tilton and Mary his wife, having been accused and committed before the governor and council of New Amsterdam, of having entertained Quakers and frequented their conventicles, were condemned, and ordered to depart from the province before the 20th November following, upon pain of corporeal punishment. It is presumed that through the influence of Lady Moody, the last sentence was either reversed or commuted for the payment of a fine, as they continued to reside at Gravesend for the remainder of their lives.

It appears from the trial, that Goody Tilton (as she is called) was not so much condemned for assisting at conventicles, as " for having, like a sorceress, gone from door to door, to lure and seduce the people, yea, even young girls, to join the quakers." Her husband had been fined the 19th of

September preceding, for "permitting quakers to quake at his house in Gravesend." (He died in 1688, and his wife in 1683). On Henry Townsend's last imprisonment for the non-payment of his fine, he was daily supplied with food, through the gratings of the jail, by his daughter Rose, then only nine years old, she being able to excite the compassion of the keeper so far as to permit the performance of this pious duty.

May 17, 1663, the governor put forth a still more severe edict, denouncing vengeance and heavy penalties upon skippers and barques, that should smuggle in any of those " abominable imposters, runaways, and strolling people, called quakers."

Many more instances, with almost equally aggravated circumstances, might be mentioned, showing that the severe reprimand which the governor received from the authorities of Holland was well merited, and ought to have been followed by his expulsion from an office he so unworthily filled. But his power was soon after terminated by the conquest of New York; yet his excellency, though deprived of the government, was nevertheless permitted to retain his large possessions upon Manhattan Island, a good portion of which is still enjoyed by his descendants.

Before closing this interesting article, we will cite an example of Quaker persecution, which took place during the administration of Lord Cornbury, a man of most detestable character, and fully equal to the Dutch Governor for religious Intolerance. He in his turn persecuted other sects as well as Quakers, instances of which are adverted to in other parts of this work. The case we now allude to is that of Samuel Bownas, a Quaker preacher, who came to America at the beginning of the eighteenth century. The facts are stated in the journal of his travels, afterwards published. He left England on the 24th of March, 1702, and landed in Maryland, where he received a challenge from George Keith, an Episcopal missionary, who had once been a Quaker. He was followed by Keith through Pennsylvania and New Jersey to Long Island, and a meeting being appointed at Hempstead, he preached November 21, 1702, at the house of one Thomas Pearsall. As Keith could not, by other means, silence his adversary, he procured Richard Smith and William Bradford of Hempstead to make an affidavit charging him with heresy, and for this a warrant was issued by Joseph Smith and Edward Burroughs, justices, for his apprehension. On the 29th, while he was attending a meeting of Friends at Flushing, Cardell, the high sheriff, with a posse armed with guns, pitchforks, swords, and clubs, entered the house and took him prisoner. He appeared before the court at Jamaica, consisting of four justices, Joseph Smith, Edward Burroughs, John Smith, and Jonathan Whitehead, the last of whom, says the prisoner, was a very moderate man, and did much to set him at liberty; but they had a priest with them, who put the worst construction upon everything he said, and had also a man secreted in a closet to note down what he should say; but the man was so drunk, that in going home he lost his papers, for which great inquiry was made. The justices ordered the prisoner to give bail in £2000, with sureties to appear and answer an indictment, which the prisoner said he would not give, " were it only three half-pence." Justice Whitehead offered himself as bail, and took the prisoner home till next day, when he was committed to jail in Jamaica for the term of three months. At the end of which, a special commission of oyer and terminer was granted to Chief Justice Bridges, and Robert Miller, Thomas Willet, John Jackson, and Edward Burroughs, associates, who met at the county hall in Jamaica. The names of the grand jury were Richard Cornell, Ephraim Goulding, John Clayer, Isaac Hicks, Robert Hubbs, Richabel Mott, Theodore Vanderwick, Samuel Denton, Joseph Mott, Richard Valentine, Nathaniel Coles, Joseph Dickerson, Isaac Doughty, Samuel Emery, John Smith, John Sering, John Oakley, Samuel Hallet, Richard Alsop, John Hunt, James Clement, and William Bloodgood. The jury presented the bill to the court, endorsed " Ignoramus "; upon which the judge was very angry, and told the jury that surely they had forgot their oaths, and for so doing he could give them some hard names, but for the present should forbear. "is this your verdict (said the judge) touching the Quaker?" "It is," said the foreman; at which the judge raged, and threatened to " lay the jury by the heels, and to impose a fine upon them"; to which one of them replied, if he did, " the matter should soon be exposed in Westminster Hall." The judge now ordered the prisoner to be kept more close than before, and threatened to send him to London, chained to the deck of a man-of-war, then ready to sail for England. " Thomas Hicks, an honest old man, who had been a justice of the province, and was well versed in the law, came to visit me (says he) and consoled me with many kind words, saying that they dare not send me out of the country." His old enemy, Keith, published a pamphlet against him, which rather increased the number of his friends. During his imprisonment he learned to make shoes, by which he earned fifteen shillings a week, refusing, at the same time, all pecuniary aid from his friends. While here, he was visited, he says, by an Indian sachem, who asked him if he was a Christian; and being told yea, " and are they not Christians who keep you here? " Being told they called themselves so, he expressed much surprise, and said, " the Mang Manetou (meaning God) looked at the heart." Then the Indian took a piece of coal, and drawing a circle, said, " they believed the Great Spirit to be all eye, that he saw everything; all ear, that he heard everything; and all mind, that he knew everything." At the sitting of the court in October, 1703, the bill was again returned " Ignoramus," and he was discharged. He visited America again in 1727, and died in England on the 2nd of April, 1753.

LONG ISLAND CANAL

An opinion has long been entertained that the interest of the island would be much advanced by a canal connecting the great bays, so as to secure an inland navigation from the Lower Bay of New York to the Peconic or Southold Bay, Gardiner's Bay, and the Sound around Oyster Pond Point. This project assumed a definite shape by an application to the State Legislature in 1824, in consequence of which a survey was ordered and made under the direction of the canal commission the next year. His excellency De Witt Clinton, the enlightened statesman and firm friend of internal improvement, in his message of 1826, earnestly recommended the plan to the favorable notice of the Legislature.

The petitioners proposed, 1st. That the canal be made by the state; if this were refused then, 2nd, That a company be incorporated to construct the same, with hauling privileges; or in failure of both these propositions, 3rd, That the state should refund to the company incorporated, one-third the costs of constructing the said canal. In lieu of all these, an act was passed April 1, 1828, and amended April 1, 1829, incorporating the Long Island Canal Company, which, not being accepted on account of the omission of the banking clause, was suffered to expire by its own limitation. In 1846 the matter was again agitated, which resulted in an act to incorporate the Long Island Canal & Navigation Company, passed April 7, 1848; capital stock, $300,000, divided into shares of $50 each. This act, among other things, authorized and empowered the corporation to survey, construct, navigate, and maintain a line of canals and water communication from Gravesend Bay to Jamaica Bay, from thence over Rockaway to the Great South Bay, and across Quogue to Southampton or Shinnecock Bay, and thence to the great Peconic Bay. Anyone who will take the trouble to examine the map of the south shore of Long Island will find it full of small bays, coves, inlets, and islands, covering a considerable surface, and it is now proposed to unite them by cuts and form them into a continuous line of canal navigation. The outline of the project is quite interesting. It is proposed to commence at Gravesend Bay, thence through the creek separating Coney Island from the main land, the creek to be deepened so as to obtain four feet water at low tide. The distance from Gravesend Bay to Jamaica Bay across Coney Island is about 8,000 feet. Near Barren Island the shoals will require deepening. Two routes are practicable: the Ocean line, 10,000 feet from the Pavilion, which will be about 30,000 feet in length on the northern line, beginning near the mouth of Hook Creek, and extending to the head of Brewer's Bay, 13,000 feet in length. Shoals and flats will have to be dredged, and creeks deepened, to connect East Bay with Shinnecock. Now when all these cuts are completed, and the creeks deepened, vessels will be able to have an inland navigation from Coney Island to Southampton, a distance of eighty miles with four feet water at low tide. The whole capital required for this interesting project is only $300,000. It is estimated that at the present time $150,000 is paid annually for freight to and from the various places on the north-east side, and at least $160,000 for freight on the Bay side. The farmers are deeply interested in this project, which will afford them a rapid conveyance for their products to market, and it opens a new route to reach all the pleasant towns and villages on the island.

We herewith append a clipping from a Brooklyn newspaper, date of January 22, 1847, which gives some further information concerning the projected canal.

In this connection it is interesting to note that the project has again been revived during the past year (1916), but with what result, the future can only tell. The need and value of such a canal is very plain to see.

" Friday, January 22, 1847.

" Long Island Canal

" The attention of our readers was called, some time ago, to the project of uniting the Bays along the South shore of Long Island. We are now enabled to give further particulars in relation to the contemplated improvement, derived from authentic sources.

" The proposed line of navigation commences at Gravesend Bay; thence through the creek separating Coney Island from the main land. — This creek is to be widened, and excavated so as to afford four feet of water at low tide. The distance from Gravesend Bay to Jamaica Bay across Coney Island is about eight thousand feet.

Near Barren Island it will probably be necessary to deepen the shoals and excavate a small piece of meadow. Through Rockaway two routes are practicable: the lower or ocean line passes about 1000 feet in front of the Pavilion, and will be about 4 ½ miles or 30,000 feet, in length; the northern line, beginning near the mouth of Hook Creek, extends to the head of Brewer's Bay, the length of which is about 13,000 feet. The shoals will need some dredging near South Oyster Bay, and no further work will be required before reaching Quogue, where it will be necessary to deepen a creek and cut for a short distance in order to connect the East Bay with Shinnecock Bay. From Canoe Place to Peconic Bay the distance is less than one mile, and the deepest cut will not exceed twenty-five feet.

" When this improvement is completed, vessels can navigate the Bays from Coney Island to Southampton, a distance of 80 miles, with 4 feet of water at low tide.

" The increase of business which must necessarily follow the opening of this new line of inland communication, will render the stock of the Company a good field for investment. It is estimated that $150,000 per annum is now paid for freights to and from the various places on the south side, without taking into consideration the amount paid for the transportation of Bay produce, the value of which annually exceeds $160,000.

" Admitting the freights to be increased one third, or amounting to $200,000 per annum, and allowing one eighth to the Company, a sum of $25,000 would accrue from this source alone. — The number of persons who would avail themselves of this new and agreeable route for visiting the pleasant villages on the southern shore during the summer months cannot be estimated but it is reasonable to suppose that the amount received from all sources would exceed $50,000 per annum, which would pay all expenses and give a remuneration of 7 per cent, on the proposed capital ($300,000).

" Our farmers are deeply interested in the success of this project, and there is no reason why it should not receive the particular attention of our State Legislature.

" Nearly one thousand inhabitants of the Island have petitioned for the privilege of undertaking this work, which cannot be made by the State according to the restrictions of the New Constitution. Our friends at Jamaica propose a canal from their village to the Bay, in connection with the main line of navigation.

" We are pleased to see that the people are aroused to the vital importance of this great improvement, and we see no reason why Long Island cannot have her resources opened and be justly called the ' Garden of the State.' Our soil is better suited for all kinds of crops than that of any immediate portion of the State. All that is required is cheap manure and an easy access to market.

" At our office a map can be seen showing the contemplated improvement, and a petition to the Legislature will also be found, to which we hope all favorable to the project will affix their names."

THE LONG ISLAND RAILROAD

This road of about ninety-six miles in length, including the Brooklyn and Jamaica railroad, is an essential link in the chain of communication between the city of New York and the commercial capital of New England. It is besides the most speedy and direct, being the straightest and most uniform road of its extent in the United States. It should be premised that the western portion is the property of the Brooklyn and Jamaica Railroad Company, incorporated April 25, 1832, with a capital of $300,000, and opened to travelers April 18, 1836. It was leased for a term of years, immediately after its completion, to the Long Island Railroad Company, which had been incorporated April 24, 1834, with a capital of $1,500,000, in shares of $50 each. It was commenced in 1836, completed to Hicksville in March, 1837, opened to Carman's River June 26, 1844, and on the 25th of July following, the first passenger train of cars passed over the whole road to Greenport, where on the 27th of the same month, the event was celebrated with great pomp and ceremony, several cars loaded with invited guests having arrived there from Brooklyn in three hours and thirty-five minutes. The travel and other patronage of the road has exceeded the general expectation, while the expenses have likewise been beyond what was calculated, so that little or no profit has thus far been realized by the stockholders. The tunnel under a part of Atlantic Street, South Brooklyn, is among the most magnificent and durable works of the kind in this country. It is 2,550 feet long with massive granite walls, sufficiently wide for a double track, and cost about $75,000. The construction of this road constitutes an important era in the history of the island, and will serve to make it better known, although it traverses the most sterile and desert portion of the country. The highest elevation of this road is at Hicksville, where it is 142 feet above tide water. The height at Brooklyn ferry is seven and at Greenport ten feet. The advantages of travel by this conveyance are very great, and it is sincerely to be wished that economy and prudence in its management may yet make it a safe and profitable investment for the holders of its stock.